Jon E. Lewis is a writer and historian, whose books on history and military history are sold world wide. A regular Mammoth author and editor, his books include the bestselling *The Mammoth Book of How It Happened* and *The Mammoth Book of How It Happened World War II*. He lives in Hertfordshire with his wife and two children.

Also available

The Mammoth Book of Bridge
The Mammoth Book of British Kings & Queens
The Mammoth Book of Celtic Myths and Legends
The Mammoth Book of Chess
The Mammoth Book of Elite Forces & SAS
The Mammoth Book of Endurance & Adventure
The Mammoth Book of Fighter Pilots
The Mammoth Book of Heroes
The Mammoth Book of How It Happened
The Mammoth Book of How It Happened: America
The Mammoth Book of How It Happened: Ancient Egypt
The Mammoth Book of How It Happened: Ancient Rome
The Mammoth Book of How It Happened: Battles
The Mammoth Book of How It Happened: Britain
The Mammoth Book of How It Happened: Everest
The Mammoth Book of How It Happened: Naval Battles
The Mammoth Book of How It Happened: The Titanic
The Mammoth Book of How It Happened: World War II
The Mammoth Book of Jack the Ripper
The Mammoth Book of Jokes
The Mammoth Book of Journalism
The Mammoth Book of Literary Anecdotes
The Mammoth Book of Maneaters
The Mammoth Book of Mountain Disasters
The Mammoth Book of Murder
The Mammoth Book of Private Lives
The Mammoth Book of Prophecies
The Mammoth Book of Puzzles
The Mammoth Book of Sex, Drugs and Rock 'n' Roll
The Mammoth Book of The Edge
The Mammoth Book of The West
The Mammoth Book of Travel in Dangerous Places
The Mammoth Book of True War Stories
The Mammoth Book of True Crime
The Mammoth Book of UFOs
The Mammoth Book of Unsolved Mysteries
The Mammoth Book of Unsolved Crimes
The Mammoth Book of War Correspondents
The Mammoth Book of Women who Kill

The Mammoth Book of
How It Happened
WORLD WAR I

Edited by
JON E. LEWIS

ROBINSON
London

Constable & Robinson Ltd
3 The Lanchesters
162 Fulham Palace Road
London W6 9ER
www.constablerobinson.com

First published in the UK by Robinson,
an imprint of Constable & Robinson Ltd 2003

A copy of the British Library Cataloguing in Publication Data is available from the British Library.

ISBN 1-84119-803-X

Printed and bound in the EU

10 9 8 7 6 5 4 3 2 1

For Tristram and Freda Lewis-Stempel. Peace be with you.

CONTENTS

TIMELINE

1914

Western Front

June 28	Assassination of Archduke Ferdinand of Austria at Sarajevo
July 23	Austria issues ultimatum to Serbia
July 28	Austria declares war on Serbia
July 30	Russian General Mobilization
July 31	Austrian General Mobilization
August 1	German and French General Mobilization; Germany declares war on Russia
August 2	Germany invades Luxembourg
August 3	Germany invades Belgium and declares war on France
August 4	Britain declares war on Germany
August 6	Austria declares war on Russia
August 12	Britain and France declare war on Austria-Hungary
August 14	French troops enter Lorraine
August 17	Germans capture fortress of Liege, Belgium
August 22	British Expeditionary Force lands in France
August 23	Battle of Mons
September 5–12	Battle of the Marne
September 15–18	Battle of the Aisne
September 27–October 10	Battle of Artois
October 18–November 20	Battle of Yser
October 3–November 24	First Battle of Ypres
December 14–24	First Battle of Champagne

Eastern Front

August 26–30	Battle of Tannenberg
September 6–15	Battle of Masurian Lakes
October 9–20	Battle of Warsaw
November 16–25	Battles of Lowicz and Lodz
November 16–December 2	Battle of Cracow
December 2	Austrians capture Belgrade
December 15	Serbs retake Belgrade

Other Theatres

October 18	U-boat attack on Scapa Flow
November 1	British defeated in naval battle of Coronel
November 2	Serbia and Russia declare war on Turkey
November 5	Britain and France declare war on Turkey
November 22	British land expeditionary force at Basra, Mesopotamia (Iraq)
December 8	Naval battle of Falkland Islands
December 17	Turks launch offensive in Caucasus

1915

Western Front

April 22	Germans use gas at launch of Second Battle of Ypres
May 9– June 18	Second Battle of Artois
May 31	First Zeppelin raid on London
July 21	US President Wilson instructs Secretaries of State for War and Navy to prepare "defense program"
September 15–November 17	Battle of Loos
September 22–November 6	Second Battle of Champagne
September 25–October 15	Third Battle of Artois

Eastern Front

February 7	German offensive in Masuria
March 22	Fortress of Przemysl falls into Russian hands
May 2–June 27	Austro-German offensive in Galicia (Gorlice-Tarnow)
June 3	Austrians retake Przemysl
June 22	Austrians capture Lemberg
July 1–September 19	Renewed Austro-German offensive drives Russians out of Poland and Courland

Other Theatres

January 14	South African forces occupy Swakopmund

January 24	Dogger Bank battle
February 2	Germany declares water around Britain a "war zone"
May 23	Italy declares war on Austria-Hungary
June 23–July 7	July First Battle Isonzo (another eleven ensue)
April 25	Anglo-French landing at Gallipoli
May 7	*Lusitania* sunk by U-boat
July 9	Surrender of German South-West Africa
July 17	Bulgaria signs secret military treaty with Germany and Austria
August 6	Sulva Bay offensive, Gallipoli
September 28	Battle of Kut-el-Amara (Mesopotamia)
October 3	Anglo-French landing at Salonika
October 12	Edith Cavell executed
November 15	Senussi tribesmen revolt against Allies, Italian Libya
December 7	Turks commence siege of Kut-el-Amara
December 19	Allies withdraw from Gallipoli

1916

Western Front

January 6	Conscription Bill passed, Britain
February 21	Battle of Verdun opens
February 25	Germans take Fort Douaumont (Verdun)
July 1–November 18	Battle of the Somme
August 29	Hindenburg appointed Supreme German Commander; Ludendorff Quarter-Master General
September 15	First use of tanks (by British, on the Somme)
October 24–December 18	French counter-attack at Verdun
November 28	First German airplane raid on London
December 4	David Lloyd George becomes PM, Britain

Eastern Front

March 19–April 30	Battle of Lake Naroch
June 4	Russian "Brusilov" offensive opens
December 17	Rasputin assassinated, Russia

Other Theatres

April 24–May 1	Eastern Rising, Ireland
May 31–June	Battle of Jutland
June 5	Field Marshal Lord Kitchener drowns at sea; Arab revolt started in Hejaz
May15–June 3	Austrian offensive, Trentino
August–December	Battle of Doiran, Florina and Monastir, Macedonia
August 9	Italian Gorizia offensive

August 27	Rumania declares war on Austria-Hungary, invades Transylvania
December 6	Austro-German counter-offensive against Rumania culminates in capture of Bucharest
December 15	British commence advance in Sinai

1917

Western Front

February 3	USA severs diplomatic relations with Germany
March 4	Germans commence withdrawal to Hindenburg Line
April 6	USA declares war on Germany
April 9–May 4	Battle of Arras
April 12	Canadians capture Vimy Ridge
April 16–May 21	Second Battle of Aisne, Third Battle of Champagne
June 7–17	Battle of Messines
June 26	US troops (1st Division) lands in France
July 31–November 10	Third Battle of Ypres (Passchendaele)
August 20–December 15	Second Battle of Verdun
October 23–November 1	Battle of Malmaison
October 24–December 26	Italians routed at Caporetto
November 16	Georges Clemenceau becomes French Premier
November 20–December 3	Battle of Cambrai
December 7	USA declares war on Austria-Hungary

Eastern Front

March 8	First Russian Revolution begins in Petrograd
March 12	Provisional Government established, Russia
March 15	Tsar Nicholas II abdicates
April 6	Lenin arrives in Petrograd
July 18–28	Battle of East Galicia; Russian offensive driven back
September 3–5	Battle of Riga Bridgehead
November 7	Bolsheviks seize power in Petrograd in "October Revolution"
December 15	Central Powers sign armistice with Russia

Other Theatres

January 9–February 24	British defeat Turks at Kut-el-Amara
March 11	Baghdad occupied by British
April	U-boat campaign at height
March 26–27	First Battle of Gaza
April 17–19	Second Battle of Gaza (British defeated)
June 27	Greece enters war on Allied side
August 17–September 12	Conclusion of fighting on the Isonzo
December 8	Jerusalem captured by British

1918

Western Front	
January 8	President Wilson announces 14 point Peace Program
March 21–April 5	German "Michael Offensive"
March 23	Germans bombard Paris
April 14	Foch appointed Allied Commander in Chief on Western Front
April 9–29	Battle of the Lys
April 23	Naval raid on Zeebrugge
May 27–June 6	Third Battle of the Aisne (Germans reach to within 37 miles from Paris)
June 4	US 2nd Division in Battle of Chateau-Thierry
June 6	US 2nd Division captures Bouresches and southern end of Belleau Wood
July 15–August 7	Second Battle of the Marne
July 18	Foch orders Allied counter-offensive
August 8	Opening of the Battle of Amiens; "Black Day" of German Army
August 21–September 3	Second Battles of the Somme and Arras
September 12	US forces in St Mihiel Offensive
September 26	Meuse-Argonne Offensive
October 5	Allied forces capture Hindenburg Line
October 27	Ludendorff resigns
November 3	Armistice signed between Austria-Hungary and Allies; German fleet mutinies at Kiel
November 7	Revolution in Munich
November 9	German Republic proclaimed in Berlin
November 10	Wilhelm II flees to Holland
November 11	Armistice on Western Front
Eastern Front	
March 3	Treaty of Brest-Litovsk
July 16	Tsar Nicholas and family shot
September 30	Armistice signed with Bulgaria
Other Theatres	
September 15	Allied offensive on Macedonian front
September 19	British offensive in Palestine (Battle of Megiddo)
October 24–November 4	Italians victorious in Battle of Vittorio Veneto
October 30	Armistice concluded with Turkey

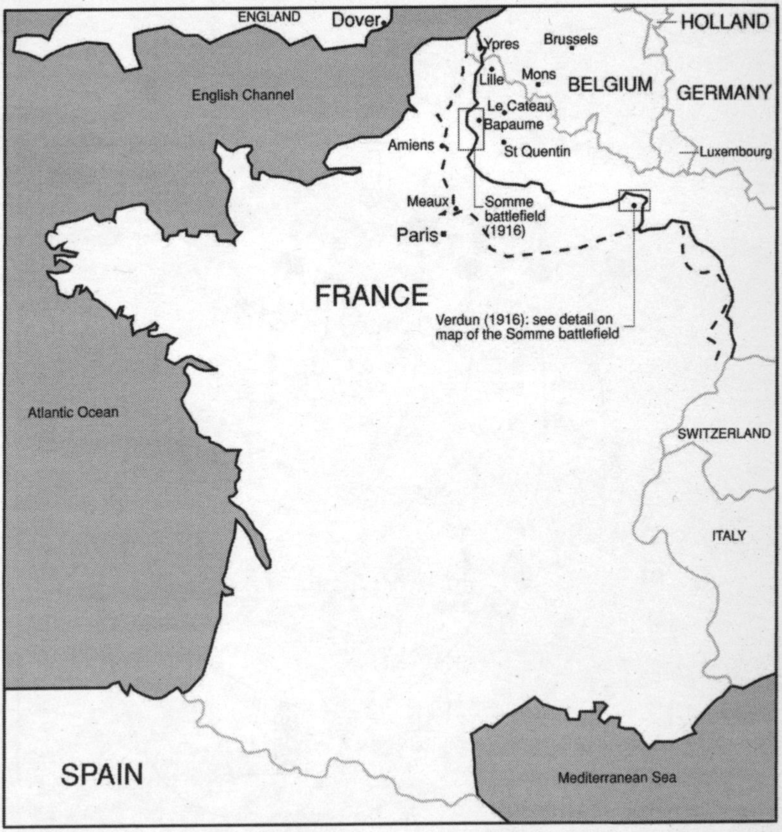

ENGLAND
Dover
HOLLAND
Ypres
Brussels
Lille
Mons
BELGIUM
GERMANY
English Channel
Le Cateau
Bapaume
Amiens
St Quentin
Luxembourg
Meaux
Somme battlefield (1916)
Paris
FRANCE
Verdun (1916): see detail on map of the Somme battlefield
Atlantic Ocean
SWITZERLAND
ITALY
SPAIN
Mediterranean Sea

The Western Front 1914

Key

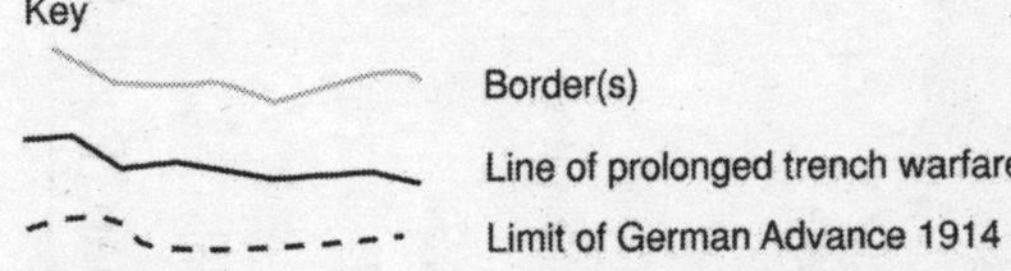

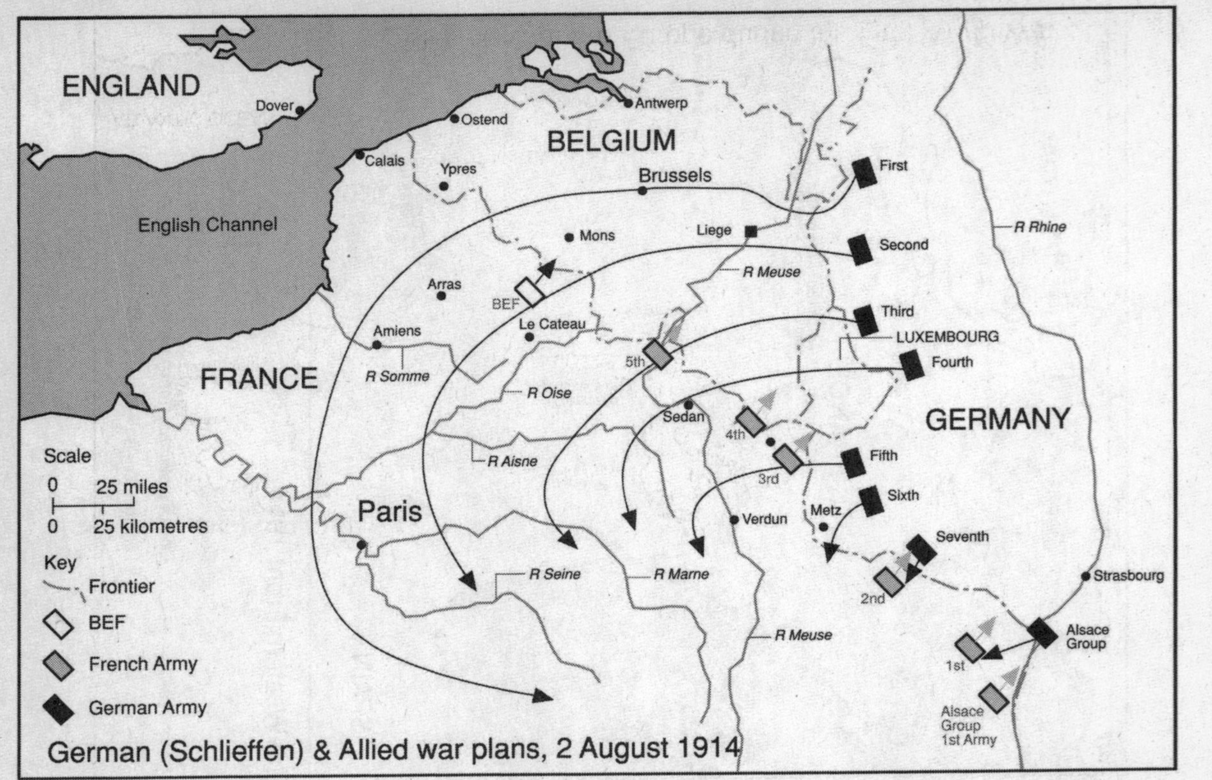

German (Schlieffen) & Allied war plans, 2 August 1914

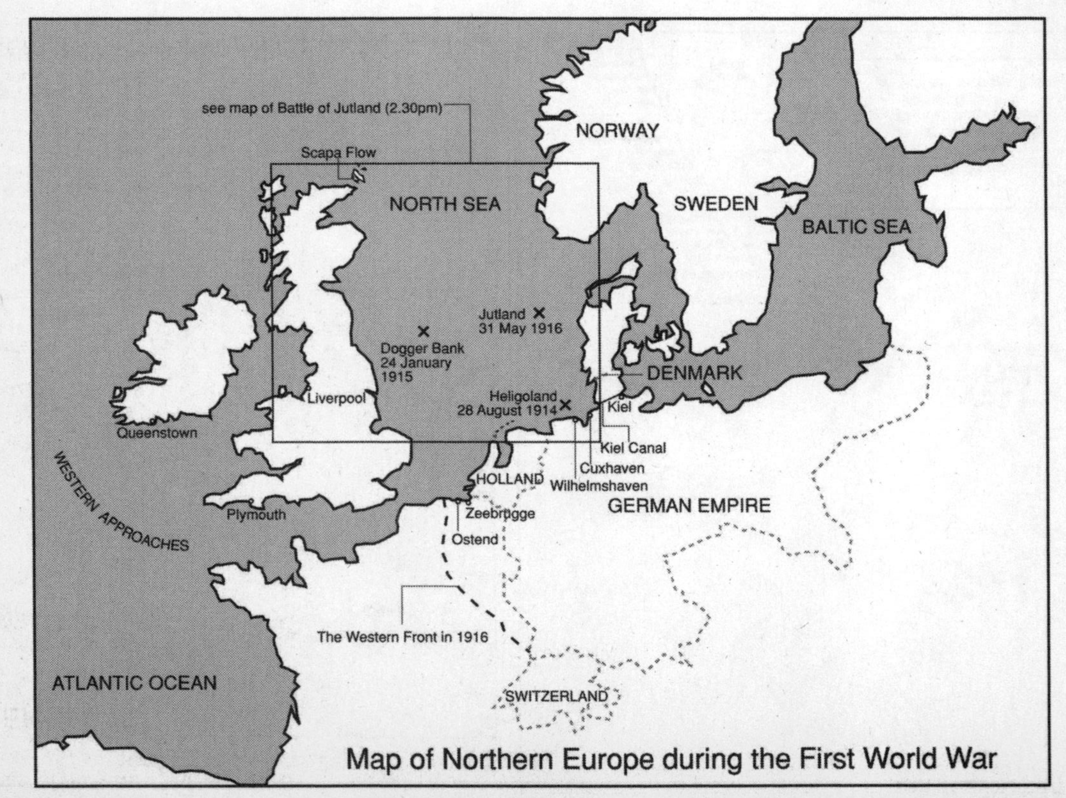

Map of Northern Europe during the First World War

Battle of Jutland 31 May 1916

Names of FLAGSHIPS shown in CAPITALS

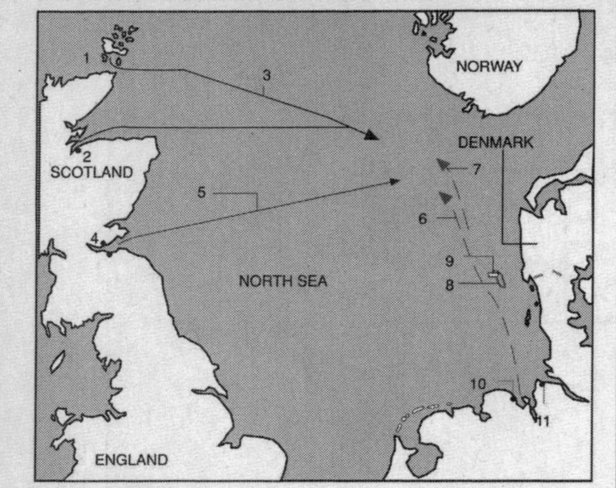

Above: Positions at 2.30 pm

Key:
1 Scapa Flow
2 Cromarty
3 Course of Grand Fleet (Jellicoe)
4 Rosyth
5 Course of British Battle cruisers & Fifth Battle Squadron (Beatty)
6 Course of German High Seas Fleet (Scheer)
7 Course of German Battle cruisers (Hipper)
8 Horn Reef
9 Horn Reef Light vessel
10 Wilhelmshaven
11 Cuxhaven

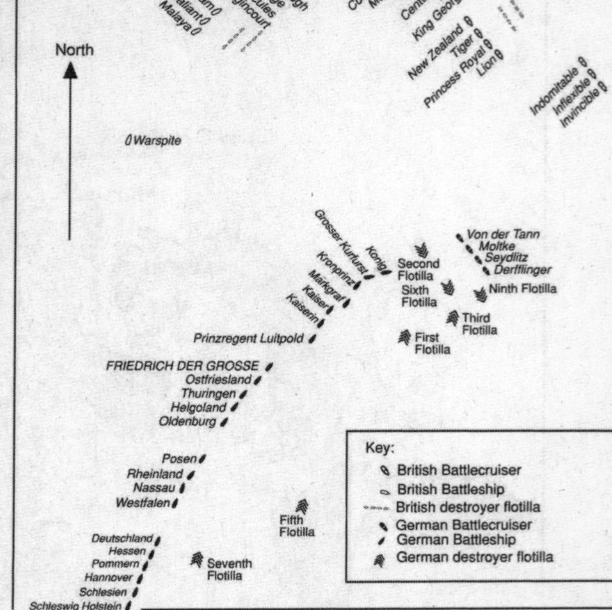

Right: Positions at 6.30 pm

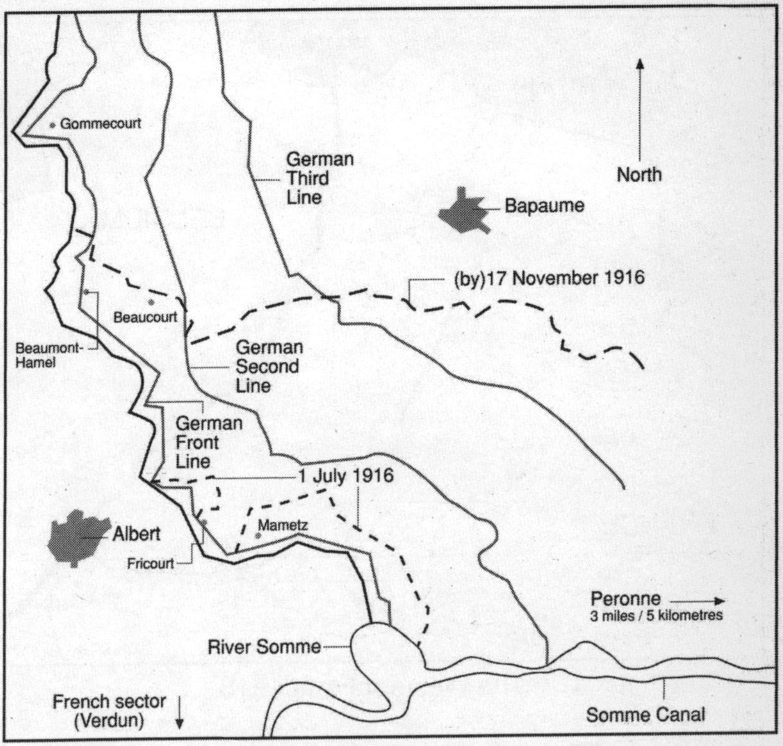

Gommecourt
German
Third
Line
North
Bapaume
(by)17 November 1916
Beaucourt
Beaumont-
Hamel
German
Second
Line
German
Front
Line
1 July 1916
Albert
Mametz
Fricourt
Peronne
3 miles / 5 kilometres
River Somme
French sector
(Verdun)
Somme Canal

The Battle of the Somme (British sector), 1 July – 17 November 1916

Key

British Front Line, 1 July 1916

German Lines 1 July 1916

British gains

German Gains
Verdun

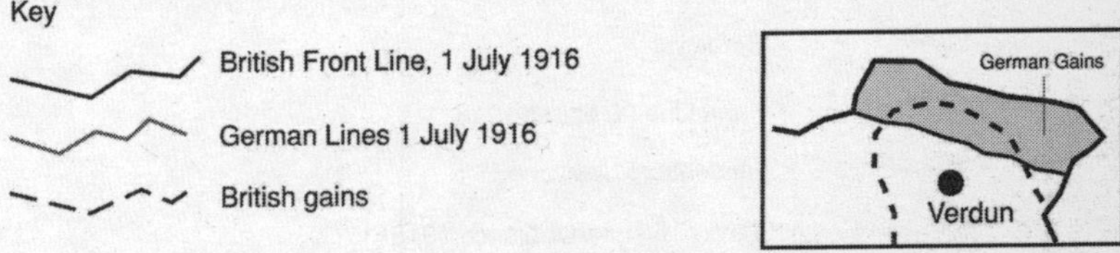

Verdun: detail showing German gains

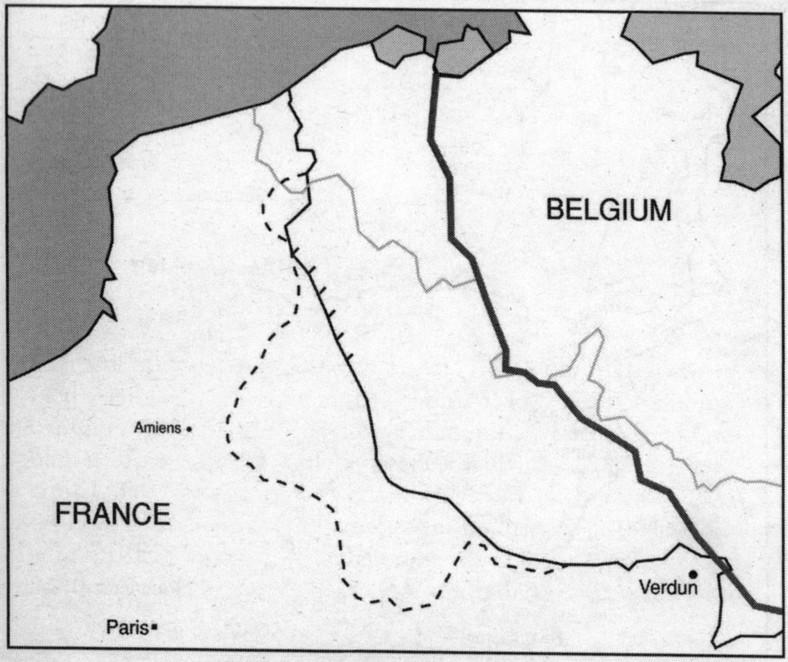

BELGIUM

Amiens

FRANCE

Verdun

Paris

The Western Front 1918

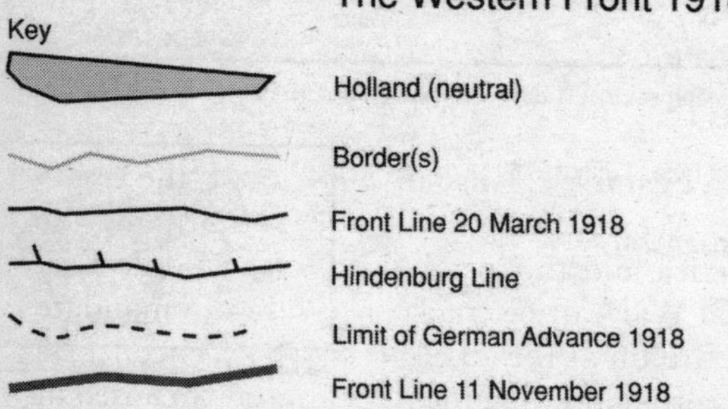

INTRODUCTION

It was, it is often forgotten, a *world* war. Despite the still haunting images of Flanders' trenches with "soldiers bent double, like sacks", the fighting of 1914–18 was not confined to a corner of northwest Europe, but took in eastern and southern Europe, the Middle East, Africa and even China and Japan. Fifty million men from thirty nations donned uniform. When the last bullet sounded on 11 November 1918, nine million of the combatants lay dead, alongside five million citizens.

The world had seen nothing like it, and it was the hope of the survivors that their war was the "war to end all wars". This hope was dashed even before the Armistice, because the Great War – as its participants called it, in awed honour of its bloody magnitude – had let roll events which ripple to this day. Out of the four-year-conflict came the Russian Revolution, the rise of Hitler, the Second World War, the decline of Britain, the supremacy of America and the instability of the Middle East (even the 2003 Gulf War can be tracked back to the mandate over Iraq given to Britain at the 1919 Peace Conference.) Less obvious, but no less profound were the ripples the war caused in the minds of men and women. In 1914 youth rushed to colours in an enthusiastic fever of patriotism and public duty. There would never be, to echo the phrase of the latter-day British poet Philip Larkin, such innocence again. Those who survived the fighting would never again be so deferential to their masters, so accepting of their lot, so reverential of the word – be it political, or religious – from on high.

Little, if any of this, was obvious as the world ran and slipped to war in July and August 1914. Almost everyone expected a quick and glorious *guerre de manoeuvre*. Seeing off his troops, the Kaiser assured them they would be home "before the leaves have fallen"; the British were only marginally less optimistic with their "Home for Christmas" cheerio.

Such self-deceit came easily, for the major European powers had next-to-no acquaintanceship with modern war, with the mass-slaughter which came courtesy of mass-produced machine-guns and artillery. Only a few leaders, notably Kitchener and Moltke, foresaw the long struggle, although even a glimpse at the history of the American Civil War would have cautioned that the industrialization of warfare tended to produce stasis on the battlefield (there had even been trenches in the Blue–Grey conflict). So it was that the soldiers of 1914, like their Civil War forbears, dug for cover in the face of modern arms, notably on the Western Front where the ratio of such arms was especially high. There, within a year, the soldiers' impromptu slits in the earth burgeoned into a trench system which stretched from the English Channel to Switzerland along which one could, in theory at least, walk "bent double" all the way.

If the Great War was not the first modern war, it was unique in its scale and in its "totality". And the more the War endured, the more "total" it became. This totality lay partly in its global nature – for the war soon spewed out from Europe to the Middle East, to the belligerents' colonies, and then entangled the USA – but more in the way it subsumed the home society, through mass conscription in the war effort, and the way in which bombing and blockades brought the war home. German U-boats almost starved Britain into surrender in early 1917, whilst Britain's reciprocal surface blockade was a factor in German's exhausted surrender in 1918. Meanwhile, 1,413 British civilians were killed in Zeppelin raids. There was no corner of life untouched by the war. Similarly, the economies of the belligerents became perverted towards the production of military *matériel*; 52% of British GNP in 1918, for example, went on defence expenditure. Over the course of the war as whole,

Britain spent approximately 23 billion dollars (at 1913 prices) on its prosecution.

For all her industrial might, Germany could not hope to match such largesse. Wars are not necessarily won by the side with the biggest pockets, but the longer a war endures the more likelihood that money will win out (another lesson from the American Civil War). Imperial Germany, in all probability, lost the war in August 1914 when she failed to deliver the KO to France; she definitely lost it in 1917, when America entered on the Allied side, with her double-sized divisions and her economy double the size of Germany's. (By 1917, incidentally, Germany was having to release men *from* the front to work in arms-related factories; the Allies, notably Britain, recruited women to make up shortfalls in the industrial and agricultural workforce). Futhermore, Germany was badly hampered by her choice of Allies, with the decrepit Austro-Hungarian Empire being a particularly weak and impecunious sister.

In hindsight, the wonder of World War I is less why Germany lost, but how Germany came so close to winning. The answer lies largely in the efficacy of the German army. Against stereotype, this was not led by clockwork Prussians, but extraordinarily effective and responsive junior officers and NCOs, who out of the long stalemate on the Western Front even conjured a new form of "storm trooper" warfare, as seen in the Michael Offensive of Spring 1918, which reached to within 37 miles of Paris.

This was the Germans' last grasp at victory. They had bested the Russians in the East, they had routed the Italians at Caporetto, but they were unable to break through in the West. They lost 973,000 men in the attempt; effectively the German army bled itself to death in March–June 1918. When the Allies counterattacked, the Germans had no reserves left on the Western Front. They could find no cheer on other fronts either, with a succession of Allied victories in Italy, Syria and Bulgaria, whilst their home front was falling into demoralization, discontent, even revolution. Suddenly, in late October the German-led Central Powers bloc collapsed. The war was over, bar the paperwork of surrender, which was duly signed on the 11th of November. The war was finished. So was the old order of things.

The following pages are a record of the Great War, from the opening shots at Sarajevo to the signing of the armistice at Compiègne, in which the participants are left to speak for themselves. For their words communicate, so much better than the second-hand sentences of historians, the experience of the war, what it felt like to be in an aerial dog-fight over the Western Front, to lead a charge of Arab irregulars, to dodge Zeppelin bombs in Sheffield, to abandon ship after a U-boat attack in the Atlantic. In keeping with an understanding of the totality of the First World War, a great diversity of witnesses has been presented from as many theatres as could be contained within the pages of this single volume, from Prussian generals in Africa to royal servants in Russia, from French officers at Verdun to English nurses in London, from American war correspondents in Belgium to Australian sappers at Gallipoli. Their accounts are testimony to the various aspects of the war in which they found themselves, but I have also tried to remember that wars, even world ones, are but the story of the fate of individual humans. Consequently, throughout the pages which follow I have sought to give the experience of particular individuals in the wider narrative. It is through such individual identification, I think, that we can better understand the suffering, the bravery, the fear and the hopes of the men and women who lived, fought and died in the Great War.

Part One

1914

The lamps are going out all over Europe; we shall not see them lit again in our lifetime.

Sir Edward Grey, British
Foreign Secretary, 3 August 1914.

INTRODUCTION

If the First World War has an exact beginning, it was the balmy Sunday of 28 June 1914 in a remote Balkan town, when a Bosnian Serb student, Gavrilo Princip, aimed his pistol at Archduke Franz Ferdinand.

Two shots rang out – the first of the First World War – and the heir to the rackety Hapsburg empire was lying dead in his car in a street in Sarajevo. In truth, the incident was obscure, only enough in itself to start another interminable Balkan War, but in a Europe riven with imperial rivalry, arms races and diplomatic alliances it served as a pretext for war. A month after Sarajevo, Austria-Hungary took her revenge and declared hostilities against Serbia. Russia mobilized to defend her Serbian ally, Germany declared war on Russia, then on Russia's ally, France. When Germany invaded "poor little Belgium" on 4 August Britain – almost against its will – was sucked into the fray on the side of France and Russia. And the world was at war.

Dare to say it, the populace of Europe – and not just its political class – was mad for the war. You only have to read Sergyei Kurnakov's account of war fever in St Petersburg to see that, or Herbert Sulzbach's account of a week in Germany in late July. Most of civilian Europe, in 1914, were poor innocents about war; Britain, for instance, had not fought a land war in Europe for a hundred years. (Professional soldiers were more sanguine in August 1914: "Send out my mother, my sister and my brother/But for Gawd's sake don't send me," sang the regular British Army). Few imagined the war would last more than a few months. "Over by Christmas" was the popular phrase. All over Europe millions of men were cheered on their way to the front lines, while millions of other, faces flushed bright with patriotism and adventure, rushed to the recruiting office. The more prescient, such as Britain's Lord Kitchener, realized that the war would likely take years – and therefore encouraged more young men to volunteer – especially after Germany's failure to knock out France in the west in the first weeks of the conflict. The doughty resistance of the French – who lost some 200,000 soldiers over seven days – and the British Expeditionary Force at the Marne in September 1914 stopped the German attack in its tracks After the "First Ypres" battle – which virtually destroyed the original 100,000-strong BEF – both sides on the Western Front tried repeated outflanking manoeuvres, with the result that by October 1914 a double line of defensive entrenchments stretched from the English Channel to Switzerland. The resultant trench warfare has become the defining image of the Great War. For four years, the combatants hurled shells and bullets across the dividing yards of No Man's Land, each in the effort to budge the other, the numerical inferiority of the Kaiser's army offset by the simple fact that it held the high ground along the front.

In the vastness of the East, the war took a more open and fluid form from the outset. Enjoying numbers if not *matériel*, the Russian "steam-roller" slowly moved laboriously into Prussia and Austrian Galicia. And was promptly de-roaded by the Prussians at Tannenberg. Against Austria-Hungary, an empire as ramshackle as itself, the Russians had more success. Until, that, the Germans came to the aid of the Hapsburg armies. Why the Germans were so successful on the Eastern Front can be put down to the brilliance of its high command, pure luck, or even the ineptness of the opponent; a more telling reason is caught in the newspaper report of Karl Von Wiegand of 8 October, which details German machine guns blowing down ill-armed Russian ranks like a "terrible gust of wind". The Germans, though still peculiarly attached to cavalry, were fighting a modern war with modern means.

The shock of the new was evident on the Western Front too, though there both sides boasted modern war machines. The result was warfare unlike any other, for it was industrialized slaughter, with armaments and munitions manufactured on fantastic scale by the belligerent powers. Small wonder, perhaps, that those who fought and survived the Western Front battles of 1914 were only too glad to call a Christmas truce. The war was not over by Christmas. It was just that those who did its fighting wished it was.

THE ASSASSINATION OF ARCHDUKE FRANZ FERDINAND, SARAJEVO, 28 June 1914

Borijove Jevtic

The spark which ignited the First World War. Franz Ferdinand was the heir to the Hapsburg throne. The assassin was Gavrilo Princip, Serbian nationalist. Jevtic was one of Princip's co-conspirators.

A tiny clipping from a newspaper mailed without comment from a secret band of terrorists in Zagreb, a capital of Croatia, to their comrades in Belgrade, was the torch which set the world afire with war in 1914. That bit of paper wrecked old proud empires. It gave birth to new, free nations.

I was one of the members of the terrorist band in Belgrade which received it and, in those days, I and my companions were regarded as desperate criminals. A price was on our heads. Today my little band is seen in a different light, as pioneer patriots. It is recognized that our secret plans, hatched in an obscure cafe in the capital of old Serbia, have led to the independence of the new Yugoslavia, the united nation set free from Austrian domination.

The little clipping was from the *Srobobran*, a Croatian journal of limited circulation, and consisted of a short telegram from Vienna. This telegram declared that the Austrian Archduke Franz Ferdinand would visit Sarajevo, the capital of Bosnia, 28 June, to direct army manoeuvres in the neighbouring mountains.

It reached our meeting place, the cafe called Zeatna Moruana, one night the latter part of April, 1914 . . . At a small table in a very humble cafe, beneath a flickering gas jet we sat and read it. There was no advice nor admonition sent with it. Only four letters and two numerals were sufficient to make us unanimous, without discussion, as to what we should do about it. They were contained in the fateful date, 28 June.

How dared Franz Ferdinand, not only the representative of the oppressor but in his own person an arrogant tyrant, enter Sarajevo on that day? Such an entry was a studied insult.

28 June is a date engraved deeply in the heart of every Serb, so that the day has a name of its own. It is called the *vidovnan*. It is the day on which the old Serbian kingdom was conquered by the Turks at the battle of Amselfelde in 1389. It is also the day on which in the second Balkan War the Serbian arms took glorious revenge on the Turk for his old victory and for the years of enslavement.

That was no day for Franz Ferdinand, the new oppressor, to venture to the very doors of Serbia for a display of the force of arms which kept us beneath his heel.

Our decision was taken almost immediately. Death to the tyrant!

Then came the matter of arranging it. To make his death certain twenty-two members of the organization were selected to carry out the sentence. At first we thought we would choose the men by lot. But here Gavrilo Princip intervened. Princip is destined to go down in Serbian history as one of her greatest heroes. From the moment Ferdinand's death was decided upon he took an active leadership in its planning. Upon his advice we left the deed to members of our band who were in and around Sarajevo under his direction and that of Gabrinovic, a linotype operator on a Serbian newspaper. Both were regarded as capable of anything in the cause.

The fateful morning dawned. Two hours before Franz Ferdinand arrived in Sarajevo all the twenty-two conspirators were in their allotted positions, armed and ready. They were distributed 500 yards apart over the whole route along which the Archduke must travel from the railroad station to the town hall.

When Franz Ferdinand and his retinue drove from the station they were allowed to pass the first two conspirators. The motor cars were driving too fast to make an attempt feasible and in the crowd were Serbians: throwing a grenade would have killed many innocent people.

When the car passed Gabrinovic, the compositor, he threw his grenade. It hit the side of the car, but Franz Ferdinand with presence of mind threw himself back and was uninjured. Several officers riding in his attendance were injured.

The cars sped to the Town Hall and the rest of the conspirators did not interfere with them. After the reception in the Town Hall General Potiorek, the Austrian Commander, pleaded with Franz Ferdinand to leave the city, as it was seething with rebellion. The Archduke was persuaded to drive the shortest way out of the city and to go quickly.

The road to the manoeuvres was shaped like the letter V, making a sharp turn at the bridge over the River Nilgacka. Franz Ferdinand's car could go fast enough until it reached this spot but here it was forced to slow down for the turn. Here Princip had taken his stand.

As the car came abreast he stepped forward from the kerb, drew his automatic pistol from his coat and fired two shots. The first struck the wife of the Archduke, the Archduchess Sofia, in the abdomen. She was an expectant mother. She died instantly.

The second bullet struck the Archduke close to the heart.

He uttered only one word; "Sofia" – a call to his stricken wife. Then his head fell back and he collapsed. He died almost instantly.

The officers seized Princip. They beat him over the head with the flat of their swords. They knocked him down, they kicked him, scraped the skin from his neck with the edges of their swords, tortured him, all but killed him.

Then he was taken to the Sarajevo gaol. The next day he was transferred to the military prison and the round-up of his fellow conspirators proceeded, although he denied that he had worked with anyone.

He was confronted with Gabrinovic, who had thrown the bomb. Princip denied he knew him. Others were brought in, but Princip denied the most obvious things.

The next day they put chains on Princip's feet, which he wore till his death.

His only sign of regret was the statement that he was sorry he had killed the wife of the Archduke. He had aimed only at her husband and would have preferred that any other bullet should have struck General Potiorek.

The Austrians arrested every known revolutionary in Sarajevo and among them, naturally, I was one. But they had no proof of my connection with the crime. I was placed in the cell next to Princip's, and when Princip was taken out to walk in the prison yard I was taken along as his companion.

"A STONE HAS BEGUN TO ROLL DOWNHILL": A GERMAN DIARY, 28 June – 25 July 1914

Herbert Sulzbach, German Army

Frankfurt-am-Main, 28 June 1914
Archduke Francis Ferdinand has been murdered, with his wife [the Duchess of Hohenberg], by two Serbs at Sarajevo. What follows from this is not clear. You feel that a stone has begun to roll downhill and that dreadful things may be in store for Europe.

I am proposing on 1 October to start my military service instead of going to Hamburg as a commercial trainee. I'm twenty, you see, a fine age for soldiering, I don't know a better.

July 14
I travel to Würzburg, report to the 2nd Bavarian Field Artillery Regiment and get accepted.

Böhm, the German airman, has scored a world record with 24½ hours of continuous flight.

July 23
Ultimatum delivered to Serbia by Austria-Hungary. No strong action by Austria appeared to have been taken since the assassination of 28 June until suddenly this note was presented, containing ten demands which among other things were supposed to allow Austria herself to take action on Serbian soil against activities hostile to Austria. Serbia has to accept the ultimatum within 48 hours, otherwise Austria reserves the right to take military action. A world war is hanging by a thread.

July 25
Unbelievably large crowds are waiting outside the newspaper offices. News arrives in the evening that Serbia is rejecting the ultimatum. General excitement and enthusiasm, and all eyes turn towards Russia – is she going to support Serbia?

The days pass from 25 to 31 July. Incredibly exciting; the whole world is agog to see whether Germany is now going to mobilize. I've hardly got enough peace of mind left to go to the bank and do my trainee job. I play truant as though it were school and stand about all day outside the newspaper offices, feeling that war is inevitable.

JEAN JAURÈS IS MURDERED, PARIS, 31 July 1914

Robert Dell

Jaurès was leader of the French Socialist Party and the founder of *L'Humanité*. He had championed the working-classes against Clemenceau and was anti-militaristic. Many considered him unpatriotic. It would turn out, in fact, that Jaurès' assassin espoused no cause, and was merely mad, but the murder only exacerbated the mood of foreboding hanging over Europe.

Grave as is the international situation even the probable imminence of war has been overshadowed for the moment in Paris by the appalling crime this evening of which I was an eye-witness. It is impossible to one who knew M. Jaurès, whom one could not help loving, to write about it calmly with the grief fresh upon one. I was dining with a member of my family and a friend at the Café du Croissant, the well-known resort of journalists in the rue Montmartre close to many newspaper offices including that of *L'Humanité*. M. Jaurès was also dining there with some Socialist deputies and members of the staff of *L'Humanité*. He came in later than we did. I spoke to him just as he entered and had a short conversation with him about the prospects of war and peace. Like everyone else, he feared that war was probable, but he still had some faith that Sir Edward Grey might succeed in inducing Germany to be conciliatory. If some sort of conference could be arranged, he thought, peace might even yet be secured: and if the French Government would bring pressure to bear on Russia and the German Government on Austria an arrangement might be possible. He added, however, that he feared the French Government might not do that. What a crime war will be and what a monstrous folly. The last words that he said to me was an inquiry about M. Anatole France, who, he said, must be deeply distressed by the situation.

At about half-past nine, when we were just finishing dinner, two pistol shots suddenly resounded in the restaurant. At first we did not understand what had happened, and for a moment thought that there was shooting in the street outside. Then we saw that M. Jaurès had fallen sideways on the bench on which he was sitting, and the screams of the women who were present told us of the murder. It should be explained that M. Jaurès and his friends were sitting on a bench with their backs to the open window of the restaurant, and the shots were fired from the street through the window. M. Jaurès was shot in the head, and the murderer must have held the pistol close to his victim. A surgeon was hastily summoned, but he could do nothing, and M. Jaurès died quietly without regaining consciousness a few minutes after the crime. Meanwhile the murderer had been seized and handed over to the police, who had to protect him from the crowd which had quickly collected in the street. At that hour in the evening the rue Montmartre is filled with newsvendors waiting for the late editions of the evening papers.

It is said that the murderer is a member of the Royalist society Action Française, but I have not yet been able to discover whether this report is true or not. A more cold-blooded and cowardly murder was never committed. The scene in and about the restaurant was heartrending; both men and women were in tears and their grief was terrible to see. It is as yet too early to say what the effect of the murder will be, but it may be considerable. M. Jaurès has died a victim to the cause of peace and humanity.

WAR FEVER IN ST PETERSBURG, 1 August 1914

Sergyei N. Kurnakov

There was a crowd in front of a newspaper office. Every few minutes a momentous phrase scribbled in charcoal appeared in the window: "ENGLAND GIVES UP PEACE NEGOTIATIONS. Germany invades Belgium. Mobilization progressing with Great Enthusiasm." And at 7.50 p.m.:

"GERMANY DECLARES WAR ON RUSSIA."

Spontaneously the crowd started singing the national anthem. The little pimply clerk who had pasted up the irrevocable announcement was still standing in the window, enjoying his vicarious importance. The people were staring at the sprawling words, as if trying to understand what they actually meant as far as each personal little life was concerned.

Then the edges of the crowd started breaking off and drifting in one direction, up the Nevsky Prospect. I heard the phrase "German Embassy" repeated several times. I walked slowly that way.

The mob pulled an officer from his cab and carried him in triumph.

I went into a telephone box and called up Stana.

"Yes, it's been declared . . . I don't know what I am going to do yet . . . All right, I'll be over about midnight."

I did not like the way her receiver clicked; there seemed to be contempt in it.

When I got to the St Isaac Square it was swarming with people. It must have been about nine o'clock, for it was pretty light yet – the enervating, exciting twilight of the northern nights.

The great greystone monstrosity of the German Embassy was facing the red granite of St Isaac's Cathedral. The crowds were pressing around waiting for something to happen. I was watching a young naval officer being pawed by an over-patriotic group when the steady hammering of axes on metal made me look up at the Embassy roof, which was decorated with colossal figures of overfed German warriors holding bloated carthorses. A flagstaff supported a bronze eagle with spread wings.

Several men were busily hammering at the feet of the Teutons. The very first strokes pitched the mob to a frenzy: the heroic figures were hollow!

"They are empty! . . . A good omen! . . . Another German bluff! . . . We'll show them! . . . Hack them all down! . . . No, leave the horses standing! . . . The national anthem! . . . Lord, Save Thy People!"

The axes were hammering faster and faster. At last one warrior swayed, pitched forward, and crashed to the pavement one hundred feet below. A tremendous howl went up, scaring a flock of crows off the gilded dome of St Isaac's. The turn of the eagle came; the bird came hurtling down, and the battered remains were immediately drowned in the nearby Moika river.

But obviously the destruction of the symbols was not enough. A quickly organized gang smashed a side door of the Embassy.

I could see flashlights and torches moving inside, flitting to the upper storeys. A big window opened and spat a great portrait of the Kaiser at the crowd below. When it reached the cobblestones, there was just about enough left to start a good bonfire. A rosewood grand piano followed, exploded like a bomb; the moan of the broken strings vibrated in the air for a second and was drowned: too many people were trying to outshout their own terror of the future.

'Deploy! . . . Trot! . . . Ma-a-arch!'

A troop of mounted *gendarmes* was approaching from the other end of the square. The crowd opened up like the Red Sea for the Israelites. A new crowd carrying the portrait of the Emperor and singing a hymn was advancing slowly towards the *gendarmes*. Their officer halted the men and stiffened at the salute; this was the only thing he did towards restoring order. The bonfire was being fed by the furniture, books, pictures, and papers which came hurtling through the windows of the Embassy.

The emblazoned crockery of state came crashing, and the shattering sound whipped the crowd into a new wave of hysteria.

A woman tore her dress at the collar, fell on her knees with a shriek, and pressed her naked breasts against the dusty boots of a young officer in campaign uniform.

"Take me! Right here, before these people! Poor boy . . . you will give your life . . . for God . . . for the Tsar . . . for Russia!"

Another shriek, and she fainted. Men and women were running aimlessly around the bonfire . . . Is it an effect of light and shadow, or do I really see high cheekbones, slanting eyes, and the conic fur caps of Aladin Mirza's horde?

Whew! . . . I let out the breath I had been holding unconsciously during the entire bacchanal.

THE DRIFT TO WAR: THE VIEW FROM 10 DOWNING STREET, LONDON, 1–3 August 1914

Herbert Asquith, Prime Minister

August 1

When most of them [the Cabinet] had left, Sir W. Tyrrell arrived with a long message from Berlin to the effect that the German Ambassador's efforts for peace had been suddenly arrested and frustrated by the Tsar's decree for a complete Russian mobilization. We all set to work, Tyrrell, Bongie, Drummond and myself, to draft a direct personal appeal from the King to the Tsar. When we had settled it I called a taxi, and, in company with Tyrrell, drove to Buckingham Palace at about 1.30 a.m. The King was hauled out of bed, and one of my strangest experiences was sitting with him, clad in a dressing gown, while I read the message and the proposed answer.

There was really no fresh news this morning. Lloyd George, all for peace, is more sensible and statesmanlike for keeping the position still open. Grey declares that if an out-and-out and uncompromising policy of non-intervention at all costs is adopted, he will go. Winston [Churchill] very bellicose and demanding immediate mobilization. The main controversy pivots upon Belgium and its neutrality. We parted in fairly amicable mood, and are to sit again at 11 to-morrow, Sunday. I am still not quite hopeless about peace, though far from hopeful, but if it comes to war, I feel sure we shall have a split in the

Cabinet. Of course if Grey went I should go and the whole thing would break up. On the other hand, we may have to contemplate, with such equanimity as we can command, the loss of Morley and possibly, though I do not think it, of Simon.

August 2

Things are pretty black. Germany is now in active war with both Russia and France, and the Germans have violated the neutrality of Luxembourg. We are waiting to know whether they are going to do the same with Belgium. I had a visit at breakfast from Lichnowsky, who was very *emotionné* and implored me not to side with France. He said that Germany, with her army cut in two between France and Russia, was far more likely to be crushed than France. He was very agitated, poor man, and wept. I told him that we had no desire to intervene, and that it rested largely with Germany to make intervention impossible if she would (1) not invade Belgium, and (2) not send her fleet into the Channel to attack the unprotected north coast of France. He was bitter about the policy of his Government in not restraining Austria and seemed quite heart-broken.

Then we had a long Cabinet from 11 till nearly two, which very soon revealed that we are on the brink of a split. We agreed at last with some difficulty that Grey should be authorized to tell Cambon that our fleet would not allow the German fleet to make the Channel a base of hostile operations. John Burns at once resigned, but was persuaded to hold on at any rate till the evening when we meet again. There is a strong party against any kind of intervention in any event. Grey, of course, will never consent to this, and I shall not separate myself from him. Crewe, McKenna and Samuel are a moderating intermediate body. Bonar Law writes that the Opposition will back us up in any measure we may take for the support of France and Russia. I suppose a good number of our own party in the House of Commons are for absolute non-interference. It will be a shocking thing if at such a moment we break up.

Happily I am quite clear in my mind as to what is right and wrong. (1) We have no obligation of any kind either to France or Russia to give them military or naval help. (2) The dispatch of the Expeditionary Force to help France at this moment is out of the question and would serve no object. (3) We must not forget the ties created by our long-standing and intimate friendship with France. (4) It is against British interests that France should be wiped out as a Great Power. (5) We cannot allow Germany to use the Channel as a hostile base. (6) We have obligations to Belgium to prevent it being utilized and absorbed by Germany . . .

August 3
This morning, two letters arrived for me, one from John Morley, the other from Simon, announcing that they must follow John Burns's example. They are both characteristic productions. At the Cabinet later in the morning Beauchamp declared that he must do likewise. That is four gone. We had a rather moving scene in which every one all round said something, Lloyd George making a strong appeal to them not to go, or at least to delay it. Anyhow, they all agreed to say nothing today and to sit in their accustomed places in the House.

Bonar Law and Lansdowne came to see me early this morning. They were in general agreement, but laid great stress upon Belgian neutrality. The Germans have delivered an ultimatum to Belgium and forced themselves on their territory, and the Belgian King has made an appeal to ours. After lunch we all went to the House of Commons. Grey made a most remarkable speech almost an hour long, for the most part almost conversational in tone and with some of his usual ragged ends, but extraordinarily well reasoned and tactful and really cogent, so much so that our extreme peace lovers were for the moment reduced to silence, though they will soon find their tongues again.

BRITAIN DECLARES WAR, 4 August 1914

King George V

With the German invasion of neutral Belgium on 4 August all chances of British non-involvement in the European conflict were washed away.

August 4th
Warm, showers & windy. At work all day. Winston Churchill came to report at 1.0 that at the meeting of Cabinet this morning we had sent an ultimatum to Germany that if by midnight tonight she did not give satisfactory answer about her troops passing through Belgium, Goschen would ask for his passports. Held a Council at 4.0. Lord Morley & John Burns have resigned & have left the Cabinet. . . . I held a Council at 10.45 to declare War with Germany, it is a terrible catastrophe but it is not our fault. . . . When they heard that War had been declared the excitement [of the crowds outside the Palace] increased & it was a never to be forgotten sight when May & I with David went on to the balcony, the cheering was terrific. Please God it may soon be over & that He will protect dear Bertie's life.

JOINING UP, Summer–Autumn 1914

Patriotic fervour caused recruiting stations all over Europe to be flooded with citizen volunteers. In Britain alone, nearly a million men enlisted for Lord Kitchener's "new army" by the end of 1914.

Oskar Kokoschka
Austrian by birth, Kokoschka went on to become one of Europe's most eminent painters.

In 1914 I was twenty-eight years old, and thus liable for military service. It seemed to me better to volunteer before I was conscripted. I had no wife or child to await my happy return. I had nothing to lose or to defend. I felt melancholy at the sight of the young bank clerks, the little office workers, whom I saw hurrying with their suitcases to enlist, and yet I did not share the doom-laden mood that prevailed on the streets. The air was thick with rumours that part of the army had gone into the field wearing peacetime clothing.

Arthur Conan Doyle
The British author of the *Sherlock Holmes* stories writes a letter to the War Office.

I have been told that there may be some difficulty in finding officers for the New Army. I think I may say that my name is well-known to the younger men of this country and that if I were to take a commission at my age it might be of help. I can drill a company – I do so every evening. I have seen something of campaigning, having served as a surgeon in South Africa. I am fifty-five but I am very strong and hardy, and can make my voice audible at great distances which is useful at drill. Should you entertain my application, I should prefer a regiment which was drawn from the South of England – Sussex for choice.

Robert Graves

At the time of writing Robert Graves was a student. He later joined the Royal Welsh Fusiliers, and wrote one of the classic memoirs of the conflict, *Goodbye to All That*.

I had just finished with Charterhouse and gone up to Harlech, when England declared war on Germany. A day or two later I decided to enlist. In the first place, though the papers predicted only a very short war – over by Christmas at the outside – I hoped that it might last long enough to delay my going to Oxford in October, which I dreaded. Nor did I work out the possibilities of getting actively engaged in the fighting, expecting garrison service at home, while the regular forces were away. In the second place, I was outraged to read of the Germans' cynical violation of Belgian neutrality. Though I discounted perhaps twenty per cent of the atrocity details as wartime exaggeration, that was not, of course, sufficient.

"THE TOMMY"

The marching song of the regular British Army in 1914.

"Send out the Army and the Navy,
Send out the rank and file.
(Have a banana!)
Send out the brave Territorials,
They'll face the danger with a smile.
(I don't think!)

Send out the boys of the girls' brigade,
They will keep old England free;
Send out my mother, my sister and my brother,
But for Gawd's sake don't send me!"

BANK HOLIDAY AT THE SEASIDE, BRIGHTLINGSEA, ENGLAND, 6 August 1914

Arnold Bennett

On arriving at Brightlingsea on Monday afternoon, I was told that petrol could not be got in the district; that it was fetching up to 10s. a tin at Clacton; and that Baggaley, the regular hirer of motor-cars at B'sea, had gone forth in an attempt to get petrol. At Clacton yesterday the price was 2s. 3d. or 2s. 4d. a gallon. I have 60 gallons in stock.

A great crowd of holiday makers at Clacton in the showers yesterday. No difficulty about getting change for a £10 note in gold and silver. At the fish shop, slight increases of price in poultry and eggs. The man said there was no chance for him to make money (in response to a friendly jibe of M's). He said he expected to get no more fish after that day.

Yesterday we heard noise of explosions destroying inconvenient houses at Harwich. The sensations of Harwich people must be poignant. Nevertheless the G.E.R. in yesterday evening's papers was advertising its Hook of Holland service (with restaurant cars, etc.) exactly as usual, and I believe the boat left last night. We also heard thunder; and the children affirm that they distinctly heard the noise of firing – not explosions. (Report of action in North Sea in evening papers). I saw one warship in the offing at Clacton; but an ordinary steamer coming to the pier, and a barge sailing northwards.

An officer came yesterday to complain of a fox terrier (? ours) which flew at despatch-riders on motor-bicycles. He said it would be shot if found loose. These despatch-riders are the most picturesque feature of the war here. They rush through the village at speeds estimated up to 50 miles an hour. I am willing to concede 40 . . .

. . . After reading the diplomatic papers leading up to the

rupture between England and Germany, this morning, one has to admit that Sir E. Grey did everything he could, once he had stated his position. The war is a mistake on our part, but other things leading to it were a mistake, and, these things approved or condoned, the war must be admitted to be inevitable . . .

Apart from Germany two countries are pre-eminently suffering at the beginning of the war – France and Belgium. Both are quite innocent; Belgium touchingly so. I can imagine the Germans among them if they get the upper hand. The Germans are evidently quite ruthless and brutal and savage in war. This is logical; but a large part of their conduct is due to the arrogant military tradition, which will one day be smashed. If Germany is smashed in this war, the man most imperilled will be the German Emperor. If she is not smashed the man most imperilled may be the Tsar.

I am told, convincingly, that a firm at Clacton is making an extra £50 a week out of bread, through increased charges for which there is no justification. It appears that the farmers all round have raised the price of butter 3d. a lb.

Miss Osborne and a girl friend came round yesterday afternoon to ask for linen or subscriptions for the local branch of the Red Cross Society. Mrs Byng is ready to lend Thorpe Hall for a hospital. These young ladies have no orders or permission yet from the War Office; but they wish to be in readiness. This instinct to do something on the part of idle young women or half-idle is satisfactory to behold.

On the day after the war the boys [his nephews] wanted a tent. They had one, beyond the pond. It cost one day's labour of a carpenter. This tent is used by everybody except me nearly all the time. The whole household seems to live in it. To-day the boys are making wooden swords. Yesterday a village boy gave me a military salute.

Edith Johnston recounts how her father is laying in ammunition against the time when the populace will raid the countryside demanding provisions; he, being a farmer, is to be called on early in the proceedings, and he is determined to give out his stores evenly and not to the strongest. Each morning he summons all his men and explains to them the course of the war, so that they shall not be misled by rumours. Edith thinks that a war is necessary and advisable, as the population is too thick . . .

TO THE FRONT: A GERMAN SOLDIER WRITES HOME, 7 August 1914

Walter Limmer, German Army

Limmer writes to his parents from Leipzig.

Dear Father, good Mother, beloved Brothers and Sisters, please, please don't think me cruel for saying this, but it would be a good thing if already you too would, with brave hearts and firm self-control, get accustomed to the idea that you will not see me or any of my brothers again. Then if bad news does come, you will be able to receive it much more calmly. But if we all do come back, then we can accept that joy as an unexpected and all the more gracious and glorious gift of God. You will believe that I really mean this. The matter is much too sacred to me for me to be capable of merely making phrases in what I have just said.

In any case I mean to go into this business "like Blücher". That is the simple duty of every one of us. And this feeling is universal among the soldiers, especially since the night when England's declaration of war was announced in the barracks. We none of us got to sleep till three o'clock in the morning, we were so full of excitement, fury, and enthusiasm. It is a joy to go to the Front with such comrades. We are bound to be victorious! Nothing else is possible in the face of such determination to win. My dear ones, be proud that you live in such times and in such a nation, and that you too have the privilege of sending several of those you love into this glorious struggle.

In the Train

Our march to the station was a gripping and uplifting experience! Such a march is hallowed by its background of significance and danger. Both those who were leaving and those who remained behind were beset by the same thoughts and feelings. It seemed as if one lived through as much in that hour as ordinarily in months and years. Such enthusiasm! – the whole battalion with helmets and tunics decked with flowers – handkerchiefs waving untiringly – cheers on every side – and over and over again the ever-fresh and wonderful reassurance from the soldiers: "*fest stetht und treu die Wacht am Rhein!*" This hour is one such as seldom strikes in the life of a nation, and it is so marvellous and moving as to be in itself sufficient compensation for many sufferings and sacrifices.

Limmer died of tetanus on 24 September 1914, at the Military Hospital in Luxemburg.

PROTEST OF A PACIFIST, LONDON, 15 August 1914

Bertrand Russell

The philosopher writes to the *Nation*.

Sir

Against the vast majority of my countrymen, even at this moment, in the name of humanity and civilization, I protest against our share in the destruction of Germany.

A month ago Europe was a peaceful comity of nations; if an Englishman killed a German, he was hanged. Now, if an Englishman kills a German, or if a German kills an Englishman, he is a patriot, who has deserved well of his country. We scan the newspapers with greedy eyes for news of slaughter, and rejoice when we read of innocent young men, blindly obedient to the word of command, mown down in thousands by the machine-guns of Liège. Those who saw the London crowds, during the nights leading up to the Declaration of War saw a whole population, hitherto peaceable and humane, precipitated in a few days down the steep slope to primitive barbarism, letting loose, in a moment, the instincts of hatred and blood lust against which the whole fabric of society has been raised. "Patriots" in all countries acclaim this brutal orgy as a noble determination to vindicate the right; reason and mercy are swept away in one great flood of hatred; dim abstractions of unimaginable wickedness – Germany to us and the French, Russia to the Germans – conceal the simple fact that the enemy are men, like ourselves, neither better nor worse – men who love their homes and the sunshine, and all the simple pleasures of common lives; men now mad with terror in the thought of their wives, their sisters, their children, exposed, with our help, to the tender mercies of the conquering Cossack.

And all this madness, all this rage, all this flaming death of our civilization and our hopes, has been brought about because a set of official gentlemen, living luxurious lives, mostly stupid, and all without imagination or heart, have chosen that it should occur rather than that any one of them should suffer some infinitesimal rebuff to his country's pride. No literary tragedy can appraoch the futile horror of the White Paper. The diplomatists, seeing from the first the inevitable end, mostly wishing to avoid it, yet drifted from hour to hour of the swift crisis restrained by punctilio from making or accepting the small concessions that might have saved the world, hurried on at last by blind fear to loose the armies for the work of mutual butchery.

And behind the diplomatists, dimly heard in the official documents, stand vast forces of national greed and national hatred – atavistic instincts, harmful to mankind at its present level, but transmitted from savage and half-animal ancestors, concentrated and directed by Governments and the Press, fostered by the upper class as a distraction from social discontent, artificially nourished by the sinister influence of the makers of armaments, encouraged by a whole foul literature of "glory", and by every text-book of history with which the minds of children are polluted.

England, no more than other nations which participate in this war, can be absolved either as regards its national passions or as regards its diplomacy . . .

It thus appears that the neutrality of Belgium, the integrity of France and her colonies, and the naval defence of the northern and western coasts of France, were all mere pretexts. If Germany had agreed to our demands in all these respects, we should still not have promised neutrality.

I cannot resist the conclusion that the Government has failed in its duty to the nation by not revealing long-standing arrangements with the French, until, at the last moment, it made them the basis of an appeal to honour; that it has failed in its duty to Europe by not declaring its attitude at the beginning of the crisis; and that it has failed in its duty to humanity by not informing Germany of conditions which would insure its non-participation in a war which, whatever its outcome, must cause untold hardship and the loss of many thousands of our bravest and noblest citizens.

THE GERMAN ARMY ENTERS BRUSSELS, 21 August 1914

Richard Harding Davis

Davis was a war reporter for the New York *Tribune*.

The entrance of the German army into Brussels has lost the human quality. It was lost as soon as the three soldiers who led the army bicycled into the Boulevard du Régent and asked the way to the Gare du Nord. When they passed the human note passed with them.

What came after them, and twenty-four hours later is still coming, is not men marching, but a force of nature like a tidal wave, an avalanche or a river flooding its banks. At this minute it is rolling through Brussels as the swollen waters of the Conemaugh Valley swept through Johnstown.

At the sight of the first few regiments of the enemy we were thrilled with interest. After for three hours they had passed in one unbroken steel-grey column we were bored. But when hour after hour passed and there was no halt, no breathing time, no open spaces in the ranks, the thing became uncanny, inhuman. You returned to watch it, fascinated. It held the mystery and menace of fog rolling toward you across the sea.

The grey of the uniforms worn by both officers and men

helped this air of mystery. Only the sharpest eye could detect among the thousands that passed the slightest difference. All moved under a cloak of invisibility. Only after the most numerous and severe tests at all distances, with all materials and combinations of colours that give forth no colour, could this grey have been discovered. That it was selected to clothe and disguise the German when he fights is typical of the German staff in striving for efficiency to leave nothing to chance, to neglect no detail.

After you have seen this service uniform under conditions entirely opposite you are convinced that for the German soldier it is his strongest weapon. Even the most expert marksman cannot hit a target he cannot see. It is a grey green, not the blue grey of our Confederates. It is the grey of the hour just before daybreak, the grey of unpolished steel, of mist among green trees.

I saw it first in the Grand Place in front of the Hôtel de Ville. It was impossible to tell if in that noble square there was a regiment or a brigade. You saw only a fog that melted into the stones, blended with the ancient house fronts, that shifted and drifted, but left you nothing at which you could point.

Later, as the army passed below my window, under the trees of the Botanical Park, it merged and was lost against the green leaves. It is no exaggeration to say that at a hundred yards you can see the horses on which the uhlans ride, but you cannot see the men who ride them.

If I appear to overemphasize this disguising uniform it is because of all the details of the German outfit it appealed to me as one of the most remarkable. The other day when I was with the rearguard of the French Dragoons and Cuirassiers and they threw out pickets, we could distinguish them against the yellow wheat or green gorse at half a mile, while these men passing in the street, when they have reached the next crossing, become merged into the grey of the paving stones and the earth swallows them. In comparison the yellow khaki of our own American army is about as invisible as the flag of Spain.

Yesterday Major General von Jarotsky, the German Military Governor of Brussels, assured Burgomaster Max that the German army would not occupy the city, but would pass through it. It is still passing. I have followed in campaigns six armies, but excepting not even our own, the Japanese, or the British, I have not seen one so thoroughly equipped. I am not speaking of the fighting qualities of any army, only of the equipment and organization. The German army moved into this city as smoothly and as compactly as an Empire State Express. There were no halts, no open places, no stragglers.

This army has been on active service three weeks, and so far there is not apparently a chin strap or a horseshoe missing. It came in with the smoke pouring from cookstoves on wheels, and in an hour had set up post-office wagons, from which mounted messengers galloped along the line of columns, distributing letters, and at which soldiers posted picture postcards.

The infantry came in in files of five, two hundred men to each company; the Lancers in columns of four, with not a pennant missing. The quick-firing guns and fieldpieces were one hour at a time in passing, each gun with its caisson and ammunition wagon taking twenty seconds in which to pass.

The men of the infantry sang "Fatherland, My Fatherland". Between each line of song they took three steps. At times two thousand men were singing together in absolute rhythm and beat. When the melody gave way the silence was broken only by the stamp of iron-shod boots, and then again the song rose. When the singing ceased, the bands played marches. They were followed by the rumble of siege guns, the creaking of wheels, and of chains clanking against the cobblestones and the sharp bell-like voices of the bugles.

For seven hours the army passed in such solid columns that not once might a taxicab or trolley car pass through the city. Like a river of steel it flowed, grey and ghostlike. Then, as dusk came and as thousands of horses' hoofs and thousands of iron boots continued to tramp forward, they struck tiny sparks from the stones, but the horses and the men who beat out the sparks were invisible.

At midnight pack wagons and siege guns were still passing. At seven this morning I was awakened by the tramp of men and bands playing jauntily. Whether they marched all night or not I do not know; but now for twenty-six hours the grey army has rumbled by with the mystery of fog and the pertinacity of a steam roller.

CAVALRY SKIRMISH, ETALLE, BELGIUM, 22 August 1914

Lieutenant Manfred von Richthofen, Uhlan Regiment 1

I will briefly describe for you what I have experienced here on the Western Front. Before the advance of the army ended, it was somewhat boring. We disembarked northeast of Diedenhofen and marched through Luxembourg and crossed the Belgian border near Arlon. In Etalle, about twenty kilometers west of Arlon, I was ordered on 21 August to reconnoitre south in the direction of Meix-devant-Virton. As I came to the edge of the forest south of Etalle, I spotted a troop of French dragoons. I only had fifteen men with me. After about a half hour the enemy troop disappeared and I led my men forward to determine where the French had gone. We found ourselves right at the exit of the forest, in the vicinity of Meix-devant-Virton. On the right was a wall of rock, on the left a stream, and about fifty metres behind was a broad meadow – then the forest's edge. Suddenly my horse stopped short, but I galloped out to see what was going on.

Just as I put the field glasses to my eye, a volley of fire cracked from the edge of the forest about fifty meters away. There were about two hundred to two hundred and fifty French riflemen over there. We couldn't move to the left or forward because the enemy was there, and to the right was the wall of rock; therefore, we had to go back. Yes, but it wasn't so simple. The way was quite narrow and it led right by the enemy-fortified forest's edge. To take cover was also useless; therefore I had to go back. I was the last one. In spite of my orders, all the others had bunched together and offered the Frenchmen a good target. Perhaps that was the reason why I escaped. I brought only four men back. This baptism of fire was not as much fun as I thought. That evening some of the others came back, although they had to come by foot, as their horses were dead.

It was really a miracle that nothing happened to me or my horse.

The same night I was sent to Virton but did not get there as that town was taken by the enemy.

During the night Division Commander Von Below decided to attack the enemy at Virton and appeared at the head of his Uhlan Regiment 1 at the exit of the forest.

The fog was so thick, one could not see more than thirty paces ahead.

One regiment after another, just as if on maneuvers, was deployed on the narrow way into the forest. Prince Oscar stood on a pile of rocks and urged his regiment, the 7th Grenadiers, onward, looking each grenadier in the eye. A splendid moment before the battle. Thus began the battle of Virton, where the 9th Division fought against an enemy six times its own number, and where, after two days, was brilliantly victorious.

In this battle Prince Oscar fought at the head of his regiment and remained unscathed. I spoke with him right after the battle, as he was presented with the Iron Cross.

WESTERN FRONT: THE RETREAT FROM MONS, 23 August–5 September 1914

Corporal Bernard Denmore, 1st Royal Berkshire Regiment

Hurried into battle against the Germans at Mons, Belgium, the British Expeditionary Force withstood six enemy divisions before being ordered to retreat alongside their French allies. The retreat lasted until 5 September. During that time Bernard Denmore marched 251 miles. The fatigue endured by the troops created mass hallucinations, most famously the "Angel of Mons".

August 23rd
We had been marching since 2.30 a.m. and about 11.15 a.m. an order was passed down for "A" Company (my company) to deploy to the right and dig in on the south bank of a railway cutting.

We deployed and started digging in, but as the soil was mostly chalk, we were able to make only shallow holes. While we were digging the German artillery opened fire. The range was perfect, about six shells at a time bursting in line directly over our heads. All of us except the company commander fell flat on our faces, frightened, and surprised; but after a while we got up, and looked over the rough parapet we had thrown up; and could not see much. One or two men had been wounded, and one was killed.

There was a town about one mile away on our left front, and a lot of movement was going on round about it; and there was a small village called Binche on our right, where there was a lot of heavy firing going on – rifle and artillery.

We saw the Germans attack on our left in great masses, but they were beaten back by the Coldstream Guards.

A squadron of German cavalry crossed our front about 800 yards distant, and we opened fire on them. We hit a few and the fact that we were doing something definite improved our *moral* immensely, and took away a lot of our nervousness.

The artillery fire from the Germans was very heavy, but was dropping behind us on a British battery. The company officer, who had stayed in the open all the time, had taken a couple of men to help get the wounded away from the battery behind us. He returned about 6.30 p.m., when the firing had died down a bit, and told us the battery had been blown to bits.

I was then sent with four men on outpost to a signal box at a level crossing, and found it was being used as a clearing station for wounded. After dark more wounded were brought in from of the 9th Battery R.F.A. (the battery that was cut up). One man was in a very bad way, and kept shrieking out for somebody to bring a razor and cut his throat, and two others died almost immediately.

I was going to move a bundle of hay when someone called out, 'Look out, chum. There's a bloke in there.' I saw a leg completely severed from its body, and suddenly felt very sick and tired.

The German rifle-fire started again and an artillery-man to whom I was talking was shot dead. I was sick then.

Nothing much happened during the night, except that one man spent the time kissing a string of rosary beads, and another swore practically the whole night.

August 25th

We started off about 5 a.m., still retiring, and so far we had had no food since Sunday the 23rd. All day long we marched, and although a lot of firing was going on, we did none of it. About 6.30 p.m. we got to a place called Maroilles, and my platoon spent the night guarding a bridge over a stream. The Germans attacked about 9 p.m. and kept it up all night, but didn't get into Maroilles.

About forty-five of the company were killed or wounded, including the company officer. A voice had called out in English, "Has anybody got a map?" and when our C.O. stood up with his map, a German walked up, and shot him with a revolver. The German was killed by a bayonet stab from a private.

August 26th

The Germans withdrew at dawn, and soon after we continued retiring, and had not been on the march very long before we saw a French regiment, which showed that all of them had not deserted us.

We marched all day long, miles and miles it seemed, probably owing to the fact that we had had no sleep at all since Saturday the 22nd, and had had very little food to eat, and the marching discipline was not good. I myself frequently felt very sick.

We had a bit of a fight at night, and what made matters worse was that it happened at Venerolles, the village we were billeted in before we went up to Mons. Anyway, the Germans retired from the fight.

August 27th

At dawn we started on the march again. I noticed that the *curé* and one old fellow stayed in Venerolles, but all the other inhabitants went the previous night.

A lot of our men threw away their overcoats while we were on the road to-day, but I kept mine.

The marching was getting quite disorderly; numbers of men from other regiments were mixed up with us.

We reached St Quentin, a nice town, just before dark, but marched straight through, and dug ourselves in on some high ground, with a battery of artillery in line with us. Although we saw plenty of movement in the town the Germans didn't attack us, neither did we fire on them. During the night a man near me quite suddenly started squealing like a pig, and then jumped out of the trench, ran straight down the hill towards the town, and shot himself through the foot. He was brought in by some artillery-men.

August 28th

Again at dawn we started on the march, and during the first halt another fellow shot himself through the foot.

The roads were in a terrible state, the heat was terrific, there seemed to be very little order about anything, and mixed up with us and wandering about all over the road were refugees, with all sorts of conveyances – prams, trucks, wheelbarrows, and tiny little carts drawn by dogs. They were piled up, with what looked like beds and bedding, and all of them asked us for food, which we could not give them, as we had none ourselves.

The men were discarding their equipment in a wholesale fashion, in spite of orders to the contrary; also many of them fell out, and rejoined again towards dusk. They had been riding on limbers and wagons, and officers' chargers, and generally looked worse than those of us who kept going all day. That night I went on outpost, but I did not know where exactly, as things were getting hazy in my mind. I tried to keep a diary, although it was against orders. Anyway, I couldn't realize all that was happening, and only knew that I was always tired, hungry, unshaven, and dirty. My feet were sore, water was scarce: in fact, it was issued in half-pints, as we were not allowed to touch the native water. The regulations were kept in force in that respect – so much so that two men were put under arrest and sentenced to field punishment for stealing bread from an empty house.

Then, again, it wasn't straight marching. For every few hours we had to deploy, and beat off an attack, and every time somebody I knew was killed or wounded. And after we had beaten off the attacking force, on we went again – retiring.

August 31st

Again we were rearguard, but did little fighting. We marched instead, staggering about the road like a crowd of gipsies. Some of the fellows had puttees wrapped round their feet instead of boots; others had soft shoes they had picked up somewhere; others walked in their socks, with their feet all bleeding. My own boots would have disgraced a tramp, but I was too frightened to take them off, and look at my feet. Yet they marched until they dropped, and then somehow got up and marched again.

One man (Ginger Gilmore) found a mouth-organ, and, despite the fact that his feet were bound in blood-soaked rags, he staggered along at the head of the company playing tunes all day. Mostly he played "The Irish Emigrant", which is a good marching tune. He reminded me of Captain Oates.

An officer asked me if I wanted a turn on his horse, but I looked at the fellow on it, and said, "No thanks."

The marching was getting on everyone's nerves, but, as I went I kept saying to myself, "If you can, force your heart and nerve and sinew." Just that, over and over again.

That night we spent the time looking for an Uhlan regiment, but didn't get in touch with them, and every time we stopped we fell asleep; in fact we slept while we were marching, and consequently kept falling over.

September 2nd

At 2 a.m. we moved off, and marched all day long. It was hot and dusty and the roads were rotten, but, as we got mixed up with hundreds of refugees, we were obliged to keep better marching order. About 6 p.m. to 8 p.m. we reached Meaux – I believe we did about twenty-five miles that day, but no fighting. We bivouacked outside Meaux, but I went into the cathedral when we halted near it, and thought it was very beautiful. Also I saw some of the largest tomatoes I have ever seen in my life, growing in a garden. I was rounding up stragglers most of the night until I a.m., and at 3 a.m. we moved off again.

September 3rd

The first four or five hours we did without a single halt or rest, as we had to cross a bridge over the Aisne before the R.E.'s blew it up. It was the most terrible march I have ever done. Men were falling down like ninepins. They would fall flat on their faces on the road, while the rest of us staggered round them, as we couldn't lift our feet high enough to step over them, and, as for picking them up, that was impossible, as to bend meant to fall. What happened to them, God only knows. An aeroplane was following us most of the time dropping iron darts; we fired at it a couple of times, but soon lost the strength required for that. About 9 a.m. we halted by a river, and immediately two fellows threw themselves into it. Nobody, from sheer fatigue, was able to save them, although one sergeant made an attempt, and was nearly drowned himself. I, like a fool, took my boots off, and found my feet were covered with blood. I could find no sores or cuts, so I thought I must have sweated blood.

As I couldn't get my boots on again I cut the sides away, and when we started marching again, my feet hurt like hell.

We marched till about 3 p.m. – nothing else, just march, march, march. I kept repeating my line, "If you can, force, etc." Why, I didn't know. A sergeant irritated everyone who could hear him by continually shouting out: "Stick it, lads. We're making history."

The Colonel offered me a ride on his horse, but I refused, and then wished I hadn't, as anything was preferable to the continuous marching.

We got right back that afternoon among the refugees again. They were even worse off than we were, or, at least, they looked it. We gave the kids our biscuits and "bully", hoping that would help them a little; but they looked so dazed and tired there did not seem to be much hope for them.

At 8 p.m. we bivouacked in a field and slept till dawn. Ye gods! what a relief.

AN OFFICER AND A GENTLEMAN: ADVICE FOR SUBALTERNS, 1914

Major-General D. O'Callaghan, British Army

From *The Young Officers "Don't", or Hints to Youngsters on Joining*, first issued in 1907, still popular in 1915.

Don't *grouse*. However irksome the duty, remember that others have been put to the same inconvenience – and worse – scores of times before. Try to do what you have to do cheerfully. It is all in a day's work.

Don't lose your temper at games. It is painful both to the other players and to the onlookers, and invariably to your disadvantage.

Don't use bad language or deal in strange oaths. The habit is easily acquired, but became bad form shortly after the withdrawal of our Army from Flanders.

A PILOT ENCOUNTERS THE ENEMY, WESTERN FRONT, August 1914

Lieutenant W. R. Read, Royal Flying Corps

At the outbreak of war, the Royal Flying Corps numbered 860 men and 63 aeroplanes. The latter were not yet armed, and were used for observation.

One day, after our reconnaissance over Mons and Charleroi, Jackson [Read's observer] spotted a German Taube machine. I had also seen him but we had done our job and I did not want a fight. Jackson was always bloodthirsty, however, and the following shouted conversation ensued:

Jackson: "Look, old boy!"

Me: "Yes, I know."

Jackson: "I think we ought to go for him, old boy."

Me: "Better get home with your report."

Jackson: "I think we ought to go for him, old boy."

Me: "All right."

I changed course for him and, as we passed the Taube, Jackson got in two shots with the rifle. We turned and passed each other again with no obvious result. This happened three or four times. Then, "Have you got a revolver, old boy? My ammunition's all gone." I, feeling rather sick of the proceedings, said "Yes. But no ammo." "Give it me, old boy, and this time fly past him as close as you can." I carried out instructions and, to my amazement, as soon as we got opposite the Taube, Jackson, with my Army issue revolver grasped by the barrel, threw it at the Taube's propeller. Of course it missed and then, honour satisfied, we turned for home.

HOME FRONT: A LONG WEEK IN THE COUNTRY, ESSEX, ENGLAND, 29 August–6 September 1914

Reverend Andrew Clark

Clark was the Rector of Great Leighs, Essex. The lack of enthusiasm for the war he records was typical of country areas; patriotic fervour was the purview of the city and the town.

Saturday, 29 August 1914
Letter received by afternoon post, 2 p.m.:

> 28, August 1914
> Dear Dr Clark,
> Now that the harvest is over I am arranging to summon a meeting of the men and women of Great and Little Leighs in the barn here on Sunday afternoon, Sept. 6, in order to make clear to them the causes and the justice of the war and the Nation's need for soldiers; and further to make an appeal to the young men to offer themselves. It is especially necessary to get the women, otherwise I would have suggested a joint parish meeting. It will be at 3 o'clock and I trust will have your approval and if possible, your presence.
> Yours truly,
> J. H. Tritton.

It is reported that after a special meeting at Great Waltham under Col. W. Nevill Tufnell, to beat up recruits, only one recruit joined. The Colonel is *the* territorial magnate of this part of the country, but is at present not in highest favour in his own parish.

Sunday, 30 August
Reports from Braintree: twenty-eight men of Courtauld's Braintree crape-works, after a recruiting meeting, volunteered

for service. The government is said to allow – per week – to each man 8*s*. 9*d*., to his wife 7*s*. 7*d*. and 1*s*. 2*d*. for each child. The hospital of the Red Cross at Braintree was very much out of pillow cases. Mrs Lave of Gosfield Hall, a very wealthy but most eccentric widow-lady, had lent four, all carefully marked with her name and stringent orders that they should be returned when no longer needed.

On my way to Church for a Christening at 6 p.m., Miss Lucy Tritton, elder daughter of H. L. M. Tritton of the Hole Farm, Great Leighs, met me, jumped off her bicycle and told me that her father had heard from someone in the "Home" office (she said) that a large Russian force from Archangel had landed in Scotland and was being speeded south by rail to take its place in the theatre of war in Belgium. I mentioned the report of Saturday's evening paper, that a train-load of 200 Russians escaped from Germany into Switzerland and France, had reached England. But Miss Tritton was positive that her information was authentic and correct.

My elder daughter, Mary Alice, attended the evening service at Fairstead, one of the ring of parish churches which lie round Great Leighs. The Rector, Thomas Sadgrove, preached a horrifying sermon, on the horrible scenes of the battlefield and exhorted all the young men to join the army. He had a big Union Jack hung in front of the pulpit, instead of the pulpit-hanging.

Tuesday, 1 September

Village lads are not very pleased at pressure put by the Squire to compel his two footmen to enlist. To use the phrase of one of the lads, the "idle sons" of the house ought to have set the example of going, though married, with children and something over the age.

Village gossip makes fun of the projected savings of Lyons Hall (Village opinion is always spiteful and disparaging and ungrateful.):

(a) either butter or jam, not both.

(b) no cake at tea – but only one seed-cake (for show) which no one cares for and is not cut.

(c) meat at only one meal a day.
(d) only fruit from Lyons Hall gardens.
(e) no cream; all cream to be made into butter which now sells at a high price.

Wednesday, 2 September

Dr H. G. K. Young of Braintree told Miss Mildred Clark that on Su. 30 Aug., the Russian troops were fed in Colchester; that the Gurkhas were in highest feather at coming to European War. King George was the greatest and wisest of Kings. He first had gone to India to be crowned there and he first had perceived that they were worthy to stand shoulder to shoulder with the British troops in the greatest of wars.

Mrs Albert Taylor, wife of Albert Taylor, postman, son of Henry Taylor, wheelwright, and Sub-Postmaster of Great Leighs – an exceptionally kindly natured, gentle-spoken woman, said (14 Sept. 1914) "Well, it may be very wrong; but I don't mind saying it, that I should be very glad if the Kaiser were shot."

At 5 p.m. an aeroplane passed over the Rectory grounds, but very high up. (Aeroplanes have been seen crossing over this parish on several days, but these occurrences have not been noted as I had no definite hours given me.)

At 5.45 p.m. James Turner, farm labourer at Lyons Hall, came for a "harvest-home". This is a traditional tip contributed by the parson to each farm towards the jollification which the men hold on their own account on completion of harvest.

Sunday, 6 September

Another day of intense heat – deep blue sky – only the faintest white clouds; pastures and gardens burnt up by the long drought. Apples, pears and acorns falling prematurely. Mr T. Stoddart, Rector's Churchwarden, tells me that although it is a time of stress and sorrow of wat, it is the wish of the parish that the Harvest Festival shall be held next Sunday just as usual in thankfulness for the extraordinary bounty of this year's harvest and unbroken harvest weather.

EASTERN FRONT: THE RUSSIAN "STEAM-ROLLER" MOVES INTO PRUSSIA, August 1914

John Morse

To relieve pressure on his French allies, the Russian commander-in-chief, the Grand Duke Nicholas, sought to immediately – hastily, perhaps – attack both the exposed German province of East Prussia and the Austrian province of Galicia. Accordingly 14.5 divisions, and 8 cavalry divisions, were sent rolling into East Prussia from August 17 onwards. John Morse was an Englishman in the Russian ranks.

Much of the scene of the operations I have been describing was very beautiful country, studded with homesteads and farms that, in normal times, must have been quiet and peaceful places, occupied by well-to-do yeomanry and peasantry, living happy and contented lives. Orchards were numerous, but the fruit had entirely disappeared, either prematurely removed by its owners to make what they could of it, or plundered by the passing troops. Frequently we rode by cornfields that had been burned; and potato fields had been dug up and wasted, thousands of potatoes the size of marbles lying on the ground. Our raiders got hold of many fowls and pigs; and for a week or two pork was always to be had at two or three meals per day.

Most of the people had fled from this country; those that remained seemed to fear their own countrymen as much as they did our Cossacks, and remained in hiding while we were passing. Generally speaking they were not ill-used when our men discovered them; but scant respect was shown to the rights of womanhood by the Germans themselves, who had become brutal. No doubt many of the German officers made great efforts to maintain order; but the licence of war is notorious, and many opportunities for wrong-doing must necessarily arise in countries under its influence.

Houses and whole villages were wrecked and burned. We were constantly passing through smouldering ruins, and at night the land resembled our "Black Country" for blazing fires, and reflections of fires. We saw bodies of civilians who appeared to have been executed by shooting; and in one wrecked and smoke-blackened street, a couple of our own Cossacks, and another Russian soldier, were seen hanging to lamp-posts – probably marauders who had wandered away from their ranks, and fallen amongst the Philistines – a fate such people often meet.

Acting on orders, the cavalry spread out into a vast screen, covering the movements of the infantry, and gradually fell back before the enemy. The movement was described as being strategical, for the purpose of drawing the Germans into a favourable position for attack; but this assertion was probably made to keep up the spirits of our troops.

The enemy fired at us a good deal; but as they could not bring their guns to bear on a group of men, very little execution was done. There were some charges between small parties, always much less than a squadron in strength: and in all these that I saw or heard of the Germans got the worst of the fight; and besides those cut down, in three or four days, our men captured more than two hundred prisoners, half a dozen of whom were officers. I believe that the Germans claimed to have captured some of our soldiers, but I much doubt if they secured as many as a score.

The Cossack has a strong disinclination to be taken prisoner; and I knew of several of them sacrificing their lives rather than fall into the hands of the Germans, who heartily detest these men, and usually murdered such as they succeeded in catching – and murdered them after preliminary tortures, according to reports which reached us. The country people certainly showed no mercy to stragglers falling into their hands. They usually pitch-forked them to death; and this lethal weapon was a favourite with the ladies on both sides of the border, many a fine Teuton meeting his end by thrusts from this implement. For in some of the fights the peasantry, including women of all ages, took part, and showed that farm instruments are as deadly as any kind of *arme blanche*. (*Arme blanche* is the term used by military scientists to include bayonets, lances and swords of all descriptions. Perhaps the nearest English equivalent is "cold steel".)

Riding through a burnt village near Neidenburg, half a *sotnia* of our fellows fell into a Prussian trap and had a third of their saddles emptied in a few seconds. The survivors were equal to the occasion; and charged so vigorously that they completely routed their opponents – about one hundred of a reservist corps with the figures 239 on their shoulder-straps.

Two of these men were impaled on the same Cossack lance, an almost incredible circumstance. The Cossacks are in the habit of lowering their lances as they charge without removing them from the buckets. Holding them loosely by the lanyards, they kick them into their enemies with such irresistible force, aided by the speed of the charging horse, that to parry the weapons is impossible. In the case mentioned, the men must have been standing one close behind the other, and the lance was driven right through bodies, packs and all. It was some time before one of the men died: in fact, not before the Cossack drew his sword and finished him off by a sabre cut. The soldier could not withdraw his lance, so firmly was it embedded in the bodies, a circumstance which much aroused his ire, for all Cossacks are much attached to their weapons.

HINDENBURG REPORTS THE GERMAN VICTORY AT TANNENBERG, EAST PRUSSIA, 31 August 1914

General Paul von Hindenburg, German Eighth Army

Tannenberg! A word pregnant with painful recollections for German chivalry, a Slav cry of triumph, a name that is fresh in our memories after more than five hundred years of history.* Before this day I had never seen the battlefield which proved so fateful to German culture in the East. A simple monument there bore silent witness to the deeds and deaths of many heroes.

On the 29th a large part of the Russian Army saw itself faced with total annihilation. On August 30th the enemy concentrated fresh troops in the south and east and attempted to break our encircling ring from without. There was danger ahead; all the more so because airmen reported that enemy columns twenty-three miles long were pressing forward from Mlawa.

Yet we refused to let go of our quarry. Samsonov's main force had to be surrounded and annihilated. While despair seized on those within the deadly ring, faint-heartedness paralysed the energies of those who might have brought their release. Our ring of fire round the Russian masses, crowded closely together and swaying this way and that, became closer and narrower with every hour that passed.

On August 31st I was able to send the following report to my Emperor and King:

"I beg most humbly to report to Your Majesty that the ring round the larger part of the Russian Army was closed yesterday. The 13th, 15th and 18th Army Corps have been destroyed. We have already taken more than 60,000 prisoners, among them the Corps Commanders of the 13th and 15th Corps. The guns are still in the forests and are now being brought in. The booty is immense, though it cannot yet be assessed in detail."

In our new Headquarters at Allenstein I entered the church, close by the old castle of the Teutonic Knights, while divine service was being held. As the clergyman uttered his closing words all those present, young soldiers as well as elderly landsturm [*Territorial units*], sank to their knees under the overwhelming impression of their experiences. It was a worthy curtain to their heroic deeds.

* At Tannenberg, in 1410, the Teutonic Knights had been defeated by a Polish-Lithuanian army.

CHILDREN'S PLAYGROUND SONG, ENGLAND, September 1914

Anonymous

General French was the commander of the British Expeditionary Force.

Kaiser Bill went up the hill
To see the British Army,
General French jumped out of a trench
And made the cows go barmy.

THE BATTLE OF THE MARNE: PRIVATE FRANK RICHARDS IN ACTION, FRANCE, 5–9 September 1914

Private Frank Richards, Royal Welsh Fusiliers

After retreat, the French and the British Expeditionary Force staged an "about turn" on the Marne. The resultant battle blunted, even reversed the German advance, and was of decisive import. "We have lost the war," noted a perspicacious Crown Prince Wilhelm of Germany. "It will go on for a long time but it is already lost."

We had finished with our retirement [from Mons] and were facing in the right direction. We marched up some rising ground. Down in the valley in front of us ran the River Marne. On each side of the river was a village. A fine bridge had spanned the river but it was now in a half, the enemy having blown it up. We advanced down the hill in extended order. The enemy were supposed to be holding the two villages, and we had to take them. We were met by a hail of bullets. The men on the right and left of me fell with bullet wounds in the legs, and a sergeant just behind me fell with one through the belly. We were having heavy casualties, but couldn't see one of the enemy. We lined the edge of a little copse and opened fire on the villages, aiming at the windows of the houses. But the hidden enemy were still keeping up an intense rifle-fire, so we doubled back up the hill and under cover. Some of the men had remarkable escapes, several having their water-bottles pierced. A man named Berry happened to ask me to undo his haversack from his shoulders, saying that he had a spare tin of bully and some biscuits in it. When I did so he found that whilst lying on the slope of the hill his haversack must have flopped up and a bullet must have just missed his head, gone through his haversack, right through the tin of bully, and through one of his folded socks; because here it was now, reposing in the other sock. No, Berry didn't know what a narrow squeak he had had until I pulled his haversack off.

When it was dusk we carried on with the attack. We advanced and got into the grounds of a big château. Everything was now quiet, and from the château my platoon advanced quietly into the village. The first house we came to was locked. We heard some groans in the yard of the house and found an officer of the King's Own Lancaster Regiment who was badly wounded. He told the Second-in-Command of the Battalion, who was with us, that the enemy was strongly entrenched the other side of the river. He said it was quite possible there were still a lot of them left in the village we were now in. We also came across the dead bodies of three other officers of the same regiment; I expect they had been reconnoitring the village earlier in the day.

Six of us and a young lance-corporal were told to occupy the nearest large house, and if we found any of the enemy inside not to fire but use the bayonet. The doors and the wooden shutters of the windows were securely fastened and we tried to burst a door open, but failed. We then knocked a panel out of the bottom of it, which left a space just big enough for one man to crawl through. The seven of us looked at one another: no doubt each one of us had thought it out that if any of the enemy were still inside the house the first man that crawled in didn't have a ghost of a chance. We were all old soldiers except the lance-corporal, who had about twelve months service. One old soldier had very nearly persuaded him that it was his duty as a lance-corporal to lead the way, when our officers came on the scene and ordered us to get in the house at once, also warning me to take the lead. It took me a couple of seconds to crawl through, but it seemed like a couple of years. I had every prospect of being shot, bayoneted, stabbed, or clubbed whilst crawling through; but nothing happened and the remainder soon followed. We searched the house. There was not a soul inside, but we found a small back door wide open which a few minutes before had been securely fastened.

I went out to report and going down the street came across one of our majors and half a dozen men knocking at the door of a house which had a Red Cross lamp hanging outside. The major had just given orders to burst the door in when it was opened and a German Red Cross nurse appeared in the doorway. We went in and found twenty-seven wounded Germans, including two officers, inside. Our major, who was an excitable man, was cursing and raving and informing the German officers that if one weapon was found in the house he would order his men to bayonet the bloody lot of them. We searched the house but did not find a weapon of any description. One of the German officers who spoke English told me that we were the first British troops he had seen in action since the War commenced. He had a slight wound in the leg.

I went back to the house I had left, with orders that the seven of us had to stay the night there. We were lucky in that house. In one room we found the remains of a big dinner – roast chickens, ducks, vegetables all nicely cooked, and bottles of wine. By the look of it half a dozen men had just sat down to dine when they were disturbed and had to leave in a hurry. One man said he was going to have a feed and chance whether it was poisoned or not, and that he didn't believe pukka soldiers would ever poison good food and drink. We all agreed with him. Stories had been going around that the Germans had been poisoning the water in the wells and we had been warned to be very careful not to eat or drink anything where they had been. We never took much notice of the stories or warnings. So now we got down to that feed and eat until we very nearly busted, and washed it down with good wine. We retired upstairs and got into some nice beds just as we were and were soon fast asleep.

We were woke up next morning by one of our own eighteen-pounder shells, which had dropped short, hitting a house a few yards away. The street below was full of our men. Some were drumming up – that is, making tea – others wandering about on the scrounge, when suddenly a machine-gun opened fire from across the river, sweeping the street. Second-Lieutenant Thompson of my battalion was badly wounded; most of the men had taken cover as soon as the gun opened out. Two men named Jackson and Edwards rushed forward, in spite of the machine-gun, and carried him to safety, Jackson getting shot through the wrist. The young lieutenant, who had been shot low down, lived about half an hour. Jackson was awarded the Distinguished Conduct Medal, also the French Medaille Militaire on the recommendation of some French staff-officers who were in the village and happened to be witnesses. Edwards only got the French Medaille Militaire, because his wrists escaped injury. Jackson went home with his wound but came back to France to the First Battalion, and I was told he got killed at Festubert; Edwards was killed at Loos.

The enemy were fighting a rearguard action and the seven of us were told to get up in the tollet of the house and make loopholes in the walls with our entrenching tools. We found a couple of picks in a toolhouse and we soon made the loopholes. We could now see right across the river and the rising ground behind the village the other side. There were a few more bursts of machine-gun fire from the other side of the river and then silence. We spotted some of the enemy making their way up the rising ground and opened out with rapid fire which we kept up until we could see no one to fire at. We had some excellent shooting practice for about five minutes and saw a lot of men fall.

A few hours later the Engineers had constructed a pontoon bridge across the river which we crossed without having a shot fired at us. There were a lot of dead Germans in the village the other side of the river and they were soon relieved of any valuables they had on them. As fast as we retired on our retirement, the Germans were equally as fast on theirs from the Marne to the Aisne. Our rations were very scarce at this time. Bread we never saw; a man's daily rations were four army biscuits, a pound tin of bully beef and a small portion of tea and sugar. Each man was his own cook and we helped our rations out with anything we could scrounge. We never knew what it was to have our equipment off and even at night when we sometimes got down in a field for an all-night's rest we were not allowed to take it off. One night just after we had got down to it a man lying beside me was spotted by a sergeant to have slipped his equipment off. He was brought up the next morning before we moved off and was sentenced to twenty-eight days Number One Field Punishment. After many days of hard marching, which we did not mind so much now because we were advancing, not running away, we crossed the Aisne and arrived at Venizel Wood. We were there a few days and on the day we left we were shelled with large shells which we called Jack Johnsons, because they burst with a black smoke.

FLEEING THE GERMAN ADVANCE, FRANCE, September 1914

Frederick Delius

At the time of the German invasion of France, the composer Delius was living at Grez-sur-Loing, some sixty miles south of Paris.

We have been having very exciting times here – During the German advance there was an ever growing panic here caused, no doubt, by the refugees from Belgium & the North of France streaming thro' Grez – The high road to Nemours was a terrifying sight & we sat for hours watching this terrified stream of humanity pass by in every sort of vehicle possible – We had hundreds every night in Grez & they told terrible tales of German atrocities – On Sept 5th it got too much for us & we also could hear the booming of the canon [Battle of the Marne] so we decided to get out also, so we left for Orleans in a cattle truck with 50 or 60 others. We took 16½ hours to go 75 kilometres & arrived in Orleans at 3.30 in the morning & as there was not a room to be had in the whole town we spent the rest of the night on a bench on the boulevard near the railway station – We had a most interesting luck to get a room at night so we decided to stay there & await further developments (*sic*) – We had a most interesting & exciting time in Orleans watching the soldiers going off to the front & the wounded coming back – trainload after trainload – this was awful – Some of the poor soldiers, carried on stretchers, with one or both legs shot off – As soon as we heard of the great Victory of the allies we quietly returned to Grez & found everything as quiet & peaceful as ever – Your uncle had gone off the same day as we did with his 2 servants en route for Guernsey – At Havre he got a steamer for Cherbourg & had a most fearful passage in a miserable little dirty boat. On arriving in some port or other they were fired on 3 times, it appears, as they had no flag up. I nearly died with laughter when Joe told me of his adventures – We are thinking of going to America until all this is over – I am entirely sick of it – We shall leave about Christmas probably from England – I may come to London a fortnight or 3 weeks before sailing & then I should just love to roam about London with you – I am glad you have not enlisted – I hate & loathe this German miiitarism & autocracy & hope it may be crushed for ever – but I can get up no enthusiasm whatever for the war. My sympathies are with the maimed & slaughtered on both sides. My North Country sketches are ready & also my "Requiem". I shall take them with me to America & perhaps conduct them myself – I shall have to make some money over there in some way or other. Music will be dead in Europe for a year or more & all countries will be ruined – It makes one despair of humanity – Lloyd Osbourne & his wife were here thro' the panic – They were seized with it 24 hours before we were & left for Nantes but they returned a fortnight ago here to Grez & are now on their way to London. We had great fun burying our best wine & silver – I would not have missed this experience for anything. The world has gone mad.

WESTERN FRONT: POUR ENCOURAGER LES AUTRES, 12 September 1914

Brigadier General E.L. Spears, British Expeditionary Force

General de Maud'huy had just been roused from sleep on the straw of a shed and was standing in the street, when a little group of unmistakable purport came round the corner. Twelve soldiers and an NCO, a firing party, a couple of gendarmes, and between them an unarmed soldier. My heart sank and a feeling of horror overcame me. An execution was about to take place. General de Maud'huy gave a look, then held up his hand so that the party halted, and with his characteristic quick step went up to the doomed man. He asked what he had been condemned for. It was for abandoning his post. The General then began to talk to the man. Quite simply he explained discipline to him. Abandoning your post was letting down your pals, more, it was letting down your country that looked to you to defend her. He spoke of the necessity of example, how some could do their duty without prompting but others, less strong, had to know and understand the supreme cost of failure. He told the condemned man that his crime was not venial, not low, and that he must die as an example, so that others should not fail. Surprisingly the wretch agreed, nodded his head. The burden of infamy was lifted from his shoulders. He saw a glimmer of something, redemption in his own eyes, a real hope, though he knew he was to die.

Maud'huy went on, carrying the man with him to comprehension that any sacrifice was worth while if it helped France ever so little. What did anything matter if he knew this?

Finally de Maud'huy held out his hand: "Yours also is a way of dying for France," he said. The procession started again, but now the victim was a willing one.

The sound of a volley in the distance announced that all was over. General de Maud'huy wiped the beads of perspiration from his brow, and for the first time perhaps his hand trembled as he lit his pipe.

A PORTRAIT OF KITCHENER, LONDON, 1914

Sir Osbert Sitwell

Appointed Britain's War Minister on 7 August 1914, Kitchener correctly intuited that the war would last four years, and placarded Britain with his poster "Your Country needs YOU". Kitchener was killed in 1916, when the ship in which he was travelling was struck by a German mine.

As the nights of 1914 wore on, their splendour increased. There was no sign of anything amiss, no sudden chilling of the blood, unless it were at the single glimpse I obtained of Lord Kitchener, sitting like a pagod shrined in flowers and exotic leaves, beneath wreaths and swags at a ball which I attended, given by the Household Cavalry at Knightsbridge Barracks. He just happened to have chosen this seat, at an angle which commanded the full length of two vistas of rooms; but there was something both intensely appropriate and inappropriate about the place he had selected: moreover, one saw only him, his partner sank into insignificance, since, whatever his faults or his merits, his genius was sufficient to concentrate attention upon him to the exclusion of all others in his neighbourhood, as if he were accompanied by an invisible limelight, with an orange slide; for the colour of his face was tawny beyond sunburn and pertained to the planet Mars. With an altogether exceptional squareness and solidity, he sat there as if he were a god, slightly gone to seed perhaps, but waiting confidently for his earthly dominion to disclose itself at the sound of the last, or, in his case, of the first trump. A large square frame, with square shoulders, square head, square face, a square line of hair at the top of a square forehead, he rested there, with a curious rectangular immobility, enfilading two perspectives of rooms with a slightly unfocused glance, which seemed, almost, in its fixity to possess a power of divination. As well as being the realization of an ideal of Kipling's – and to that writer, except for his stature, he bore a certain affinity, of head, hair, eyebrow –, he plainly belonged to some different creation from those round him; a rare, distinguished sect such as the Four Marshals of China, vast figures with angry, bulging eyes, daubed faces and drawn swords, who, fashioned of painted wood, guard the entrance to every Chinese temple, or, again, he could claim kinship to the old race of gigantic German Generals, spawned by Wotan in the Prussian plains, and born with spiked helmets ready on their heads. Though his pose offered the same suggestion of immense strength, and even of latent physical fury, yet, just as he could have been nothing but a soldier, and a great soldier, so, too, every trait in his appearance, his blue eyes, and the cut of his features, unusual as it was, proclaimed him to be English: not an English leader of patrician type such as Wellington, but one from the class that had, since the Reform Bill, monopolized power. And you could, in the mind's eye, see his image set up as that of an English god, by natives in distant parts of the Empire which he had helped to create and support, precisely as the Roman Emperors had formerly been worshipped. Within a few months' time, when from every hoarding vast posters showed Lord Kitchener pointing into perspectives in space, so steadily perceived, if focused with uncertainty, and below this portrait the caption "He wants YOU!", I often thought of that square figure glowering under the wreaths and festoons of smilax, from among the ferns and palms and flowers . . .

U-9 SINKS THE *ABOUKIR, CRESSY* AND *HOGUE*, NORTH SEA, 22 September 1914

Lieutenant Otto Weddigen, U-9

I set out from a North Sea port on one of the arms of the Kiel Canal and set my course in a south-westerly direction. Thus I was soon cruising off the coast of Holland. I had been lying in wait there only a few days before the morning of September 22nd arrived, the day on which I fell in with my quarry.

When I started from home the fact was kept quiet and a heavy sea helped to keep the secret, but when the action began the sun was bright and the water smooth – not the most favourable conditions for submarine work.

I had sighted several ships during my passage, but they were not what I was seeking. English torpedo boats came within my reach, but I felt there was bigger game further on, so on I went. I travelled on the surface except when we sighted vessels, and then I submerged, not even showing my periscope, except when it was necessary to take bearings. It was ten minutes after 6 on the morning of last Tuesday when I caught sight of one of the big cruisers of the enemy.

I was then eighteen sea miles northwest of the Hook of Holland. I had then travelled considerably more than 200 miles from my base. My boat was one of an old type, but she had been built on honour, and she was behaving beautifully.

I had been going ahead partly submerged, with about five feet of my periscope showing. Almost immediately I caught sight of the first cruiser and two others. I submerged completely and laid my course so as to bring up in the centre of the trio, which held a sort of triangular formation. I could see their grey-black sides riding high over the water.

When I first sighted them they were near enough for torpedo work, but I wanted to make my aim sure, so I went down and in on them. I had taken the position of the three ships before submerging, and I succeeded in getting another flash through my periscope before I began action. I soon reached what I regarded as a good shooting point.

Then I loosed one of my torpedoes at the middle ship. I was then about twelve feet under water, and got the shot off in good shape, my men handling the boat as if she had been a skiff. I climbed to the surface to get a sight through my tube of the effect, and discovered that the shot had gone straight and true, striking the ship, which I later learned was the *Aboukir*, under one of her magazines, which in exploding helped the torpedo's work of destruction.

There were a fountain of water, a burst of smoke, a flash of fire, and part of the cruiser rose in the air. Then I heard a roar and felt reverberations sent through the water by the detonation. She had been broken apart, and sank in a few minutes. The *Aboukir* had been stricken in a vital spot and by an unseen force; that made the blow all the greater.

Her crew were brave, and even with death staring them in the face kept to their posts, ready to handle their useless guns, for I submerged at once. But I had stayed on top long enough to see the other cruisers, which I learned were the *Cressy* and the *Hogue*, turn and steam full speed to their dying sister, whose plight they could not understand, unless it had been due to an accident.

The ships came on a mission of inquiry and rescue, for many of the *Aboukir*'s crew were now in the water, the order having been given, "Each man for himself."

But soon the other two English cruisers learned what had brought about the destruction so suddenly.

As I reached my torpedo depth I sent a second charge at the nearest of the oncoming vessels, which was the *Hogue*. The English were playing my game, for I had scarcely to move out of my position, which was a great aid, since it helped to keep me from detection.

On board my little boat the spirit of the German Navy was to be seen in its best form. With enthusiasm every man held himself in check and gave attention to the work in hand.

The attack on the *Hogue* went true. But this time I did not have the advantageous aid of having the torpedo detonate under the magazine, so for twenty minutes the *Hogue* lay wounded and helpless on the surface before she heaved, half turned over and sank.

But this time, the third cruiser knew of course that the enemy was upon her and she sought as best she could to defend herself. She loosed her torpedo defence batteries on boats, starboard and port, and stood her ground as if more anxious to help the many sailors who were in the water than to save herself.

In common with the method of defending herself against a submarine attack, she steamed in a zigzag course, and this made it necessary for me to hold my torpedoes until I could lay a true course for them, which also made it necessary for me to get nearer to the *Cressy*.

I had come to the surface for a view and saw how wildly the fire was being sent from the ship. Small wonder that was when they did not know where to shoot, although one shot went unpleasantly near us.

When I got within suitable range I sent away my third attack. This time I sent a second torpedo after the first to make the strike doubly certain. My crew were aiming like sharpshooters and both torpedoes went to their bulls-eye.

My luck was with me again, for the enemy was made useless and at once began sinking by her head. Then she careened far over, but all the while her men stayed at the guns looking for their invisible foe. They were brave and true to their country's sea traditions. Then she eventually suffered a boiler explosion and completely turned turtle.

With her keel uppermost she floated until the air got out from under her and then she sank with a loud sound, as if from a creature in pain.

The whole affair had taken less than one hour from the time of shooting off the first torpedo until the *Cressy* went to the bottom. Not one of the three had been able to use any of its big guns.

I knew the wireless of the three cruisers had been calling for aid. I was still quite able to defend myself, but I knew that news of the disaster would call many English submarines and torpedo boat destroyers, so, having done my appointed work, I set my course for home.

My surmise was right, for before I got very far some British cruisers and destroyers were on the spot, and the destroyers took up the chase. I kept under water most of the way, but managed to get off a wireless to the German fleet that I was heading homeward and being pursued.

I hoped to entice the enemy, by allowing them now and then a glimpse of me, into the zone in which they might be exposed to capture or destruction by German warships, but, although their destroyers saw me plainly at dusk on the 22nd and made a final effort to stop me, they abandoned the attempt, as it was taking them too far from safety and needlessly exposing them to attack from our fleet and submarines.

How much they feared our submarines and how wide was the agitation caused by good little U-9 is shown by the English reports that a whole flotilla of German submarines had attacked the cruisers and that this flotilla had approached under cover of the flag of Holland.

These reports were absolutely untrue. U-9 was the only submarine on deck, and she flew the flag she still flies – the German naval ensign – which I hope to keep forever as a glorious memento and as an inspiration for devotion to the Fatherland.

I reached the home port on the afternoon of the 23rd, and on the 24th went to Wilhelmshaven, to find that news of my effort had become public. My wife, dry-eyed when I went away, met me with tears. Then I learned that my little vessel and her brave crew had won the plaudit of the Kaiser, who conferred upon each of my co-workers the Iron Cross of the second class and upon me the Iron Cross of the first and second classes.

"THE MEN WENT DOWN LITERALLY LIKE DOMINOES IN A ROW": MACHINE GUNS IN ACTION, RUSSIAN POLAND, 8 October 1914

Karl H. Von Wiegand, United Press war correspondent

At sundown tonight after four days of constant fighting, the German Army holds its strategic and strongly entrenched position east of Wirballen. As I write this in the glare of a screened automobile headlight several hundred yards behind the German trenches, I can catch the occasional high notes of a soldier chorus. For days, these soldiers have lain cramped in these muddy ditches, unable to move or to stretch except under cover of darkness. And still they sing. They believe they are on the eve of a great victory.

Today I saw a wave of Russian flesh and blood dash against a wall of German steel . . .

From the outset of the advance the German artillery began shelling the onrushing mass with wonderfully timed shrapnel.

On came the Slave swarm – into the range of the German trenches, with wild yells and never a waver. Russian battle flags, the first I had seen, appeared in the front of the charging ranks.

Then came a new sound. First I saw a sudden, almost grotesque melting of the advancing line. It was different from anything that had taken place before. The men literally went down like dominoes in a row. Those who had kept their feet were hurled back as though by a terrible gust of wind. Almost in the second that I pondered, puzzled, the staccato rattle of machine guns reached us. My ear answered the query of my eye.

For the first time, the advancing lines here hesitated, apparently bewildered. Mounted officers dashed along the line urging the men forward. Horses fell with the men. I saw a dozen riderless horses dashing madly through the lines, adding a new terror . . . Then with the withering fire raking them even as they faltered, the lines broke. Panic ensued.

HOME FRONT: RUMOURS AND JANGLED NERVES, ENGLAND, 19 October 1914

Michael MacDonagh, Times *journalist*

A large section of the public continue to suffer from the first bewildering shock of being at war. Their nerves are still jangling, and they are subject to hallucinations. They seem to be enveloped in a mysterious darkness, haunted by goblins in the form of desperate German spies, and they can find no light or comfort afforded them by Press or Government . . . The wildest stories are being circulated by these people of outrages committed by Germans in our midst. Attempts have been made to destroy the permanent ways of railways and wreck trains! Signalmen in their boxes, armed sentries at bridges, have been overpowered by bands of Germans who arrived speedily on the scene and, their foul work done, as speedily vanished! Germans have been caught red-handed on the East Coast, signalling with lights to German submarines! More damnable still, bombs have been discovered in the trunks of German governesses in English county families!

"FIRST YPRES": SERGEANT BELL LOSES HIS LEG, 29 October 1914

Sergeant J.F. Bell, 2nd Gordon Highlanders

After the battles of the Marne and the Aisne, the British Expeditionary Force moved to a new sector, Ypres, in Belgium. A series of frontal attacks by the Germans from 20 October to 24 November was stopped by the "thin khaki line" of the BEF in the first battle of Ypres.

On that night there was no sleep, as we had to dig and dig to improve the trench, and were being fired at all night. At 5 a.m. a group of us were standing in the open – everything had turned peaceful – admiring our now almost perfect trench when hell seemed let loose. All the guns in Flanders seemed to have suddenly concentrated on our particular sector of the British front. When the artillery fire subsided, Germans sprang from everywhere and attacked us. My platoon held fast; we lost some good comrades. Then we were ordered to evacuate the trench, and assist to hold a trench on the flank where the fighting was fiercest. I was a sergeant, and was told to take and hold a certain part of the trench where the occupants had just been driven out. On rushing the trench, and leaping into it, I found that the dead were lying three deep in it. After taking bearings, I told the men to keep under cover and detailed one man, Ginger Bain, as "look out". After what seemed ages Ginger excitedly asked, "How strong is the German army?" I replied, "Seven million." "Well," said Ginger, "here is the whole bloody lot of them making for us."

We were driven from the trench, and those of us who were unscathed joined Lieutenant Brook, who had come up with cooks, transport men, and men who had been wounded but could still use a rifle. Lieutenant Brook was (outwardly) quite unperturbed, walking about the firing line issuing orders as if on the barrack square. I had served under him for nine years and, seeing him such a target for the enemy riflemen, I asked him to lie down as I felt if he was hit his loss at that particular time would be disastrous. He told me we must retake the trench I had been driven from, and to pick twenty men to do so. All the men were alike to me – men I had known for years – so I told ten men on my right and ten on my left to get ready to rush the trench. We succeeded in this. No artist or poet can depict a trench after fighting in its stark hellishness.

If we could not be driven out of the trench, it seemed certain that we would be blown out of it. Shells kept landing near enough in front of or behind the trench to shake us almost out of it. Many got killed by rifle-fire, Ginger Bain being the first, then Big Bruce whom I boxed in a competition before going to France. I passed a message to Lieutenant Brook, informing him our numbers were so reduced that if attacked we could not hold the trench, and received back word that he had just been killed. (The V.C. was posthumously awarded him.) A message was then sent to me to retire and join a platoon entrenched near us. I gave instructions to the few men (eight I think) to retire along the communication trench, and I would join them at the head of it, and lead them to our new position. I slipped over the rear of the trench, to cut across and meet the lads as they emerged from the communication trench, but had only gone about six yards when I received what in the regiment was called the "dull thud". I thought I had been violently knocked on the head, but, feeling I was not running properly, I looked down and discovered that my right foot was missing. Somehow, I stood watching men running along the communication trench. My power of speech had left me, so I could speak to none of them, then I swooned into the trench. No one had seen me being wounded, but one of the men, "Pipe" Adams, on missing me, returned to look for me.

On seeing me lying quite helpless, he prepared to lift and carry me out of the trench. I told him I was too heavy, that it was too dangerous, and that in time our regiment would retake all the ground lost, when I would be safe. When I think of the War comradeship, of unaffected and unknown bravery, I think of "Pipe" Adams (killed later) telling me, "Christ, Jerry [my nickname], I could not leave you here." However, confident that our people would return, I persuaded him to go. I then put a field dressing and a shirt from my pack over my stump and lay down to wait further developments. In this trench there would be about sixty badly wounded British soldiers (mostly Gordons) of all ranks. The soldier nearest me was a sergeant of the Grenadiers who was severely wounded in both arms and both legs. I noticed a watch quite close to me; on looking at it I found the time was 9 a.m.

I must have dropped into a kind of stupor, and I woke suddenly with the noise of great shouting. I thought it was our fellows returned to their old position, imagined I heard voices I knew, also that of my company officer, Captain Burnett, shouting, "Where are you, Sergeant Bell?" I tried to rise, failed, but kept shouting," Here I am, in this trench, sir." Judge my surprise when two German infantrymen jumped into the trench. One of them got quite excited, raised his rifle, levelled at and within a yard of me, but the other knocked his mate's rifle up and asked me when and where I was wounded. I asked them to try and do something for the wounded Grenadier, but they seemed in great haste as they jumped out of the trench. It was then twelve noon. So ended one morning in Flanders.

NIGHT PATROL, YPRES, October 1914

Private Frank Richards, Royal Welsh Fusiliers

That night we heard the enemy working on our front, but we didn't know whether they were entrenching themselves or not. The next morning a heavy mist hung over everywhere and it was impossible to see ten yards ahead. Buffalo Bill decided to send a patrol out, consisting of a corporal and two men; in my battalion throughout the whole of the War no privates were ever warned to go out on patrol – volunteers were always called for. Corporal Pardoe, Private Miles and I went out on that patrol; our orders were simply to proceed as far as we could up the willow ditch and to discover what we could. We had gone a considerable way past our listening-post when we halted. Pardoe said: "How far do you think we have come?" "Over 200 yards," said Miles, and I agreed with him. The mist was still heavy and we were listening intently. Presently we heard voices not far off and the sounds of men working. We were wondering whether to work up closer or to go back and report, when all of a sudden the mist blew away, and there, a little over 100 yards in front of us, were new enemy trenches. The enemy were taking advantage of the mist and working on the parapet: some were a good thirty yards from their trench – they had been levelling some corn-stacks so as to have a clear line of fire. Pardoe got one side of the ditch, and Miles and I on the other, and opened out with rapid fire. We had our rifles resting on the bank. The three of us had been marksmen all through our soldiering: each of us could get off twenty-five aimed rounds a minute and it was impossible to miss at that distance. We had downed half a dozen men before they realized what was happening; then they commenced to jump back in the trench. Those that were out in front started to run, but we bowled them over like rabbits. It put me in mind of firing at the "running man" on a peace-time course of musketry. Against we had expended our magazines which held ten rounds there wasn't a live enemy to be seen, and the whole affair had not lasted half a minute. We quickly reloaded our magazines, which took us a couple of seconds, turned around, and ran towards our trench, each of us in turn halting to fire five rounds covering fire at the enemy's trench.

The mist had now lifted everywhere: we could see our own trench quite plainly and bullets were zipping around us. Our men on the extreme left of the platoon had opened fire on the enemy's trench, but the men in line with the ditch were not allowed to fire for fear of hitting us (we learned this when we got back). We arrived at our listening-post, jumped the little bank and laid down, properly winded. We were not out of the soup yet: we still had forty yards to travel before we got back in our trench. We were safe from rifle-fire as long as we crawled on our bellies to the parapet but when we got to the end of the ditch we would have to jump out in the open before getting into the trench, and we knew full well that the enemy would be waiting for that move. We arrived at the end of the ditch and there we heard Buffalo Bill shouting over for us to remain where we were for a couple of minutes, and then to get back in the trench one by one. He passed word up the trench for the whole platoon to open out with rapid fire which would make the enemy keep their heads down and give us a decent chance to get home without being hit. We got back safely; I never knew how well I could jump until that morning. I was out of the ditch and into the trench in the twinkling of an eye: Duffy said that I cleared the parapet like a Grand National winner. The corporal made his report to Buffalo Bill who was delighted at our brush-up. Miles and I did not know what narrow squeaks we had had until someone noticed a bullet-hole through Miles's trousers and two more through the right sleeve of my tunic.

A SONG OF LAMENT TO THE OLD REGULAR ARMY, Autumn 1914

Anonymous

Written in the aftermath of "First Ypres", the graveyard of the old professional British Army.

If you want the old battalion,
I know where they are, I know where they are,
If you want the old battalion,
I know where they are,
They're hanging on the old barbed wire.
I've seen 'em, I've seen 'em,
Hanging on the old barbed wire,
I've seen 'em,
Hanging on the old barbed wire.

WESTERN FRONT: LIFE IN THE TRENCHES, Autumn–Winter 1914

After the first battle of Ypres ("Wipers," as it became known to the British soldier), the opposing sides on the Western Front settled down to digging for a double line of entrenchments that stretched from the Channel to Switzerland.

Alan Seeger, French Foreign Legion
Killed at the Somme in 1916.

This style of [trench] warfare is extremely modern and for the artillerymen is doubtless very interesting, but for the poor common soldier it is anything but romantic. His role is simply to dig himself a hole in the ground and to keep hidden in it as tightly as possible. Continually under the fire of the opposing batteries, he is yet never allowed to get a glimpse of the enemy. Exposed to all the dangers of war, but none of its enthusiasms or splendid élan, he is condemned to sit like an animal in its burrow and hear the shells whistle over his head and take their little daily toll from his comrades . . . His feet are numb, his canteen frozen, but he is not allowed to make a fire . . . he is not even permitted to light a candle, but must fold himself in his blanket and lie down cramped in the dirty straw to sleep as best he may. How different from the popular notion of the evening campfire, the songs and good cheer.

Private Frank Richards, Royal Welsh Fusiliers
Our dead we used to put on the back of the parapet and we carried them at night to a place just behind the line and buried them there. All companies carried their dead to the same place. If a dead man's clothes or boots were in good condition we never hesitated to take them off him, especially when they would fit a man. My own puttees were in ribbons, so I took the Corporal's, which were in good condition. In a belt that Corporal Pardoe wore next to his skin they found about sixty English sovereigns, besides French money. None of it went back to his next-of-kin. I could have had some but I didn't want to touch it: I was satisfied with his puttees. We began to sap out to our left and right platoons and dug a trench from the officers' bay back to a dip in the ground about twenty yards from a farmhouse. We used to fill our water-bottles at the farm at night, and each man's water-bottle had to last him twenty-four hours.

There was no such thing as cooked food or hot tea at this stage of the War, and rations were very scarce: we were lucky if we got our four biscuits a man daily, a pound tin of bully between two, a tin of jam between six, and the rum ration which was about a tablespoonful and a half. Even at this early period the jam was rotten and one firm that supplied it must have made hundreds of thousands of pounds profit out of it – the stuff they put in instead of fruit and sugar! One man swore that if ever he got back to England he would make it his first duty to shoot up the managing director and all the other heads of that particular firm. Tobacco, cigarettes and matches were also very scarce. We had plenty of small-arm ammunition but no rifle-oil or rifle-rag to clean our rifles with. We used to cut pieces off our shirts for use as rifle-rags, and some of us who had bought small tins of vaseline (in villages we passed through during our Aisne advance) for use on sore heels or chafed legs, used to grease our rifles with that. A rifle soon got done up without oil in these conditions. Our sanitary arrangements were very bad: we used empty bully-beef tins for urinating in, throwing it over the back of the parapet. If a man was taken short during the day he had to use the trench he was in and then throw it over the back of the trench and throw earth after it.

One night there was an enemy attack which we beat off and the next morning some corpses were to be seen lying just out in front of us: they were wearing spiked helmets. We crawled out the next night and went through their packs, taking anything they had of value from them. The spiked helmets we intended to keep as souvenirs, but we soon came to the conclusion that it was no good keeping souvenirs of that sort when any moment we may be dancing a two-step in another world. So we used them as latrine buckets, throwing them over the parapet at the back when we had used them.

Fritz Meese, German Army

Killed at Loretto Hill, 1915.

. . . For the last week in a trench which is a mere ruin through which water flows in wet weather – stiff with clay and filth, and thereby supposed to protect us from the awful shell-fire. A feeble human defence against powerful forces. I am still alive and unwounded though my pack and my clothes are torn to rags by bullets. I can't say that I am enjoying myself, but I have not lost my sense of humour. Pray for fine weather and food for me, for wet and hunger are the worst enemies. You simply can have no idea what it is like, to be in the trenches for days and weeks on end under enemy fire. Never again shall I be able to shout a thoughtless "hurrah" in a café at the news of a victory – oh the poor patriots!

I have been on sentry-duty for five hours and shall probably be awake all night, but, anyhow, to sleep standing up or half sitting on the wet clay is a very doubtful pleasure. My letter has of course been written like this: five words and then a long look at the enemy, now and then up with the "cannon" and a shot.

Boys, you don't realize how well off we were in Berlin! Truly and honestly, if I ever felt inclined to moralize about my past life, every such thought has vanished now. I am quite convinced that everybody who gets home safe and sound will be a totally different fellow in every way. He will certainly be more considerate towards other people, especially in the matter of exploiting them for his own ends. The habit of comradeship necessitated by the war will have that result.

Life here isn't worth a damn, one thinks nothing of losing it. To-day, for instance, I walked for half an hour through violent rifle-fire just to have a wash and because I hoped to get one or two cigarettes . . .

"IT IS ALL *THE* BEST FUN": THE HON. JULIAN GRENFELL WRITES HOME, FLANDERS, 3 November 1914

Captain the Hon. Julian Grenfell, 1st Royal Dragoons

Julian Grenfell was killed in action in 1915.

. . . I have not washed for a week, or had my boots off for a fortnight . . . It is all *the* best fun. I have never felt so well, or so happy, or enjoyed anything so much. It just suits my stolid health, and stolid nerves, and barbaric disposition. The fighting-excitement vitalizes everything, every sight and word and action. One loves one's fellow man so much more when one is bent on killing him. And picnicing in the open day and night (we never see a roof now) is the real method of existence.

There are loads of straw to bed-down on, and one sleeps like a log, and wakes up with the dew on one's face . . . The Germans shell the trenches with shrapnel all day and all night: and the Reserves and ground in the rear with Jack Johnsons, which at last one gets to love as old friends. You hear them coming for miles, and everyone imitates the noise; then they burst with a plump, and make a great hole in the ground, doing no damage unless they happen to fall into your trench or on to your hat. They burst pretty nearly straight upwards. One landed within ten yards of me the other day, and only knocked me over and my horse. We both got up and looked at each other and laughed . . .

We took a German Officer and some men prisoners in a wood the other day. One felt hatred for them as one thought of our dead; and as the officer came by me, I scowled at him, and the men were cursing him. The officer looked me in the face and saluted me as he passed; and I have never seen a man look so proud and resolute and smart and confident, in his hour of bitterness. It made me feel terribly ashamed of myself . . .

CHRISTMAS IN THE TRENCHES, WESTERN FRONT, December 1914

Captain Sir Edward Hamilton Westrow Hulse, Scots Guards

Killed in action, March 1915.

28/12/14

My Dearest Mother, Just returned to billets again, after the most extraordinary Christmas in the trenches you could possibly imagine. Words fail me completely in trying to describe it, but here goes!

On the 23rd we took over the trenches in the ordinary manner, relieving the Grenadiers, and during the 24th the usual firing took place, and sniping was pretty brisk. We stood to arms as usual at 6.30 a.m. on the 25th, and I noticed that there was not much shooting; this gradually died down, and by 8 a.m. there was no shooting at all, except for a few shots on our left (Border Regt.). At 8.30 a.m. I was looking out, and saw four Germans leave their trenches and come towards us; I told two of my men to go and meet them, unarmed (as the Germans were unarmed), and to see that they did not pass the half-way line. We were 350–400 yards apart, at this point. My fellows were not very keen, not knowing what was up, so I went out alone, and met Barry, one of our ensigns, also coming out from another part of the line. By the time we got to them, they were $^3/_4$ of the way over, and much too near our barbed wire, so I moved them back. They were three private soldiers and a stretcher-bearer, and their spokesman started off by saying that he thought it only right to come over and wish us a happy Christmas, and trusted us implicitly to keep the truce. He came from Suffolk where he had left his best girl and a 3½ h.p. motor-bike! He told me that he could not get a letter to the girl, and wanted to send one through me. I made him write out a postcard in front of me, in English, and I sent it off that night. I told him that she probably would not be a bit keen to see him again. We then entered on a long discussion on every sort of thing. I was dressed in an old stocking-cap and a man's overcoat, and they took me for a corporal, a thing which I did not discourage, as I had an eye to going as near their lines as possible . . . I asked them what orders they had from their officers as to coming over to us, and they said *none*; they had just come over out of goodwill.

They protested that they had no feeling of enmity towards us at all, but that everything lay with their authorities, and that being soldiers they had to obey. I believe that they were speaking the truth when they said this, and that they never wished to fire a shot again. They said that unless directly ordered, they were not going to shoot again until we did . . . We talked about the ghastly wounds made by rifle bullets, and we both agreed that neither of us used dum-dum bullets, and that the wounds are solely inflicted by the high-velocity bullet with the sharp nose, at short range. We both agreed that it would be far better if we used the old South African round-nosed bullet, which makes a clean hole . . .

They think that our Press is to blame in working up feeling against them by publishing false "atrocity reports". I told them of various sweet little cases which I have seen for myself, and they told me of English prisoners whom they have seen with soft-nosed bullets, and lead bullets with notches cut in the nose; we had a heated, and at the same time, good-natured argument, and ended by hinting to each other that the other was lying!

I kept it up for half an hour, and then escorted them back as far as their barbed wire, having a jolly good look round all the time, and picking up various little bits of information which I had not had an opportunity of doing under fire! I left instructions with them that if any of them came out later they must not come over the halfway line, and appointed a ditch as the meeting place. We parted after an exchange of Albany cigarettes and German cigars, and I went straight to H.-qrs. to report.

On my return at 10 a.m. I was surprised to hear a hell of a din going on, and not a single man left in my trenches; they were completely denuded (against my orders), and nothing lived! I heard strains of "Tipperary" floating down the breeze, swiftly followed by a tremendous burst of "Deutschland über Alles", and as I got to my own Coy. H.-qrs. dug-out, I saw, to my amazement, not only a crowd of about 150 British and Germans at the half-way house which I had appointed opposite my lines, but six or seven such crowds, all the way down our lines, extending towards the 8th Division on our right. I bustled out and asked if there were any German officers in my crowd, and the noise died down (as this time I was myself in my own cap and badges of rank).

I found two, but had to talk to them through an interpreter, as they could neither talk English nor French . . . I explained to them that strict orders must be maintained as to meeting half-way, and everyone unarmed; and we both agreed not to fire until the other did, thereby creating a complete deadlock and armistice (if strictly observed) . . .

Meanwhile Scots and Huns were fraternizing in the most genuine possible manner. Every sort of souvenir was exchanged, addresses given and received, photos of families shown, etc. One of our fellows offered a German a cigarette; the German said, "Virginian?" Our fellow said, "Aye, straight-cut", the German said, "No thanks, I only smoke Turkish!" (Sort of 10*s.* a 100 me!) It gave us all a good laugh. A German N.C.O. with the Iron Cross, gained, he told me, for conspicuous skill in sniping – started his fellows off on some marching tune. When they had done I set the note for "*The Boys of Bonnie Scotland, where the* *heather and the bluebells grow*", and so we went on singing everything from "*Good King Wenceslaus*" down to the ordinary Tommies' song, and ended up with "*Auld Lang Syne*", which we all, English, Scots, Irish, Prussian, Wurtembergers, etc., joined in. It was absolutely astounding, and if I had seen it on a cinematograph film I should have sworn that it was faked! . . .

From foul rain and wet, the weather had cleared up the night before to a sharp frost, and it was a perfect day, everything white, and the silence seemed extra-ordinary, after the usual din. From all sides birds seemed to arrive, and we hardly ever see a bird generally. Later in the day I fed about 50 sparrows outside my dug-out, which shows how complete the silence and quiet was.

I must say that I was very much impressed with the whole scene, and also, as everyone else, astoundingly relieved by the quiet, and by being able to walk about freely. It is the first time, day or night, that we have heard no guns, or rifle-firing, since I left Havre and convalescence! Just after we had finished "*Auld Lang Syne*" an old hare started up, and seeing so many of us about in an unwonted spot, did not know which way to go. I gave one loud "View Holloa", and one and all, British and Germans, rushed about giving chase, slipping up on the frozen plough, falling about, and after a hot two minutes we killed in the open, a German and one of our fellows falling together heavily upon the completely baffled hare. Shortly afterwards we saw four more hares, and killed one again; both were good heavy weight and had evidently been out between the two rows of trenches for the last two months, well-fed on the cabbage patches, etc., many of which are untouched on the "no-man's land." The enemy kept one and we kept the other. It was now 11.30 a.m. and at this moment George Paynter arrived on the scene, with a hearty "Well, my lads, a Merry Christmas to you! This is d—d comic, isn't it?" . . . George told them that he thought it only right that we should show that we could desist from hostilities on a day which was so important in both countries; and he then said, "Well, my boys, I've brought you over something to celebrate this funny show with," and he produced from his pocket a large bottle of rum (not ration rum, but the proper stuff). One large shout went up, and the nasty little spokesman uncorked it, and in a heavy unceremonious manner, drank our healths, in the name of his "camaraden", the bottle was then passed on and polished off before you could say knife . . .

During the afternoon the same extraordinary scene was enacted between the lines, and one of the enemy told me that he was longing to get back to London: I assured him that "So was I". He said that he was sick of the war, and I told him that when the truce was ended, any of his friends would be welcome in our trenches, and would be well-received, fed, and given a free passage to the Isle of Man! Another coursing meeting took place, with no result, and at 4.30 p.m. we agreed to keep in our respective trenches, and told them that the truce was ended. They persisted, however, in saying that they were not going to fire, and as George had told us not to, unless they did, we prepared for a quiet night, but warned all sentries to be doubly on the alert.

During the day both sides had taken the opportunity of bringing up piles of wood, straw, etc., which is generally only brought up with difficulty under fire. We improved our dugouts, roofed in new ones, and got a lot of very useful work done towards increasing our comfort. Directly it was dark, I got the whole of my Coy, on to improving and re-making our barbed-wire entanglements, all along my front, and had my scouts out in front of the working parties, to prevent any surprise; but not a shot was fired, and we finished off a real good obstacle unmolested.

On my left was the bit of ground over which we attacked on the 18th, and here the lines are only from 85 to 100 yards apart.

The Border Regiment were occupying this section on Christmas Day, and Giles Loder, our Adjutant, went down there with a party that morning on hearing of the friendly demonstrations in front of my Coy., to see if he could come to an agreement about our dead, who were still lying out between the trenches. The trenches are so close at this point, that of course each side had to be far stricter. Well, he found an extremely pleasant and superior stamp of German officer, who arranged to bring all our dead to the half-way line. We took them over there, and buried 29 exactly half-way between the two lines. Giles collected all personal effects, pay-books and identity discs, but was stopped by the Germans when he told some men to bring in the rifles; all rifles lying on their side of the half-way line they kept carefully!

They apparently treated our prisoners well, and did all they could for our wounded. This officer kept on pointing to our dead and saying, "*Les Braves, c'est bien dommage.*" . . .

When George heard of it he went down to that section and talked to the nice officer and gave him a scarf. That same evening a German orderly came to the half-way line, and brought a pair of warm woolly gloves as a present in return for George.

The same night the Borderers and we were engaged in putting up big trestle obstacles, with barbed wire all over them, and connecting them, and at this same point (namely, where we were only 85 yards apart) the Germans came out and sat on their parapet, and watched us doing it, although we had informed them that the truce was ended . . . Well, all was quiet, as I said, that night; and next morning, while I was having breakfast, one of my N.C.O's came and reported that the enemy were again coming over to talk. I had given full instructions and none of my men were allowed out of the trenches to talk to the enemy. I had also told the N.C.O. of an advanced post which I have up a ditch, to go out with two men, *unarmed*; if any of the enemy came over, to see that they did not cross the half-way line, and to engage them in pleasant conversation. So I went out, and found the same lot as the day before; they told me again that they had no intention of firing, and wished the truce to continue. I had instructions not to fire till the enemy did; I told them; and so the same comic form of temporary truce continued on the 26th, and again at 4.30 p.m. I informed them that the truce was at an end. We had sent them over some plum-puddings, and they thanked us heartily for them and retired again, the only difference being that instead of all my men being out in the "no-man's zone", one N.C.O. and two men only were allowed out, and the enemy therefore sent fewer.

Again both sides had been improving their comfort during the day, and again at night I continued on my barbed wire and finished it right off. We retired for the night all quiet and were rudely awakened at 11 p.m. A H.-qr. orderly burst into my dug-out, and handed me a message. It stated that a deserter had come into the 8th Division lines, and stated that the whole German line was going to attack at 12.15 midnight, and that we were to stand to arms immediately, and that reinforcements were being hurried up from billets in rear. I thought, at the time, that it was a d—d good joke on the part of the German deserter to deprive us of our sleep, and so it turned out to be. I stood my Coy, to arms, made a few extra dispositions, gave out all instructions, and at 11.20 p.m. George arrived . . . Suddenly *our* guns all along the line opened a heavy fire, and all the enemy did was to reply with 9 shell (heavy howitzers), *not one of which exploded*, just on my left. Never a rifle shot was fired by either side (except right away down in the 8th Division), and at 2.30 a.m. we turned in half the men to sleep, and kept half awake on sentry.

Apparently this deserter had also reported that strong German reinforcements had been brought up, and named a place just in rear of their lines, where, he said, two regiments were in billets, that had just been brought up. Our guns were informed, and plastered the place well when they opened fire (as I mentioned). The long and the short of it was that absolutely *nixt* happened, and after a sleepless night I turned in at 4.30 a.m., and was woken again at 6.30, when we always stand to arms before daylight. I was just going to have another sleep at 8 a.m. when I found that the enemy were again coming over to talk to us (Dec. 27th). I watched my N.C.O. and two men go out from the advanced post to meet, and hearing shouts of laughter from the little party when they met, I again went out myself.

They asked me what we were up to during the night, and told me that they had stood to arms all night and thought we were going to attack them when they heard our heavy shelling; also that our gups had done a lot of damage and knocked out a lot of their men in billets. I told them a deserter of theirs had come over to us, and that they had only him to thank for any damage done, and that we, after a sleepless night, were not best pleased with him either! They assured me that they had heard nothing of an attack, and I fully believed them, as it is inconceivable that they would have allowed us to put up the formidable obstacles (which we had on the two previous nights) if they had contemplated an offensive movement.

Anyhow, if it had ever existed, the plan had miscarried, as no attack was developed on any part of our line, and here were

> these fellows still protesting that there was a truce, although I told them that it had ceased the evening before. So I kept the same arrangement, namely, that my N.C.O. and two men should meet them half-way, and strict orders were given that no other man was to leave the lines . . . I admit that the whole thing beat me absolutely. In the evening we were relieved by the Grenadiers, quite openly (not crawling about on all fours, as usual), and we handed on our instructions to the Grenadiers in case the enemy still wished to pay visits! . . .

By the following year the respective high commands had curtailed Christmas fraternizations, although some local ones broke out intermittently over the next three years.

Part Two

1915

In Flanders Fields, 1915

In Flanders fields the poppies blow
Between the crosses, row on row
That mark our place; and in the sky
The larks, still bravely singing, fly
Scarce heard amid the guns below.

We are the Dead. Short days ago
We lived, felt dawn, saw sunset glow,
Loved and were loved, and now we lie
In Flanders fields.

Take up our quarrel with the foe:
To you from failing hands we throw
The torch; be yours to hold it high.
If ye break faith with us who die
We shall not sleep, though poppies grow
In Flanders fields.

– Lieutenant-Colonel John McCrae,
Canadian Expeditionary Force

INTRODUCTION

1915 was the year of deadlock on the Western Front. There were limited offensives – Champagne, Neuve Chapelle, Loos, for instance – but these only nibbled into enemy territory at the costs of millions of men; the French lost 1.5 million, the British 300,000 in 1915 in frontal assaults on the defensively minded Germans.

Up against the seemingly impenetrable barrier of the trenches, the belligerents sought means to win the war other than a mad scamble through mud and wire and shell and shot on the Western Front.

Of these the most unorthodox, terrible even, was the use of poison gas by the Germans, first used successfully at Ypres on 22 April. (The British were not above foul means; they responded in kind at Loos.) Seemingly more technologically imaginative than the Allies, the Germans also used Zeppelins in a bombing offensive against England, and intensified their U-boat campaign against Allied shipping.

Then there was diplomacy. Even by the end of 1914, the Central Powers of Germany and Austria had inveigled Turkey onto their side; in October 1915 they wooed Bulgaria, which promptly began a brilliantly ruthless onslaught on Serbia. In diplomatic counter-attack, the Allies wedded Italy to their cause in May 1915.

Yet the most dramatic attempt to break the stalemate in the war came with the diversionary British attack on Turkey, at the Dardenelles. In theory, this would have reduced pressure on the

Russian army which was suffering catastrophic losses – a million men indeed – to the Germans in Russian Poland, Galicia and Lithuania. Some 252,000 British, Australian and New Zealand casualties were incurred before the Gallipoli campaign was given up, defeated by poor execution, poorer generalship. Nothing became the Gallipoli campaign like its leaving, for it was one of the truly great military evacuations of history.

And so, all these other ways exhausted, the focus of the war swung back in the fall of 1915 to the trenches, with more attacks by the French at Champagne and the BEF at Loos. (With the old BEF almost extinct through blood-loss, the brunt of the BEF's fighting was done by the first divisions of Kitchener's "New Army"). These but presaged the offensives of 1916, the year of the "Big Pushes".

THE BATTLE OF NEUVE CHAPELLE: A PRIVATE'S DIARY, FRANCE, 10–12 March 1915

Private Montague S. Goodbar, 4th Battalion Cameron Highlanders

Goodbar later transferred to the Royal Flying Corps. He was killed in action in 1917.

Diary: Wednesday, March 10 [1915]

The battle of Neuve Chapelle commences. At 4 a.m. our Artillery commences to bombard the German trenches until 7 a.m. when their guns were elevated they continued to bombard the rear for the remainder of the day. During the 3 hours from 4 to 7 a.m. were had orders to pour rapid fire in to the "Allemands" who were retreating from their trench to [?] safer quarters. With the constant rapid fire my rifle steamed like a boiling kettle and became so hot that I could scarcely hold it. During this time I think we managed to bag a good few of the enemy between us. Their parapet was so badly damaged by our high explosives that they stuffed the gaps up with their dead . . .

Thursday, March 11

After a fairly quiet night the bombardment was again opened this morning. During the night however they have brought some artillery up and started giving us a few back. About 11o/c it gets too hot for them and up go "white flags", (shirts etc on their rifles). We get the order to cease fire and our captain tells them to come over to us which they do after a little hesitation, each holding his hands high above his head. We took about 300 prisoners, a great many of them wounded. We now take possession of their trenches.

Friday, March 12
We have to change our position temporarily, a little further south. In order to do so the men have to wade through trenches waist deep in water, which is like syrup and as cold as ice. We are however not a bit worried by our personal discomfort as the excitement is so great – this is our first glimpse of real warfare. What a sight! I cannot describe it . . . At about 4 o/c we return to our old position, things now having quietened down a bit. Hungry, wet and smothered in mud. At 7, 7–30 p.m. we get the order to agin leave our trench in order to make a bayonet charge. We proceed to cross the field which was behind the original German trench. What a gruesome sight! Dead and wounded are strewn everywhere, the latter groaning and moaning in a most heartbreaking manner, there are British and Germans mixed up lying side by side, rifles and equipment everywhere. We eventually get the order to lie down and await orders, the "Warwicks" are already in position on our left and the "Grenadiers" in our rear in reserve. We are about 100 yards in front of the new German position, it is pitch dark and we are lying in a field of rotten turnips. We are unopposed by the Germans and intend taking them by surprise. After waiting about ½ an hour we are discovered and for reasons I am unable to to find out we get the order to get back on the road as quick as we can, the road is about ½ mile in our rear. As soon as the Hun discovered us they opened a terrific fire of machine guns, rifles, artillery, cries of chaps getting hit go up on all sides. Eventually myself and three pals get clear but find we have lost touch with our Battalion and are mixed up with lots of "Warwicks". We decide we had better make for headquarters which we find after a great deal of tramping

and arrive there at 5.30 a.m. Saturday . . . absolutely done up. All day long chaps keep turning up which had got lost in a similar manner to ourselves.

KITCHENER'S ARMY: A SELF-PORTRAIT, 1915

Donald Hankey, 1st Royal Warwickshire Regiment

"The New Army", "Kitchener's Army", we go by many names. The older sergeants – men who have served in regular battalions – sometimes call us "Kitchener's Mob," and swear that to take us to war would be another "Massacre of the Innocents". At other times they affirm that we are a credit to our instructors (themselves); but such affirmations have become rarer since beer went up to three-pence a pint.

We are a mixed lot – a triumph of democracy, like the Tubes. Some of us have fifty years to our credit, and only own to thirty; others are sixteen and claim to be eighteen. Some of us enlisted for glory and some for fun, and a few for fear of starvation. Some of us began by being stout, and have lost weight; others were seedy, and are filling out. Some of us grumble, and go sick to escape parades; but for the most part we are aggressively cheerful, and were never fitter in our lives. Some miss their glass of claret, others their fish-and-chips; but as we all sleep on the floor, and have only one suit, which is rapidly becoming very disreputable, you would never tell t'other from which.

We sing as we march. Such songs we sing! All about coons and girls, parodies about Kaiser Bill, and sheer unadulterated nonsense. We shall sing:

"Where's yer girl?
Ain't yer got none?"

as we march into battle.

Battle! Battle, murder and sudden death! Maiming, slaughter, blood, extremities of fear and discomfort and pain! How incredibly remote all that seems! We don't believe in it really. It is just a great game we are learning. It is part of the game to make little short rushes in extended order, to lie on our bellies and keep our heads down, snap our rifles and fix our bayonets. Just a game, that's all, and then home to tea.

Some of us think that these young officers take the game a jolly sight too seriously. Twice this week we have been late for dinner, and once they routed us out to play it at night. That was a bit too thick! The canteen was shut when we got back and we missed our pint.

Anyhow, we are Kitchener's Army, and we are quite sure it will be all right. Just send us to Flanders, and see if it ain't. We're Kitchener's Army, and we don't care if it snows ink!

THE RUSIANS CAPTURE PRZEMYSL, GALICIA, 30 March 1915

Bernard Pares, war correspondent

Long-besieged, the fortress of Przemysl garrisoned 120,000 Austro-Hungarian troops.

The fall of Przemysl, which will no doubt be called by its Russian name of Peremyshl, is in every way surprising.

Even a few days before, quite well-informed people had no idea that the end was coming so soon. The town was a first-class fortress, whose development had been an object of special solicitude to the late Archduke Franz Ferdinand. Of course it was recognized that Peremyshl was the gate of Hungary and the key to Galicia; but, more that that, it was strengthened into a great point of debouchment for an aggressive movement by Austro-Hungary against Russia; for the Russian policy of Austria, like her original plan of campaign, was based on the assumption of the offensive. It was generally understood that Peremyshl was garrisoned by about 50,000 men, that the garrison was exclusively Hungarian, and that the commander Kusmanek, was one of the few really able Austrian commanders in this war. The stores were said to be enough for a siege of three years. The circle of the forts was so extended as to make operations easy against any but the largest blockading force; and the aerodrome, which was well covered, gave communication with the outside world. An air post has run almost regularly, the letters (of which I have some) being stamped

"Flieger-Post" . . . The practical difficulties offered to the Russians by Peremyshl were very great; for the one double railway line westward runs through the town so that all military and Red Cross communications have been indefinitely lengthened . . .

For weeks past the fortress had kept up a terrific fire which was greater than any experienced elsewhere from Austrian artillery. Thousands of shell yielded only tens of wounded, and it would seem that the Austrians could have had no other object than to get rid of their ammunition. The fire was now intensified to stupendous proportions and the sortie took place; but, so far from the whole garrison coming out, it was only a portion of it, and was driven back with the annihilation of almost a whole division.

Now followed extraordinary scenes. Austrian soldiers were seen fighting each other, while the Russians looked on. Amid the chaos a small group of staff officers appeared, casually enough, with a white flag, and announced surrender. Austrians were seen cutting pieces out of slaughtered horses that lay in heaps, and showing an entire indifference to their capture. Explosions of war material continued after the surrender.

The greatest surprise of all was the strength of the garrison, which numbered not 50,000 but 130,000, which makes of Peremyshl a second Metz. Different explanations are offered; for instance, troops which had lost their field trains and therefore their mobility are reported to have taken refuge in Peremyshl after Rava Russka, but surely the subsequent withdrawal of the blockade gave them ample time for retreat. A more convincing account is that Peremyshl was full of depots, left there to be supports of a great advancing field army. In any case no kind of defense can be pleaded for the surrender of this imposing force.

The numbers of the garrison of course reduced to one-third the time during which the food supplies would last; but even so the fortress should have held out for a year. The epidemic diseases within the lines supply only a partial explanation. The troops, instead of being all Hungarians, were of various Austrian nationalities; and there is good reason to think that the conditions of defense led to feuds, brawls and, in the end, open disobedience of orders. This was all the more likely because, while food was squandered on the officers, the rank and file and the local population were reduced to extremes and because the officers, to judge by the first sortie, took but little part in the actual fighting. The wholesale slaughter of horses of itself robbed the army of its mobility. The fall of Peremyshl is the most striking example so far of the general demoralization of the Austrian army and monarchy.

Peremyshl, so long a formidable hindrance to the Russians, now a splendid base for an advance into Hungary.

ONE MAN'S WAR: SERGEANT S.V. BRITTEN AT YPRES, 17–26 April 1915

Sergeant S.V. Britten, 13th Battalion, Royal Highlanders of Canada

Serving with the Canadian Division at Ypres, Britten was one of the first to witness the successful use of poison gas in World War I (see also page 85).

Diary: 17 April 1915
Rose at 8.30, went down to Ypres with Capt. Morrisey & Rae, & spent day there, saw over the ruins of the Cathedral & Cloth Hall etc. Stopped all the afternoon, bought a handkerchief of Flemish Lace (& sending it to Vera as a souvenir), brought back a quantity of stuff for ourselves, including two bottles of wine. Witnessed an exciting battle between a British & a German biplane. The latter was brought down about 7 p.m. Terrific artillery fire started about 6 p.m., & lasted all night.

22 April
Left at 6.30 p.m. for reserve trenches and reached our reserve dugouts via St Julien. Just rat holes! One hell of accommodation! Got to the trenches as a fatigue party with stake & sandbags, and thought they were reserve trenches, they were so rotten. No trenches at all in parts, just isolated mounds. Found German's feet sticking up through the ground. The Gurkhas had actually used human bodies instead of sandbags.

Right beside the stream where we were working were the

bodies of two dead, since November last, one face downwards in full marching order, with his kit on his back. He died game! Stench something awful and dead all round. Water rats had made a home of their decomposed bodies. Visited the barbed wire with Rae – ordinary wire strung across. Quit about 1 a.m., came back to our dugouts and found them on fire. Had to march out to St Julien, & put up in a roofless house – not a roof left on anything in the whole place. Found our sack of food had been stolen and we were famished. Certainly a most unlucky day, for I lost my cherished pipe in the evening also. Bed at 4 a.m.

23 April
Up about noon and had no breakfast. Had a good view of the village of the dead, everything in a most heartbreaking state. We found a piano and had music. Furious shelling started about 4.30 p.m., and we took to the dugouts. Almost suffocated by the poisonous fumes! Got into marching order (without packs) & lined for action outside the village. Got to No. 7 station & found Captain Morrisey there, almost suffocated. Brought Lieutenant Molson out to St Jean, & we came to St Julien, getting a lift in an ambulance. Village a mess of dead horses, limbers and men. Went on ration fatigue & tried to get up to the trenches but failed. Scouted the road, waited under heavy shell fire for about two hours, then moved off, & made a circumference up to the trenches via 48th communication trench. Getting there at almost daybreak.

23 April
Terrible day, no food or water, dead & dying all around.

24 April
Dug ourselves in with entrenching tools on left flank approaching St Julien. Just got finished about 3 p.m. (4½ feet deep and a little later the artillery opened fire). At 7.30, trench blown to hell, and we were terribly cut up. Rae & I got separated from the rest, and I helped Gardiner (wounded) who got wounded again, and finally reaching reserve trench found Captain Ross and Sergeant-Major Jeffries there. At 8.10, took message with Rae to Colonel through

artillery fire, entered St Julien, and found him transferred to a farmhouse outside. Brought him, and Sergeant Claridge, Colonel Batemare and four others up to trenches with all the ammunition we could. No casualties. Reached trenches, our left flank broke, and orders to fire on them. Captain Kenway killed on the road. Then went with the Colonel to relay message for him. Met Colonel Currie on way. Left Rae at farm, and went on to General Head Quarters (General Turner) with the Colonel, then back to local Head Quarters, and back again to General Head Quarters, with the Germans already in village of St Julien. Brought back General Retirement order from General Head Quarters, and gave same to Major Buchanan, and finally to the Colonel. Left the Colonel with Rae, to advise everyone in front of us. Then on the way back to General Head Quarters, met Irish Rifles extended, ready to attack village of St Julien. Shell fire most awful – never such known before. Knee gave way through a cut by shrapnel, so lay down and rested.

26 April
In canvas rest Camp Hospital at Etaples, in bed next to Fred. Many Canadians here. Division pretty nearly wiped out.

RECRUITING POSTER FOR THE WOMEN'S LAND ARMY, BRITAIN, 1915

Beneath God's smiling sun
The gentlest women in the world
Shall overthrow the Hun.

GAS! THE ATTACK AT YPRES, 22 April 1915

Anthony R. Hossack, Queen Victoria Rifles

Although the Germans had used poison gas as early as 27 October 1914, its employment had been so defective as to be unnoticeable. This could not be said of their discharge of poison gas against the French trenches at Ypres on 22 April 1915.

As the sun was beginning to sink, this peaceful atmosphere was shattered by the noise of heavy shell-fire coming from the north-west, which increased every minute in volume, while a mile away on our right a 42-cm shell burst in the heart of the stricken city of Ypres.

As we gazed in the direction of the bombardment, where our line joined the French, six miles away, we could see in the failing light the flash of shrapnel with here and there the light of a rocket. But more curious than anything was a low cloud of yellow-grey smoke or vapour, and, underlying everything, a dull confused murmuring.

Suddenly down the road from the Yser Canal came a galloping team of horses, the riders goading on their mounts in a frenzied way; then another and another, till the road became a seething mass with a pall of dust over all.

Plainly something terrible was happening. What was it? Officers, and Staff officers too, stood gazing at the scene, awe-struck and dumbfounded; for in the northerly breeze there came a pungent nauseating smell that tickled the throat and made our eyes smart. The horses and men were still pouring down the road, two or three men on a horse, I saw, while over the fields streamed mobs of infantry, the dusky warriors of French Africa; away went their rifles, equipment, even their tunics that they might run the faster. One man came stumbling through our lines. An officer of ours held him up with levelled revolver, "What's the matter, you bloody lot of cowards?" says he. The Zouave was frothing at the mouth, his eyes started from their sockets, and he fell writhing at the officer's feet. "Fall in!" Ah! we expected that cry; and soon we moved across the fields in the direction of the line for about a mile. The battalion is formed into line, and we dig ourselves in.

It is quite dark now, and water is being brought round, and we hear how the Germans have, by the use of poison gas, driven a French army corps out of the line, creating a huge gap which the Canadians have closed *pro tem.*

GALLIPOLI, THE LANDINGS: THE VIEW FROM THE BOATS, 25 April 1915

Midshipman Eric Bush, Royal Navy

The landing of Allied troops – predominantly British and Anzac (Australian and New Zealand Army Corps) – at the entrance to the Dardenelles, the straits between the Mediterranean and Sea of Marmara, giving access to Istanbul, was intended to open a front against the Turks and so lessen the pressure on the Russian army. It was one of the most audacious moves of the war (its instigators included Winston Churchill at the Admiralty) but inept execution translated the Gallipoli campaign into one of the war's great military disasters. For months Allied troops were unable to break out of a narrow bridgehead on the rocky, sun-beaten peninsula, and eventually in December 1915 the Allied survivors were evacuated. Behind they left the bodies of 46,000 compatriots.

Eric Bush was midshipman of HMS *Bacchante*'s picket boat.

Oars, muffled to prevent any noise, are being lowered carefully, without making a splash. The men are starting to row. Some of the soldiers are helping with the oars, others are adjusting their equipment, tightening their chin-stays, slinging their rifles. I take all this in at a glance, but what stirs my imagination is the look on the men's faces.

A bugle call from on shore gives the alarm. We've been seen! Very lights are set off and a star-shell, too. The enemy opens fire and down comes a rain of bullets. It is just dark enough to see the flashes of the rifles and machine-guns and light enough to recognize Turks moving about on shore. The time is 4.30 a.m.

There is no cover for our soldiers, and several are wounded before shore is reached. I see some of them fall back into the crowded boats as they stand up to jump out. Thank goodness, there are only a few more yards to go.

The moment their boats ground, they leap out. In some cases it is further out than they imagine, and they have to wade ashore up to their waists in water. A few unlucky ones are completely out of their depth, and their heavy equipment is carrying them under. But the majority are reaching the shore in safety, and I have a glimpse of them lying flat on the sand behind their packs and firing, then rising with a cheer and charging up the beach.

It is almost daylight now, and our destroyers with troops are close behind us. We pick up our launch first. Her casualties are very distressing. Unfortunately there is nothing we can do to help them. As we round the stern of the nearest destroyer, I notice that they are having casualties, too. Some wounded are being carried along the upper deck by sailors to a place of safety. As we turn to recover our other two boats, I see fresh troops clambering down into our launch. There is no time to take out the wounded, so they, poor chaps, have to make another trip inshore, in fact several more before anyone can attend to them.

There were thirty-six boats in the original landing, and most of them seem to have got off again somehow. But those left behind are a sad sight.

Glancing up at the high ground in front of us, we see violent and bloody skirmishes going on as the Australians and New Zealanders with their bayonets drive the Turks before them. It is broad daylight now, and the sun is up.

All day long we ferry backwards and forwards, making ourselves as useful as we can. Some Turkish snipers annoy us as we lie off shore. The Turks have brought up several 15-pounder guns and have obtained an accurate range of the beach. Our picket boat has just received a direct hit from one of them but no one is hurt.

Soon it is late afternoon, and shelling of the beaches is increasing. Suddenly we hear the noise of a warship firing rapid salvoes. Soldiers ashore are cheering and pointing to the southward. We look round and see it is our dear old *Bacchante* absolutely plastering a hill in the direction from which the shelling has been coming. Rear-Admiral Cecil Thursby in the *Queen* has told Captain Boyle to see what he can do to silence the guns. Taking the *Bacchante* so close inshore is a fine feat of seamanship. As she fires, her bows are actually touching the bottom. The old naval spirit of 'close action' never fails. Thanks to *Bacchante*, the enemy's guns have stopped firing and the moral effect on us all is tremendous.

A start is at last being made to evacuate the wounded. There are hundreds to be taken off and many have been lying about in the sun all day. It is a long and painful task to which service boats are not suited. The work is also hindered by a shortage of stretchers. But the wounded don't complain.

We have just heard that the landing has been made in the wrong place. Apparently, during the approach and without our knowledge, we were swept by a current a mile too far north. Instead of finding low-lying ground in front of them, our soldiers are confronted with mountainous country.

Some destroyers are now coming in with men from a New Zealand Regiment. As we finish unloading them, the sun sets behind the horizon and it is dark once more. More destroyers arrive with troops during the night. It is difficult work landing them in the dark when no lights are allowed, not even on the beaches.

GALLIPOLI, THE LANDINGS: THE VIEW FROM THE BEACH, 25 April 1915

Major Shaw, 29th Division

About 100 yards from the beach the enemy opened fire, and bullets came thick all around, splashing up the water. I didn't see anyone actually hit in the boats, though several were; e.g. my Quartermaster-Sergeant and Sergeant-Major sitting next to me; but we were so jammed together that you couldn't have moved, so that they must have been sitting there, dead. As soon as I felt the boat touch, I dashed over the side into three feet of water and rushed for the barbed wire entanglements on the beach; it must have been only three feet high or so, because I got over it amidst a perfect storm of lead and made for cover, sand dunes on the other side, and got good cover. I then found Maunsell and only two men had followed me. On the right of me on the cliff was a line of Turks in a trench taking pot shots at us, ditto on the left. I looked back. There was one soldier between me and the wire, and a whole line in a row on the edge of the sands. The sea behind was absolutely crimson, and you could hear the groans through the rattle of musketry. A few were firing. I signalled to them to advance. I shouted to the soldier behind me to signal, but he shouted back "I am shot through the chest". I then perceived they were all hit.

Chief Petty Officer Johnson, Royal Naval Division

For quite an hour the huge guns blazed away, whilst we in the trenches lay full length on the ground or stuffed ourselves into small holes cut in the trench side. It was good if two fellows could get together in one of these holes – it meant company. Your feet and legs stuck well out into the trench, but your back and head were safely protected by perhaps two feet of earth which any ordinary size of shell would cut a way through in the hundredth part of a second. You are both squeezed together, you don't dare think how easily a piece of shell would penetrate your shelter. You light a cigarette, look at each other, and wait . . . You press your back harder against the wall and your head harder into the roof. You know you are not safe, but you press harder and that seems to help a bit. You can only see in front of you the opposite side of the sandy trench, at which you gaze in a vacant stare. The shells scream louder and more often, the screeches, whistles and bangs are hopelessly intermingled, and the ground beneath and around you is rocking and trembling.

Thick fumes float into your hole and you cough and your pal coughs. Your knees and legs are covered with pieces of dirt and a layer of dust, and half of the ground that was above your head has gone by way of your neck to the seat of your trousers. You wonder if the bombardment will ever cease . . .

The crashes suddenly cease, the air becomes clearer at once, and you realize that for the time being at any rate the bombardment is over. You wait a few minutes to make quite sure, and then you struggle out of the hole into the trench . . . You look over the parapet, and see a stretch of country with no sign of life.

WESTERN FRONT: LANCE CORPORAL BAXTER SAVES A WOUNDED MAN, 27 April 1915

Robert Graves, Royal Welsh Fusiliers

From the morning of September 24th to the night of October 3rd, I had in all eight hours of sleep. I kept myself awake and alive by drinking about a bottle of whisky a day. I had never drunk it before, and have seldom drunk it since; it certainly helped me then. We had no blankets, greatcoats, or waterproof sheets, nor any time or material to build new shelters. The rain poured down. Every night we went out to fetch in the dead of the other battalions. The Germans continued indulgent and we had few casualties. After the first day or two the corpses swelled and stank. I vomited more than once while superintending the carrying. Those we could not get in from the German wire continued to swell until the wall of the stomach collapsed, either naturally or when punctured by a bullet; a disgusting smell would float across. The colour of the dead faces changed from white to yellow-grey, to red, to purple, to green, to black, to slimy.

On the morning of the 27th a cry arose from No Man's Land. A wounded soldier of the Middlesex had recovered consciousness after two days. He lay close to the German wire. Our men heard it and looked at each other. We had a tender-hearted lance-corporal named Baxter. He was the man to boil up a special dixie for the sentries of his section when they came off duty. As soon as he heard the wounded Middlesex man, he ran along the trench calling for a volunteer to help fetch him in. Of course, no one would go; it was death to put one's head over the parapet. When he came running to ask me I excused myself as being the only officer in the company. I would come out with him at dusk, I said – not now. So he went alone. He jumped quickly over the parapet, then strolled across No Man's Land, waving a handkerchief; the Germans fired to frighten him, but since he persisted they let him come up close. Baxter continued towards them and, when he got to the Middlesex man, stopped and pointed to show the Germans what he was at. Then he dressed the man's wounds, gave him a drink of rum and some biscuit that he had with him, and promised to be back again at nightfall. He did come back, with a stretcher party, and the man eventually recovered. I recommended Baxter for the Victoria Cross, being the only officer who had witnessed the action, but the authorities thought it worth no more than a Distinguished Conduct Medal.

THE SINKING OF THE *LUSITANIA*, NORTH ATLANTIC, 7 May 1915

Viscountess Rhonda

The British liner *Lusitania* was sunk by a German U-boat with the loss of over one thousand lives. The German submarine campaign against shipping eventually entangled the USA into the War in 1917.

. . . Since my father could never bear to be away from Llanwern during the two most perfect weeks of the year, the second and third weeks of May, we decided to return by the *Lusitania*, which sailed on May 1st. In New York, during the weeks preceding the last voyage of the *Lusitania*, there was much gossip of submarines. It was freely stated and generally believed that a special effort was to be made to sink the great Cunarder so as to inspire the world with terror. She was at that time the largest passenger boat afloat. The few pre-war passenger-boats of greater tonnage had been commandeered for war service of various kinds.

On Saturday, May Ist (the day on which the *Lusitania* was to sail), in order that there might be no mistake as to German intentions, the German Embassy at Washington issued a warning to passengers couched in general terms, which was printed in the New York morning papers directly under the notice of the sailing of the *Lusitania*. The first-class passengers, who were not due on board till about ten o'clock, had still time after reading the warning, unmistakable in form and position, to cancel their passage if they chose. For the third-class passengers it came too late. As a matter of fact, I believe that no British and scarcely any American passengers acted on the warning, but we were most of us very fully conscious of the risk we were running. A number of people wrote farewell letters to their home folk and posted them in New York to follow on another vessel.

There were some two thousand people aboard altogether, counting passengers and crew. Curiously enough, there were a large number of children on the passenger list. We noticed this with much surprise. I think that the explanation lay in the fact that a number of the families of Canadians serving in the war were coming over to join them.

My father and I made friends with our table-neighbours, an American doctor coming over on Red Cross service and his young sister-in-law who had enrolled as a nurse. We used to discuss our chances. "I can't help hoping," said the girl, "that we get some sort of thrill going up the Channel."

We were due to arrive in Liverpool on Saturday, May 8th, and we had all imagined that the attempts would be made in the Irish Sea during our last night. We were wrong. On the Friday afternoon, at about two o'clock, we were off the south-west coast of Ireland, the Old Head of Kinsale was visible in the distance; my father and I had just come out of the dining-room after lunching and were strolling into the lift on "D" deck. "I think we might stay up on deck to-night to see if we get our thrill," he said. I had no time to answer. There was a dull, thud-like, not very loud but unmistakable explosion. It seemed to come from a little below us and about the middle of the vessel on the port side, that was the side towards the land. I turned and came out of the lift; somehow, the stairs seemed safer. My father walked over to look out of a porthole. I did not wait. I had days before made up my mind that if anything happened one's instinct would be to make straight for the boat deck (it is a horrible feeling to stay under cover even for a few moments in a boat that may be sinking), but that one must control that and go first to one's cabin to fetch one's lifebelt and then on to the boat deck. As I ran up the stairs, the boat was already heeling over. As I ran, I thought, "I wonder I'm not more frightened," and then, "I'm beginning to get frightened, but I mustn't let myself."

My cabin was on "B" deck some way down a passage. On my way I met a stewardess; by this time the boat had heeled over very much, and as we each ran along holding the rail on the lower side of the passage we collided, and wasted a minute or so making polite apologies to each other.

I collected my lifebelt, the "Boddy" belt provided by the Cunard Company. On my way back I ran into my father's cabin and took out one of his belts, fearing that he might be occupied with his papers and forget to fetch one for himself. Then I went up on to "A" deck (the boat deck). Here there was, of course, a choice of sides. I chose the starboard side, feeling that it would somehow be safer to be as far away from the submarine as possible. The side further from the submarine was also the higher out of the water, as the boat had listed over towards the side on which she had been hit and the deck was now slanting at a considerable angle; and to be as high as possible out of the water felt safer too.

As I came out into the sunlight, I saw standing together the American doctor, Dr F—, and his sister-in-law, Miss C—, I asked if I might stay beside them until I caught sight of my father, which I made sure of doing soon. I put on my own lifebelt and held the other in my hand. Just after I reached the deck a stream of steerage passengers came rushing up from below and fought their way into the boat nearest us, which was being lowered. They were white-faced and terrified; I think they were shrieking; there was no kind of order – the strongest got there first, the weak were pushed aside. Here and there a man had his arm round a woman's waist and bore her along with him; but there were no children to be seen; no children could have lived in that throng. They rushed a boat before it was ready for them. A ship's officer made some feeble attempt to prevent them, but there was no real attempt at order or discipline. As we watched, I turned to the American girl. . . . "I always thought a shipwreck was a well-organized affair." "So did I," said she, "but I've learnt a devil of a lot in the last five minutes." Two seamen began to lower the boat, which was full to overflowing, but no one was in command of them. One man lowered his end quickly, the other lowered his end slowly; the boat was in an almost perpendicular position when it reached the water. Half the people fell out, but the boat did not capsize, and I think most of them scrambled back afterwards. I do not know. We turned away and did not look. It was not safe to look at horrible things just then. Curious that it never for a moment struck any of us as possible to attempt to get into the boat ourselves. Even at that moment death would have seemed better than to make part of that terror-infected crowd. I remembered regretfully thinking something of this sort.

That was the last boat I saw lowered. It became impossible to lower any more from our side owing to the list on the ship. No one else except that white-faced stream seemed to lose control. A number of people were moving about the deck, gently and vaguely. They reminded one of a swarm of bees who do not know where the queen has gone. Presently Dr F—decided to go down and fetch lifebelts for himself and his sister-in-law. Whilst he was away, the vessel righted herself perceptibly, and word was passed round that the bulkheads had been closed and the danger was over. We laughed and shook hands, and I said, "Well, you've had your thrill all right." "I never want another," she answered. Soon after, the doctor returned bearing two life-belts. He said he had had to wade through deep water down below to get them.

Whilst we were standing, I unhooked my skirt so that it should come straight off and not impede me in the water. The list on the ship soon got worse again, and, indeed, became very bad. Presently Dr F— said he thought we had better jump into the sea. (We had thought of doing so before, but word had been passed round from the captain that it was better to stay where we were.) Dr F— and Miss C— moved towards the edge of the deck where the boat had been and there was no railing. I followed them, feeling frightened at the idea of jumping so far (it was, I believe, some sixty feet normally from "A" deck to the sea), and telling myself how ridiculous I was to have physical fear of the jump when we stood in such grave danger as we did. I think others must have had the same fear, for a little crowd stood hesitating on the brink and kept me back. And then, suddenly, I saw that the water had come over on to the deck. We were not, as I had thought, sixty feet above the sea; we were already under the sea. I saw the water green just about up to my knees. I do not remember its coming up further; that must all have happened in a second. The ship sank and I was sucked right down with her.

The next thing I can remember was being deep down under the water. It was very dark, nearly black. I fought to come up. I was terrified of being caught on some part of the ship and kept down. That was the worst moment of terror, the only moment of acute terror, that I knew. My wrist did catch on a rope. I was scarcely aware of it at the time, but I have the mark on me to this day. At first I swallowed a lot of water; then I remembered that I had read that one should not swallow water, so I shut my mouth. Something bothered me in my right hand and prevented me striking out with it; I discovered that it was the lifebelt I had been holding for my father. As I reached the surface I grasped a little bit of board, quite thin, a few inches wide and perhaps two or three feet long. I thought this was keeping me afloat. I was wrong. My most excellent lifebelt was doing that. But everything that happened after I had been submerged was a little misty and vague; I was slightly stupefied from then on.

When I came to the surface I found that I formed part of a large, round, floating island composed of people and débris of all sorts, lying so close together that at first there was not very much water noticeable in between. People, boats, hencoops, chairs, rafts, boards and goodness knows what besides, all floating cheek by jowl. A man with a white face and yellow moustache came and held on to the other end of my board. I did not quite like it, for I felt it was not large enough for two, but I did not feel justified in objecting. Every now and again he would try and move round towards my end of the board. This frightened me; I scarcely knew why at the time (I was probably quite right to be frightened; it is likely enough that he wanted to hold on to me). I summoned up my strength – to speak was an effort – and told him to go back to his own end, so that we might keep the board properly balanced. He said nothing and just meekly went back. After a while I noticed that he had disappeared. I don't know what had happened to him. He may have gone off to a hencoop which was floating near by. I don't know whether he had a lifebelt on or not. Somehow I think not.

Many people were praying aloud in a curious, unemotional monotone; others were shouting for help in much the same slow, impersonal chant: "Bo-at . . . bo at . . . bo-at . . ." I shouted for a minute or two, but it was obvious that there was no chance of any boat responding, so I soon desisted. One or two boats were visible, but they were a long way away from where I was, and clearly had all they could do to pick up the people close beside them. So far as I could see, they did not appear to be moving much. By and by my legs got bitterly cold, and I decided to try to swim to a boat so as to get them out of the cold water, but it was a big effort swimming (I could normally swim a hundred yards or so, but I was not an expert swimmer). I only swam a few strokes and almost immediately gave up the attempt, because I did not see how I could get along without letting go of my piece of board, which nothing would have induced me to abandon.

There was no acute feeling of fear whilst one was floating in the water. I can remember feeling thankful that I had not been drowned underneath, but had reached the surface safely and thinking that even if the worst happened there could be nothing unbearable to go through now that my head was above the water. The lifebelt held one up in a comfortable sitting position, with one's head lying rather back, as if one were in a hammock. One was a little dazed and rather stupid and vague. I doubt whether any of the people in the water were acutely frightened or in any consciously unbearable agony of mind. When Death is as close as he was then, the sharp agony of fear is not there; the thing is too overwhelming and stunning for that. One has the sense of something taking care of one – I don't mean in the sense of protecting one from death; rather of death itself being a benignant power. At moments I wondered whether the whole thing was perhaps a nightmare from which I should wake, and once – half laughing, I think – I wondered, looking round on the sun and pale blue sky and calm sea, whether I had reached heaven without knowing it – and devoutly hoped I hadn't.

One was acutely uncomfortable, no more than that. A discomfort mainly due to the intense cold, but further – at least so far as I was concerned – to the fact that, being a very bad sailor, when presently a little swell got up, I was seasick. I remember, as I sat in the water, I thought out an improvement which I considered should be adopted for all lifebelts. There should be, I thought, a little bottle of chloroform strapped into each belt, so that one could inhale it and lose consciousness when one wished to. I must have been exceedingly uncomfortable before I thought of that.

The swell of the sea had the effect of causing the close-packed island of wreckage and people to drift apart. Presently I was a hundred yards or more away from anyone else. I looked up at the sun, which was high in the sky, and wished that I might lose consciousness. I don't know how long after that I did lose it, but that is the last thing I remember in the water.

The next thing I remember is lying naked between blankets on a deck in the dark. (I was, I discovered later, on a tiny patrol steamer named *The Bluebell*). Every now and again a sailor came and looked at me and said, "That's better". I had a vague idea that something had happened, but I thought that I was still on the deck of the *Lusitania*, and I was vaguely annoyed that some unknown sailor should be attending to me instead of my own stewardess. Gradually memory came back. The sailor offered me a cup of lukewarm tea, which I drank (we were on a teetotal vessel). There did not seem much wrong with me except that my whole body was shaking violently and my teeth were chattering like castanets, as I had never supposed teeth could chatter, and that I had a violent pain in the small of my back, which I suppose was rheumatism. The sailor said he thought I had better go below, as it would be warmer. "We left you up here to begin with," he explained, "as we thought you were dead, and it did not seem worth while cumbering up the cabin with you." There was some discussion as to how to get me down the cabin stairs. "It took three men to lift you on board," someone explained. I said that I thought I could walk; so, supported on either arm and with a third man holding back my dripping hair, I managed to get down. I was put into the captain's bunk, whence someone rather further recovered was ejected to make room for me. The warmth below was delicious; it seemed to make one almost delirious. I should say that almost all of us down there (I do not know how many rescued were on board; I can remember noticing five or six, but probably there were thirty or forty) were a little drunk with the heat and the light and the joy of knowing ourselves to be alive. We were talking at the tops of our voices and laughing a great deal. At one time I was talking and laughing with some woman when a sailor came in and asked us if we had lost anyone in the wreck. I can remember the sudden sobering with which we answered. I did not then know what had happened to my father; she was almost sure that her husband was drowned. He was, she had already told me (there are no veils just after a shipwreck), all she had in the world. It seemed that his loss probably meant the breaking up of her whole life, yet at that moment she was full of cheerfulness and laughter.

I can remember two exceptions to the general merriment. The captain of the *Lusitania* was amongst those rescued on our little boat, but I never heard him speak. The other exception was a woman, who sat silent in the outer cabin. Presently she began to speak. Quietly, gently, in a low, rather monotonous voice, she described how she had lost her child. She had, so far as I can now recollect, been made to place him on a raft, which, owing to some mismanagement, had capsized. She considered that his death had been unnecessary: that it had been due to the lack of organization and discipline on board, and gently, dispassionately, she said so to the captain of the *Lusitania*. She further stated her intention of saying so publicly later. It seemed to me, fresh from that incompetent muddle on the *Lusitania's* deck, that she entirely proved her case. A sailor who came in to attend to me suggested that she was hysterical. She appeared to me to be the one person on board who was not.

It must have been about half-past nine at night when I came to myself on board *The Bluebell*. As to the interval, I heard afterwards that I had been picked up at dusk by a rowing-boat; that in the gathering darkness they had very nearly missed me, but that by some curious chance a wicker chair had floated up under me (it must have happened after I lost consciousness); that this had both helped to raise me further out of the water than I should otherwise have floated (and so likely enough saved my life by lessening the strain on me) and had made a slightly larger mark which had been noticed in the water, and they had rowed to it. The little boat had transferred me to *The Bluebell*. I was handed up to it along with a lot of dead bodies, but the midshipman who handed me on board said, "I rather think there's some life in this woman; you'd better try and see."

So they did. They told me that when I recovered I went straight off to sleep without regaining consciousness, and had slept for two hours before I came to myself on the deck of *The Bluebell* in the dark.

When we came alongside, the captain of *The Bluebell* came in and asked if I could go ashore, as he wanted to move on again. I said certainly, but not wrapped in one tiny blanket. Modesty, which had been completely absent for some hours, was beginning faintly to return. I said I could do it if only I had a couple of safety-pins to fasten the thing together; but it was a man's ship, and the idea of safety-pins produced hoots of laughter. Finally someone went ashore and borrowed a "British Warm" from one of the soldiers on the quay. Clad in this, with the blanket tucked round my waist underneath it, and wearing the captain's carpet slippers, I started for the shore. The gangway was a difficult obstacle. It was so placed that it meant stepping up eighteen inches or possibly a couple of feet. I must have been pretty weak, for I had to get down on to my hands and knees and crawl on to it.

At the other end of the gangway my father was waiting . . .

HUN BAITING, LONDON, 12 May 1915

E. Sylvia Pankhurst

Sparked off by Londoners' anger at the sinking of the *Lusitania*.

Crowds, mostly made up of women, gathered before each ruined home. One, where a child had been killed, was still inhabited. A soldier in khaki stood at the door striving in vain to keep back the press of human bodies surging against it. The people who lived there were scarcely able to force a way to their own door. A bomb had descended upon a brewery; from the roof to the cellar all had fallen, only the outer walls remained, and a mass of charred wood in the basement. Many dwellings were thus completely gutted. In the ashes left by the fires which had ravaged them nothing save the twisted ironwork of the bedsteads could be identified. A chorus of wailing stirred amongst the women: "Oh, my God! Look at the home! Oh, my God!"

Rumour raced hot-foot: "There were little lights signalling, telling them where to drop the bombs!" . . . "Germans!" . . . "Beasts." . . . "Germans!" . . . "I saw taxi-cabs driving up and down signalling!" . . . "Germans!" . . .

"They should all have been cleared out at the beginning of the War!" . . . "The Government has nowhere to put them!" . . . "They go and give themselves up to the police and they tell them to go home. . . . Everywhere a bomb is dropped you'll find one of their shops was wrecked near!"

Alas, where in the East End would one fail to find a German shop which had been wrecked in the anti-German riots? Near to the brewery was a baker's shop with a German name on the fascia; the door, the shutters, the very window-frames had been torn off. It was boarded up now with new, unpainted wood. The crowds as they passed it growled imprecations; wild stories grew there . . .

In Hoxton Street was a rush of excitement. A German baker's, one of the few still remaining, had just been raided. "They were serving bread there an hour ago!" a surprised voice uttered. "They go in to buy bread from them, and they wreck the shop," another answered. The windows were smashed, only a few jagged bits of glass still attached to the framework. The pavement was littered with glass and flour. The shop had been cleared of everything portable. A policeman stood at the door. Two soldiers came out, laughing. "There is plenty of new bread downstairs if you want it; it will only be wasted there!" they called as they went off, seeking new quarry.

Down the street police whistles sounded vociferously: a babel of shouting, tremendous outcry. A crowd was advancing at a run, a couple of lads on bicycles leading, a swarm of children on the fringes, screaming like gulls. Missiles were flying. In the centre of the turmoil men dragged a big, stout man, stumbling and resisting in their grasp, his clothes whitened by flour, his mouth dripping blood. They rushed him on. New throngs closed round him . . .

From another direction arose more shouting. A woman's scream. The tail of the crowd dashed off towards the sound. Crowds raced to it from all directions . . . fierce, angry shouts and yells . . . A woman was in the midst of a struggling mob; her blouse half torn off, her fair hair fallen, her face contorted with pain and terror, blood running down her bare white arm. A big, drunken man flung her to the ground. She was lost to sight . . . "Oh, my God! Oh! They are kicking her!" a woman screamed.

"Do help her!" I pleaded with a soldier who stood watching. He shrugged his shoulders. "I can't do anything." "You are a soldier; they will respect you!" "Why should I?" he asked with a curl of the lip. "Look, there's another soldier: can't you get on to *him*?"

"She is covered with blood!" a woman's voice cried again. I struggled to reach her, but the closely packed onlookers would not make way for me. An Army motor drove up and was halted by the press. An officer, hawk-eyed, aquiline, sat in the front; there were vacant seats behind. I sprang to the step: "A woman is being hurt here. Will you take her away from the crowd?" "I don't think we can; we are on military business," he answered curtly. The horn was sounded, the people made way, the car drove on . . .

The woman on the ground was unconscious. Those who a moment before had shrieked imprecations, were seized with pity. The nearest raised her and rested her on a fruiterer's upturned barrel. A couple of women supported her with their arms; another was fastening up her hair. She drooped, still nerveless, her colour gone, her eyes closed. They chafed her hands, the crowd about them silent and awed. Passion was spent. "I believe in all things being done in a proper manner." "Killing the woman won't do any good!" Two voices were heard . . .

"Make a way there! Make a way there! Move on! Move on!" The police came shouting and pushing through the throng, hustling away with equal roughness the onlookers, the fainting woman and those who bore her.

Another mob swept round the corner, hot in fury, baiting a man in flour-covered clothing, wrenched and jerked by the collar, thumped on the back, kicked from the rear. "All right, Gov'ner; all right," he articulated between the blows, in humble and reasoning Cockney-tones fully typic as that of his assailants. Alas, poor Patriotism, what foolish cruelties are committed in thy name!

ONE MAN'S WAR: THE DIARY OF PRIVATE HORACE BRUCKSHAW, GALLIPOLI, 9 May–13 July 1915

Private Horace Bruckshaw, Royal Marine Light Infantry

Bruckshaw volunteered in 1914. He was killed at Arleux on the Western Front in 1917.

Diary: Sunday, 9 May 1915
Spent a rotten night of it. This is a terrible place simply infested with snipers. Nine of us went out with Capt. Andrews hunting them during the morning. Could find nothing however although we were sniped at every step we took. Luckily we all got safely back to our trench. Chapman wounded in chest this morning just as he got up to go to the assistance of another wounded man. It made us a wee bit nervous as he was sitting against me. After dark we went over the back of the trench to a point about a mile back to fetch rations up. We had just returned when the Turks greeted us with a fusillade of rapid fire. This they kept up all night.

Monday, 10 May
Things went quieter by breakfast time but the snipers kept very busy. We laid pretty low all day. We have lost nearly all our officers with these blessed snipers. Captain Tetley is the latest victim having been hit in both legs while leading a party sniper hunting. Very few of them got back again. Heavy firing commenced at dusk and continued all night.

Tuesday, 11 May
Getting our full share of casualties. Poor Capt. Andrews killed by a sniper just after dinner. We have lost our best friend. We have only about five officers left. We are to be relieved today sometime. Left the trenches after dark and made our way back to some open ground about a mile and a half back. We had to doss down in the open. To make things worse it started raining.

Wednesday, 12 May

It poured with rain all night but we were tired out and slept through it all. We got some breakfast and then made ourselves as comfortable as we could in some vacated trenches waiting for further orders. We buried Captain Andrews this morning together with Lieut. Barnes. The Colonel read the service and was very much cut up. The poor Captain's men felt it very much, most of us turning away before the service was finished. A mound, a small wooden cross and a few pebbles alone mark the last resting place of as brave a gentleman as ever walked. In the afternoon we moved further back and dug rest trenches for ourselves. Sir Ian Hamilton paid us a visit and complimented Col. Matthews on the work he and his men had done.

Thursday, 13 May

Enjoyed a good, long night's sleep for we were very tired. Our artillery has been bombarding since yesterday afternoon. We dug a hole in the ground first thing and put a waterproof sheet in it, which we filled with water. Stripping ourselves we then enjoyed a much needed bath. Soon after we had completed our rough and ready toilet a big shell dropped right in amongst us knocking out seven or eight. Pollard and Madden were two victims out of our section. Duckworth, the man who did such good work in the landing was blown to atoms. It gave us a terrible shaking up. We got shelled all the afternoon so were obliged to remain in the trenches. It went quieter towards evening however. The Turks very rarely fire the big guns after dark, thank goodness, so that we can get a bit of peace at night.

Friday, 14 May

Got shells for breakfast and got the meal crouching down in the trench. Some of the shells, which were for the most part shrapnel, did not burst, but buried themselves. Went trench digging elsewhere in the afternoon. At tea time the enemy started putting some big shells into us. We were bobbing in and out of the trench all tea time. In the evening they shifted their range to the aeroplane base at the back of us. It was a lively evening but we were consoled with a quiet night.

Saturday, 15 May

Turks seem to be attacking this morning. Very heavy firing is going on. We are getting our fair share of shells in our camp. We spent the morning cleaning our ammunition. Went to W. Beach in the afternoon gathering big stones for road making etc. In the evening heavy firing recommenced and the artillery started on both sides. Our chaplain arranged an open air concert to take place after dark. It was the most weird concert I have ever attended. It went very dark and lightning was playing in the sky. The artillery were roaring a solo with a chorus of rifle fire, stray bullets even reaching the spot where we were. Every now and then Veras Lights were shot up from the French and our own lines, bursting into a shower of stars when in the air. All the while our fellows were in turn singing comic, secular and sacred songs. The limit however was reached when Gilbert Wilson, a chum of mine, and who is a professional sang Will o' th' Wisp. He sang it splendidly but the effect was almost unearthly. We piped down about 10 p.m. to dream of Turks, Germans, goblins and goodness knows what.

Sunday, 16 May

We are commencing the week well with the usual shelling. They kept it up nearly all the morning. We had an early dinner today and spent the afternoon making a new road. The rough and ready way of making a new road employed here is to dig a trench having sloping sides on either boundary. These trenches are about three feet wide and eighteen inches deep. All the earth is taken from these trenches and utilized to make a camber on the roadway. We got back for tea about 5 p.m. and were quite ready for it.

Seeing that it is Sunday and that I have now had time to look round I cannot do better than give a few of my impressions of the peninsula of Gallipoli.

The ideas I had formed of the peninsula were altogether wrong in most respects. I had always imagined a rocky, barren land, but instead I found it quite fertile, cultivated, in many parts with orchards, vineyards and fields sprouting up with good crops of barley. There is plenty of good sandy soil. The uncultivated portions are covered with heather and wild sage for the most part, the latter giving off an odour which reminds one of last Christmas dinner.

The place lends itself naturally to defensive purposes. On all sides there are very steep cliffs right from the edge of the sea. From the southern end of the peninsula to Achi Baba is a stretch of plain or plateau extending four or five miles. Achi Baba rises here, not to a very great height, but extends itself across the peninsula in such a way that it effectively bars the way to an intruder. It has barred it to us anyway. The ground is broken up by deep ravines and gullies most of them having a stream running in the bed. These gullies abound with frogs which make the nights lively indeed with their continual and loud croaking. Lizards of the common variety are to be plentifully found. I have seen snakes as big as four feet in length and as thick as my wrist. I am no naturalist but should take them to be the ordinary grass snake.

The only two towns on this, the southern side of Achi Baba, are Sedd-el-Bahr and Krithia. Sedd-el-Bahr is on the mouth of the Straits and was the Turkish fortress. Our ships soon laid that base. Krithia is a small town on the slopes of Achi Baba and looks very quaint and picturesque from our front line of trenches. I have not yet had the privilege of seeing it from a nearer point owing to the strenuous resistance of the Turks.

Tuesday, 13 July

We spent the remainder of the night in our old spot on the gully after aimlessly wandering about half the night as usual. At dawn we moved from here, which now were the supports and went into the new fire position which was taken from the Turks yesterday. We just had to go into a Turkish communication trench which now formed part of our supports. This was in a terrible state, simply full of dead bodies and filth of all kinds. Up to dinner time all our time was taken in burying the dead and cleaning up. Where some of the dead had already been half buried was a sight awful to witness and the stench was terrific. Heads, arms and legs were sticking up from the ground and out of the parapets. It was terrible and a sight I can never forget. In addition to cleaning all this mess up we had to make this trench possible for a fire trench should it be necessary.

OVER THE TOP, YPRES, Summer 1915

H.S. Clapham, British Army

At 4.15 a whistle blew. The men in the front line went over the top, and we scrambled out and took their places in the front trench. In front of us was a small field, with grass knee-high, split diagonally by an old footpath. On the other side of the field was a belt of trees, known as Y Wood, in which lay the first Hun trench.

In a few moments flags went up there, to show that it had been captured and that the troops were going on. Another whistle, and we ourselves scrambled over the parapet and sprinted across the field. Personally, I was so overweighted that I could only amble, and I remember being intensely amused at the sight of a little chap in front of me who seemed in even worse case than myself. Without thinking much about it, I took the diagonal path, as the line of least resistance, and most of my section did the same.

When I dropped into the Hun trench I found it a great place, only three feet wide, and at least eight deep, and beautifully made of white sandbags, back and front. At that spot there was no sign of any damage by our shells, but a number of dead Huns lay in the bottom. There was a sniper's post just where I fell in, a comfortable little square hole, fitted with seats and shelves, bottles of beer, tinned meats, and a fine helmet hanging on a hook.

Our first duty was to change the wire, so, after annexing the helmet, I slipped off my pack, and, clambering out again, started to move the wire from what was now the rear to the new front of the trench. It was rotten stuff, most of it loose coils, and the only knife-rests were not more than a couple of feet high. What there was movable of it we got across without much difficulty, and we had just finished when we were ordered to move down the trench as our diagonal advance had brought us too far to the right.

We moved down along the belt of woodland, which was only a few yards broad, to a spot where one of our companies was already hard at work digging a communication trench back to our old front line. Here there was really no trench at all. One or more of our own big shells had burst in the middle, filling it up for a distance of ten yards and practically destroying both parapet and parados. Some of us started building up the parapet with sandbags, and I saw the twins merrily at work hauling out dead Huns at least twice their own size.

There was a hedge along the back of the trench, so I scrambled through a hole in it, piled my pack, rifle and other things, including the helmet, on the farther side, and started again on the wire. Hereabouts it was much better stuff, and it took us some time to get it across and pegged down. We had just got the last knife-rest across when I saw a man who was placing sandbags on the parapet from the farther side swivel round, throw his legs into the trench and collapse in a heap in the bottom. Several others were already lying there, and for the first time I realised that a regular hail of machine-gun bullets was sweeping over the trench.

I made a dive for my pack, but though I found that, my pet helmet had disappeared. Quite a string of wounded and masterless men had passed down the back of the hedge while I was working, and one of them must have thought it a good souvenir to take into hospital.

We all started work at a feverish pace, digging out the trench and building up some sort of shelter in front. One chap, a very nice kid, was bowled over almost at once with a bullet in the groin, and lay in the trench, kicking and shrieking, while we worked.

A PRISONER-OF-WAR OF THE GERMANS, 1915

Brian Horrocks, Middlesex Regiment

I was judged fit to be sent back to a prisoner-of-war camp in Germany. My escort turned out to be a *Feldwebel* of the Imperial Guard who had been at the front since the beginning of the war, and was now on his way back to Germany to do some course or other; he spoke a little English, and had once been in London to take part in a swimming race.

At the station I was leaning out of the carriage window when a German Red Cross girl passed along the platform, carrying a large bowl of soup with an appetising smell. She stopped, and then, seeing that I was an Englishman, spat into the soup and threw it on the platform. There was a bellow of rage from my escort. He made me sit well down in the carriage while he leant out and collected food from all who passed, every bit of which was passed back to me.

On another occasion we went into the station-master's office to find out about trains. As there was no one in the room, my *Feldwebel* pushed forward a chair for me to sit on. Suddenly the door burst open and in came a typical fat, German railway official.

"Why is this English swine seated in my office?" he shouted. "Get up!"

The *Feldwebel* walked slowly over to him, bent down towards the little turkey-cock and said: "This is a British officer who was wounded fighting, which you are never likely to be. He will remain seated."

And I did.

Afterwards he apologized for his fellow countryman, saying: "All front-line troops have a respect for each other, but the farther from the front you get, the more bellicose and beastly the people become."

How right he was. I have always regarded the forward area of the battlefield as the most exclusive club in the world, inhabited by the cream of the nation's manhood – the men who actually do the fighting. Comparatively few in number, they have little feeling of hatred for the enemy – rather the reverse.

EASTERN FRONT: AN ENGLISH DOCTOR WITH A RUSSIAN MOBILE HOSPITAL UNIT, GALICIA, 2 June 1915

Hugh Walpole

Have been in the thick of things for nearly a month, under fire several times, and have decided that a dentist is much more alarming. The worst part of a battle is its invisibility and never knowing what it's going to do next. Waiting with a cart under shrapnel for wounded is depressing if it lasts long, but doing anything definite is highly inspiring, and amusing sometimes in most unexpected ways. I had the other night a race from the Austrians in a haycart that was Gilbertian, quite especially as I'd lost my braces and my glasses were crooked! Day before yesterday eight hundred wounded in twelve hours. I cut off fingers with a pair of scissors as easily as nothing.

GALLIPOLI: BURYING THE DEAD, June 1915

Leonard Thompson, British Army

We arrived at the Dardanelles and saw the guns flashing and heard the rifle-fire. They heaved our ship, the River Clyde, right up to the shore. They had cut a hole in it and made a little pier, so we were able to walk straight off and on to the beach. We all sat there – on the Hellespont! – waiting for it to get light. The first things we saw were big wrecked Turkish guns, the second a big marquee. It didn't make me think of the military but of the village fêtes. Other people must have thought like this because I remember how we all rushed up to it, like boys getting into a circus, and then found it all laced up. We unlaced it and rushed in. It was full of corpses. Dead Englishmen, lines and lines of them, and with their eyes wide open. We all stopped talking. I'd never seen a dead man before and here I was looking at two or three hundred of them. It was our first fear. Nobody had mentioned this. I was very shocked. I thought of Suffolk and it seemed a happy place for the first time . . .

We set to work to bury people. We pushed them into the sides of the trench but bits of them kept getting uncovered and sticking out, like people in a badly made bed. Hands were the worst: they would escape from the sand, pointing, begging – even waving! There was one which we all shook when we passed, saying, "Good morning", in a posh voice. Everybody did it. The bottom of the trench was springy like a mattress because of all the bodies underneath. At night, when the stench was worse, we tied crêpe round our mouths and noses. This crêpe had been given to us because it was supposed to prevent us being gassed. The flies entered the trenches at night and lined them completely with a density which was like moving cloth. We killed millions by slapping our spades along the trench walls but the next night it would be just as bad. We were all lousy and we couldn't stop shitting because we had caught dysentery. We wept, not because we were frightened but because we were so dirty.

MARCHING SONG OF THE BRITISH ARMY, 1915

Anonymous

I like to hear the news from the Dardanelles,
I like to hear the whistle of the Allyman's shells.
I like to hear the rifle-fire,
I like to see the blinking Allymans retire.
I like to hear the click-click of the pick and spade,
(the French they are no bon.)
Look out, look out, the gas clouds are coming:
Go get your respirator on.

WESTERN FRONT: A LOVE LETTER HOME, 3 July 1915

Private Jack Mackenzie, Cameron Highlanders

Mackenzie was killed in action in 1916.

3/7/15 [France]

My Own Darling Wife,

Your dear letters all safely to hand. I am please to see you are keeping so well. Your parcel also arrived last night and I am just delighted with the contents many thanks for it Minnie but I really can't thank you enough here and will do better when we meet, the cake is just delightful darling, just like a wedding cake, the boys enjoyed it so well, and the papers were nearly fought for, you will be please to know that your shirt and socks just arrived in the very nick of time as the visitors [lice] had just arrived. You know we have been in the trenches for nearly a week now and under fire the whole time, the shells are flying round thick now and I am writing this in my dug out, so you will have to excuse the dirty paper sweetheart. There are three of us in the same dug out and we are so closely packed that we cant turn. We relieved our fourth battalion in here, these are the trench which they lost so many men in capturing, & is just one vast deadhouse, the stench in some places is something awfull, the first thing we had to do was dig the trenches deeper & otherwise repair them & we came across bodies all over the place, you know the Germans occupied these trenches nearly the whole winter and have been losing heavily & has had to bury their killed in the trenches, there were legs and arms sticking out all over the place when we arrived but we have buried the most of them properly now. The ground behind us us [sic] is covered yet by dead Camerons and Germans who fell on the seventeenth of May & we go out at night & bury them, it is a rotten job as they are very decomposed, but it has to be done . . . and we think it only right to their relatives at home, to put their poor bodies under the ground properly. The smell is a lot better now & we hope to have all the dirty work finished by tomorrow night. Our chaps are just grand sweetheart, it is an honour to be amongst such a crowd, they are all cheery and always in good humour, & always willing to help each other. We have only had about eight casualties so far that is a very light bill. We are going to be relieved on Monday night & are going down to a rest camp, so will write to you better from there. One good thing darling we get our letters delivered to us & can get writing home, so that is great consulation is'nt it, did you get the pc [postcard] view I sent you Min, it was of a village which had been shelled, all the villages round here are like that, it is awfull darling the damage done to innocent people, & it makes me feel ten times more proud that I enlisted when I did. The arrangements in the trenches are good & we are as comfortable as it is to be under the circumstances, we are very well looked after & not allowed to take any unnecessary risks or anything, the only thing is it is always bully beef & sea biscuits & one gets very tired of that, could you send me a tin of cocoa in your next parcel, & a candle, candles & sugar are the things we are most short of, & when you send anything sweetheart could you put it in a tin box, as the trenches are swarming with big blue bottles, which one sees in thousands on the dead bodies & then they come crawling over the food. Our officers are just grand & every one of us would do anything for them, especially Mr Ellice our junior officer, he is always smiling & has a kind word for everyone. We[ll] dear heart it is not half so bad being under fire as some people say at least I did not feel so jumpy as expected to be, dont you fret about me dear heart it is not half so dangerous in the trenches as one would expect, the worst danger is the snipers. This is the first time I have ever wished I was a wee chap, I feel as if I am going to get a kink in my back. Well Minnie sweetheart the pants will do alright but would have been beter if they had been dark, even black, as the white shows the dirt up so much, but many thanks dearest for sending them they will do fine.

P.S. I am always thinking of you lassie night & day, you are never out of my thoughts, always remember darling that I love you dearly & don't worry too much about me, mind & write to me often. Give my love to Father & Mother & all the rest, tell father that I got his letter. I am addressing this to Straiton, you might let me know when to adress them to our wee home. Mind & enjoy yourself, remember me to all; write often to me, with best love and kisses, hoping this finds you well. So ta ta just now & God bless you darling.

Your ever loving sweetheart
Jack.

PROSTITUTION, BÉTHUNE, FRANCE, Summer 1915

Robert Graves, Royal Welsh Fusiliers

I was now back in Béthune. Two officers of another company had just been telling me how they had slept in the same room with a woman and her daughter. They had tossed for the mother, because the daughter was a "yellow-looking scaly little thing like a lizard". The Red Lamp, the army brothel, was around the corner in the main street. I had seen a queue of a hundred and fifty men waiting outside the door, each to have his short turn with one of the three women in the house. My servant, who had stood in the queue, told me that the charge was ten francs a man – about eight shillings at that time. Each woman served nearly a battalion of men every week for as long as she lasted. According to the assistant provost-marshal, three weeks was the usual limit: "after which she retired on her earnings, pale but proud."

I was always being teased because I would not sleep even with the nicer girls; and I excused myself, not on moral grounds or on grounds of fastidiousness, but in the only way that they could understand: I said that I didn't want a dose. A good deal of talk in billets concerned the peculiar bed-manners of Frenchwomen. "She was very nice and full of games. But when I said to her: '*S'il vous plaît, ôtes-toi la chemise, ma chérie,*' she wouldn't. She said: '*Oh, no'-non, mon lieutenant. Ce n'est convenable.*' "

ZEPPELIN RAID ON LONDON, Summer 1915

Freiharr Treusch von Buttlar Brandenfels

Raids by Zeppelin airships on England began in January 1915, the worst of which came in October 1915 (see pp 125–6). From 1917 England also endured bomber attacks.

We were flying at a height of 15,000 feet. Suddenly the steersman called out to me: "Searchlights on our starboard bow!" Then the whole car became alive, and with our binoculars to our eyes we leant out of the control car down to our waists.

What a magnificent sight! How wonderful to see the beams of the searchlights exploring the heavens inch by inch, intersecting one another, then collecting into groups of three, four and five from different directions, and cutting each other again, and at last, at the point where they interesected, possibly finding a Zeppelin hanging like a huge incandescent cigar in the sky!

In a moment red lights were scattered through the blackness. They were the shrapnel-bursts.

Soon corresponding red lights appeared below on the ground. They were our own bombs.

There could not be the slightest doubt that our ship, too, was now quite close to the English coast.

Suddenly I staggered and was enveloped in blackness. In the heat of the fight I had lost my liquid-air pipe. It had dropped off the mouthpiece. It grew darker and darker. I felt I was going to be sick. I groped madly about the floor and seized hold of legs, cables, machine-gun belts. At last, just as I felt I should faint from the leaden weight on my head, I found the pipe!

It was marvellous. The moment I was able to breathe in the liquid air again I felt I could have knocked down whole barricades of brick walls, or lifted our tender with my little finger, or juggled with the machine-gun as though it were a billiard-cue, so elemental and powerful is the sudden fresh breath of life that is breathed into one!

"Climb to 18,000 feet!"

Minus twenty-one degrees, thirty degrees, thirty-five degrees Centigrade! Splendid! We met with no inversion. On the contrary, the temperature decreased appreciably the higher we rose.

A quarter of an hour later we had made the coast. We could see the lights of towns and villages, and of railways with their red and green signals, quite plainly. Suddenly everything below went black again. The district was certainly very skilful at putting out or concealing lights. It knew all about airship raids!

Ahead of us, I should say about ten miles away, one of our ships was attacking, and it immediately occurred to me that I ought to keep a more southerly course. So I changed my direction, intending, as soon as I had the attacking ship on my starboard beam, to course about and, flying north-east, to attack the same objective.

Everything depended on our reaching our objective unobserved. We were lucky. It was not long before we located the brightly illumined ship four points abaft the starboard beam, and I gave the order to steer north-east with rudder hard aport. The attack could begin.

The trap-doors for the bombs, which were in the catwalk, could be opened by the *Wachoffizier* by simply pressing a button. We were on the western edge of our objective. I gave the order for action!

Schiller pressed the first button and the first ten-pounder bomb whistled down to the depths. In spite of the buzz of the engines we could hear it whizzing through the air. The whole thing happened in a flash; the next bomb followed, then the third and fourth.

The bombs were plainly visible. A tiny blob of light appeared 18,000 feet below us, a few seconds later we heard the dull thud above the hum of the engines.

There could be no doubt that we were well over our objective, so the heavier fellows, the one-hundredweight and two-hundredweight bombs, were also dropped. They were released at regular intervals and crashed down below with a loud whine, followed quite rhythmically by a heavy thud as they reached the ground. The last three bombs were released simultaneously, and a heavy roll of thunder resounded below.

The crew knew what to do. Out with the ammunition!

It was so light that my eyes began to smart. Immediately after the first burst the searchlights had found us. One, two, three, four! We were flying through a cloud of glaring light. I could read the smallest print on the map before me.

How magnificent the huge, dazzlingly bright form of the ship must have looked 18,000 feet up in the sky, as she steered her way across the heavens!

The shrapnel salvoes drew nearer and nearer. At first they burst 3000 feet below us. Oh, so the man in front of us had been flying at 15,000 feet!

But they corrected their range damnably quickly. Now they were getting very close indeed. We could hear the shells bursting all round and the whine of the splinters as they hurtled through space—high-explosive shells.

Should we climb higher, exhaust our last reserve strength, and, for the sake of 300 feet, risk being brought down by a hit, in which case all would be lost?

Suddenly on our port bow we saw a brilliant light, but no searchlight beam. It was deep and broad, a regular bank of light. The searchlight was penetrating a cloud.

"All engines full throttle." We were saved! Up we climbed into the cloud. The next salvo would certainly have hit the ship if we had not been able to hide.

WESTERN FRONT: FACTORING THE RISK, LAVENTIE SECTOR, July 1915

Robert Graves, Royal Welsh Fusiliers

Like everyone else, I had a carefully worked out formula for taking risks. In principle, we would all take any risk, even the certainty of death, to save life or to maintain an important position. To take life we would run, say, a one-in-five risk, particularly if there was some wider object than merely reducing the enemy's man-power; for instance, picking off a well-known sniper, or getting fire ascendancy in trenches where the lines came dangerously close. I only once refrained from shooting a German I saw, and that was at Cuinchy, some three weeks after this. While sniping from a knoll in the support line, where we had a concealed loop-hole, I saw a German, perhaps seven hundred yards away, through my telescopic sights. He was taking a bath in the German third line. I disliked the idea of shooting a naked man, so I handed the rifle to the sergeant with me. "Here, take this. You're a better shot than I am." He got him; but I had not stayed to watch.

About saving the lives of enemy wounded there was disagreement; the convention varied with the division. Some divisions, like the Canadians and a division of Lowland territorials, who claimed that they had atrocities to avenge, would not only avoid taking risks to rescue enemy wounded, but go out of their way to finish them off. The Royal Welsh were gentlemanly: perhaps a one-in-twenty risk to get a wounded German to safety would be considered justifiable. An important factor in calculating risks was our own physical condition. When exhausted and wanting to get quickly from one point in the trenches to another without collapse, we would sometimes take a short cut over the top, if the enemy were not nearer than four or five hundred yards. In a hurry, we would take a one-in-two-hundred risk, when dead tired, a one-in-fifty risk. In battalions where morale was low, one-in-fifty risks were often taken in laziness or despair. The Munsters of the First Division were said by the Welsh to "waste men wicked" by not keeping properly under cover while in the reserve lines. The Royal Welsh never allowed wastage of this sort. At no time in the war did any of us believe that hostilities could possibly continue more than another nine months or a year, so it seemed almost worth while taking care; there might even be a chance of lasting until the end absolutely unhurt.

GALLIPOLI: TURKISH ATTACK, 22–23 July 1915

H.W. Nevinson, war correspondent

It was Ramadan, and the sacred moon, three-quarters full, gave light for climbing the precipitous cliffs. By eleven I was at the highest point. Through deeply cut saps and "communications", the work of Australian miners, the way runs in winding labyrinth, and the length of sap and trench comes to much over a hundred miles. The point I reached had served for a machine-gun emplacement, but that evening it was watched by a Sikh sentry, who stood in the shadow, silent as the shadow. Mounted on the firing-step, I looked over the sandbag parapet upon a peculiar scene.

Far on my right lay the sea, white with the pathway of the setting moon. Up from the shore ran the lines of our position. Close outside the lines, north, south, and east, the Turks stood hidden in their trenches – 25,000 to 35,000 of them, as estimates say – and all the time they kept up a casual rifle fire. Some six miles away, in the centre of the peninsula south, I could see the long and steep position of Kilid Bahr plateau where the Turks drill new troops daily, and three or four miles still further away rose the dangerously gentle slopes and the low flat summit of Achi Baba. Beyond it gleamed the sudden flashes of Turkish and British guns defending or assaulting the sand-blown point of land between Krithia and Cape Helles. Sometimes, too, a warship's searchlight shot a brilliant ray across the view.

At one o'clock the moon set in a deep red haze over the sea. But still nothing happened. The enemy merely kept up a casual fire against our sandbags, shaking the sand down upon my face as I lay upon a kind of shelf in the parapet. Then suddenly, just on the stroke of two, an amazing disturbance arose.

Every Turk who held a rifle or commanded a machine-gun began to fire as fast as he could. From every point in their lines arose such a din of rifle fire as I have seldom heard, even at the crisis of a great engagement. It was one continuous blaze and rattle. From a gap in the parapet I could see the sharp tongues of flame flashing all along the edges, like a belt of jewels. Minute followed minute, and still the incomprehensible din continued. Now and again one of our guns flung up a shell which burst like a firework into brilliant stars, as though to ask, "What on earth is the matter with you?" Now and again another gun threw a larger shell which came lumbering up "Shrapnel Gully" with a leisurely note, to burst crashing among the enemy's trenches. And still the roar of rifles and machine-guns went on incessantly and still nothing occurred. Suddenly, after just a quarter of an hour, the tumult ceased, with as little reason as it began.

When the storm subsided, we and the Turkish snipers settled down again to normal relations, and all was star-lit peace. At half-past three the phantom of false dawn died into daylight, and the men who had been "standing to" all night sank to sleep in the bottom of the trenches. Picking my way over them, I climbed down the yellow and slippery cliffs again to my cavern beside the sea. General Birdwood told me afterwards that, as an attack had been expected that night (spies so reported), not a single man in the Anzac force had gone sick. It is one of the domestic virtues not to go sick at a crisis.

AN ANZAC AT GALLIPOLI, July–August 1915

Major Oliver Hogue, 14th Australian Light Horse

Hogue, a former journalist, was commissioned from the ranks. He survived the war but succumbed to the great influenza pandemic of 1918–19.

3 August, 1915
Ryrie's Post, Anzac

My Bonie Jean,

You'll be sorry to hear that poor Harry Robson is dead, killed on 24 July by a shrapnel shell. He was one of the patriots, well off, with a wife and family, automobile and everything that makes life worth living. Yet when Britain stepped in to defend Belgium and when Australia offered 20,000 men, Lieutenant Robson heard the Empire call and buckled on his sword. (By the bye, Australia will have sent nearly 250,000 men to the war soon.)

Robson was all over South Africa with Colonel Cox during the South African War and was a splendid transport officer. He could do anything with horses and cattle. On various occasions when the columns were stuck up and bogged in the drifts he managed to improvise some scheme for getting the wagons through. He was a great swordsman and won several prizes at the big tournaments when he went to London with the New South Wales Lancers. We put up a cross with crossed swords over the little shallow grave on Shell Green. May poor old Robbo rest in peace!

Tresilian has gone – top-sergeant Tresilian, whom you met at the camp. He was reckoned quite the best of all the non-coms in our regiment and was generally looked upon as certain for a commission. He was game as a pebble, a regular dare-devil, and he never knew what fear was. He came from down Wagga way originally, but of late had been a station manager in the north-west of New South Wales. He got a bullet in his brain, when looking over the parapet on Holly Ridge, and died without a sound.

Did I tell you about Major Midgley? He is one of the very best officers in our brigade, got the D.S.O. in the Zulu War, went through the South African War, and is a regular little fire-eater. He is in charge of Chatham's Post and is always pulling the Turks' leg. He conceives the most wonderful ruses and tricks to worry the Turks and draw their fire. He sends out fiery arrows and rockets and flares, and by simulating preparations for attack at all times, he has the Turks in the Gaba Tepe zone worried to death.

The other night, however, one of his patrols nearly got cut off. They went out under Lieutenant Bolingbroke to try and snare a prisoner, but as they went south along the beach a strong Turkish patrol tried to sneak in behind them and cut them off from our lines. Our lads streaked back like startled wallabies. The men on the post could not give covering fire for fear of hitting our patrol. However, they all got back safely, and the moment they were in, Chatham's Post opened a hot fire and sent the venturesome patrol about their business. They must have thought that the Post was only lightly held, for some time after midnight a couple of hundred Turks made a dash at the Beach Post. They gave us warning by accidentally kicking the tins we had scattered in the grass. Our chaps were ready and the first Turkish shot was answered by a veritable fusillade from our lines, and after a half-hour's hot firing the enemy drew off.

We have come to the conclusion here that only about 10 per cent of the Turks are good shots and snipers, while about 90 per cent of the Light Horsemen are crack marksmen. This being so, we are able to keep their snipers well in subjection. Lately in front of Ryrie's Post and Chatham's, the Turks cannot show a periscope without having it smashed, and our lads now are actually shooting them through their loopholes and smashing the mud bricks with which the Turks surround their fire recesses.

Several of our snipers are putting up fine records in the matter of bagging Turks. But the champion sniper of them all is Trooper Sing of the 5th Light Horse. He is a champion shot, terrible quick on the up-take (as your mither would say), has keen eyesight, and abundant patience. He has now shot over one hundred Turks; and every one is vouched for by an officer or the sergeant on duty, who sits by Sing all day with a telescope and never gives him credit for a kill unless he actually sees the Turk fall. Some of the infantry on our left are rather inclined to be sceptical as to Sing's performances, but there is not the slightest doubt about it. Major Midgley reckons that Sing must have killed at least one hundred and twenty and wounded thirty more, but he only gives credit for those the observer sees actually fall. But Sing never shoots at a stretcher-bearer. He will wait for hours for a sniper. "There is always tomorrow," he says.

Our sharpshooters always get a bag when a batch of Turkish reinforcements arrive. The newcomers don't know the ropes.

They are always very inquisitive, and will go poking their heads up over the parapets, or round sandbags. They don't know that while they may not be visible in front they are "wide open" from either flank, and with trenches rather zigzagging here and there, well, as Sing says, "It's a shame to take the money." One old Turk yesterday was fixing his overhead cover, when one of the Fifth smashed a brick and the thing toppled down on top of him. He lay quite exposed, kicking and yelling and waving his arms frantically. Sing exclaimed, "I'll put the poor cuss out of his agony", and promptly put a bullet through his brain.

Doesn't all this sound shockingly cruel and callous, my darling? But you made me promise to tell you everything; anyhow I have broken my promise time and time again. I simply can't tell you about the aftermath of battle – the shockingly mangled bodies and the comrades maimed and crippled, and the agonies of those poor wounded fellows left between the two firing lines. Yet we are all erring mortals, when we try to gloss over the horrors of war. It's only when the women of the world realize all war's wickedness and misery that there will be even a faint chance of turning our swords into plough-shares . . . Yet I remember when poor Belgium was trodden beneath the iron heel of the Hun, her shrines desecrated, her citizens butchered and her women outraged, it was the women of Great Britain that gladly sent their men to avenge the wrongs of the plucky little kingdom. And when the Empire called, the women of Australia gladly bade their sons and brothers "Go and God-speed". You, too, are not blameless in this regard, my angel, for if you had lifted your little finger to hold me back, I would have been numbered amongst the shirkers . . .

When will it all end, I wonder? How long, O Lord, how long? Yet I know we cannot sheathe the sword till the Hun is humbled and the spirit of Prussian Militarism quenched for good and all.

As for the poor turbaned and malignant Turk, he's merely the unhappy dupe of the German intriguers. Our Australians don't hate the Turk like they do the Hun. The Turkish prisoners have taken quite a liking to the Australians but they all voice their fear of the Australian bayonets. They call us the "White Gurkhas".

I'm getting long-winded today. Au revoir.

Yours ever,
J.B.

EASTERN FRONT: A CAVALRYMAN IS WOUNDED, August 1915

Oskar Kokoschka, Austro-Hungarian Army

There was something stirring at the edge of the forest. Dismount! Lead horses! Our line was joined by volunteers, and we beat forward into the bushes as if we were going out to shoot pheasant. The enemy was withdrawing deeper into the forest, firing only sporadically. So we had to mount again, which was always the worst part, for since conscription had been introduced the requisitioned horses were as gun-shy as the reservists who had been called up were wretched horsemen. After all, most of them were used to sitting only on an office chair. In the forest suddenly we were met by a hail of bullets so near and so thick that one seemed to see each bullet flitting past; it was like a startled swarm of wasps. Charge! Now the great day had come, the day for which I too had been longing. I still had enough presence of mind to urge my mount forward and to one side, out of the throng of other horses that had now gone wild, as if chased by ghosts, the congestion being made worse by more coming up from the rear and galloping over the fallen men and beasts. I wanted to settle this thing on my own and to look the enemy straight in the face. A hero's death – fair enough! But I had no wish to be trampled to death like a worm. The Russians had lured us into a trap. I had actually set eyes on the Russian machine-gun before I felt a dull blow on my temple.

The sun and the moon were both shining at once and my head ached like mad. What on earth was I to do with this scent of flowers? Some flower – I couldn't remember its name however I racked my brains. And all that yelling round me and the moaning of the wounded, which seemed to fill the whole forest – that must have been what brought me round. Good lord, they must be in agony! Then I became absorbed by the fact that I couldn't control the cavalry boot with the leg in it, which was moving about too far away, although it belonged to me. I recognized the boot by the spur: contrary to regulations, my spurs had no sharp rowels. Over on the grass there were two captains in Russian uniform dancing a ballet, running up and kissing each other on the cheeks like two young girls. That would have been against regulations in our army. I had a tiny round hole in my head. My horse, lying on top of me, had lashed out one last time before dying, and that had brought me to my senses. I tried to say something, but my mouth was stiff with blood, which was beginning to congeal. The shadows all round me were growing huger and huger, and I wanted to ask how it was that the sun and moon were both shining at the same time. I wanted to point at the sky, but my arm wouldn't move. Perhaps I lay there unconscious for several days.

EASTERN FRONT: THE SOLDIER'S LOT, September 1915

Karl Liebknecht, German Army

Liebknecht, along with Rosa Luxemburg, was to lead the abortive Spartacist Uprising in Berlin in January 1919, during which he was murdered by army officers.

The way we are being used is careless and criminal. Please inform Hugo Haase [socialist member of the Reichstag] if necessary. The whole battalion has only one doctor, and what kind of! . . . For our company of 500 men there are two medical orderlies – and what kind of! . . . The food leaves much to be desired, only potatoes are in the fields plentifully, and very good ones. No tobacco – that hurts especially, because it is the only stimulant. In the rear area there are all sorts of things, for instance two cigars and two cigarettes per day. Aside from this the greatest hardship is the lack of lighting. After half past six it is dark. No candles, nothing. You hang around, cannot read or write and crawl into your "bed", that is your straw and wrap yourself in the unheated stable or barn into your coat or a thin blanket, often dripping wet, freezing all night . . .

LONDON BOMBED, 8 October 1915

Beatrice Webb

The Zeppelin attack on London of 8 October killed thirty-eight people.

October 8th [1915] – The window rattled behind me: then all the windows rattled and we became conscious of the booming of guns getting nearer. "At last the Zeppelins," Sidney said, with almost boyish glee. From the balcony we could see shrapnel bursting over the river and beyond, somewhat aimlessly. In another few minutes a long sinuous airship appeared high up in the blue black sky, lit up faintly by the searchlights. It seemed to come from over the houses just behind us – we thought along Victoria Street – but it was actually passing along the Strand. It moved slowly, seemingly across the river, the shells bursting far below it – then there were two bursts that seemed nearly to hit it and it disappeared – I imagine it bounded upwards. The show was over. It was a gruesome reflection afterwards that while we were being pleasantly excited, men, women and children were being killed and maimed. At the time it was impossible not to take it as a "Sight". Julia, who was with us, suddenly remarked that she would go and get her morphine tablets in case we were wounded. But by that time the Zeppelin was just disappearing. My main desire was to see inside the Zeppelin, to see and speak with the German officers as they were sailing back from their adventure.

There was apparently no panic, even in the crowded Strand. The Londoner persists in taking Zeppelin raids as an entertainment – a risky entertainment – but no more risky than some forms of sport. "Did you see the Zeppelins?" was the first question, in the most cheerful voice, which every man, woman and child asked each other for at least four and twenty hours afterwards.

SHOOTING DOWN A ZEPPELIN, POTTERS BAR, LONDON, October 1915

Lieutenant W. J. Tempest, Royal Flying Corps

I decided to dive at her . . . firing a burst straight into her as I came. I let her have another burst as I passed under her and then banked my machine over, sat under her tail and flying along underneath her pumped lead into her for all I was worth . . . As I was firing, I noticed her to begin to go red inside like an enormous Chinese lantern. She shot up about 200 feet, paused, and came roaring down straight on to me before I had time to get out of the way. I nose-dived for all I was worth, with the Zeppelin tearing after me . . . I put my machine into a spin and just managed to corkscrew out of the way as she shot past me, roaring like a furnace . . . then proceeded to fire off dozens of green Very lights in the exuberance of my feelings.

NURSE CAVELL BEFORE HER EXECUTION, BRUSSELS, 11 October 1915

Rev. H. Stirling T. Gahan, British Chaplain at Brussels

Cavell, an English nurse working in Brussels, was arrested by the German authorities for helping British soldiers to escape. She was executed by firing squad at 7 am on 12 October 1915.

On Monday evening, October 11, I was admitted by special passport from the German authorities to the prison of St Gilles, where Miss Edith Cavell had been confined for ten weeks. The final sentence had been given early that afternoon.

To my astonishment and relief I found my friend perfectly calm and resigned. But this could not lessen the tenderness and intensity of feeling on either part during the last interview of almost an hour.

Her first words to me were upon a matter concerning herself personally, but the solemn asseveration which accompanied them was made expressedly in the light of God and eternity. She then added that she wished all her friends to know that she willingly gave her life for her Country, and said: "I have no fear nor shrinking; I have seen death so often that it is not strange or fearful to me." She further said: "I thank God for this ten weeks' quiet before the end. Life has always been hurried and full of difficulty. This time of rest has been a great mercy. They have all been very kind to me here. But this I would say, standing as I do in view of God and eternity: I realise that *patriotism is not enough. I must have no hatred or bitterness toward any one*."

We partook of the Holy Communion together, and she received the Gospel message of consolation with all her heart. At the close of the little service I began to repeat the words "Abide with me" and she joined softly in the end.

We sat quietly talking until it was time for me to go. She gave me parting messages for relations and friends. She spoke of her soul's needs at the moment and she received the assurance of God's Word as only the Christian can do.

Then I said "Good-bye," and she smiled and said, "We shall meet again."

The German military chaplain was with her at the end and

afterwards gave her Christian burial. He told me: "She was brave and bright to the last. She professed her Christian faith and that she was glad to die for her country. She died like a heroine."

SERBIA: THE GREAT RETREAT, October–December 1915

Miss M.I. Tatham, Stobart Field Hospital, Serbian Relief Unit

Offered financial and territorial inducements by the Central Powers, Bulgaria joined them in October 1915 in attacking Serbia.

The Bulgarians declared war early in October. Simultaneously the Austrians attacked on the north, and the field hospital had to retreat with the Army. We were in the town of Kraguyevatz, arsenal of Serbia, which had suffered the bombardment of Austrian aeroplanes for weeks before the evacuation, and was left an open city. Having sent off every man who had sound feet, and left those who were unable to move in charge of American doctors (who were then neutrals) the trek southwards began. It was southwards at first, for we had been told that, if we could reach Monastir, there was the possibility of transport to Salonika. The single railway line from Belgrade to Salonika had been cut the first day after the declaration of war by the Bulgarians; and there was the life-line, as it were, severed, for on that railway line all the stores, men, and ammunition were transported.

We started off with bullock-wagons with as much of the hospital equipment as we could carry, and for three weeks we trekked south – a long, slow procession of springless carts, each drawn by oxen, moving deliberately at the rate of two miles an hour – day or night was all one. Several times the unit halted, hoping that the retreat was stayed, for all the telephone wires were down, and no one knew exactly what was happening. There we would rig up a dressing station, and dress the wounds of the men as they marched by, and there we were invariably sent to join the retreating mass again, as the sound of the guns drew nearer and the towns behind were occupied by the enemy. The stream of the refugees grew daily greater – mothers, children, bedding, pots and pans, food and fodder, all packed into the jolting wagons; wounded soldiers, exhausted, starving, hopeless men, and (after the first few days) leaden skies and pitiless rain, and the awful, clinging, squelching mud.

The roads were obliterated by the passage of big guns – those guns served by that wonderful "Last Hope" of the Serbians, the old men, the *Cheechas*, the "uncles", who held the enemy for the priceless few days or even hours, and so saved the youth of the country. For every Serbian boy – every man-child over twelve – had to retreat. The Serbians had at last realized that the enemy were out to finish her as a nation, and the only way to save herself was to run away. And at first all those battalions of boys, gay with the coloured blankets they carried coiled across their backs, camping round the great camp-fires at night, were happy – until the days grew into weeks, and the rain fell and fell and there was no bread anywhere. But the rain, which churned up the mud, and soaked the ill-clad people, was called by the Serbians "the little friend of Serbia", for it held up the Austrian advance, and consequently saved practically the whole of Serbia's remaining Army.

We camped one night in an old monastery, deep in the heart of the mountains, the residence of the Metropolitan, dating back to the thirteenth century. Here it was decided we might stop for a time, and the monks gave us their new school-house for a dressing station. We had high hopes of being able to remain the winter, so entirely ignorant were we all of the real conditions, and we actually did remain for a fortnight, amongst the most beautiful hills, clothed in their gorgeous autumn colours, for the country thereabouts was one glowing wonder of beech-woods. Until again came the order to evacuate, and in haste, for we were not on the beaten track, and were in danger of being cut off.

We had orders to go to a town called Rashka, and we trudged there in a jam of ox-wagons and soldiers, big guns and refugees, in the most appalling mud and pelting rain – and quite unquenchable good spirits. Until we were nearly there, when one of our number was shot through the lungs – an accidental shot, fired by an irate farmer after some flying refugees who were stealing his horses. The injured girl was taken to a Serbian dressing station about eight miles back along the road, with two doctors and a nurse; after which the rest of us tramped unhappily on, knowing that they would inevitably be taken prisoners, which they were two days later. They were well treated, however, by the Austrians, and when the girl who had been shot was sufficiently recovered to undertake the journey, they were all passed through Vienna and Switzerland, and so home to England. But that is another story.

Meanwhile, the rest of us arrived, soaked to the skin, at Rashka, and were cheered by hot soup and cocoa, in the awful little hovel in which the earlier arrivals were housed. We slept that night under a roof, but infinitely preferred our previous nights under the stars, for about twenty of us were crammed into an indescribably filthy room, over a stable full of Army horses, and next to a larger room in which they were making shells! In those days there was no time for factories. Things were made anywhere. Most of the Army had no uniforms. The country had not recovered from the Balkan Wars of 1912 and 1913, and there was no help outside the country when all Europe was engaged in her own bitter struggle.

Then, two days before we would have reached Monastir, the Bulgarians took it. We had no choice no but to cross the mountains – the mountains of Albania and Montenegro, which we had been told were impassable for women in the winter. The three weeks' trek south had made us three weeks later in the beginning of the attempt, and the very first night we got to the narrow ways, the snow came. The roads were now too narrow for wagons, even though at the beginning they had been sawn laboriously in half, so that two wheels might pass where four would not, and the only means of transport were pack-mules or donkeys. These carried what food we had, and the blankets without which we would have perished. For many died on those pitiless mountains, and the snow fell and covered up their misery for ever.

Yet, with all hope gone, their country left behind, their women left behind (for when we reached the mountains the only women were the Red Cross units), starving, beaten, miserable, how wonderful were those soldiers! Peasants, driven from the soil which bred them, these men had no high education to tell them how to hold themselves in this disaster. But every Serbian is a poet: how else had they kept their souls free under 500 years of the Turkish yoke? And ever down those years, entirely through their songs and stories, and through their religion (for, to give the Turks their due, they did not interfere with that), they had kept alive and burning bright the flame of the belief that one day their country would be free. And in the year 1912 it came true, for the small Balkan states banded together and pushed the Turks out of their country – back to Constantinople. But for a pitiful short time, for in 1914 came Armageddon.

These retreating men, even if they won through wounds and starvation and exposure and hardship unspeakable, had only hope of exile. For us who were with them, the end of our journey was home. So it was easier to bear things cheerily, though hearts could hold no more of pity. Simple as children, with the unquestioning gratitude of such, no one ever saw them other than forbearing with each other, when men fell dead of starvation while waiting for the ration of bread and were laid by the roadside and left for the snow to shroud; no one ever saw them other than courteous to women. And when one remembers how the conditions of retreat can turn men into animals, when things are down to the bed-rock of primitive passions and desire for life, then it is a proud thing to remember also the high courage with which this people bore their disaster.

To add to the horrors of the retreat, there fell upon the mountains in that December one of the worst snow-storms for decades, and then was the pathway indeed bordered by death. We were crossing the higher passes, and only a 2-foot track wound upwards. On the right were snow-covered cliffs, on the left a sheer drop to the river 1,000 feet below. Two mules could not pass each other on that path, deep in snow or slippery with ice, and when a pack mule fell and died (brave little faithful beasts of burden) there they froze and the trail passed over them. The worst night of the storm we sheltered in an Albanian hut. The fire smouldered in the middle of the mud floor, the smoke escaping through a hole in the roof – and round the fire squatted the family – unto the third and fourth generation! Around them again, the refugees, soldiers, and nurses, and the live-stock of the little farm. (My neighbour on one side was a warm and comfortable calf!) Everything that could be sheltered was sheltered; those that had no shelter remained out on the mountain and died. In the morning, the pack-mules, which were under the lee of the hut, were frozen stiff; and again the blankets and gear were reduced. At the last, when the mountains were crossed, and the weary, muddy miles to the sea lay before us, nothing remained to most of us but what we carried ourselves. But we had our lives, and many had left theirs on those cruel heights. But for those exiles, literally bereft of everything that made life worth living – family, home, country – what use, after all, seemed even that?

Those last days, towards the sea and the ultimate hope of rest, were even more dreadful than the rest. For now it was not the snow which covered death and corruption, but mud. It seemed as though there never had been and never again could be anything else than rain, rain, rain. And in all the world there is surely nothing more depressing than rain which falls soddenly on mud, and mud which receives all sullenly the rain.

Then, as the uttermost depths seemed reached, the skies of the nearly-last night cleared. It was late, nearly midnight, but the little fishing village on the Adriatic coast had somehow to be reached by morning – for a ship was to be there to take us off. (It was torpedoed, and we sat on the shore, as it happened, for three more days.) And suddenly, out of the welter of misery, the road burst out on to the sea – lying dark and shining under stars; and perhaps the most vivid memory of all those weeks of adventure is the sight of her – sudden, beautiful, clean. "Who hath desired the sea, the immense and contemptuous surges"; after all, what was starvation and death?

The Italian ship which was to meet us at San Giovanni di Medua was, as I said, torpedoed, along with every food-ship which was being sent by the Italian Government to meet the refugees. The little harbour was full of the sprouting masts and funnels of unhappy ships which had been sunk, a pitiful sight at the ebb of the tide. And the surrounding hills were quivering at night with the little fires of innumerable soldiers, who had survived starvation on the mountains only to meet it again on the shore. While overhead the Austrian aeroplanes circled, and dropped their bombs.

Then, after three days, a ship got through. Little as she was, she was able to take off all the Red Cross units. The soldiers had to set off again on that everlasting trek, down to Alassio and the further ports. No man of military age was allowed on board, but many refugees who were quite hopelessly smashed, and women of the coast as well, filled the little ship literally to overflowing. There was not room for all to lie down. Twice she was attacked, and tacking, swerving, zigzagging across the Adriatic, we came at last at dawn to Brindisi. And as the light grew, to port and starboard of the little ship, loomed in the mist first one and then another protecting form. And hearts at last believed in safety, for they were British gunboats. We landed at Brindisi, and had our first real meal for over two months.

SHELLED, HEBUTERNE TRENCHES, WESTERN FRONT, 19 October 1915

Second-Lieutenant Graham Greenwell, 4th Battalion, Oxford and Buckinghamshire Light Infantry

A letter home.

Thank God, in two or three hours' time I shall have left these trenches for billets.

Since I wrote to you yesterday we have had a ghastly time. The German bombardment, for so it became after lunch, grew extremely violent; they were using some of their largest shells, which shook the earth and sent splinters flying hundreds of yards away.

At 4.30 p.m. a white-faced officer, one of our subalterns, came up to my trench from somewhere behind and told me that the front line trenches were completely wrecked: the officer in charge buried and killed in the signallers' dug-out, all the telephone wires were cut, and that I, in fact, was virtually the front line. This news was certainly depressing and I gave up Conny for lost as he had gone up there a few minutes before.

About a quarter of an hour later the Colonel came up, called me out and ordered me to take my Platoon down to the front line as quickly as possible, as it had been reported that the German front line and saps were full of men; they might be in our trench now for all he knew. I hastily turned them out and rushed down the communication trench with only about two men at my heels, hearing appalling explosions ahead of me.

The trench was blocked in one place by a stretcher with a wounded or dead signaller on it, and this delayed us until I got him removed. Finally, when I reached the front trench the most terrible scene of destruction confronted me; it was impossible to see the old trench line. Then Conny came running up very dishevelled and shouted to me to take my men down one of the front trenches at once and stand to, ready to be attacked. As it was impossible to get to this trench except overland – the communication trench being filled in – it was a nasty job. The Huns had turned on to the spot which we had to pass their most appalling of all engines – the meinenwerfer or mine-thrower. As I was about to go across I saw a blinding flash in front of me and a great column of flame and earth rose into the sky: the concussion hurled me backwards into a deep German dug-out. I felt shaken to pieces: it was a most horrible feeling of being absolutely dazed and helpless just at the wrong moment. A corporal who was with me pulled me up and we went back to get the rest of my men up, as they were straggling behind and getting lost in the confusion. As we were waiting about a few minutes later Conny saved our lives by yelling out "Look out for the meinenwerfer!" He had just heard the faint sound of its discharge. There was a rush backwards and every-one flung themselves face downwards under any sort of protection that offered. There was another terrific explosion and we were covered with filthy smoke and falling mud and earth. However, after this I ran the gauntlet and got safe into the trench, which I found quite intact, thank Heaven, though it was cut off at the end. It was now mercifully too dark for the shelling to continue, so we had the meinenwerfer instead. About three fell in it, all of which, by some extraordinary chance, did no damage to life. I felt most frightfully shaken and pretty rotten, but after about half an hour it passed off.

Two other Platoons had by this time reinforced the front line; the enemy had ceased every kind of fire and there was dead quiet. We posted sentries all the way along a[illegible] work like niggers to try to rebuild the trenches b[illegible] luckily we got plenty of sand-bags. A large party [illegible] up and a few Gloucesters. The men worked splendid[illegible] on duty all night without a stop, building up to the [illegible], renewing the wire in front, and clearing the entranc[illegible] to the trench so that we could get out when it became light.

The wreckage was awful, dug-outs completely smashed in and everything pitched up all over the shop. It is a miracle how few the casualties were. Captain Treble, who was taking charge of our Platoon in the front line, as we had an officer away, was killed sitting by the telephone in the signallers' dug-out. The shell scored a direct hit on it and his head was smashed in by the timbers. The signaller was, I think, mortally wounded and one bomber broke down. There were no other casualties.

During the worst part of the show I saw a young subaltern of the Seaforths, the battalion on our right, who had actually come round to have a look. They had had it as badly as we had, but had only three casualties. He seemed pretty cool and was wearing a squash hat – a Homburg. We fraternized over the wreckage and voted the Huns rotten beasts.

Twenty minutes later

I thought this letter would end abruptly at "beasts". For just after I had written that word I heard to my horror one of those awful explosions which made yesterday so hideous, followed by two or three others. They were again firing, away to the right this time. I telephoned back to Conny to ask him where the shells were actually falling, and he said that it was a good way over to the right on the next Division. It turns out that they were not the heavy guns as I had thought, but only that formidable meinenwerfer firing from the German front trench. Our heavy guns then put shells into their front trench with wonderful accuracy; the ground shook, huge clouds of yellow smoke arose and some of the fragments flew back to our trench. Since then we have had peace; it looks like raining and I pray that it will pour. We have only another two hours here and then freedom.

The row these things make is incredible and I can hear

nothing but the low whistle of heavy shells; every puff of the wind startles me and I feel as nervous as a cat. It is the sitting still throughout a solid day listening the whole time to shells and wondering if the next will be on the dug-out or not which is so unnerving. I cannot understand what sort of men they are who can stand three or four days of continued bombardment. Of course, at the end the ones who are alive are absolutely demoralized.

EASTERN FRONT: WINTER BATTLE IN THE CARPATHIAN PASSES, GALICIA, 17–25 November 1915

Lieutenant Octavian Taslaunau, Austro-Hungarian Army

November 17th

We had some frightful news this morning. The fighting Hungarian Lieutenant Szinte's company had been scattered, and he himself had bolted at top speed, thereby crushing one of his feet and taking all the skin off his nose.

Michaelis, the bookseller, had gone forward with fifty men to a wooded height. A few men of my company, including Sergeant Corusa, told me that they saw some thirty Russians stealing away in front of their line. They began to call out, "*Feuer einstellen – Tuzet seuntes*" ("Cease fire!").

At this double command, in German and Hungarian, our men got up and left their shelter behind the trees. Then the Russians were head to whisper: "*Brzo, brzo!*" ("Quick, quick!"), and they fired rapidly on our poor simpletons and then bolted.

In a few seconds we had only dead and wounded left, for hardly fifteen came back untouched. Poor Michaelis, hit in the left shoulder by a bullet which came out the other side, was killed and buried on the frontier. A Rumanian stretcher-bearer laid him on straw at the bottom of a trench and recited a paternoster over him. That was a real good soul, in a man devoted to his duty. God rest it. His brother, the engineer, had had his forehead scraped by a bullet. Two other officers had been seriously wounded.

I was left alone, of all those who had left Fagaras with the battalion. Michaelis, my last companion, had just left me for ever.

In the afternoon I took fifty men to hold a slope covered with juniper trees. The men hastily dug trenches, and I manufactured a shelter of boughs and branches. Once more it snowed, and there was no question of making fires.

Everything was wrapped in a mantle of snow, whose virginal whiteness soothed us and made our thoughts turn calmly to death, which we longed for as never before. The men dug coffin-shaped trenches, so that when in the evening I went to inspect them lying in these ditches covered with juniper, they looked to me as if they had been buried alife. Poor Rumanians!

November 20th

An unforgettable day, I doubt if fiction has ever recorded scenes more comic, and yet more interesting, than those of November 20th.

First, a description of the situation is necessary.

We were holding the hills between the road from Radoszyce in Hungary and that which passes through Dolzyca to the frontier.

The terrain was very uneven and thickly wooded. Here and there a clearing or meadow could be seen, though even these were invaded by junipers. The line of our positions was prolonged over the wooded height opposite us, so that we had to fire to our left straight through the woods without seeing anything.

The reports of our patrols did not enable us to get any very clear idea of the extent of our front, so Major Paternos and I went out to confirm their news from the spot.

The forest began in face of us, thirty or forty paces down the slope. We made our way into it and reached a stream. On the other side of the stream the woods became thicker, and we could get up the slope only with the assistance of projecting tufts and branches.

Beyond the top we found a battalion, about 300 strong, of the 47th Infantry. They had all gone to ground, and their Captain showed us thirty paces away, the crest covered with junipers, and told us: "Russians are there."

But the undergrowth was so thick that nothing could be seen and no one could get through. This Captain was in despair, feeling that he had no chance of getting away. We understood it. His situation was very difficult. We shivered even as we listened.

Our sector was broken on the right, but on our left, three hundred paces off, the next sector had good trenches, which wound round in a bend to the Dolzyca road. The gaps were due to our lack of men.

In the morning the 12th Company was on duty. Mine rested in shelters in the woods, and we were served out with bread, tinned stuffs, winter underclothes, boots – even children's elastic slippers – and other luxuries.

The men, cold or no cold, lost no time in undressing to change their linen. I then saw human bodies which were nothing but one great sore from the neck to the waist. They were absolutely eaten up with lice. For the first time I really understood the popular phrase, "May the lice eat you!"

One of the men, when he pulled off his sthirt, tore away crusts of dried blood, and the vermin were swarming in filthy layers in the garment. The poor peasant had grown thin on this. His projecting jaws and sunken eyes were the most conspicuous features of him.

Even we officers were regular hives. Fothi yesterday counted fifty. He pulled them one by one from the folds of his shirt collar. He counted them, threw them in the fire, and while we drank our tea and smoked, we scratched ourselves and laughed.

About midday I decided to change also. I began by washing, for I was filthy and black. From the time of our arrival at Laszki-Murowane, six weeks before, I had not known what it was to wash my mouth.

The post had brought me from Hungary a toothbrush and some paste. What a joy once more to have white teeth and a clean mouth! In one's daily life at home one cannot imagine that such pleasures can exist. One thing at least war teaches us – to appreciate as never before the pleasures of peace!

I had just put on my shirts again – I always wore two or three – when I heard a shout from all sides: "The Russians are on us!"

Private Torna came to our shelter to announce: "Sir, the Russians are breaking through our line on the top!"

I did not yet believe it, but, at any cost, I asked my friend Fothi to conduct the company to the trenches. Meanwhile I hastily put on my boots, took my rifle and rejoined the company as it was emerging from the wood.

There I stopped. I could hardly believe my eyes. What was it I saw? Along the whole front, the Russians and our men were in contact, staring at, threatening (with bayonets fixed), shouting at, and, in places, blazing away at each other.

Among the junipers, near to the trench we had dug three days back, the Russians and our men were scrambling together, fighting and kicking, around a supply of bread intended for the 12th Company. This struggle of starving animals for food only lasted a few seconds. They all got up, each man having at least a fragment of bread, which he devoured voraciously.

With a rapid glance I counted the Russians. They were not more numerous than ourselves, and I saw them drag our men away one by one by pulling at the corners of their blankets – for our shepherds had turned their blankets into overcoats.

One or two of them, a little more knowing than the rest, unfastened these coverings and, with a shake of the shoulders, left them in the hands of the Russians. The latter, well content with their prize, went their way laughing, while our men came back to us. I thought to myself that, after all, it could not be much worse in Siberia than it was here.

Some of the Russians now tried to surround us. One raw young recruit came quite close up to us and raised his rifle at me. I held mine to the ready in response. It was a thrilling moment. I don't know what it was, but something in my look prevented him from firing, and I too refrained.

He took to his heels and fled. But the shock had been too much for me, and, like a savage, I yelled in a fury: "Disarm them!"

I threw myself on to the group nearest to us, and Fothi and I together wrenched the rifles out of the hands of the two Russian soldiers. They all surrendered forthwith like lambs. We took sixty of them. All our men wished to escort the prisoners.

I selected three as a guard, the third to walk behind and carry the Russian's rifle. I was obliged to have recourse to threats before I could induce them to enter the trench, and I then marched them off in file to the Commander-in-Chief.

And this is how bread, holy bread, reconciles men, not only in the form of Communion before the holy altar, but even on the field of battle. The peasants, who, in their own homes, whether in Russia or elsewhere, sweat blood in order to insure the ripening of the golden ear of corn which is to feed their masters, once they are on the battlefield forget the behests of these masters who have sent them forth to murder their fellows, and they make peace over a scrap of bread.

The bread which they have produced and harvested makes them brothers. After this scene not a single shot disturbed the forest, and those who had been able to preserve a whole loaf, quickly shared it in brotherly fashion with the prisoners, the latter offering them tobacco in exchange. All this, of course, took place in front of our bivouacs in the heart of the forest.

I sent Fothi to the Major to ask for reinforcements, as I was expecting a second attack. The prisoners told me that the Russians had come about four hundred strong.

I did not have long to wait. An hour later, on the edge of the wood, a party of Russians appeared. They were standing with their rifles at the slope, beckoning to us to approach. One of our men left his party and came to tell us that the Russians wished to surrender, but that we ought to surround them.

It was no doubt a fresh ruse. A quarter of an hour before I had sent out a patrol of two men – a Rumanian and a Saxon – and they had not returned. The Rumanian had surrendered and the Saxon had been killed.

My reinforcements arrived, sixty men of the 10th Company, under Second Lieutenant Szollosy, the man who was always the best hand at cursing and belabouring our Rumanians. I sent his sergeant-major, a brutal and thoroughly repellent Saxon, together with twenty men, to the right to surround the Russians.

I certainly doomed them to death. I reckoned that if the Russians wished to surrender they would not wait for us to surround them first. They would lay down their arms and give themselves up. On the other hand, if they did fire on our men, all who had gone out to the corner of the forest would fall victims. But calculations are all very fine; on the field of battle they are apt to be misleading.

Surrender was the last thing in the world that the Russians

against whom our men were advancing with fixed bayonets had in mind.

I went over the top, clambering over the body of a man whose brains were sticking out of his head, and signed them to surrender – they were at most 200 yards away.

But they still continued to call to us without attempting to move. I thereupon gave the command, "Fire!" and held my own rifle at the ready. At this point my calculations broke down. My Rumanians refused to fire, and, what was more, prevented me from firing either. One of them put his hand on my rifle and said "Don't fire, sir; if we fire, they will fire too. And why should Rumanians kill Rumanians?" (he was thinking of the Bessarabians.)

I accordingly refrained, but, beside myself with rage, tried to rejoin my right wing, where incredible things were happening.

The schoolmaster Catavei and Cizmas barred my way, exclaiming: "Stop, don't go and get yourself shot, too!"

Our men were advancing towards the Russians, and at the slope, were shaking hands with them; and the fraternizing business started again.

"Surrender, and we will surrender, too. We're quite ready."

Our men were bringing in Russians, and vice versa. It was a touching sight.

I saw one of my Rumanians, towards Saliste, kiss a Russian and bring him back. Their arms were round each other's necks as though they were brothers. They were old friends, who had been shepherd boys together in Bessarabia.

We took ninety Russians as prisoners in this way; whilst they took thirty of our men.

But this was not the last of the adventures of that wonderful day.

I was afraid of a third attack. A Moldavian from Bessarabia, noticing what a handful we were, said to me: "If we had known there were so few of you we should have gone for you with sticks."

I again applied to the Major for reinforcements and a machine gun. As it happened, he had just called up a company of the 96th Infantry Regiment; they arrived almost immediately – 125 men, under Lieutenant Petras – and went to lengthen our right wing.

As for me, the Major sent me to a bank on the left, to direct two machine guns where to fire in order to cut off the retreat of those Russians who had remained in the wood. I had hardly advanced a hundred yards before I heard a shout of "Hurrah!" in my sector.

I called out to the Major to find out what it meant, and went on. In a hollow I found a field officer – unfortunately, I have forgotten his name – who sent a lieutenant to accompany me to the machine guns.

But it was a Russian machine gun that welcomed us as soon as we reached the trenches. The bullets whizzed by, thick and fast. One grazed my leg, another came within a hand's-breadth of my head.

The Russians employ detachments of snipers, who creep into advanced positions and pick off officers only. Major Paternos had the fingers of his left hand shot off in his observation post. They are wonderful shots. I showed my respect for them by not leaving the trench until nightfall, when I returned to my sector.

Lieutenant Petras had attacked the Russians in the wood. That was the meaning of the cheers I had heard, of which the most patent result was the reduction of the relieving company of the 96ths to twenty-five men. Those who had entered the wood never returned, and had certainly fallen prey to the Russians.

Once again I had escaped the dangers of that fateful day, which the Commander-in-Chief assured us, in a special Army Order, would be inscribed on the page of history.

Our scrap with the Russians may have been extremely comic, but at least we had held our positions – and that alone was a victory. We had been allotted the task of keeping the crest, from which, if they had been able to seize it, the Russians would have threatened our line in the rear and on the flank; and we had fulfilled it.

Major Paternos told us to draw up a list of the men who had distinguished themselves. We all received the second-class medal for valour, and three officers – Fothi, Szollosy and myself – were also awarded the *Signum Laudis* bar.

The Hungarian deserved it perhaps least of any of us. He was not even present when we took the prisoners; but he had the impudence to go to the Major and declare, in front of us all, that it was he who captured the first Russian.

We marched through a huge forest to Hocra, where the Command of the Twentieth Division was stationed. We only got there late at night, and our strength had dwindled to a quarter of what we had at the start.

Our little Budapest gentleman had littered the road like flies. Many of them remained behind in the woods, weeping, and no one bothered about them. Some of our veterans had dropped behind, too. It was by the mercy of God if they escaped the frost and the wolves.

November 25th

All these villages of the Galician frontier were crammed with Jewish refugees from the Galician frontier. We found rooms filled by thirty to forty persons, men, women, little girls, children, and, of course, a seasoning of soldiers all sleeping together in a heap. It is difficult to imagine a more complete picture of misery.

Our numbers were so seriously reduced that we were obliged to form two companies, a half-battalion, the last unit which preserved its individual supply arrangements, for although we were attached to the 1st Regiment of Honveds, we were messed by ourselves.

Here my company was dissolved, as it had now only the strength of a platoon, of which I was still the Commander. There were only two officers with precedence over me, and both of these were Hungarians – Szinte and Szollosy – so that in spite of the regret of my men and the indignation of many of my friends, I still remained a subaltern.

The dispersion of my company was the last straw. I made up my mind to say goodbye to battlefields, as I was nothing but a shadow and it was all I could do to drag myself along.

November 27th

At night we returned to Havaj. We left early for Stropka-Polena in a thick mist, cold and penetrating. Marching was a difficult business, for the men were worn out.

At Polena, a halt. But Austrian bureaucracy could not even

leave us alone in the field. We had to get out a return of all the men's belongings which were missing, and ever would be.

What was there that our poor fellows did not lack? Everything they had on them was in rags, and filthy beyond words. Lice swarmed over them like bees in a hive. Most of them were barefooted, and had wrapped up their feet in rags tied round their tattered socks.

The feet of many were terribly torn and sore, but it was useless for them to go to the doctors. Strict orders had been issued that only those half dead should be admitted to hospital. One of our men remained in action for two weeks with his left arm broken by a piece of shrapnel, so he said. He was actually afraid to go to the doctor. There was, in fact, no question that the bone of his forearm was broken, but no flesh wound was to be seen.

About midday we once more took the northwest road for Galicia. We climbed hills which had been well ploughed by Russian artillery. To get through a wood we had to swing by the trees. At the top we were stopped by Colonel Gombosh.

It was useless to tell him that we had our Major's orders to occupy another hill. He would not hear of it. He needed a reserve, and we must stay. Shells of all kinds fell thick and fast in the forest, and there was violent fighting everywhere, the swish of machine gun bullets being conspicuous.

Colonel Gombosh sent Szinte to take a house about 1,000 metres behind the Russian front line. Then he showed me a knoll from which I was to watch for his return and shoot his company wholesale if he returned with it. We then began to realize that we were dealing with one who had lost his wits. But Szinte's men went off to the Russian trenches – and few of them came back.

Night fighting in forests, where it is almost impossible to see even in daytime, has something quite unreal about it. All is confusion, and fear reigns supreme. Only the flashes can be seen, and it is by them that the enemy, his strength and position, can be seen. Group fights with group. Often enough you come upon your enemy from behind without knowing that it is your enemy. I once met a lieutenant whose cap was absolutely cut up at the back. He had got up to the Russians, crawling at full length. Bullets had sliced through his clothes. But he had come, dragging himself along from tree to tree.

The men passed the night in a wide trench, dug specially for the reserve, and I myself sheltered behind a tree, shivering with cold. The bullets struck the tree-trunks with a sound like the cracking of a whip. We heard that the Russians were using explosive bullets.

The minute you got up or moved from your protecting tree, you were gambling with your life. It was indeed a night of horror. At two o'clock in the morning certain platoons received an order to fix bayonets and drive the Russians from a trench. They approached, sent out scouts ahead, and found the trench full of the – 24th Territorials!

They were within an ace of executing their orders and killing every single occupant. The Colonel's information was defective. The trench had been only partly occupied by the Russians, and was actually held both by our men and them. In fact, they had been having a shooting-match down the same communication trench. In the morning we returned to Havaj.

November 28th

We went back to the trenches. Towards five o'clock in the afternoon the Russians were at Stropko-Polena. They bade us goodnight by sending over four shells, which burst round the village church. We did trench duty that night, relieving each other every two hours.

In the night one of our patrols brought us in three Russian soldiers, well-clad, healthy young men, two of whom were Russians, the third a Jew, "master of the Hebrew tongue." I can't say where he came from. It was he who had persuaded the others to surrender.

Our popular Major Paternos left us at last. He got poisoning in the wound on his hand and had a sharp fever.

That night I felt ill myself: I was reduced to skin and bones – I could hardly stand up. I had had quite enough of soldiering, and so made up my mind to go.

November 29th

In the morning with tears in my eyes I said goodbye to my men. Then, having gone through all the formalities, I walked as far as

Buckocz and drove to Eperjes in two days, and from there took the last train to Budapest.

Both Eperjes and Cassorie were empty of inhabitants. I was the officer of the unit who had started out with the battalion from Fagaras and had left the fighting area. After myself there was none left but Dr Schuller.

Of our regiment of more than 3,500 men I had left only 170 at Havaj. On the 11th Company, which had left Fagaras 267 strong, only five now remained, and six counting myself.

God had willed that I should return alive.

GALLIPOLI: THE ALLIED EVACUATION, 18–19 December 1915

Commander Roger Keyes, Royal Navy

. . . By the afternoon of the 18th, 44,000 men, 130 guns and several thousand animals had been embarked without apparently causing the slightest suspicion. Nothing was done until it was dark, and by dawn everything was normal again. There were still 40,000 men and 50 guns on shore, and it was arranged to withdraw 20,000 men and 30 guns on the night of the 18th if the weather looked promising. Thus throughout the 19th the whole front would be very lightly held by 20,000 men and 20 guns with a force of about 100,000 enemy in close proximity. In some places the opposing trenches were only a few yards apart.

Generals Byng and Godley were each provided with a sloop from which to direct the retirement, and at either flank of the two positions cable connections from every point of command were brought off to buoys, which could be picked up by the Corps Commander's sloop. Wireless communication was reserved for the fire control of the supporting ships, which was of the utmost importance in the absence of artillery.

Everything went without a hitch during the night of the 18th. On the morning of Sunday, 19th, I went over to the Peninsula with Lambart and General Birdwood, and after landing the latter at Anzac we went to Suvla, where I spent some hours walking round with General Byng, who was cheerful and optimistic. He had spent the night on board his sloop. His Chief of Staff, Brigadier-General Read, would remain there to keep in cable communication with the front, but he told me that he intended to spend the night of 18th on shore and be the last to leave. I told him that he would have trouble with Unwin, who would claim the Navy's prerogative, since the last to leave must be the naval beach party. He said that he would gladly give way to Unwin, for whom he had an unbounded admiration.

I congratulated him on the wonderful arrangements for evacuation at Suvla; there seemed to be nothing for his Corps to do but march down to the boats and set light to the bonfires – large piles of provisions, stores, fodder and petrol, which it was decided to abandon rather than prolong the evacuation. He said, "Don't congratulate me; my Chief of Staff has thought of nothing else but evacuation for the last four months!"

The naval arrangements were excellent; Unwin had provided for every possible contingency. Thanks to the long spell of fine weather since the heavy southerly blow at the end of November, it had been possible to make wonderful preparations for rapid embarkation; but one southerly blow would have wrecked everything. The blockship harbour on the north shore of Suvla Bay, which was connected by a light railway with the depots inland, was equipped with piers, pontoons and ramps, which enabled guns, heavy wagons and lorries to run down to the lighters, and animals could walk straight on board. There were berths for five motor lighters, capable of carrying 500 men apiece. The main embarkation was to take place in motor lighters here, two adjacent beaches, and under Lala Baba where a new pier had been constructed. A number of steam pinnaces, each with two cutters in tow, were stationed along the foreshore ready to pick up any stragglers.

General Byng told me that the enemy had been seen digging, rolling out new wire, and generally preparing to resist an attack, and during the previous night two deserters had come into our lines with the same story of depression and low *morale*.

The field hospital tents were left standing, well equipped with medical stores and comforts, in which to leave the wounded who could not be embarked. It was hoped that we should be able to get the badly wounded off the following day under a flag of truce.

There was a certain amount of desultory shelling, and at about noon, the Turks shelled the beach under Lala Baba pretty heavily for about half an hour, evidently registering on to it. Otherwise it was a very quiet day.

The battleships *Cornwallis and Prince George* were anchored in Suvla Bay inside the nets, the *Theseus*, three monitors and two destroyers covered the position from outside. The *Grafton, Talbot, Humber*, two monitors and five destroyers were off Anzac. Several ships were standing by at short notice at Kephalo.

We could hear a battle in progress at Helles during the afternoon. General Davies had been ordered to carry out a minor offensive to distract the attention of the Turks from the northern area. After blowing up a series of mines on the left of our line, our troops delivered a successful attack, seized several Turkish trenches and resisted all counter-attacks. They were supported by the *Edgar*, three heavy monitors and two destroyers, which greatly contributed to the success.

Lambart and I left Suvla about 2 p.m. and went to Anzac, where we remained until dusk. General Godley had embarked in his sloop during the previous night, and General Birdwood had returned to Imbros. I went round with an Australian Colonel.

It was distressing to find enormous piles of boots, clothing, stores and provisions, which might have been destroyed if arrangements had been made for bonfires, but I was told that they had orders not to run any risks, as the enemy, by a very short advance, could seize the position on the crest of a hill overlooking the beach, from which they could command it with machine guns at a range of less than 500 yards, if they discovered we were evacuating.

I suggested that they might make piles and surround them with fodder and petrol, as at Suvla, in order that we might destroy them by gunfire later, but they said they did not want to risk an accidental bonfire as the enemy were registered on to all the beaches and might open fire at any moment.

The main evacuation was to be carried out by motor lighters from the only two piers it had been possible to maintain on the exposed shelving foreshore, but the troops from the flanks were to be embarked in a number of pulling boats, towed by picket boats. On the right flank the embarkation would be in full view of the Turkish observation post on Gaba Tepe, which could bring down a devastating fire on to the beach. Captain Boyle had arranged for the destroyer *Rattlesnake* to lie off there and switch her searchlight on to the foreshore, to the southward of our most southerly position, at intervals throughout the night – and several preceding nights – thus making it impossible for the Turks to see through the screen of light she placed between them and our troops. Although the *Rattlesnake* had often been shelled, and had had to switch her light off and shift berth occasionally, the enemy were pretty well used to her by the night of the evacuation, and her intervention was invaluable to the troops, who were withdrawn unseen, though within full view of the Turks.

The Anzacs were determined to give the enemy a "shake up" before they left, and had undermined Russell Top with a ton of ammonal, which was to be blown up ten minutes after it was evacuated.

The motor lighters were all in their berths before we left, and an armada of troop carriers and boats was approaching as we stood across to Kephalo in a destroyer. We joined Admiral Wemyss on board the *Chatham*, in which he had hoisted his flag, and embarked the General and his Staff, We spent the night off the northern area, where there appeared to be a normal amount of firing for a quiet night, but the time passed very slowly to us onlookers. At 3.30 a.m. there was a heavy explosion – the Russell Top mine – followed by a tremendous outburst of rifle and machine-gun fire in its vicinity, which went on for half an hour or so, but by that time the troops must have been well on their way to the beach. At 4.30 a.m. we learnt that the last man had left Anzac, where all was quiet for the rest of the night except for spasmodic rifle fire and a few shells on the beaches.

At Suvla our guns fired as usual for some time before withdrawing, and there was a certain amount of rifle fire. At 5 a.m. the bonfires were lit, Suvla Point was ablaze, and we knew that the evacuation had been successfully completed. The enemy fired heavily at the bonfires, presumably thinking that our people would be endeavouring to extinguish them. When dawn broke about 6.30, all the troop carriers and small craft were well on their way to Imbros and Mudros; only the covering ships were off the Peninsula. A mist hung over the beaches and it was not until about 7 a.m. that the enemy began to realize that something had occurred. Under cover of a very heavy bombardment small parties were then seen to advance, and our ships opened fire on them and on the piles of stores at Anzac and the burning dumps at Suvla. The enemy must have suffered heavily, particularly at Anzac, where our fire was withheld until they were well exposed.

Our total casualties on that last night were one man wounded early in the evening at Anzac. At Suvla not a gun, wagon or animal was left on shore. The stores were completely destroyed by fire, and the only things that fell into the enemy's hands were the hospital tents and equipment.

At Anzac a vast quantity of valuable material was left behind, and though the ships made every effort to destroy it by gunfire, a good deal must have been serviceable to the enemy. It was not, however, until nightfall that they could examine their capture with comparative safety; even then they were frequently disturbed by destroyers running in to very close range, switching on their searchlights and opening fire with guns, machine guns and rifles. Twenty mules and 50 donkeys which were required until the last moment were killed. Nine old howitzers and guns were left behind, as they were considered necessary for the security of the position until the end; they were practically worn out and were destroyed. All the ammunition which could not be brought away was thrown into the sea.

Although every available small craft was brought into service the main evacuation had to be carried out in three trips, and there was a very small margin for either a naval or a military error in the time-table, if the work was to be completed before dawn. However, ever, everything went like clockwork, and to quote the German military correspondent of the *Vossische Zeitung:* "As long as wars last this evacuation of Suvla and Anzac will stand before the eyes of all strategists as a hitherto unattained masterpiece . . ."

HOME FRONT: DEATH OF A FIANCÉ, Christmas 1915

Vera Brittain

Brittain was a nurse with the Volunteer Aid Detachment (VAD). Her fiance was Roland Leighton. He was due home on leave from the Western Front on Christmas Day 1915.

Certainly the stage seemed perfectly set for his leave. Now that my parents had at last migrated temporarily to the Grand Hotel at Brighton, our two families were so near; the Matron had promised yet again that my own week's holiday should coincide with his, and even Edward wrote cheerfully for once to say that as soon as the actual date was known, he and Victor would both be able to get leave at the same time.

"Very wet and muddy and many of the communication trenches are quite impassable," ran a letter from Roland written on December 9th. "Three men were killed the other day by a dug-out falling in on top of them and one man was drowned in a sump hole. The whole of one's world, at least of one's visible and palpable world, is mud in various stages of solidity or stickiness . . . I can be perfectly certain about the date of my leave by to-morrow morning and will let you know."

And, when the final information did come, hurriedly written in pencil on a thin slip of paper torn from his Field Service note-book, it brought the enchanted day still nearer than I had dared to hope.

"Shall be home on leave from 24th Dec. – 31st. Land Christmas Day. R."

Even to the unusual concession of a leave which began on Christmas morning after night-duty the Matron proved amenable, and in the encouraging quietness of the winter's war, with no Loos in prospect, no great push in the west even possible, I dared to glorify my days – or rather my nights – by looking forward. In the pleasant peace of Ward 25, where all the patients, now well on the road to health, slept soundly, the sympathetic Scottish Sister teased me a little for my irrepressible excitement.

"I suppose you won't be thinking of going off and getting married? A couple of babies like you!"

It was a new and breath-taking thought, a flame to which Roland's mother – who approved of early marriages and believed that ways and means could be left to look after themselves far better than the average materialistic parent supposed – added fuel when she hinted mysteriously, on a day off which I spent in Brighton, that *this* time Roland might not be content to leave things as they were . . . Suppose, I meditated, kneeling in the darkness beside the comforting glow of the stove in the silent ward, that during this leave we *did* marry as suddenly, as, in the last one, we became "officially" engaged? Of course it would be what the world would call – or did call before the War – a "foolish" marriage. But now that the War seemed likely to be endless, and the chance of making a "wise" marriage had become, for most people, so very remote, the world was growing more tolerant. No one – not even my family now, I thought – would hold out against us, even though we hadn't a penny beyond our pay. What if, after all, we did marry thus foolishly? When the War was over we could still go back to Oxford, and learn to be writers – or even lecturers; if we were determined enough about it we could return there, even though – oh, devastating, sweet speculation! – I might have had a baby.

I had never much cared for babies or had anything to do with them; before that time I had always been too ambitious, too much interested in too many projects, to become acutely conscious of a maternal instinct. But on those quiet evenings of night-duty as Christmas approached, I would come, half asleep, as near to praying as I had been at any time, even when Roland first went to France or in the days following Loos.

"Oh, God!" my half-articulate thoughts would run, "do let us get married and let me have a baby – something that is Roland's very own, something of himself to remember him by if he goes . . . It shan't be a burden to his people or mine for a moment longer than I can help, I promise I'll go on doing war-work and give it all my pay during the War – and as soon as ever the War's over I'll go back to Oxford and take my Finals so that I can get a job and support it. So *do* let me have a baby, dear God!"

The night before Christmas Eve, I found my ward transformed into the gay semblance of a sixpenny bazaar with Union Jacks, paper streamers, crinkled tissue lampshades and Christmas texts and greetings, all carried out in staggering shades of orange and vivid scarlet and brilliant green. In the cheerful construction of red paper bags, which I filled with crackers and sweets for the men's Christmas stockings, I found that the hours passed quickly enough. Clipping, and sewing, and opening packets, I imagined him reading the letter that I had written him a few days earlier, making various suggestions for meeting him, if he could only write or wire me beforehand, when the Folkestone train arrived at Victoria, and travelling down with him to Sussex.

"And shall I really see you again, and so soon?" It had concluded. "And it will be the anniversary of the week which contained another New Year's Eve – and *David Copperfield*, and two unreal and wonderful days, and you standing alone in Trafalgar Square, and thinking of – well, what *were* you thinking of? When we were really both children still, and my connection with any hospital on earth was unthought-of, and your departure for the front merely the adventurous dream of some vaguely distant future date. And life was lived, at any rate for two days, in the Omar Khayyámesque spirit of

> Unborn to-morrow and dead yesterday–
> Why fret about them if To-day be sweet?

But we are going to better that – even that – *this* time. Au revoir."

When I went to her office for my railway-warrant in the morning, the Matron smiled kindly at my bubbling impatience, and reminded me how lucky I was to get leave for Christmas. At Victoria I inquired what boat trains arrived on Christmas Day, and learnt that there was only one, at 7.30 in the evening. The risk, I decided, of missing him in the winter blackness of a wartime terminus was too great to be worth taking: instead, I would go straight to Brighton next morning and wait for him there.

As Christmas Eve slipped into Christmas Day, I finished

tying up the paper bags, and with the Sister filled the men's stockings by the exiguous light of an electric torch. Already I could count, perhaps even on my fingers, the hours that must pass before I should see him. In spite of its tremulous eagerness of anticipation, the night again seemed short; some of the convalescent men wanted to go to early services, and that meant beginning temperatures and pulses at 3 a.m. As I took them I listened to the rain pounding on the tin roof, and wondered whether, since his leave ran from Christmas Eve, he was already on the sea in that wild, stormy darkness. When the men awoke and reached for their stockings, my whole being glowed with exultant benevolence; I delighted in their pleasure over their childish home-made presents because my own mounting joy made me feel in harmony with all creation.

At eight o'clock, as the passages were lengthy and many of the men were lame, I went along to help them to the communion service in the chapel of the college. It was two or three years since I had been to such a service, but it seemed appropriate that I should be there, for I felt, wrought up as I was to a high pitch of nervous emotion, that I ought to thank whatever God might exist for the supreme gift of Roland and the love that had arisen so swiftly between us. The music of the organ was so sweet, the sight of the wounded men who knelt and stood with such difficulty so moving, the conflict of joy and gratitude, pity and sorrow in my mind so poignant, that tears sprang to my eyes, dimming the chapel walls and the words that encircled them: "I am the Resurrection and the Life: he that believeth in Me, though he were dead, yet shall he live: and whosoever liveth and believeth in Me shall never die."

Directly after breakfast, sent on my way by exuberant good wishes from Betty and Marjorie and many of the others, I went down to Brighton. All day I waited there for a telephone message or a telegram, sitting drowsily in the lounge of the Grand Hotel, or walking up and down the promenade, watching the grey sea tossing rough with white surf-crested waves, and wondering still what kind of crossing he had had or was having.

When, by ten o'clock at night, no news had come, I concluded that the complications of telegraph and telephone on a combined Sunday and Christmas Day had made communication impossible. So, unable to fight sleep any longer after a night and a day of wakefulness, I went to bed a little disappointed, but still unperturbed. Roland's family, at their Keymer cottage, kept an even longer vigil; they sat up till nearly midnight over their Christmas dinner in the hope that he would join them, and, in their dramatic, impulsive fashion, they drank a toast to the Dead.

The next morning I had just finished dressing, and was putting the final touches to the pastel-blue crêpe-de-Chine blouse, when the expected message came to say that I was wanted on the telephone. Believing that I was at last to hear the voice for which I had waited for twenty-four hours, I dashed joyously into the corridor. But the message was not from Roland but from Clare; it was not to say that he had arrived home that morning, but to tell me that he had died of wounds at a Casualty Clearing Station on December 23rd.

CHRISTMAS AT MAMETZ WOOD, 25 December 1915

Llewellyn Wyn Griffith, Royal Welsh Fusiliers

The night was fine and starry, with little wind. The front-line trench was wet and poor, flimsier even than Fort Erith – technically speaking it was a breastwork, not a trench. If Fort Erith seemed unfinished, this could not be rated higher than half-begun, with its evil-smelling wet walls, undrained sump-pits and ramshackle dug-out. There were five officers to share the watch, and when the company commander allotted to me a two-hour period, from one in the morning till three, I felt proud to command a stretch of the front line on my first visit. At dinner that evening a bottle of champagne gave spurious glow to an ordinary meal, if a first meal in the front line can ever be called ordinary. Towards midnight we heard voices from the German trenches and some snatches of song: they were making merry. The night was still, and its quiet was unbroken by rifle or machine-gun fire. The artillery on both sides sent over a few shells towards the rear of the lines. The firing could rightly be described as desultory, for there was little desire on either side to create trouble; some rounds must of course be fired, otherwise questions would follow.

The battalion on our right was shouting to the enemy, and he was responding. Gradually the shouts became more deliberate, and we could hear "Merry Christmas, Tommy", and "Merry Christmas, Fritz". As soon as it became light, we saw hands and bottles being waved at us, with encouraging shouts that we could neither understand nor misunderstand. A drunken German stumbled over his parapet and advanced through the barbed wire, followed by several others, and in a few moments there was a rush of men from both sides, carrying tins of meat, biscuits and other odd commodities for barter. This was the first time I had seen No Man's Land, and now it was Every Man's Land, or nearly so. Some of our men would not go, they gave terse and bitter reasons for their refusal. The officers called our men back to the line, and in a few minutes No Man's Land was once again empty and desolate. There had been a feverish exchange of "souvenirs", a suggestion for peace all day, and a football match in the afternoon, and a promise of no rifle-fire at night. All this came to naught. An irate Brigadier came spluttering up to the line, thundering hard, throwing a "court martial" into every other sentence, ordering an extra dose of militant action that night, and breathing fury everywhere. We had evidently jeopardised the safety of the Allied cause. I suspect that across No Man's Land a similar scene was being played, for later in the day the guns became active. The artillery was stimulating the infantry to resume the War. Despite the fulminations of the Generals, the infantry was in no mood for offensive measures, and it was obvious that, on both sides, rifles and machine-guns were aimed high.

A few days later we read in the papers that on Christmas Day, 1915, there was no fraternizing with the enemy – hate was too bitter to permit of such a yielding.

VERDUN: GERMAN GENERAL HEADQUARTERS DECIDES TO ATTACK, Christmas 1915

General Erich von Falkenhayn, Chief of the General Staff of the Army in the Field

Throughout 1915, German strategy on the Western Front had been to absorb repeated – and fruitless – Allied attacks. At the end of the year Falkenhayn decided to reverse the strategy, and have France "bled white" by repeated attacks on the exposed fortress of Verdun.

It is true that we have succeeded in shaking England severely – the best proof of that is her imminent adoption of universal military service. But that is also a proof of the sacrifices England is prepared to make to attain her end – the permanent elimination of what seems to her the most dangerous rival. The history of the English wars against the Netherlands, Spain, France and Napoleon is being repeated. Germany can expect no mercy from this enemy, so long as he still retains the slightest hope of achieving his object. Any attempt at an understanding which Germany might make would only strengthen England's will to war as, judging others by herself, she would take it as a sign that Germany's resolution was weakening.

England, a country in which men are accustomed to weigh up the chances dispassionately, can scarcely hope to overthrow us by purely military means. She is obviously staking everything on a war of exhaustion. We have not been able to shatter her belief that it will bring Germany to her knees, and that belief gives the enemy the strength to fight on and keep on whipping their team together.

What we have to do is to dispel that illusion.

With that end in view, it will not, in the long run, be enough for us merely to stand on the defensive, a course in itself quite worthy of consideration. Our enemies, thanks to their superiority in men and material, are increasing their resources much more than we are. If that process continues a moment must come when the balance of numbers itself will deprive Germany of all remaining hope. The power of our allies to hold out is restricted, while our own is not unlimited. It is possible that next winter, or – if the Rumanian deliveries continue – the winter after the next, will bring food crises, and the social and political crises that always follow them, among the members of our alliance, if there has been no decision by then. Those crises must and will be overcome. But there is no time to lose. We must show England patently that her venture has no prospects.

In this case, of course, as in most others involving higher strategic decisions, it is very much easier to say what has to be done than to find out how it can and must be done.

The next method would be an attempt to inflict a decisive defeat on England on land. By that I do not mean here the island itself, which cannot be reached by our troops. Of that the navy is profoundly convinced. Our efforts can therefore be directed only against one of the continental theatres where England is fighting.

It is all the more necessary that we should ruthlessly employ every weapon that is suitable for striking at England on her own ground. Such weapons are the submarine war and the conclusion of a political and economic union between Germany and not her allies only, but all States which are not yet entirely under England's spell. The review is not concerned with the formation of such a union. The solution of that problem is the exclusive sphere of the political leaders.

The submarine war, on the other hand, is a weapon to itself. It is the duty of those who are conducting the war to explain their attitude on this question.

Submarine warfare strikes at the enemy's most sensitive spot, because it aims at severing his oversea communications. If the definite promises of the naval authorities, that the unrestricted submarine war must force England to yield in the course of the year 1916, are realized, we must face the fact that the United States may take up a hostile attitude. She cannot intervene decisively in the war in time to enable her to make England fight on when that country sees the spectre of hunger and many another famine rise up before her island. There is only one shadow on this encouraging picture of the future. We have to assume that the naval authorities are not making a mistake. We have no large store of experiences to draw on in this matter. Such as we have are not altogether reassuring. On the other hand, the basis of our calculations will be materially changed in our favour if we can increase the number of our submarines and make progress with the training of their crews. For all these reasons there can be no justification on military grounds for refusing any further to employ what promises to be our most effective weapon. Germany has every right to use it ruthlessly after England's unconscionable behaviour at sea. The Americans, England's secret allies, will not recognize that, but it is doubtful whether, in face of a determined diplomatic representation of Germany's standpoint, they will decide to intervene actively on the Continent of Europe. It is even more doubtful whether they could intervene in sufficient strength in time. If we refuse to adopt unrestricted submarine warfare, it means that we are abandoning what all competent experts assure us is a sure advantage of inestimable value for a draw-back which is serious but only problematical. In Germany's position that course is not permissible.

As I have already insisted, the strain on France has almost reached the breaking-point – though it is certainly borne with the most remarkable devotion. If we succeeded in opening the eyes of her people to the fact that in a military sense they have nothing more to hope for, that breaking-point would be reached and England's best sword knocked out of her hand. To achieve that object the uncertain method of a mass breakthrough, in any case beyond our means, is unnecessary. We can probably do enough for our purposes with limited resources. Within our reach behind the French sector of the Western Front there are objectives for the retention of which the French General Staff would be compelled to throw in every man they have. If they do so the forces of France will bleed to death – as there can be no question of a voluntary withdrawal – whether we reach our goal or not. If they do not do so, and we reach our objectives, the moral effect on France will be enormous. For an operation limited to a narrow front Germany will not be compelled to spend herself so completely that all other fronts are practically drained. She can face with confidence the relief attacks to be expected on those fronts, and indeed hope to have sufficient troops in hand to reply to them with counter-attacks.

For she is perfectly free to accelerate or draw out her offensive, to intensify it or break it off from time to time, as suits her purpose.

The objectives of which I am speaking now are Belfort and Verdun.

Part Three

1916

We beat them on the Marne
We beat them on the Aisne
We gave them hell
At Neuve Chapelle
And here we go again

– Sung by British soldiers
on the eve of the
Somme battle

INTRODUCTION

By the end of 1915 the High Commands of all the main belligerents were convinced that decision in the war would only come on the Western Front. So it was that in December 1915 an inter-Allied military conference at Chantilly decided on a Anglo-French offensive for the summer of 1916, with diversionary attacks in the East and in Italy.

But the Germans got their big blow in first. Following their Christmas 1915 pontification they fell on Verdun in February 1916, having taken the precaution of transferring nearly a million men from the East, where the Russians and the Serbs lay conveniently routed. The attack on Verdun marked a change of strategy by the German High Command, who had hitherto taken a defensive stance in the West. The new aim was to "bleed" France into a separate peace treaty, leaving Britain – adjudged to be the main menace to the Central Powers – weakened and alone. As an aperitif, the Germans submitted Verdun to unparalleled saturation shelling (it was the hope, even the *idée fixé*, of both sides in the West in 1916 that artillery would demolish the enemy to allow a simple stroll to victory). Even though Verdun withstood the ten-month onslaught, it was indeed the cemetery of the French army; henceforth the main brunt of the Allied fighting on the Western Front was undertaken by the British.

Accordingly, it was the British who led the great summer offensive of 1916 at the Somme – a name which soon became a byword for senseless slaughter. More than 20,000 British troops died on the first day of the battle alone – for the sake of a few yards of mud. This not withstanding, British GHQ poured more and more men in the maws of the battle until winter caused the Germans to make a tactical withdrawal and the battle fluttered out. (Having bloodied themselves, as well as the French, at Verdun, the Germans had reverted to their old defensive posture in the West.) Such blood-letting meant that the combatant nations were becoming pitifully short of arms and the men to wield them. In response, ever more desperate measures were introduced; conscription in Britain in January 1916; forced labour in German-occupied France in April 1916; the Hindenburg Programme of expansion of the war-industry (especially munitions) in August 1916; the replacement of the Asquith government by the more war-minded Lloyd George administration in Britain in December 1916.

Outside the Western Front, the war in the rest of the world was not quite dead, even if the blinkered concentration of French, German and British minds upon Flanders fields suggested it. But it was a year of anti-climax the globe over. In the East the Russians launched their last gasp Brusilov offensive, which sent the Austrians reeling – capturing 200,000 men in two weeks of June – but then spent itself against two natural obstacles, the Carpathian mountains and the German army. And then, after persuading Rumania to their side, the Allies let her be overrun in a matter of months. In the Middle East, the British garrison at Kut hauled up the white flag to the Turks, in an almost unrivalled embarrasment to British arms, which was only effaced by the courage of its soldiers in the subsequent "death march" to the POW camps in Anatolia. At sea, the British and German fleets met in what should have been a climactic encounter at Jutland, but what turned out to be a score-draw.

And so the year closed in depression for the Allies.

TRENCH LIFE: AN OFFICER'S DUG-OUT, WESTERN FRONT, January 1916

Second Lieutenant J.S. Tatham, 9th King's Royal Rifle Corps

We are up here now in a large dug-out behind the line – came up the night before last. The quarters are quite good and there is ample room for 4 of us, but it is rather a bore not being able to undress or take off one's boots. However, we can arrange to sleep moderately well. We are, I suppose, about 500 yards from the Boches, it may be less. Pat and his platoon are a little higher up in front, but he returns to us to-night, I believe. The men are hard at it all day, and there is plenty of work for them to do. Of course we have got our servants up here, and we get our food just the same as if we were back in billets. I always think porridge and eggs and bacon sound rather funny so close up. They send our mail up as well. There is not a great deal of opportunity for writing, but I have got a chance now.

I have just had a prehistoric wash in a Huntley and Palmer's biscuit tin. It's wonderful what uses Mr H. and P.'s biscuit tins can be put to. Our table is a trench floor-board nailed on to legs and covered with sandbags, and our chairs are disinfectant tins also upholstered with sandbags.

VERDUN: THE BARRAGE, 21–22 February 1916

General Artois Pétain, French Army

On February 21st, 1916, a hurricane of iron and steel broke over the defences of Verdun. The Germans attacked with a force and violence never before equalled. The French accepted the challenge, for Verdun to them is even more than a great fortress, an outpost intended to bar the path of the invader on the east; it is the moral bulwark of France. The German onrush at first overwhelmed all our advanced positions, but we quickly found our feet, and from that time on we held in check by our unaided strength the formidable attacks that the Germans launched unremittingly for five months. Thus the Verdun region became the scene of a terrific duel between the two chief adversaries on the Western Front.

The struggle was carried on with heroic courage, both by the troops and by their leaders. Bombardments by the German heavy artillery, during February 21st and the night of the 21st–22nd, preceded the charge of the shock divisions. Nowhere before, on any front, in any battle, had anything like it been seen. The Germans aimed to create a "zone of death", within which no troops could survive. An avalanche of steel and iron, of shrapnel and poisonous gas shells, fell on our woods, ravines, trenches and shelters, destroying everything, transforming the sector into a charnel field, defiling the air, spreading flames into the heart of the town, damaging even the bridges and Meuse villages as far as Genicourt and Troyon. Heavy explosions shook our forts and wreathed them in smoke. It would be impossible to describe an action of the kind. I believe that it has never been equalled in violence, and it concentrated the devastating fire of more than two million shells in the narrow triangle of land between Brabant-on-Meuse, Ornes and Verdun.

During the afternoon of the 21st and the morning of the 22nd, after a night in which the artillery had incessantly kept up its infernal pounding, the German troops advanced in small formations, the different waves pushing one another forward, hoping to progress without opposition. Imagine their amazement and their disappointment to see everywhere along their route the French rising from the wreck, exhausted and in tatters to be sure, but still formidable, defending the ruins from every possible point of vantage . . .

The mass of combatants was composed of seasoned men, "grown old in experience of war", whose average age was from twenty-five to twenty-six years. Like the "grognards" of the First Empire, they constituted a generation of veterans whose physical vigour and moral strength were altogether extraordinary. They had made up their minds that they would save Verdun, and endured superhuman ordeals with stoicism, resigning themselves wholeheartedly, perhaps not without a touch of fatalism, to the strenuous tasks imposed upon them. Their spirit was not so much enthusiasm as virile determination, and their strength was founded principally on their inflexible purpose to defend their families and their homes from the invader. They were soldiers in the highest sense of the word, grim and resolute, accepting in their day's work both danger and suffering. When their time came to enter the line, they advanced with unfaltering steps to meet their fate, fully knowing what was in store for them. No one who saw these men at Verdun could ever forget them!

They had the implicit confidence of the French people, who thought of them as supermen, ready and able at any time to perform deeds of marvellous valour. There was something fantastic in the ideas of the general public, which, as it believed in the intervention of mysterious forces, was prone to under-estimate the true wretchedness and suffering of our soldiers, and to over-estimate their powers. Hence came the feverish impatience with which a stroke of deliverance, for which the time was not yet ripe, was expected. Nevertheless we appreciated at its full value the high esteem in which we were held by our countrymen, and in order to be worthy of it we strove each day to do better than before.

Our superhuman resistance cast a beam of light beyond the bounds of our own land, and everywhere in the camps of the Allies new hope was born. Since France by herself was capable of accomplishing so much, it was felt that nothing was impossible to the united armies of the coalition. From the capital cities of the friendly nations and from the headquarters of their staffs, messages of congratulation poured in to Chantilly. The English were the first to join in our gratification and they attempted to hasten their entry into the lists at our side in the co-operative offensive that had been decided upon. General Cadorna visited the French front and spoke with admiration of the "calm tenacity" of our troops. The Italian Chamber of Deputies applauded the French Army and stated its conviction that we had saved Europe. Prince Alexander of Serbia, after having seen the battlefield of Verdun, expressed his enthusiasm to our Ministerial Council. Our ambassador at Petrograd received from our powerful eastern allies the most affecting expressions of admiration and the promise of prompt and vigorous collaboration.

To sum up, Verdun held.

It held, although the German onslaught against Verdun continued unabated.

VERDUN: STORMING FORT DOUAUMONT, 25 February 1916

Werner Beumelburg, 15th Bavarian Infantry Regiment

The German 210-millimetre shells were exploding on the fort with formidable crashes. The Brandenburgers, massed against the fort's limits, kept sending off their flares to have the artillery fire lengthened. Unfortunately, the battlefield was shrouded by the thick smoke of shell explosions, so that our artillery observers were unable to see anything. The terrific bombardment went on unabated.

Seeing his men's predicament, Captain Haupt, who had just reached the barbed-wire entanglements, shouted: "We'll take the fort by assault!" In such perilous circumstances, his words sounded like a bad joke. Already, however, some men were busy cutting the wire with shears, and soon had opened a few gaps. The Brandenburgers stumbled over the tangle of wires, only to run into the still greater barbed-wire network set up immediately around the fort.

Not a shot came from the fort, all was deathly quiet. What was going on inside? Had the fort been evacuated or were the French prevented by our artillery from firing on us? Or, again, was there such a confusion in the fort that the French were unaware of the enemy's presence? . . .

Our captain was weighing the risks. With every passing minute, however, they would become greater. An immediate and fully conscious decision was called for. Standing upright in the trench, his cane held high, the captain shouted: "Forward! The fort is ours! Fall who must!" Some men followed him, others, undecided, held behind. He came back toward them, and exclaimed: "My boys! You are not going to let me down, are you?"

The assault then began in earnest. An officer of the Engineers, noticing that the barbed-wire network seemed to be electrified, shattered a number of glass isolators with his pick, and the wire-cutters once more began their work. Many eager soldiers could not wait till gaps were opened, and began stepping over the wires, leaving shreds of clothes and flesh on them. They rushed feverishly through the obstacle, expecting enemy fire to break loose at any moment, and bending low at each new explosion of our shells. After a few minutes, the assailants found themselves before an eight-foot iron grating planted on the counterscarp of the fifteen-foot deep ditch running all around the fort. A new moment of indecision ensued.

Fortunately, a heavy German shell had destroyed part of the grating on the north slope, and at the same time had opened a gap in the counterscarp itself. The spot was located soon, and our men began rushing in, some sliding into the ditch over the wall's rubble, others jumping fifteen feet directly down.

In the ditch, there was the same alarming silence. Not one shot was fired from the counterscarp's pillboxes. For the third time, our assault was paralyzed by irresolution. The men huddled closely together. A single heavy shell – any of those which kept falling on the fort – would have blown all of us to bits. . . .

We tried to enter the fort through the counterscarp's pillboxes, but they were closed. All we could do was to crawl out of the ditch and over the slope of the escarp, without paying too much attention to our heavy artillery fire. With some difficulty we reached the top of the fort. A fusilier stood up next to the main turret, and waved toward the rear the liaison flag with our artillery. It was of no avail. The bombardment continued unabated. From the village of Douaumont, the French had seen our grey silhouettes on the fort and presently opened a violent machine-gun fire. Our losses were increasing. It was really frustrating not to be able to have our artillery fire lengthened.

Groups of assailants then began, without liaison, to enter the fort from different sides. They met inside, where, unbelievably, all was still. Suddenly, a Frenchman carrying a flashlight and whistling a song came along. He was quite unaware of our presence and was practically rivered to the ground when he suddenly saw us. We made him a prisoner and used him as our guide.

As we advanced toward the center of the fort, French voices began to be heard. We shouted to the enemy to surrender, as the fort was in our hands, but there was no answer. We had no idea of the number of defenders, and there was hardly a dozen of us at the time. Petroleum lamps lit the corridors. Above us, the explosions of our shells thundered with a dull rumble. We began searching the fort's rooms, one after the other. Sappers cut the electric wiring, to prevent the French from blowing up the fort once they realized that it was in our hands. The prisoners kept coming in, and before long numbered over a hundred. The fort's commander, too, surrendered, after he had convinced himself that any further resistance was useless.

By nightfall the fort was solidly in the hands of our Brandenburgers, who in the meantime had been reinforced by other groups. Our artilery fire, too, finally stopped . . .

EASTERN FRONT: EMPEROR NICHOLAS II DEMANDS RENEWED EFFORTS FROM HIS TROOPS, March 1916

General A.A. Noskoff, Russian Army

Toward the end of March, several large-scale operations were launched on the broad Russian front extending from Niya to Baranovich. On the front's right wing, in particular, a considerable force attacked the German positions near Lake Naroch, east of Vilna. The attack, if successful, would have rolled up the German front along the Dvina, from both the flank and the rear. Our advance toward Kovno in fact created a difficult situation for the Germans, compelling them to fall back on the Dvina and Riga fronts, which were so important to them . . .

My recollection of all the painful details concerning our offensive is still very vivid. When, at the end of March, operations began, there was a light frost. After a short artillery bombardment, the Russian troops moved forward. Although they ran into a heavy enemy barrage and sustained enormous losses, they reached the enemy lines and broke the front. At that moment, however, an entirely unexpected thaw changed the country into one vast marshland, in which it became impossible to bring in supplies or move the artillery ahead. Still, the Russian troops, soaked to the skin and without any warm food for two days, accomplished their duty faithfully. The Germans, once they had recovered from their surprise, brought up reinforcements and their artillery caused havoc in our ranks. Many of our casualties, even the lightly wounded, could not be carried from the battlefield.

Two or three days later, the thaw was followed by a sudden cold, and a violent and icy wind began blowing. All over the ice-coated battlefield, great numbers of wounded men died from the cold. The still able-bodied men made a supreme effort to keep holding their rifles in their numbed hands. One could only admire the poor fellows' courage and patience . . .

The result of these operations was not decisive, and even mediocre in importance. Still, the Germans were compelled to reinforce their front with several divisions withdrawn from France during the most critical days of the battle at Verdun. Our losses were very high, numbering some two hundred and fifty thousand men.

That was the amount of blood and suffering which the Russian people sacrificed to the common Allied victory. The sacrifices resulted from the personal intervention of Emperor Nicholas II.

WESTERN FRONT: EXECUTIONS AT DAWN, 14 April–21 July 1916

Captain T.H. Westmacott, First Indian Cavalry Division

There were 346 Allied executions during the war, mostly for desertion. The Australians, incidentally, refused use of the death penalty.

14 April, 1916

I was staying with Bowring of the 51st Division, and we received orders to attend the execution of a deserter in the Cheshire Regiment. The man had deserted when his battalion was in the trenches and had been caught in Paris. He was sentenced to death, but the sentence was remitted, and he was sent back to his battalion. He did so well in the trenches that he was allowed leave to England. He deserted again, and after being arrested was sent back to his battalion in France, when he was again sentenced to death. This time he was shot. We got up at 3.30 a.m., and Bowring and I were driven to the HQ of the 5th Division, the car breaking down on the way. When we got to DHQ Coates, of the 15th Hussars, the APM had gone on with the firing party. We caught them up, and I found Coates, the firing party and a company of the Cheshires drawn up opposite a chair under a railway embankment. The condemned man spent the night in a house about half a mile away. He walked from there blindfolded with the doctor, the parson and the escort. He walked quite steadily on to parade, sat down in the chair, and told them not to tie him too right. A white disc was pinned over his heart. He was the calmest man on the ground. The firing party was 15 paces distant. The officer commanding the firing party did everything by signal, only speaking the word "Fire!" The firing party was twelve strong, six kneeling and six standing. Before the condemned man arrived, the firing party about turned after grounding arms, and the OC firing party and the APM mixed up the rifles and unloaded some of them.

On the word "Fire!" the man's head fell back, and the firing party about turned at once. The doctor said the man was not quite dead, but before the OC firing party could finish him with his revolver he was dead, having felt nothing. The company was then marched off. The body was wrapped in a blanket, and the APM saw it buried in a grave which had been dug close by, unmarked and unconsecrated.

26 June, 1916

A Sowar in the 29th Lancers shot the Wordi Major (native Adjutant) of the Regiment dead. He then threw away his rifle, tore off most of his clothes, and rushed off to the HQ of the Lucknow Brigade, where he happened to catch General Morton Gage, the Brigadier, in the street. He told the General a long story, but as the General was British service he could not understand a word. The man was a Delhi policeman, and a Jat, who enlisted for the period of the war. He is a sulky kind of fellow but there is no doubt that the Wordi Major, who was an absolute rotter, goaded the wretched fellow to desperation.

After this date we moved down to the neighbourhood of

Doullens for the battle of the Somme. Until the 13th of July the man was in my charge and I had to drag him about with DHQ until that date, very hard luck on the man. He behaved very well the whole time and one day he said to me, "Sahib, I am quite certain now that I shall not be shot, as you have kept me so long."

19 July
Had a long ride of about 28 miles to Villers Chatel, north of Aubigny, Yadram, the murderer, riding with me under escort the whole way. On arrival, orders came in for his execution.

20 July
Rode over to the Lucknow Brigade HQ and to the 29th Lancers and arranged everything including the place of execution.

Sent Yadram to the Regiment under escort to have the sentence promulgated. Gibbon, the Divisional Chaplain, was a great nuisance, as he obtained leave from the Divisional Commander to visit Yadram during the night. As Yadram was a Jat and not a Christian we all considered it a great piece of impertinence on Gibbon's part.

21 July
Got up at 2.45 a.m. and went over to the 29th Lancers with Gordon, the General's ADC, and Winckworth, my assistant. The Regiment was drawn up dismounted in hollow square with the firing party and the chair in front. The firing party consisted of twenty men, five from each squadron. They grounded arms and faced about and moved 3 paces to the rear, while I mixed up the rifles and unloaded some of them. Then they marched back and picked up their arms. The prisoner was then brought up under escort blindfolded with a white disc pinned over his heart, and he sat down in the chair. As Sergeant Walsh, my provost sergeant was tying him to the chair, he shouted in Hindustani, "Salaam, O Sahibs! and Salaam, all Hindus and Mahometans of this regiment! There is no justice in the British Sirkar. I did this deed because I was abused. Those of you who have been abused as I was go and do the same, but eat your own bullet and do not be shot as I shall be."

Then the OC firing party gave the signal, and the party came to the present, and on the word "Fire" they fired a volley. The regiment and the firing party then faced about and marched off. Five bullets had gone through the disc, but the man still breathed, and I had to shoot him through the heart with my revolver, a horrid job. The grave had already been dug at the firing point, and Yadram was put straight into it and the grave was filled in and levelled by a fatigue party from the regiment.

OCCUPIED FRANCE: CIVILIANS ARE ROUNDED UP FOR FORCED LABOUR, LILLE, 24 April 1916

Pierre Baucher, civilian

During the month of April, an official announcement informed us that in view of the population's lack of eagerness in volunteering to work for the Germans, and because England's attitude was making the supplying of food difficult, the city was to be evacuated. Actual evacuation operations would begin on Easter Sunday and would be completed by May 1st.

The Lillois were filled with apprehension and anxiety, as the evacuation was going to be effected according to districts, but without forewarning. For many days, people's faces revealed their deep worries and despondency.

At 4:30 a.m. on April 24th, I was awakened by noises from the outside: the turn of my district had come. Armed soldiers were posted at the end of every street, and a sad-looking French policeman knocked at every door, telling people to get ready for the fateful visit. It seemed as though he was handing a death-sentence on every one of us. A young non-commissioned German officer, who spoke but little, had been assigned to the unpleasant task. He went about his business quietly, entering each house and, having been given the official list containing the names of its inhabitants, he designated, more or less haphazardly, those who were to go. The painful scene in a way was comparable to the slave market episode described in *Uncle Tom's Cabin.*

People were given half an hour to get ready, under the watchful eyes of German sentries, and then were herded along like convicted criminals. At the end of my boulevard, a man and his son in his mid-teens were tearing themselves away from the crying mother. Elsewhere, a man walking with bent head and carrying a small suitcase, was accompanying the son who had been designated. Here and there, some people succeeded in escaping exile by using supplications or ruses, or thanks to special protection granted for one reason or another. The German officer kept telling people that he had to fill his evacuation quota. The last ones he took were the most heart-broken. At last we saw the Germans leave with their victims. No one knew where they were going to be taken, what use would be made of them, and what sort of ordeals were in store for them.

Most of those forcibly evacuated were deported to Germany to work as farm labourers, allowing the Germans to release more able-bodied men for the front.

U-202 SINKS A STEAMER, April 1916

Adolf K.G.E. von Spiegel, U-202

The steamer appeared to be close to us and looked colossal. I saw the captain walking on his bridge, a small whistle in his mouth. I saw the crew cleaning the deck forward, and I saw, with surprise and a slight shudder, long rows of wooden partitions right along all the decks, from which gleamed the shining black and brown backs of horses.

"Oh, heavens, horses! What a pity, those lovely beasts!

"But it cannot be helped," I went on thinking. "War is war, and every horse the fewer on the Western front is a reduction of England's fighting power." I must acknowledge, however, that the thought of what must come was a most unpleasant one, and I will describe what happened as briefly as possible.

There were only a few more degrees to go before the steamer would be on the correct bearing. She would be there almost immediately; she was passing us at the proper distance, only a few hundred metres away.

"Stand by for firing a torpedo!" I called down to the control room.

That was a cautionary order to all hands on board. Everyone held his breath.

Now the bows of the steamer cut across the zero line of my periscope – now the forecastle – the bridge – the foremast – funnel—

"FIRE!"

A slight tremor went through the boat – the torpedo had gone.

"Beware, when it is released!"

The death-bringing shot was a true one, and the torpedo ran towards the doomed ship at high speed. I could follow its course exactly by the light streak of bubbles which was left in its wake.

"Twenty seconds," counted the helmsman, who, watch in hand, had to measure the exact interval of time between the departure of the torpedo and its arrival at its destination.

"Twenty-three seconds." Soon, soon this violent, terrifying thing would happen. I saw that the bubble-track of the torpedo had been discovered on the bridge of the steamer, as frightened arms pointed towards the water and the captain put his hands in front of his eyes and waited resignedly. Then a frightful explosion followed, and we were all thrown against one another by the concussion, and then, like Vulcan, huge and majestic, a column of water two hundred metres high and fifty metres broad, terrible in its beauty and power, shot up to the heavens.

"Hit abaft the second funnel," I shouted down to the control room.

Then they fairly let themselves go down below. There was a real wave of enthusiasm, arising from hearts freed from suspense, a wave which rushed through the whole boat and whose joyous echoes reached me in the conning tower. And over there? War is a hard task master. A terrible drama was being enacted on board the ship, which was hard hit and in a sinking condition. She had a heavy and rapidly increasing list towards us.

All her decks lay visible to me. From all the hatchways a storming, despairing mass of men were fighting their way on deck, grimy stokers, officers, soldiers, grooms, cooks. They all rushed, ran, screamed for boats, tore and thrust one another from the ladders leading down to them, fought for the lifebelts and jostled one another on the sloping deck. All amongst them, rearing, slipping horses are wedged. The starboard boats could not be lowered on account of the list; everyone therefore ran across to the port boats, which, in the hurry and panic, had been lowered with great stupidity either half full or overcrowded. The men left behind were wringing their hands in despair and running to and fro along the decks; finally they threw themselves into the water so as to swim to the boats.

Then – a second explosion, followed by the escape of white hissing steam from all hatchways and scuttles. The white steam drove the horses mad. I saw a beautiful long-tailed dapple-grey horse take a mighty leap over the berthing rails and land into a fully laden boat. At that point I could not bear the sight any longer, and I lowered the periscope and dived deep.

"STICK HIM BETWEEN THE EYES . . .": HOW TO USE A BAYONET, 25 April 1916

Siegfried Sassoon, Royal Welsh Fusiliers

Some phrases used by a major during a lecture on the uses of the bayonet.

"If you don't kill him, he'll kill you."

"Stick him between the eyes, in the throat, in the chest, or round the thighs."

"If he's on the run, there's only one place; get your bayonet into his kidneys; it'll go in as easy as butter."

"Kill them, kill them; there's only one good Bosche and that's a dead un!"

"Quickness, anger, strength, good fury, accuracy of aim. Don't waste good steel. Six inches are enough – what's the use of a foot of steel sticking out of a man's neck? Three inches will do him, and when he coughs, go find another."

IRELAND, THE EASTER RISING: THE COMMANDER'S PROCLAMATION, 28 April 1916

James Connolly

The Easter Rebellion in Dublin was led by Sinn Fein and the Irish Volunteers. It was suppressed and fourteen of its leaders, including Connolly, were executed.

Army of the Irish Republic
(Dublin Command)
Headquarters, April 28th, 1916.

To Soldiers,

This is the fifth day of the establishment of the Irish Republic, and the flag of our country still floats from the most important buildings in Dublin, and is gallantly protected by the officers and Irish soldiers in arms throughout the country. Not a day passes without seeing fresh postings of Irish soldiers eager to do battle for the old cause . . .

Let me remind you of what we have done. For the first time in 700 years the flag of a free Ireland floats triumphantly in Dublin City. The British Army, whose exploits we are for ever having dinned in our ears, which boasts of having stormed the Dardanelles and the German lines on the Marne, behind their artillery and machine guns, are afraid to advance or storm any position held by our forces . . .

As you know I was twice wounded yesterday, and am unable to move about, but have got my bed moved into the firing line, and with the assistance of your officers, will be just as useful to you as ever . . .

MESOPOTAMIA: THE DEATH MARCH OF THE PRISONERS OF KUT, May 1916

On 29 April more than 9000 British and Indian troops surrendered to the Turks at Kut, in a debacle to rival Gallipoli. A week later the garrison was marched into captivity at Anatolia. More than

4000 of the surrendered died on the march or in the POW camps of Anatolia.

Captain E.O. Mounsley, Royal Field Artillery

We tingled with anger and shame at seeing on the other bank a sad little column of British troops who had marched up from Kut driven by a wild crowd of Kurdish horsemen who brandished sticks and what looked like whips. The eyes of our men stared from white faces, drawn long with suffering of a too tardy death, as they held out their hands towards our boat. As they dragged one foot after another some fell, and those with the rearguard came in for blows from cudgels and sticks. I saw one Kurd strike a British soldier who was limping along. He reeled under the blows. We shouted out, and if ever men felt like murdering their guards we did . . . It seemed that half their number were a few miles ahead and the rest strewed the road to Kut . . .

The padre (the Rev. H. Spooner) was awfully good and diligent in assisting men, but, nevertheless, from out of the night one heard the high Indian wail, "*margaya, sahib, margaya,*" "lying, sahib, dying." For the most part British soldiers stayed with their friends until they were dead. I saw some of the finest examples history could produce of British soldiers' self-sacrifice for and fidelity to his friend. I shall never forget one soldier who could go no further. He fell resignedly on to the ground, the stump of a cigarette in his mouth, and with a tiredness born of long suffering, buried his head in his arms to shut out the disappearing column and smoked on.

Francis Yeats-Brown, British Army

I saw some hundred men, prisoners from Kut and mostly Indians, gathered on the platform [at Bozanti station]: one of them was sitting on this heap of sacks: he was sitting here rocking himself to and fro in great pain and sorrow, for a guard had struck him with a rifle butt and broken his arm. Not only his bone but the spirit within him was shattered: no hope remained: he had done that which is most terrible to a Hindu, for he had eaten the flesh of cows and broken the ordinances of his caste. His companions had died in the desert without the lustral rites prescribed by the Vedas, and he would soon die also, a body defiled, to be cast into outer darkness. For a time the terror of that alien brain was mine: I shared its doom and knew its death.

TRENCH LIFE: SNIPING, WESTERN FRONT, 1916

Lieutenant Stuart Cloete, 9th King's Own Yorkshire Light Infantry

I spent most of the day in the trenches, checking snipers' reports, sniping myself and watching the German line from behind a heavy iron loophole plate with a high-powered telescope. We often saw Germans moving about a mile or more away. It gave me a curious feeling to watch them. Watching and reporting all movement was part of the sniper's job. I sent a report of what we had seen to Divisional Intelligence by runner every night. We looked for their snipers' posts and when we found them we tried to destroy them. There were no armour-piercing bullets then. So we used a heavy sporting rifle – a 600 Express. These heavy rifles had been donated to the army by British big-game hunters and when we hit a plate we stove it right in, into the German sniper's face. But it had to be fired from a standing or kneeling position to take up the recoil. The first man who fired it in the prone position had his collar-bone broken. I hit two Germans at long range – about four hundred yards – with telescopic sights, and fired at a good many others. My best sniper turned out, when his parents at last traced him, to be only fourteen years old. He was discharged as under age. He was the finest shot and the best little soldier I had. A very nice boy, always happy. I got him a military medal and when he went back to Blighty and, I suppose, to school, he had a credit of six Germans hit. He was big for his age and had lied about it when he enlisted under a false name, and then had had sufficient self-restraint to write to no one. I had noticed that he received no mail and wrote no letters but had never spoken to him about it. The snipers worked in pairs, one observer with a telescope and one with the rifle. They changed over every half hour as it is very tiring to use a telescope for a long period. In action the sniper's job was to work independently and try to pick off any enemy leaders he could see. That was what the Germans did to us and they had no difficulty as we wore officers' uniforms with long tunics, riding breeches, trench boots and Sam Browne belts. This was one reason why the officers' casualties were so high. The Germans had a further advantage in their sniping. With them it was done by their Jaeger battalions, picked sharpshooters who in peacetime had been gamekeepers and guides. They wore green uniforms insted of grey and were permanently stationed in one sector, so that they knew every blade of grass in front of them and spotted the slightest change; this gave them a big edge on us because we were moved quite often.

WESTERN FRONT: NIGHT RAID, SOMME SECTOR, 25 May 1916

Siegfried Sassoon, Royal Welsh Fusliliers

Sassoon won the Military Cross in the action below.

Twenty-seven men with faces blackened and shiny – Christy-minstrels – with hatchets in their belts, bombs in pockets, knobkerries – waiting in a dug-out in the reserve line. At 10.30 they trudge up to Battalion H.Q. splashing through mire and water in the chalk trench, while the rain comes steadily down. The party is twenty-two men, five N.C.O.s and one officer (Stansfield). From H.Q. we start off again, led by Compton-Smith: across the open to the end of 77 street. A red flashlight winks a few times to guide us thither. Then up to the front line – the men's feet making a most unholy tramp and din; squeeze along to the starting-point, where Stansfield and his two confederates (Sergeant Lyle and Corporal O'Brien) loom over the parapet from above, having successfully laid the line of lime across the craters to the Bosche wire. In a few minutes the five parties have gone over – and disappear into the rain and darkness – the last four men carry ten-foot light ladders. It is 12 midnight. I am sitting on the parapet listening for something to happen – five, ten, nearly fifteen minutes – not a sound – nor a shot fired – and only the usual flare-lights, none very near our party. Then a few whizz-bangs fizz over to our front trench and just behind the raiders. After twenty minutes there is still absolute silence in the Bosche trench; the raid is obviously held up by their wire, which we thought was so easy to get through. One of the bayonet-men comes crawling back; I follow him to our trench and he tells me that they can't get through: O'Brien says it's a failure; they're all going to throw a bomb and retire.

A minute or two later a rifle-shot rings out and almost simultaneously several bombs are thrown by both sides: a bomb explodes right in the water at the bottom of left crater close to our men, and showers a pale spume of water; there are blinding flashes and explosions, rifle-shots, the scurry of feet, curses and groans, and stumbling figures loom up from below and scramble awkwardly over the parapet – some wounded – black faces and whites of eyes and lips show in the dusk; when I've counted sixteen in, I go forward to see how things are going, and find Stansfield wounded, and leave him there with two men who soon get him in: other wounded men crawl in; I find one hit in the leg; he says O'Brien is somewhere down the crater badly wounded. They are still throwing bombs and firing at us: the sinister sound of clicking bolts seems to be very near; perhaps they have crawled out of their trench and are firing from behind their advanced wire. Bullets hit the water in the craters, and little showers of earth patter down on the crater. Five or six of them are firing into the crater at a few yards' range. The bloody sods are firing down at me at point-blank range. (I really wondered whether my number was up). From our trenches and in front of them I can hear the mumble of voices – most of them must be in by now. After minutes like hours, with great difficulty I get round the bottom of the crater and back toward our trench; at last I find O'Brien down a very deep (about twenty-five feet) and precipitous crater on my left (our right as they went out). He is moaning and his right arm is either broken or almost shot off: he's also hit in the right leg (body and head also, but I couldn't see that then). Another man (72 Thomas) is with him; he is hit in the right arm. I leave them there and get back to our trench for help, shortly afterwards Lance-Corporal Stubbs is brought in (he has had his foot blown off). Two or three other wounded men are being helped down the trench; no one seems to know what to do; those that are there are very excited and uncertain: no sign of any officers – then Compton-Smith comes along (a mine went up on the left as we were coming up at about 11.30 and thirty (R.E.s) men were gassed or buried). I get a rope and two more men and we go back to O'Brien, who is unconscious now. With great difficulty we get him half-way up the face of the crater; it is now after one o'clock and the sky beginning to get lighter. I make one more journey to our trench for another strong man and to see to a stretcher being ready. We get him in, and it is found that he has died, as I had feared. Corporal Mick O'Brien (who often went patrolling with me) was a very fine man and had been with the Battalion since November 1914. He was at Neuve Chapelle, Festubert and Loos.

I go back to a support-line dug-out and find the unwounded men of the raiding-party refreshing themselves: everyone is accounted for now; eleven wounded (one died of wounds) and one killed, out of twenty-eight. I see Stansfield, who is going on all right, but has several bomb-wounds. On the way down I see the Colonel, sitting on his bed in a woollen cap with a tuft on top, and very much upset at the non-success of the show, and the mine disaster; but very pleased with the way our men tried to get through the wire.

TRENCH LIFE: LICE, WESTERN FRONT, 1916

Private Henry Gregory, 119th Machine Gun Company

We got a shock after tea; the "old sweats" in the hut had their shirts off. They were catching lice, and were all as lousy as cuckoos. We had never seen a louse before, but they were here in droves. The men were killing them between their nails. When they saw us looking at this performance with astonishment, one of the men remarked, "You will soon be as lousy as we are, chum!" They spent the better part of an hour in killing lice and scratching themselves. We soon found out that this took the better part of an hour daily. Each day brought a new batch; as fast as you killed them, others took their place.

JUTLAND: "A" TURRET, HMS *Collingwood*, 31 May–1 June 1916

Prince Albert (later King George VI), Royal Navy

The sea battle of Jutland was the major naval encounter of World War I. Both sides claimed victory; the Germans because they sank – through superior gunnery – more shipping (14 warships, 6097 men killed, to their own loss of 11 warships, 2545 men), the British because they retained control of the North Sea. The next major excursion of the German fleet was in November 1918, when it sailed to surrender.

We went to "Action Stations" at 4.30 p.m. and saw the Battle Cruisers in action ahead of us on the starboard bow. Some of the other cruisers were firing on the port bow. As we came up the *Lion*, leading our Battle Cruisers, appeared to be on fire the port side of the forecastle, but it was not serious. They turned up to starboard so as not to cut across the bows of the Fleet. As far as one could see only 2 German Battle Squadrons and all their Battle Cruisers were out. The *Colossus* leading the 6th division with the *Collingwood* her next astern were nearest the enemy. The whole Fleet deployed at 5.0 and opened out. We opened fire at 5.37 p.m. on some German light cruisers. The *Collingwood*'s second salvo hit one of them which set her on fire, and sank after two more salvoes were fired into her. We then shifted on to another light cruiser and helped to sink her as well. Our next target was a battle cruiser, we think the *Derrflinger* [*sic*] or *Lützow*, and one of the *Collingwood*'s salvoes hit her abaft and after turret, which burst into a fierce flame. After this she turned away from us and disappeared into the mist. By this time it was too dark to fire and we went to Night Defence stations. The 4″ guns were manned to repel destroyer attacks. Our 12″ firing was very good, though rather slow, as we could only fire at the flashes of the German guns. The range at the commencement was 10,000 yds. and ceased at 8,000 yds. The Germans fired some of their torpedoes but only one of them took effect in the *Marlborough*, the flagship of the 1st Battle Squadron. One of her boiler rooms, one of her hydraulic rooms, and one of her dynamo rooms were flooded, and her speed was reduced to 14 knots. She succeeded in getting into the Humber. One torpedo passed ahead of the *Collingwood* and another astern. We had no casualties and no damage done to us, though we were "straddled" several times. That is some of the shots in a salvo falling short of the ship and others over.

The *Colossus* was hit once in the superstructure which wounded 9 men, and put the main derrick out of action. The *Barham* and *Malaya* and *Warspite* in the 5th Battle Squadron were hit. The latter had to go to Rosyth at once. The 2 former had a good many killed and wounded. The *Barham* 28 killed, 41 wounded, and the *Malaya* 38 killed, 53 wounded. The dead were buried at sea. The cruiser *Defence* was concentrated on by the German battle cruisers, and was hit by several salvoes at once. She blew up in a huge sheet of flame and smoke, and when this sank down, she had utterly disappeared.

The *Warrior* was totally disabled and had to be abandoned. Several of our destroyers were sunk and some were taken in tow by others. Whether they have all got in is not yet known.

The German Fleet all turned away from us after dark, followed by our light cruisers and destroyers who attacked them during the night. The result is not yet known as to whether they accounted for any more of the enemy. We were not attacked at all during the night and everything was very quiet.

The Fleet steamed south 40 miles off the Danish coast all night. The Action was fought about 40 miles south of the Skaggerak and 40 miles off the Danish coast. We went to action stations at 2.0 a.m. on Thursday, June 1st, but there was no sign of the enemy to be seen. We saw a Shütze-Lanz airship at 4.0 a.m. who came out to make a report as to where we were. She was fired at by several ships. Her range was about 12,000 yds. She made off as soon as we fired at her. We remained at action stations all day till 5.30 p.m. We returned to Scapa Flow at noon on Friday, June 2nd, and coaled and ammunitioned at once.

JUTLAND: THE *QUEEN MARY* IS BLOWN UP, 31 May 1916

Petty Officer Ernest Francis, HMS Queen Mary

The guns crew were absolutely perfect, inclined to be a little slow in loading, but I gave them a yell and pointed out to them that I wanted a steady stride. After that everything went like clockwork until both rammers gave out, my gun going first. This was caused by number 3 opening the breech before the gun had run out after firing: the carrier arm must have hit the rammer head and slightly metal bound it. I dropped the elevating wheel, got hold of a steel bar, forced the end in behind the rammer head, at the same time putting the lever to "Run out". Out went the rammer, and I rushed it back again, and it all went gay again; then the lever was over at the right gun and both rammers were again in working order.

I was pleased to get them both going, as it would have been such a damper on the crew if we had to go into hand loading. My number 3 said "PO Francis, can you see what we are up against?" Well I had been anxious to have a look round, but could not spare the time, but as soon as my gun had fired and while the loading was being completed, I had a look through the periscopes, and it seemed to me that there were hundreds of masts and funnels. I dropped back into my seat and laid my gun by pointer, being in director firing, and while the loading was being completed again, I told them there were a few battle cruisers out, not wishing to put a damper on them in any way; not that I think it would have done so, as they were all splendid fellows and backed me up magnificently.

Up till now I had not noticed any noise, such as being struck by a shell, but afterwards there was a heavy blow, struck, I should imagine, in the after 4-inch battery, and a lot of dust and pieces flying around on the top of "X" turret. My attention was called by the turret trainer, AB Long, who reported the front glass of his periscope blocked up. This was not very important because we were in director training, but some one in rear heard him report his glass foul and without orders dashed on top and cleared it. He must have been smashed up as he did, for he fell in front of the periscope and then apparently fell on to the turret: I wish I knew his name, poor chap, but it's no use guessing.

Another shock was felt shortly after this, but it did not affect the turret, so no notice was taken. Then the T.S. reported to Lieutenant Ewert that the third ship of the line was dropping out. First blood to *Queen Mary*. The shout they gave was good to hear. I could not resist giving a quick look at her, at their request, and I found that the third ship of the line was going down by the bows. I felt the turret travel a bit faster than she had been moving, and surmised we must have shifted on to the fourth ship of the line; being in director firing, no orders were required for training.

I looked again and found the third ship of the line was gone, so I turned to the spare gun layer, PO Killick, who was recording the number of rounds fired, and he said thirty some odd figures, I didn't catch the exact number. A few more rounds were fired when I took another look through my telescope and there was quite a fair distance between the second ship and what I believed was the fourth ship, due I think to the third ship going under. Flames were belching from what I took to be the fourth ship of the line, then came the big explosion which shook us a bit, and on looking at the pressure gauge I saw the pressure had failed. Immediately after that came, what I term, the big smash, and I was dangling in the air on a bowline, which saved me from being thrown down on the floor of the turret. These bowlines were an idea I brought into my turret and each man in the gunhouse was supplied with one, and as far as I noticed the men who had them on were not injured in the big smash. Nos. 2 and 3 of the left gun slipped down under the gun and the gun appeared to me to have fallen through its trunnions and smashed up these two numbers.

Everything in the ship went as quiet as a church, the floor of the turret was bulged up and the guns were absolutely useless. I must mention here that there was not a sign of excitement. One man turned to me and said, "What do you think has happened?" I said, "Steady, everyone, I will speak to Mr Ewert." I went back to the Cabinet and said, "What do you think has happened, Sir?" He said, ("God knows!" "Well, Sir," I said, "it's no use keeping them all down here. Why not send them up on the 4-inch guns, and give them a chance to fight it out? As soon as the Germans find we are out of action they will concentrate on us and we shall all be going sky high." He said, "Yes, good idea, just see if the 4-inch guns aft are still standing."

I put my head through the hole in the roof of the turret and nearly fell through again. The after 4-inch battery was smashed out of all recognition, and then I noticed that the ship had got an awful list to port. I dropped back again into the turret and told Lieutenant Ewert the state of affairs. He said, "Francis, we can do no more than give them a chance, clear the turret."

"Clear the turret," I said, and out they went. PO Stares was the last I saw coming up from the Working Chamber, and I asked him whether he had passed the order to the Magazine and Shell Room, and he told me it was no use as the water was right up to the trunk leading to the shell room, so the bottom of the ship must have been torn out of her. Then I said, "Why didn't you come up?" He simply said, "There was no order to leave the turret."

I went through the Cabinet and out on top and Lieutenant Ewert was following me; suddenly he stopped and went back into the turret. I believe he went back because he thought someone was inside . . .

I was halfway down the ladder at the back of the turret when Lieutenant Ewert went back. The ship had an awful list to port by this time, so much so that men getting off the ladder went sliding down to port. I got to the bottom rung of the ladder and could not, by my own efforts, reach the stanchions lying on the deck from the ship's side, starboard side. I knew if I let go I should go sliding down to port like some of the others must have done, and probably get smashed up sliding down. Two of my turret's crew, seeing my difficulty, came to my assistance. They were AB Long, Turret Trainer, and AB Lane, left gun No 4. Lane held Long at full length from the ship's side and I dropped from the ladder, caught Long's legs and so gained the starboard side. These two men had no thought for their own safety; they knew I wanted assistance and that was good enough for them. They were both worth a VC twice over.

When I got to the ship's side, there seemed to be quite a fair crowd, and they didn't appear to be very anxious to take to the water. I called out to them, "Come on you chaps, who's coming for a swim?" Someone answered, "She will float for a long time yet," but something, I don't pretend to know what it was, seemed to be urging me to get away, so I clambered over the slimy bilge keel and fell off into the water, followed I should think by about five more men. I struck away from the ship as hard as I could and must have covered nearly fifty yards when there was a big smash, and stopping and looking round, the air seemed to be full of fragments and flying pieces.

A large piece seemed to be right above my head, and acting on impulse, I dipped under to avoid being struck, and stayed under as long as I could, and then came to the top again, and coming behind me I heard a rush of water, which looked very like surf breaking on a beach and I realized it was the suction or backwash from the ship which had just gone. I hardly had time to fill my lungs with air when it was on me. I felt it was no use struggling against it, so I let myself go for a moment or two, then I struck out, but I felt it was a losing game and remarked to myself, "What's the use of you struggling, you're done," and I actually ceased my efforts to reach the top, when a small voice seemed to say, "Dig out."

I started afresh, and something bumped against me. I grasped it and afterwards found it was a large hammock, but I felt I was getting very weak and roused myself sufficiently to look around for something more substantial to support me. Floating right in front of me was what I believe to be the centre bulk of our Pattern 4 target. I managed to push myself on the hammock close to the timber and grasped a piece of rope hanging over the side. My next difficulty was to get on top and with a small amount of exertion I kept on. I managed to reeve my arms through a strop and I must have become unconscious.

When I came to my senses again I was halfway off the spar but I managed to get back again. I was very sick and seemed to be full of oil fuel. My eyes were blocked up completely with it and I could not see. I suppose the oil had got a bit crusted and dry. I managed by turning back the sleeve of my jersey, which was thick with oil, to expose a part of the sleeve of my flannel, and thus managed to get the thick oil off my face and eyes, which were aching awfully. Then I looked and I believed I was the only one left of that fine Ship's Company. What had really happened was the *Laurel* had come and picked up the remainder and not seeing me got away out of the zone of fire, so how long I was in the water I do not know. I was miserably cold, but not without hope of being picked up, as it seemed to me that I had only to keep quiet and a ship would come for me.

After what seemed ages to me, some destroyers came racing along, and I got up on the spar, steadied myself for the moment, and waved my arms. The *Petard*, one of our big destroyers, saw me and came over, but when I got on the spar to wave to them, the swell rolled the spar over and I rolled off. I was nearly exhausted again getting back. The destroyer came up and a line was thrown to me, which, needless to say, I grabbed hold of for all I was worth, and was quickly hauled up on to the deck of the destroyer.

JUTLAND: ABOARD THE *DERFFLINGER*, 31 May 1916

Commander Georg von Hase, First Gunnery Officer, the Derfflinger

From 6:17 p.m., I was engaging the *Queen Mary*. Certain difficulties in the fire-control now occurred, as a result of the dense smoke from the guns and funnels, which continually blurred the lenses of the periscopes over the deck of the fore-control, making it almost impossible to see anything. When this occurred I was entirely dependent on the observations of the spotting officer in the fore-top, Lieutenant-Commander von Stosch. This excellent officer observed and reported the fall of shot with astonishing coolness, and by his admirable observation, on the correctness of which I had to rely absolutely, he contributed very considerably to the success of our gun-fire. While we could see nothing, Lieutenant-Commander von Stosch, in his draughty observation post, thirty-five meters above sea-level, kept his fore-top periscope trained dead on the enemy . . .

At 6:15 p.m. we observed that the enemy was sending his destroyers to the attack. A little later our destroyers and the light cruiser *Regensburg* passed through our line and pressed home an attack. Between the lines of fighting battle-cruisers a small independent action developed. Here about twenty-five English destroyers and almost as many of ours waged a stubborn action and successfully prevented each other respectively from using torpedoes against the battle-cruisers. About 6:30 p.m. several torpedoes were fired against the lines on both sides, but no hit was made. This destroyer action was a magnificent spectacle for us.

During the destroyer action the two lines were continually converging, and now came what was, from the point of view of gunnery, the most interesting struggle of the day. I established that the *Queen Mary* had selected the *Derfflinger* as her target. The *Queen Mary* was firing less rapidly than we, but usually full salvoes. As she had an armament of eight 13.5-inch guns, this meant that she was mostly firing eight of these powerful "coffers," as the Russians called the heaviest guns during the Russo-Japanese War, against us as the same time! I could see the shells coming and I had to admit that the enemy was shooting superbly. As a rule all eight shells fell together. But they were almost always over or short – only twice did the *Derfflinger* come under this infernal hail, and each time only one heavy shell hit her.

We were firing as at gunnery practice. The head-telephones were working splendidly, and each of my orders was correctly understood. Lieutenant-Commander von Stosch reported the exact fall of each shot with deadly accuracy: "Straddling! Two hits!" "Straddling! The whole salvo in the ship!" I was trying to get in two salvoes to the enemy's one . . .

And so the *Queen Mary* and the *Derfflinger* fought out a regular gunnery duel over the destroyer action that was raging between us. But the poor *Queen Mary* was having a bad time. In addition to the *Derfflinger*, she was being engaged by the *Seydlitz*! And the gunnery-officer of the *Seydlitz*, Lieutenant-Commander Foerster, was our crack gunnery expert, tried in all the previous engagements in which the ship had taken part, cool-headed and of quick decision . . .

About 6:26 p.m. was the historic moment when the *Queen Mary*, the proudest ship of the British fleet, met her doom. Since 6:24 p.m. every one of our salvoes had straddled the enemy. When the salvo fired at 6h. 26m. 10s. fell, heavy explosions had already begun in the *Queen Mary*. First of all a vivid red flame shot up from her forepart. Then came an explosion forward which was followed by a much heavier explosion amidships, black debris of the ship flew into the air, and immediately afterwards the whole ship blew up with a terrific explosion. A gigantic cloud of smoke rose, the masts collapsed inwards, the smoke cloud hid everything and rose higher and higher. Finally, nothing but a thick, black cloud of smoke remained where the ship had been.

JUTLAND: NIGHT FIGHT, 31 May–1 June 1916

Navigating Officer, HMS Broke

We now found ourselves steaming full-speed into the darkness, with nothing in sight except a burning mass on the starboard quarter, which must have been the remains of the unfortunate *Tipperary*. The captain accordingly ordered me to bring the ship back to the original course south and to reduce to 17 knots, the speed of the fleet, in order to have a look round and see if we could collect our destroyers together again. His intention was to attempt another attack on the three enemy ships before they had time to get too far away, and we hoped that the rest of our destroyers had fired torpedoes when we did, and would, therefore, not be far off. As we turned *Sparrowhawk* was sighted, and took station astern of us.

Almost as soon as the ship was steadied on her course south, the hull of a large ship was sighted on the starboard bow on a more or less parallel course, but this time well before the beam and not more than half a mile away. The captain immediately gave the order to challenge, but almost as he spoke the stranger switched on a vertical string of coloured lights, some green and some red, an unknown signal in our service.

"Starboard 20; full-speed ahead both; starboard foremost tube fire when your sights come on; all guns – Green 40 – a battleship," and various other orders were simultaneously shouted down the various voice pipes on the bridge, but the German had evidently been watching our movements and we were too late.

Within a few seconds of our seeing his recognition signal, he switched on a blaze of searchlights straight into our eyes, and so great was the dazzling effect that it made us feel quite helpless. Then after another interval of about a second, shells could be heard screaming over our heads, and I vaguely remember seeing spashes in the water short of us and also hearing the sound of our 4-inch guns returning the fire of this German battleship, which we afterwards had strong reason to believe was *Westfalen.* I then remember feeling the ship give a lurch to one side as a salvo hit us, and hearing the sound of broken glass and débris flying around, after which the searchlights went out, and we were once more in the darkness.

At this moment I became conscious of the fact that I could get no answer from the quartermaster at the wheel, so shouting to the captain that I was going below, I jumped down on to the lower bridge. There, in the darkness, I found complete chaos. The quartermaster and telegraph-man were both killed, and the wheel and telegraphs were shattered and apparently useless. I found our midshipman had followed me down to assist, and we were both just starting to strike matches to make certain that communication with the engineroom was gone, when I heard the captain's voice down the pipe shouting: "Full-speed astern both."

I looked up for an instant and saw a green bow light of some other ship just ahead of us, and then with a terrific crash the ship brought up all standing, and we were hurled against the bridge screens by the force of the collision.

On picking myself up I at once saw that we had one of our own destroyers bumping alongside, and an ugly-looking rent in her side abreast of the bridge showed where we had hit her. Steam was roaring out of our foremost boiler-rooms, and it was extremely difficult to see or hear anything. Our ship appeared to be settling by the bow, and at intervals gave unpleasant lurches from side to side, which for the moment made me feel that she might be sinking.

VERDUN: THE FALL OF FORT VAUX, 1–7 June 1916

General Artois Pétain, French Army

In the so-called "May Cusp" offensive of June, the Germans mounted a powerful thrust on the right bank of the Meuse aimed at lifting the last defences around Verdun – Fort Vaux, Fort Souville, Thiamont and the Fleury Ridge.

Three army corps were consequently hurled against our positions at Fort Vaux during the first part of June, the three being, in order from west to east, the First Bavarian Corps, the Tenth Reserve Corps and the Fifteenth Corps. All three had a thorough acquaintance with the terrain, where they had been fighting hard for weeks and months. They succeeded after a terrific bombardment in gaining a foothold for several groups of assault troops on the superstructure of the fort, and these men then attacked each of our isolated resistance centres in turn. Conditions were more favourable to them than they had been to us a few days earlier at Douaumont, and thanks to the fact that our position at that point formed a salient, they were able to surround the earthwork on three sides. Within a short time our communications with the rear were irremediably endangered. To attempt to hold their position under such circumstances was, on the part of our men, simply a matter of honour. Inspired by this noble ambition, Major Raynal and his heroic comrades in arms refused to yield the fort, and in recognition of their self-sacrifice, General Joffre sent them his congratulations and conferred upon their leader, as a reward, a high rank in the Legion of Honour. There can be no memory more affecting than that of their last stand, when, cut off from us with no hope of assistance, they sent us their final reports.

The following message came to us on the morning of June 4th by carrier-pigeon:

"We are still holding our position, but are being attacked by gases and smoke of very deadly character. We are in need of immediate relief. Put us into communication with Souville at once for visual signalling. We get no answer from there to our calls. This is our last pigeon!"

Then during the morning of June 5th came this message, relayed by visual signal through Souville:

"The enemy is working on the west side of the fort to construct a mine in order to blow up the vaults. Direct your artillery fire there quickly."

At eight o'clock came another:

"We do not hear your artillery. We are being attacked with gas and liquid fire. We are in desperate straits."

Then this one, at nightfall on June 5th:

"I must be set free this evening, and must have supplies of water immediately. I am coming to the end of my strength. The troops, enlisted men and officers, have done their duty to the last, in every case."

On the 6th came only these few words:

". . . you will intervene before we are completely exhausted. Vive la France!"

And finally, on June 7th, at half-past three in the morning, these last words, whose meaning we could not make out:

". . . must go on."

Order of the Day

"Every man of you should be mentioned by name, soldiers of Verdun, soldiers in the line and soldiers in the rear. For if I gave the place of honour, as is meet, to those who fell in the front of the battle, still I know that their courage would have availed nothing without the patient toil, continued day and night, to the last limit of their strength, on the part of the men to whose efforts were due the regular arrival of the reinforcements, of munitions, and of food, and the evacuation of the wounded: the truck-drivers along the Sacred Way, the railroad engineers, the ambulance force.

"Of what steel was forged the soldier of Verdun, the man whom France found ready in her need to meet the grave crisis that confronted her, the man who could calmly face the most severe of trials? Had he received some special grace which raised him instinctively to the heights of heroism?

"We who knew him can answer that he was but a man after all, with human virtues and human weaknesses. One of our own people, a man whose thoughts and affections still clung, after eighteen months of warfare, to his family, to his workshop, to his village, or to the farm on which he had been brought up.

"These same personal bonds, which, taken altogether, constituted his devotion to his country, laid him under obligation to protect those people and those things which in his eyes made life worth living. They inspired him to the complete sacrifice of himself. Other sentiments as well contributed to his state of mind – love of the soil, in the peasant who gave his life as a matter of course in defence of his ancestral field; devout submission to the decree of Providence in the heart of the true believer; the impulse to defend an ideal of civilisation in the intellectual.

"But the noblest feelings do not suffice to instil in men the ability to fight. This is something that comes only little by little, with a knowledge of what one goes through on a battlefield, and with experience in all the conditions of warfare. We must bear in mind that the War, already an old story, had in 1916 moulded our French everyday citizen and had made him a soldier in the fullest sense of the word.

"The suffering that he had already borne steeled him against emotion, and gave him extraordinary powers of endurance. The prospect of death, which he continually faced, filled him with a resignation that bordered on fatalism. Long practice in fighting had taught him that success is the most tenacious, and had developed in him qualities of patience and persistence. He had also learned that in a battle each man is one link in a chain that is forged of all, and he had sacrificed his individualistic ways and class prejudices, thus cementing the splendid spirit of comradeship that made our fighting men work as one.

"An experienced and tried soldier, believing in himself and in his comrades, proud of his renown, he went up into the line certainly without enthusiasm but also without hesitation. Feeling that he carried the burden of his country's need, more important than his own, he did his duty to the very limit of his powers.

"It is impossible to believe that the soldier could have risen to such heights of heroism if he had not felt behind him the inspiration of the whole nation. Our country as a whole took up the struggle and accepted all its consequences, material and moral. It was only because the soldier had the spirit of the nation behind him to drive him on that he won the battle. It was his country's will that he fulfilled."

After the fall of Fort Vaux, disaster at Verdun seemed imminent for the French. They were saved at the eleventh hour by the Russian General Alexei Brusilov's surprise offensive on the Eastern Front – which diverted German troops from the West to shore up the Austrians – and the Somme offensive of the British. That said, the battle of Verdun continued until December 1916.

VERDUN: LIEUTENANT HENRI DESAGNEAUX IN ACTION, 10 June–5 July 1916

Lieutenant Henri Desagneaux, French 2nd Infantry Regiment

Diary: Saturday, 10 June [1916]
At one in the morning, order for departure at 4 a.m. We are to march in the direction of Verdun. That gives us an extra day of life! We are billeted at Rosières near Bar.

Monday, 12 June
Issoncourt, Last stage before Verdun. There is not much room as car-load upon car-load of supplies and munitions speed past us.

Tuesday, 13 June
Reveille at 2 a.m. At 5, we travel by car and are put down at Nixéville, 6 kilometres from Verdun. We bivouac in a wood in a lake of mud. The guns fire angrily, it's pouring down. At 3 p.m. we are ordered to stand by to leave. We don't, however. We spend the night and the day of the 14th waiting, in torrential rain with mud up to our ankles. Our teeth chatter with cold, we are very uncomfortable. Although the troops have been stopping here for the last four months to go to and from verdun, there is not one single hut or shelter. We camp in individual tents in thick mud. You should hear what the men say about it!

At 5 p.m., order for departure at 6.30. We are going to be quartered in the Citadel of Verdun. Faces are grave. The guns are thundering over there. It's a real furnace. Everyone realizes that perhaps tomorrow death will come. Numerous rumours are circulating; we are going to "Mort-Homme" which has been captured by the Boches; or to the Fort at Vaux . . . What is certain, nothing good lies in store for us.

We arrive at the Citadel at 10 p.m. after a difficult march through the mud.

Thursday, 15 June

We spend the day in the Citadel waiting. The guns fire ceaselessly. Huge shells (380s–420s) crash down on Verdun causing serious damage. I walk as far as the town; it's in ruins and deserted. One can't stay outside for long as shells are dropping everywhere.

The Citadel is a real underground town, with narrow-gauge railway, dormitories, and rooms of every type; it's safe here, but very gloomy.

At 9 in the evening, we leave, not knowing our destination. We advance slowly through the night. At every moment huge shells come and explode on Verdun, at the crossroads, and in the direction of our gun-batteries which are stationed on all sides. We march in silence, everyone conscious of the seriousness of the moment.

At 1 a.m. we arrive at the Bras-Ravin Quarries, where we remain in reserve. No shelter, nothing, we are in the open fields at the mercy of the first shell.

Friday, 16 June

Superb weather, but not far from us, it's a furnace of artillery fire. The Boches pump their shells at us, and our guns reply. What a racket! 150s and 210s scour the land on all sides and there is nothing anyone can do but wait. The battalion is massed in the ravine without any shelter, if their shelling was not at random it would be dreadful for us. The German observation balloons scan the horizon. Up in the sky, their planes search for us; we curl up in a hole when a shell bursts near us and it's like this until evening when orders arrive.

At 6 p.m. my company and another (the 24th) receive the order to advance with a view of reinforcing the 5th Battalion which is to attack on the following day. We leave, not knowing exactly where we are going; and no one has a map. We have a vague idea where the command posts are; guides are rare in this area where death stalks at every step. With difficulty, we move along crumbling trenches, cross a ridge to take up our position in the Ravin des Dames. The shells rain down, still no shelter.

We haven't eaten for twenty-four hours and don't know if supplies can arrive tonight.

Saturday, 17 June

The attack is due at 9 a.m. The 106th is in charge with the 5th Battalion of the 359th as support. We have to recapture a trench at the top of the ravine that the Boches took from us the day before. We spend the night in the Bras-Ravin; hurriedly we dig a trench to give our men some shelter. Just beside us there is a cemetery where the dead are being brought at every moment. The guns fire furiously, from 3 o'clock it's hell. One cannot imagine what the simple phrase of an official statement like "We have recaptured a trench" really means! The attack is prepared from 4 to 9 o'clock; all guns firing together. The Germans fire non-stop, ammunition dumps blow up, it's deadly. There are so many explosions around us that the air reeks of powder and earth; we can't see clearly any more. We wait anxiously without knowing whether we shall be alive an hour later.

At 9, the gunners' range lengthens. We can't see anything up in front any more. The planes fly low, signalling all the time.

At 11, after a relative pause, the cannonade starts up again. At 2 p.m. it's worse still, it's enough to drive you mad; the Boches are only firing their 210s and 150s, shrapnel explodes above us, we have no idea of what is happening or of the result. We are infested by huge black flies. You don't know where to put yourself.

At 6 p.m. I receive the order to reconnoitre the gun emplacements in the front line, as our battalion is relieving tonight. The shell-bursts are so continuously heavy that we cannot advance before nightfall and it is impossible to cross the ridge.

The wounded from this morning's attack are beginning to arrive, we learn what happened: our artillery fired too short and demolished our front line trench (evacuated for the attack), instead of firing on the Boches. When we attacked the Germans let us advance to 15 metres and then caught us in a hail of machine-gunfire. We succeeded in capturing several parts of the trench but couldn't hold them; at the moment our troops are scattered here and there in shell-craters. During the attack, the German planes bombed our men ceaselessly. Our losses are enormous: the 106th already has 350–400 men out of action, two captains killed and a large number of officers wounded. The 5th Battalion of the 359th, which was advancing in support was caught by gunfire and suffered heavily. The 19th Company hasn't got one officer left, in the 18th, three are missing. We have 32 Boches as prisoners. The positions are the same as before the attack – with our troops only being able to maintain the front-line position which they had previously evacuated.

At nightfall, the dead arrive on stretchers at the cemetery. In this, the Ravine of Death, they lay there, lined up, waiting to be put into the holes that are being hastily dug for them: Major Payen, his head red with blood; Major Cormouls, black with smoke, still others unrecognizable and often in pieces. A sad spectacle, which is repeated here every day.

Sunday, 18 June

We have had to leave to occupy our new positions before our food arrived. It's the second day without food. We eat what little we've got amid huge black flies.

We are now stuck at the top of the ridge in a half-collapsed trench, without any shelter. The whole night there is terrible shelling; we lie flat and pray for any hole to shelter in. At every moment we are sprayed with clouds of earth and stone splinters. There must be an attack on the right, as one can hear the chatter of machine-guns! How many men are afraid! How many "Croixes de Guerre" are weak at the knees!

The 210s make the ground quake, it's hellish, and explains the dazed looks of those who return from such a sector.

It's Sunday! day breaks amid bursts of gunfire. We await orders. One can't think of washing or sleeping. No news: neither papers, nor letters. It's a void, we are no longer in a civilized world. One suffers, and says nothing; the night has been cold;

lying on the damp earth one just shivers, not being able to breathe properly because of the smell.

The afternoon doesn't pass too badly. It's an artillery duel, where the infantry is not spared.

At 8 p.m. I receive the order to relieve in the front line a company of the 106th.

At 9 p.m. this order is countermanded, I am to relieve a company of the 5th Battalion of the 359th in the ravine, at the "Boyau-Marie", near the "Trois Cornes" wood where there are attacks every day . . .

Orders and counter-orders follow each other; no-one has a map, or even a sketch. We don't know where the Boches are, but there is some fear that they will attack us on our right.

My company is all in a line in this trench which collapsed yesterday under the bombardment following our attack. A squad of machine-gunners of the 5th Battalion is buried in it; the following day at dawn we will discover all along the trench, corpses, then legs and arms protruding out of the ground.

Scarcely are we in position when the shelling restarts; the only shelter is small crannies in which one must curl up. We are being shelled from the front and from the flank. What fire! The ground trembles, the air is unbreathable; by midnight I have already eight wounded in my company.

Monday, 19 June

We are expecting an attack at any moment. There is talk of recapturing the trenches with grenades. But what are our leaders doing? Ah, we don't see them here. We are left to ourselves, they won't come and bother us.

We try and make ourselves as comfortable as possible but the more we dig, the more bodies we find. We give up and go elsewhere, but we just leave one graveyard for another. At dawn we have to stop as the German planes are up above spying on us. They signal and the guns start up again, more furiously than before.

No sleep, no water, impossible to move out of one's hole, to even show your head above the trench. We are filthy dirty and have only cold tinned food to eat. We are not receiving supplies any more and have only been here for four days!

The afternoon and the evening are dreadful, it's an inferno of fire. The Germans are attacking our front line, we expect at any instant to be summoned to help. The machine-guns sputter; the ground trembles, the air is full of dust and smoke which scorch the throat. This lasts until 10 p.m. The fatigue party has to leave under a hail of fire to go and fetch our food just outside Verdun – 6 kilometres there and 6 more back. The men go without saying a word!

Tuesday, 20 June
The food supplies only arrive with great difficulty at 2 this morning. Still no water. When one has exhausted one's ration of coffee and wine, you have to go thirsty. By day, the heat is overpowering, we are surrounded by flies and corpses which give off a nauseating smell.

On the alert the whole night. Our position is critical. The Boches harass us. On our right the ravine cannot be occupied because of the shelling. The Thiaumont and the Vaux works are being bombarded continuously. On the left, too, Bras and Mort-Homme are being shelled.

Yesterday my company had 2 men killed and 10 wounded.

The morning is calmer, but at 1 p.m. the firing starts up again. It's a battle of extermination – Man against the Cannon.

8 p.m. Night falls; time doesn't go fast enough – we would like it to be tomorrow already.

10 p.m. Great commotion, red and white flares, chatter of machine-guns, thunder of artillery. 400 metres from us, a new attack is unleashed upon our lines. Every man is at his post waiting, the whole night through. Will the Boches rush us from the top of the ridge? Shells explode only metres from us and all around men fall wounded. We are blinded by the shells and by the earth they throw up, it's an inferno, one could write about such a day minute by minute.

Meanwhile, orders to stand by arrive. Ready we are, but those who are sending these orders, without knowing what is happening, would do better to come here to see the position we are in.

Today again, I killed and 9 wounded in my company.

Wednesday, 21 June

Impossible to sleep, even an hour, the deluge of shells continues and the whole night frantic orders follow each other: you may be attacked, be ready! We have been ready for three days.

The night passes in an inferno of fire. Near Mort-Homme, calm has returned, the Boches are concentrating on Hill 321 and Vaux – it's hell out there – you wonder how anyone will come out alive. The shells, the shrapnel, the 210s fall like hail for twenty-four hours non-stop, only to start again; everything trembles, one's nerves as well as the ground. We feel at the end of our tether.

And what a responsibility! The chiefs tell us: keep watch, but no one can give you any indication about the terrain; on our right, there's the ravine of Hill 321, but we don't even know the positions occupied by our troops and by the Boches. Our artillery itself, is firing without knowing our positions.

8 p.m. We have been bombarded by 210s for exactly twenty-four hours. The Germans have been attacking on our right since 6 p.m. My company at every moment receives the order to stand by to advance. It's a state of perpetual anguish, not a moment's respite.

We crouch there, with our packs on our backs, waiting, scanning the top of the ridge to see what is happening and this lasts until nightfall. We are haggard, dazed, hungry, and feverishly thirsty, but there is no water. In some companies there have been cases of madness. How much longer are we going to stay in this situation?

Night comes and the guns still fire; our trenches have collapsed, it's a tangle of equipment and guns left by the wounded, there's nothing human about it. Why don't they send the deputies, senators, and generals here?

9 p.m. 210s still, our nerves can't take much more. Can't move or sleep. There are no more shelters, one just clings to the wall of the trench. We wait. At 9.15 the bombardment starts again: the front line troops are so fatigued and jumpy that at every moment they believe they are being attacked and ask for artillery support. Red flares follow, our artillery does its best, it's hellish.

Thursday, 22 June
At last in the evening I receive the order to relieve the 24th Company in the front line. The whole afternoon there has been a deluge of shells on the ravine, perhaps we will be calmer in the front line? But where to go to relieve? A reconnaissance is impossible, no one has an idea where the troops are exactly.

At 9 p.m. an avalanche of fire bursts on the ridge, the relief has to be delayed, it would be impossible to pass. Is it an attack? There is gas as well as shells, we can't breathe and are forced to put on our masks.

At 11 p.m. we leave. What a relief! Not knowing our front line positions we advance haphazardly and over the top we find our men crouching in shell holes.

My company is placed in one line, without any trench, in shell craters.

It's a plateau, swept continously by machine-gunfire and flares. Every ten steps one has to fall flat on the ground so as not to be seen. The terrain is littered with corpses! What an advance! It's dark, one feels something soft beneath one's feet, it's a stomach. One falls down flat and it's a corpse. It's awful; we start again with only one desire – to get there.

My company occupies a broken line. Impossible to move around in daylight. To the left, no communication with the neighbouring company; just a hole 100 metres long; we don't know if the Boches are there. In the centre, the same hole – occupied or not? I have a squad which is completely isolated and stay with it.

The captain I am relieving (Symian) tries to show me the terrain. He doesn't know it himself, dazed by four days spent up front amid dead and wounded.

In a nightmare advance, we stumble forwards falling in shell-craters, walking on corpses, flinging ourselves repeatedly to the ground.

Ground where there lie forever men of the 106th, of the 359th still others of regiments who preceded us. It's a graveyard, a glimpse of hell.

Friday, 23 June

5 a.m. The bombardment starts up again fiercely. I get a shell splinter in my lip. Nothing serious fortunately, as the wounded have to wait until evening to get their wounds dressed. One cannot leave the shell-hole even by crawling on one's stomach.

7 a.m. Alert. Commotion. The Boches attack. They are driven back by our return of fire. In the direction of Hill 321 huge attack which lasts three hours with wave upon wave of them.

The heat is oppressive. Around us the stench of the corpses is nauseating. We have to live, eat, and wait in it. Do or die! It's six days now since we had a moment's rest or sleep. The attacks follow each other. The Boches have succeeded in advancing towards Hill 321 and in occupying a part of the ravine behind us, where our reinforcements are.

The shelling has completely destroyed the trench where we were yesterday; the dead and the wounded are too numerous to count.

Saturday, 24 June

Big German offensive on the right bank of the Meuse. This news arrived during the night. There is no question of our being relieved. Everything is silent and behind us, on Fleury ridge, the Boches continue infiltrating. We have been turned! There is no longer any doubt, as we can see enemy columns invading the terrain and their machine-guns are attacking us from behind while our artillery has had to move back.

Now something worse: my men, who have been suffering all sorts of hardships for the last seven days, are becoming demoralized. The word "prisoner" is being whispered. For many this would seem salvation. We must fight against this notion, raise morale. But how? We can't move around, and only those near us can hear. They are all good chaps, devoted, who won't leave us and will form a bodyguard.

What are we waiting for? We don't know. Yet we can only wait for it: perhaps the attack which will kill us, or the bombardment to bury us, or exile even. We spend some anxious hours, without knowing how long this will last.

At 11 a.m. artillery is heard. Our batteries have taken up new positions and are opening fire, the Boches reply.

Impossible to eat, our nerves can't stand it. If we have a call of nature to satisfy, we have to do it in a tin or on a shovel and throw it over the top of our shell-hole. It's like this every day.

Sunday, 25 June

Terrible day and night.

At 3 a.m, without warning, our own troops attack us from behind in order to recapture the terrain lost the day before on our right. These troops, without precise orders, without maps, without even knowing where our lines are, ventured off. They fell upon us,. believing they had found the Boches. But the Boches were 100 metres in front, lying in wait and bursts of machine-gunfire cut them down in our trench. We thus have another heap of corpses and wounded crying out, but whom we are powerless to help. Trench! – well almost every evening we bury the dead on the spot and it's they who form the parapets!

At 6 a.m., the guns fire furiously and to add to our plight, our 75s fire at us. Terrible panic; six wounded at one go from a shell-burst, everyone wants to run for it. Agnel and I have to force these poor devils back by drawing our revolvers.

Major David is killed in turn by our 75s. Our green flares ask for the range to be lengthened, but with all the dust our artillery can't see a thing. We don't know where to put ourselves, we are powerless. Isolated from everything with no means of communication. There's blood everywhere; the wounded have sought refuge with us, thinking that we could help them; the blood flows, the heat is atrocious, the corpses stink, the flies buzz – it's enough to drive one mad. Two men of the 24th Company commit suicide.

At 2 p.m., our 75s start firing on us again, our situation is critical. It is only improved when I send a loyal man at full speed with a report to the Colonel. Luckily he gets through.

Monday, 26 June

Our 220 mortars bombard Thiaumont: we must recapture some terrain to give ourselves some room and to drive the enemy back in its advance on Fleury. We attack incessantly. It's four days since we have been in the front line and the relieving troops have been annihilated this morning during the attacks.

Rain replaces the sun; filthy mud. We can't sit down any more. We are covered in slime and yet we have to lie flat. I haven't washed for ten days, my beard is growing. I am unrecognizable, frighteningly dirty.

Tuesday, 27 June

The guns thunder the whole night: the men who left to fetch the food at 10 last night haven't come back. Still longer without food or drink.

4.30 a.m., first attack on Thiaumont and Hill 321.

9 a.m., second attack. All around us, men are falling: there are some only 5 metres from us in shell-holes, yet we can't help them. If you show your head, you get a burst of machine-gun bullets.

The whole day, incessant firing: the Boches counter-attack; we drive them back by our rifle fire and with grenades.

My company is rapidly diminishing, we are about sixty left now, with this small number we still have to hold our position. In the evening, when the men go to fetch supplies we are really at the mercy of an attack. Still no relief.

Wednesday, 28 June

Hardest day to endure. The Boches begin to pound our positions, we take cover; some try to flee, we have to get our revolvers out again and stand in their way. It's hard, our nerves are frayed and it's difficult to make them see reason.

At midday, while we are trying to eat a bit of chocolate, Agnel's orderly has his back broken beside us; the poor chap is groaning, there is nothing we can do except to wait for nightfall, and then, take him to the first-aid post, and will we be able to? The wounded are so numerous and we have so few men left that those who can't walk sometimes have to wait for forty-eight hours before being taken away. The stretcher-bearers are frightened and don't like coming to us. Furthermore, the nights are so short, that they can only make one trip. One trip: four men to take one wounded on a stretcher!

1 p.m., it's an inferno: the Boches undoubtedly are preparing to attack us. Shells scream down on every side: a new panic to be checked. At 6 p.m. when we are dazed and numb, the firing

range lengthens and suddenly everyone is on his feet, shouting, the Boches are coming. They attack in massed formation, in columns of eight!

These troops who, moments ago were in despair, are at their posts in a twinkling; we hold our grenades until the Boches are at 15 metres, then let them have it. Guns bark, and a machine-gun which survived the avalanche of shells is wreaking havoc.

The Boches are cut down; amid the smoke, we see dozens of dead and wounded, and the rest retreating back to their trenches. Our commanding officer, thinking that we are hard-pressed, sends welcome reinforcements. They will be useful for supplies and taking the wounded away.

Only around 9 p.m. is it quieter. We help the wounded who are waiting to be taken away. Our shell-holes are lakes of mud. It is raining and we don't know where to put ourselves: our rifles don't work any more, and we can only rely upon our grenades which are in short supply.

This evening, still no relief; another twenty-four hours to get through. It gets colder at night, we lie down in the mud and wait.

Thursday, 29 June

Our fourteenth day in this sector. The bombardment continues, our nerves make us tremble, we can't eat any more, we are exhausted.

Yet still no relief.

Friday, 30 June

Attacks and counter-attacks. Frightful day – the shelling and the fatigue are becoming harder to bear. At 10 a.m., French attack on Thiaumont; the artillery fires 12,000 rounds of 255s, 550 of 220s, and the 75s fire at will.

The din began at 6 this morning; the Boches reply furiously. It's hell, we are getting hit more and more often, as our position is the favourite enemy target. The majority of the shells fall on or around us. The shelling will last ten hours! And during this time we expect an attack at any moment. To make it worse, my own company is hard hit. A 210 falls directly on a group of men sheltering in a hole: 3 killed and 2 seriously wounded who drag themselves up to me to plead for help. A minute later, a second shell sends a machine-gun flying, killing 2 more men and wounding a third. It's panic stations – the men run, and under a hail of gunfire, I have to force them back again with a revolver in my hand. Everyone goes back to his post, we set up another machine-gun and keep watch.

At 10 a.m. and 2 p.m. first and second French attacks on Thiaumont. The Boche harass us with their fire. Our heads are buzzing, we have had enough. Myself, Agnel, and my orderly are squashed in a hole, protecting ourselves from splinters with our packs. Numb and dazed, without saying a word, and with our hearts pounding, we await the shell that will destroy us. The wounded are increasing in numbers around us. These poor devils not knowing where to go come to us, believing that they will be helped. What can we do? There are clouds of smoke, the air is unbreathable. There's death everywhere. At our feet, the wounded groan in a pool of blood; two of them, more seriously hit are breathing their last. One, a machine-gunner, has been blinded, with one eye hanging out of its socket and the other torn out: in addition he has lost a leg. The second has no face, an arm blown off, and a horrible wound in the stomach. Moaning and suffering atrociously one begs me, "Lieutenant, don't let me die. Lieutenant, I'm suffering, help me." The other, perhaps more gravely wounded and nearer to death, implores me to kill him with these words, "Lieutenant, if you don't want to, give me your revolver!" Frightful, terrible moments, while the cannons harry us and we are splattered with mud and earth by the shells. For hours, these groans and supplications continue until, at 6 p.m., they die before our eyes without anyone being able to help them.

At this moment, the hurricane of fire ceases, we prepare to receive an attack, but fortunately nothing happens.

We look at one another, our eyes haggard, trembling all over, half-crazy. Is it going to start all over again?

At last, at 8 p.m., an order: we are to be relieved. What a cry of joy from those of us left. We wait anxiously and it's 2 a.m. before the replacements arrive. Our information is quickly passed on. Soon it will be dawn and we have to cross the zone before sunrise. Tiredness disappears, and our limbs regain enough strength to escape from these plains where at every step the guns have done their work; corpses of men, carcasses of horses, overturned vehicles, it's a horrific graveyard all the way to Verdun. We halt, the guns are rumbling in the distance, we can breathe at last; we call the roll, how many are missing when their names are called!

Our time at Verdun has been awful. Our faces have nothing human about them. For sixteen days we have neither washed nor slept. Life has been spent amongst dead and dying, hardships of every sort and incessant anguish. Our cheeks are hollow, beards long and our clothes thick with mud. And, above all, we have a vision of these horrific days, the memory of a comrade fallen in action; each one of us thinks of those who have not returned. Despite our joy at being alive, our eyes reveal the crazy horror of it all.

During the struggle, whole regiments have melted away. The 129th Division doesn't exist any more. The 359th has lost 33 officers and 1,100 men. My company, with the 22nd, had the heaviest pressure to bear. Both resisted all the German attacks. They prevented their descent into the ravine and therefore the complete encirclement of the area.

Saturday, 1 July
After being relieved, we are quartered at Bois-la-Villee, in the same camp where we stopped on the way here. We arrive at 2 p.m., exhausted. We fall into bed and sleep like brutes.

Sunday, 2 July
At 8 a.m., we pile into cars, glad to leave this ill-fated region far behind. We get out at Ligny-en-Barrois at 2 p.m. We spend the evening at ablutions.

Wednesday, 5 July
Promoted captain.

Verdun did, as Falkenhayn hoped, "bleed" the French, to the count of 377,231 men between February and December 1916. But it bled the Germans too, to the count of 337,000. Verdun was turned into a veritable wasteland by saturation shelling, the French alone having fired 12 million artillery rounds.

HOME FRONT: DEATH OF A BROTHER, 15 June 1916

Vera Brittain

I had just announced to my father, as we sat over tea in the dining room, that I really must do up Edward's papers and take them to the post office before it closed for the weekend, when there came the sudden loud clattering at the front-door knocker that always meant a telegram.

For a moment I thought that my legs would not carry me, but they behaved quite normally as I got up and went to the door. I knew what was in the telegram – I had known for a week – but because the persistent hopefulness of the human heart refuses to allow intuitive certainty to persuade the reason of that which it knows, I opened and read it in a tearing anguish of suspense.

"Regret to inform you Captain E. H. Brittain M.C. killed in action Italy June 15th."

"No answer," I told the boy mechanically, and handed the telegram to my father, who had followed me into the hall. As we went back into the dining room I saw, as though I had never seen them before, the bowl of blue delphiniums on the table; their intense colour, vivid, ethereal, seemed too radiant for earthly flowers.

Then I remembered that we should have to go down to Purley and tell the news to my mother.

Late that evening, my uncle brought us all back to an empty flat. Edward's death and our sudden departure had offered the maid – at that time the amateur prostitute – an agreeable opportunity for a few hours' freedom of which she had taken immediate advantage. She had not even finished the household handkerchiefs, which I had washed that morning and intended to iron after tea; when I went into the kitchen I found them still hanging, stiff as boards, over the clothes-horse near the fire where I had left them to dry.

Long after the family had gone to bed and the world had grown silent, I crept into the dining room to be alone with Edward's portrait. Carefully closing the door, I turned on the light and looked at the pale, pictured face, so dignified, so steadfast, so tragically mature. He had been through so much – far, far more than those beloved friends who had died at an earlier stage of the interminable War, leaving him alone to mourn their loss. Fate might have allowed him the little, sorry compensation of survival, the chance to make his lovely music in honour of their memory. It seemed indeed the last irony that he should have been killed by the countrymen of Fritz Kreisler, the violinist whom of all others he had most greatly admired.

And suddenly, as I remembered all the dear afternoons and evenings when I had followed him on the piano as he played his violin, the sad, searching eyes of the portrait were more than I could bear, and falling on my knees before it I began to cry, "Edward! Oh, Edward!" in dazed repetition, as though my persistent crying and calling would somehow bring him back.

THE SOMME: OVER THE TOP WITH THE ROYAL WARWICKSHIRE REGIMENT, 7.30 a.m., 1 July 1916

Private Sidney Williamson, 1/8th Battalion, Royal Warwickshire Regiment

In the memorable phrase of historian Basil Liddell Hart, the Somme was the "glory and the graveyard" of Kitchener's Army. After a week's heavy shelling British troops went "over the top" on the morning of 1 July 1916 on a fifteen-mile sector of the Western front, expecting little German opposition. They met instead a hurricane of German fire, and 60,000 British casualties were sustained on this day alone. Their deaths secured 100,000 yards of ground. By the battle's end in mid-November 1916 420,000 British and 200,000 French casualties had been sustained. German casualties were 650,000 killed and wounded.

Diary; 1 July 1916 [on the Somme]

It was a lovely bright morning, but the feelings of the men were tense. We had breakfast at 5.0 a.m., afterwards the officers were going round to see all the men and have a talk with us. The shelling was terrific and the Germans started to shell our lines. At 7.20 a mine was exploded under the German trenches. An officer detailed me and another soldier standing by me to carry forward with us a box containing a signalling lamp. At 7.30 a.m. whistles were blown and the attack started. What did I see! To the left as far as Gommecourt and to the right as far as Beaumont Hamel, lines of soldiers going forward as though on parade in line formation. Just "over the top" the soldier helping me with the box stopped and fell dead. I had to go on but without the box. Lt Jones was the next officer I saw to fall, then CSM Haines was calling for me, he had been wounded. I reached the first German line and dropped into it where there were many German dead. The battlefield was nothing but shell holes and barbed wire, but now I noticed many dead and dying, and the lines of soldiers was not to be seen. With no officers or NCO near I felt alone and still went forward from shell hole to shell hole. Later Cpl Beard joined me and he asked me to hold down a ground signalling sheet so that he could get a message to the observing aeroplane flying overhead. He asked for "MORE BOMBS" and the Pilot of the aeroplane asked "Code please". This was flashed back and the aeroplane flew away.

Things were now getting disorganised and at this point we could not go any further. The machine-gun fire was deadly. And our bombs had all been used up. The Colonel of the Seaforths came up and took charge of all the odd groups of men belonging to various Regiments. He told us to dig ourselves in and eventually there must have been 50 or 60 men at this spot, and it all started from the one small shell hole Cpl Beard and myself were first in.

Now there was a lull in the fighting till 3.0 p.m. At one time a shout went up that we were surrounded by Germans, but they were Germans running from the dugouts in the first line and giving themselves up. I do not think they made it.

With Cpl Beard we started to get back to our lines shell hole by shell hole, but we soon got parted. I managed to reach the British lines at 7.30 p.m., but the sight that met my eyes was terrible. Hundreds of dead soldiers were everywhere, and the

Germans kept up their heavy shelling. Met Sam and Bob Patterson in the trench, the only two of my own Battalion. Stayed in the British trench all night.

THE SOMME: DAY ONE – THROUGH GERMAN EYES, 1 July 1916

Matthaus Gerster, German Army

The intense bombardment was realized by all to be a prelude to the infantry assault. The men in the dug-outs therefore waited ready, a belt full of hand grenades around them gripping their rifles and listening for the bombardment to lift. Looking towards the British trenches through the long trench periscopes held up out of the dug-out entrances, there could be seen a mass of steel helmets above their parapet showing that their storm-troops were ready for the assault. At 7.30 a.m. the hurricane of shells ceased as suddenly as it had begun. Our men at once clambered up the steep shafts leading from the dug-outs to daylight and ran singly or in groups to the nearest shell craters. The machine guns were pulled out of the dug-outs and hurriedly placed into position, their crews dragging the heavy ammunition boxes up the steps and out to the guns. A rough firing line was thus rapidly established. As soon as in position, a series of extended lines of British infantry were seen moving forward from the British trenches. The first line appeared to continue without end to right and left. It was quickly followed by a second line, then a third and fourth . . .

"Get Ready!"

A few minutes later, when the leading British line was within one hundred yards, the rattle of machine guns and rifle fire broke out from along the whole line of craters. Some fired kneeling so as to get a better target over the broken ground, while others in the excitement of the moment, stood up regardless of their own safety to fire into the crowd of men in front of them. Red rockets sped up into the blue sky as a signal to the artillery, and immediately afterwards a mass of shells from the German batteries in rear tore through the air and burst among the advancing lines. Whole sections seemed to fall, and the rear formations, moving in closer order, quickly scattered. The advance rapidly crumbled under this hail of shells and bullets. All along the line men could be seen throwing their arms into the air and collapsing, never to move again. Badly wounded rolled about in their agony, and others less severely injured crawled to the nearest shell-hole for shelter.

The British soldier, however, has no lack of courage, and once his hand is set to the plough he is not easily turned from his purpose. The extended lines, though badly shaken and with many gaps, now came on all the faster. Instead of a leisurely walk they covered the ground in short rushes at the double. Within a few minutes the leading troops had reached within a stone's throw of our front trench, and while some of us continued to fire at point-blank range, others threw hand grenades among them. The British bombers answered back, while the infantry rushed forward with fixed bayonets. The noise of battle became indescribable. The shouting of orders and the shrill British cheers as they charged forward, could be heard above the violent and intense fusillade of machine guns and rifles and the bursting bombs, and above the deep thunderings of the artillery and the shell explosions. With all this were mingled the moans and groans of the wounded, the cries for help and the last screams of death. Again and again the extended lines of British infantry broke against the German defence like waves against a cliff, only to be beaten back.

It was an amazing spectacle of unexampled gallantry, courage and bull-dog determination on both sides.

THE SOMME: AT 21ST CASUALTY CLEARING STATION, 1–3 July 1916

Reverend John Stanhope Walker, Chaplain 21st Casualty Clearing Station

21st Casualty Clearing Station was at Crombie, on the junction of the Somme and Ancre rivers. The rector of Kettlethorpe, Lincolnshire, Walker volunteered for the Western Front in December 1915.

Saturday, 1 July
7.30, the heavens and earth were rolling up, the crazy hour had begun, every gun we owned fired as hard as ever it could for more than an hour. From a hill near Veils over us to left and right great observation balloons hung, eighteen in view. Aeroplanes dashed about, morning mist and gun smoke obscured the view. We got back for a late breakfast and soon the wounded by German shells came in, then all day long cars of dying and wounded, but all cheerful for they told us of a day of glorious successes. They are literally piled up – beds gone, lucky to get space on floor of tent, hut or ward, and though the surgeons work like Trojans many must yet die for lack of operation. All the CCS's are overflowing.

Later. We have 1,500 in and still they come, 3–400 officers, it is a sight – chaps with fearful wounds lying in agony, many so patient, some make a noise, one goes to a stretcher, lays one's hand on the forehead, it is cold, strike a match, he is dead – here a Communion, there an absolution, there a drink, there a madman, there a hot water bottle and so on – one madman was swearing and kicking, I gave him a drink, he tried to bite my hand and squirted the water from his mouth into my face – well, it is an experience beside which all previous experience pales. Oh I am tired, excuse writing.

2 July
What a day, I had no corner in the hospital even for Holy Communion, the Colonel said that no services might be under cover, fortunately it was fine so rigged up my packing case altar in a wood behind the sisters' camp. Then all day squatting or kneeling by stretchers administering Holy Communion etc. Twice I went to bury, of course we used the trench we had prepared in a field adjoining. I first held a service of consecration, when I turned round the old man labouring in the field was on his knees in the soil. I buried thirty-seven but have some left over till tomorrow. Saddest place of all is the moribund ward, two large tents laced together packed with dying officers and men, here they lie given up as hopeless, of course they do not know it. But I can't write, I am too tired and I have some patients' letters.

3 July
Now I know something of the horrors of war, the staff is redoubled but what of that, imagine 1,000 badly wounded per diem. The surgeons are beginning to get sleep, because after working night and day they realize we may be at this for some months, as Verdun. We hear of great successes but there are of course setbacks and one hears of ramparts of dead English and Germans. Oh, if you could see our wards, tents, huts, crammed with terrible wounds – see the rows of abdominals and lung penetrations dying – you meet a compound fracture of femur walking about – in strict confidence, please, I got hold of some morphia and I go to that black hole of Calcutta (Moribund) and use it or I creep into the long tents where two or three hundred Germans lie, you can imagine what attention they get with our own neglected, the cries and groans are too much to withstand and I cannot feel less pity for them than for our own. Surgeons and sisters are splendid and I go and bother them and they come without grumbling. But one cannot drag them away from lifesaving to death-easing too often. Now 4 am, the Jewish chief rabbi has joined us.

GERMAN PRISONERS, THE SOMME, July 1916

Sidney Rogerson, British Army

We had now more energy to look about us and to note details of the vast concentration of men, beasts and machines which spread as far as the eye could see across the countryside. We saw strange-looking guns, great hump-backed howitzers being drawn along by tractors. We looked out eagerly but without success for those new monsters, the "tanks", which had burst so dramatically upon friend and enemy alike at Flers some six weeks before. So far we had not seen one, and our only idea of what they looked like had been gleaned from very foggy newspaper illustrations. We passed through lines of Australians, seeing them at close quarters for the first time, and marvelled at the difference in their physiognomy, their stature and their equipment. The slouch-hats we knew already, but how odd their shirt-like jackets looked! We commented on their dirty, slipshod appearance, which we did not then realize masked a deadly efficiency as fighting men, and on the curious lope of their long-maned horses. German prisoners were working on the roads under lanky Anzac guards. Few of them were our idea of "Square-heads". Some were mere boys, others myopic bespectacled scarecrows. Many were bearded, some having fringes of whiskers framing their faces after the manner of the great-crested grebe. All wore the long-skirted field-grey coats, the trousers stuffed into clumsy boots. It gave us a strange feeling to see our enemies at such close range. Except for dead ones, for an occasional miserable prisoner dragged back half-dead with fright from some raid, or for groups seen through field-glasses far behind their lines, many of us had never seen any Germans. That was one of the oddest aspects of the War. There must have been hundreds of men who were in France and in the trenches for months, even years, who never set eyes on the men they were fighting. The enemy early became a legend. The well-wired trenches that faced ours, frequently at a distance of only a few yards, gave shelter, we understood, to a race of savages, Huns, blond beasts who gave no quarter, who crucified Canadians and bayoneted babies, raped Belgian women, and had actually built kadaver works where they rendered down the bodies of their dead into fats! It was perhaps as well that we should believe such tales. But were these pallid, serious youths really capable of such enormities?

ONE MAN'S WAR: A MONTH IN THE LIFE OF AN AUSTRALIAN SIGNALLER, WESTERN FRONT, July 1916

Lance Corporal Thomas Part, 6th Infantry Battalion, 2nd Division, Australian Imperial Forces

Diary July 3

Relieved by the N.Z. Rifle brigade, the 4th Bn. taking over our position in trenches at CHAPELLE ARMENTIERES. Relief completed at 11.40 p.m. 2/7/16.

All very quiet. Raining all the time during relief & after a 10 mile march through water & slush we finally landed at LA CRECHE at 5 a.m.

4
Visited BAILIEUL a large town & had a good time.

July 8
Left "LA CRECHE" at 1.30 p.m. & arrived at "MERRIS" (a small village of "PRADELLE") at 7 p.m.

9
Left "PRADELLE" at 11 a.m. & arrived at "EBBLINGHEM" & put up at the Mayor's residence.

10
Left "EBBLINGHEM" at 10 a.m. for "WARDRECQUES".

11
Left "WARDRECQUES" at 7.15 a.m. with transports (in charge of panniers) & arrived at "ARQUES" at 9 a.m. to entrain.

12
Left "ARQUES" at 11.30 a.m. by train passed through St OMER thence through BOLOGNE, past ETAPLES (the Aust. training camp) thence through St ELOI. The railway practically follows the RIVER SOMME all the way. We finally arrived at ARMIENS where we dis-entrained. The scenery of the country was unsurpassed & the trip one to be always remembered. It was like the MARSEILLE-PARIS-AIRE trip. We arrived at ARMIENS at 8 p.m. & untrucked transports etc. From the railway siding the whole body marched through the main streets of ARMIENS. The French people especially the girls were hilarious with joy, they threw kisses & pressed wine etc. upon us. "VOOLAY VOU MOMBRASSAY" was what most girls asked, hand shakes & souvenirs collectors in galore. This was the first occasion of Australian troops passing through their City. We marched past nearly 4 miles of buildings & splendid avenues. It was a never-to-be-forgotten sight & experience. We had a spell about 3½ miles out & had tea & then proceeded on to "St SAVAEUR".

13
We are now billeted at ST SAVAEUR. This is a fair sized village & 3 of our Bns. are camped here.

16
Bn. moved this morning at 10.30 a.m. for RAINNEVILLE 8¼ miles march, arrived at 2.40 p.m.

17
This morning lined up & inspected by a French woman who was trying to identify some suspected individual who stole 400 Francs from her shop. This village has rather a forlorn & delapidated appearance.

18
Left RAINVILLE at 11 a.m. & rested by roadside for lunch, some cows even close by & some of our chaps milked them. Gen. BIRDWOOD has just passed us.

19
Arrived at TOUTENCOURT at 4 p.m. yesterday light showers falling.

July 19
Sleeping in huts, no sleep last night on a/c of extreme cold so got up & promenaded for a spell.

21
Left TOUTENCOURT at 9 a.m. & arrived at VARANNES at 1 p.m. & then went for a walk to German prisoners camp.

27
Left VARANNES at 5 a.m. & arrived at ALBERT at 8 a.m. Our Bde. takes over firing line tonight; we in supports. We are busy cleaning rifles & having tin diamond discs put on our backs.

28
Arrived at destination last night 5½ miles from "Albert" & have taken over trenches. Lost & wandering in No Mans land.

Shrapnel & H.Es is simply hellish sigs acting as runners & guides. Sigs are in deep German dugout 20 ft deep electric lights were used here, fittings still remain. In large hand painted letters over the mess room are the words "GOTT, STRAFF ANGLAIS".

29
6th & 7th Bdes charged & endeavoured to take 2 lines of trenches. There was a bollocks up, 7th Bde. failed to take their position & 23 Bn. had to fall back one trench on a/c of their Right flank not being covered.

July 29
Our Bn. casualties up to now today 168. Both yesterday & today it was a perfect "HELL". This evening while returning to "SAUSAGE VALLEY" (after having guided a party in) BILLY HILL was shot through the heart by machine gun bullet. Bn. now camped in saps at SAUSAGE VALLEY near the "CRATER" on the Albert-Bapaume Rd.

30
Last night I had the first nights sleep for 4 nights. I slept only 10 yds from guns of battery which were going all night. We've had plenty to eat since being here. An aeroplane left FRANCE & flew to BERLIN & dropped "PAMPHLETS" thence on to RUSSIA & when over AUSTRIA had to descend on a/c of dirty sparkling plugs & he was captured. He did 850 miles in one lap. At POZIERES, one could take a 1000 acre patch & you wouldn't a piece of ground not turned up, on which you could place a threepenny piece, so heavy are the bombardments in this area. A chap feels like shaking hands with himself when he gets out. Today the weather is very hot. Our casualties in this area to date approx 250.

THE SOMME: WALKS AMONGST THE DEAD, 4–17 July 1916

Philip Gibbs, war correspondent

It looked like victory, because of the German dead that lay there in their battered trenches and the filth and stench of death over all that mangled ground, and the enormous destruction wrought by our guns, and the fury of fire which we were still pouring over the enemy's lines from batteries which had moved forward. I went down flights of steps into German dug-outs astonished by their depth and strength. Our men did not build like this. This German industry was a rebuke to us – yet we had captured their work, and the dead bodies of their labourers lay in those dark caverns, killed by our bombers who had flung down hand-grenades. I drew back from those fat corpses. They looked monstrous, lying there crumpled up, amidst a foul litter of clothes, stick bombs, old boots, and bottles. Groups of dead lay in ditches which had once been trenches, flung into chaos by that bombardment I had seen. They had been bayoneted. I remember one man – an elderly fellow – sitting up with his back to a bit of earth with his hands half raised. He was smiling a little, though he had been stabbed through the belly, and was stone dead.

Victory! . . . Some of the German dead were young boys, too young to be killed for old men's crimes, and others might have been old or young. One could not tell because they had no faces, and were just masses of raw flesh in rags of uniforms. Legs and arms lay separate without any bodies thereabouts.

Robert Graves, Royal Welsh Fusiliers

We were in fighting kit and felt cold at night, so I went into the wood to find German overcoats to use as blankets. It was full of dead Prussian Guards Reserve, big men, and dead Royal Welch and South Wales Borderers of the New Army battalions, little men. Not a single tree in the wood remained unbroken. I collected my overcoats, and came away as quickly as I could, climbing through the wreckage of green branches. Going and coming, by the only possible route, I passed by the bloated and stinking corpse of a German with his back propped against a tree. He had a green face, spectacles, close-shaven hair; black blood was dripping from the nose and beard. I came across two other unforgettable corpses: a man of the South Wales Borderers and one of the Lehr Regiment had succeeded in bayoneting each other simultaneously.

WESTERN FRONT: SONG OF THE AUSTRALIAN ARMY, July 1916

Anonymous

A diversionary attack north of the Somme, at Fromelles, was the Australians' first offensive on the Western Front. The song below was sung to the tune of "The Church's One Foundation".

We are the Anzac Army,
The A.N.Z.A.C.,
We cannot shoot, we don't salute,
What bloody good are we.
And when we get to Ber-lin
The Kaiser he will say,
"*Hoch, Hoch! Mein Gott, what a bloody odd lot*
To get six bob a day!"

A NOVELIST IS EXCUSED MILITARY SERVICE, ENGLAND, July 1916

D.H. Lawrence

The author of *Women in Love* and *Lady Chatterley's Lover* writes to Catherine Carswell. Lawrence was consumptive.

My Dear Catherine,

I never wrote to tell you that they gave me a complete exemption from all military service, thanks be to God. That was a week ago last Thursday. I had to join the Colours in Penzance, be conveyed to Bodmin (60 miles), spend a night in barracks with all the other men, and then be examined. It was experience enough for me, of soldiering. I am sure I should die in a week, if they kept me. It is the annulling of all one stands for, this militarism, the nipping of the very germ of one's being. I was very much upset. The sense of spiritual disaster everywhere was quite terrifying. One was not sure whether one survived or not. Things are very bad.

Yet I liked the men. They all seemed so decent. And yet they all seemed as if they had chosen wrong. It was the underlying sense of disaster that overwhelmed me. They are all so brave, to suffer, but none of them brave enough, to reject suffering. They are all so noble, to accept sorrow and hurt, but they can none of them demand happiness. Their manliness all lies in accepting calmly this death, this loss of their integrity. They must stand by their fellow man: that is the motto.

This is what Christ's weeping over Jerusalem has brought us to, a whole Jerusalem offering itself to the Cross. To me, this is infinitely more terrifying than Pharisees and Publicans and Sinners, taking *their* way to death. This is what the love of our neighbour has brought us to, that, because one man dies, we all die.

REPORTED DEAD, THE SOMME, 22 July 1916

Robert Graves, Royal Welsh Fusiliers

One piece of shell went through my left thigh, high up, near the groin; I must have been at the full stretch of my stride to escape emasculation. The wound over the eye was made by a little chip of marble, possibly from one of the Bazentin cemetery headstones. (Later, I had it cut out, but a smaller piece has since risen to the surface under my right eyebrow, where I keep it for a souvenir.) This, and a finger-wound which split the bone, probably came from another shell bursting in front of me. But a piece of shell had also gone in two inches below the point of my right shoulder-blade and came out through my chest two inches above the right nipple.

My memory of what happened then is vague. Apparently Dr

Dunn came up through thc barrage with a stretcher-party, dressed my wound, and got me down to the old German dressing-station at the north end of Mametz Wood. I remember being put on the stretcher, and winking at the stretcher-bearer sergeant who had just said: "Old Gravy's got it, all right!" They laid my stretcher in a corner of the dressing-station, where I remained unconscious for more than twenty-four hours.

Late that night, Colonel Crawshay came back from High Wood and visited the dressing-station; he saw me lying in the corner, and they told him I was done for. The next morning, 21 July, clearing away the dead, they found me still breathing and put me on an ambulance for Heilly, the nearest field hospital. The pain of being jolted down the Happy Valley, with a shell hole at every three or four yards of the road, woke me up. I remember screaming. But back on the better roads I became unconscious again. That morning, Crawshay wrote the usual formal letters of condolence to the next-of-kin of the six or seven officers who had been killed. This was his letter to my mother:

> Dear Mrs Graves, 22.7.16
>
> I very much regret to have to write and tell you your son has died of wounds. He was very gallant, and was doing so well and is a great loss.
>
> He was hit by a shell and very badly wounded, and died on the way down to the base I believe. He was not in bad pain, and our doctor managed to get across and attend to him at once.
>
> We have had a very hard time, and our casualties have been large. Believe me you have all our sympathy in your loss, and we have lost a very gallant soldier.
>
> Yours sincerely,
> G. Crawshay, Lt-Col.

Then he made out the official casualty list – a long one, because only eighty men were left in the battalion – and reported me "died of wounds". Heilly lay on the railway; close to the station stood the hospital tents with the red cross prominently painted on the roofs, to discourage air-bombing. Fine July weather made the tents insufferably hot. I was semi-conscious now, and aware of my lung-wound through a shortness of breath. It amused me to watch the little bubbles of blood, like scarlet soap-bubbles, which my breath made in escaping through the opening of the wound. The doctor came over to my bed. I felt sorry for him; he looked as though he had not slept for days.

I asked him: "Can I have a drink?"

"Would you like some tea?"

I whispered: "Not with condensed milk."

He said, most apologetically: "I'm afraid there's no fresh milk."

Tears of disappointment pricked my eyes; I expected better of a hospital behind the lines.

"Will you have some water?"

"Not if it's boiled."

"It is boiled. And I'm afraid I can't give you anything alcoholic in your present condition."

"Some fruit then?"

"I have seen no fruit for days."

Yet a few minutes later he returned with two rather unripe greengages. In whispers I promised him a whole orchard when I recovered.

The nights of the 22nd and 23rd were horrible. Early on the morning of the 24th, when the doctor came round the ward, I said: "You must send me away from here. This heat will kill me." It was beating on my head through the canvas.

"Stick it out. Your best chance is to lie here and not to be moved. You'd not reach the Base alive."

"Let me risk the move. I'll be all right, you'll see."

Half an hour later he returned. "Well, you're having it your way. I've just got orders to evacuate every case in the hospital. Apparently the Guards have been in it up at Delville Wood, and they'll all be coming down tonight." I did not fear that I would die, now – it was enough to be honourably wounded and bound for home.

BOMBING THE RUSSIAN LINES, July–August 1916

Rittmeister Manfred von Richthofen, Imperial German Air Service

A former cavalry officer (see pp 30), Richthofen took a turn as a bomber pilot before his celebrated career as a fighter "ace" over the Western Front.

In Russia our battle squadron dropped many bombs. We busied ourselves with angering the Russians and dropped our "eggs" on their finest railway installations. On one of these days our whole squadron set out to bomb a very important train station called Manjewicze, about thirty kilometers behind the Front. The Russians were planning an attack, so this station was filled with trains standing side by side. A whole stretch of track was covered with engines and cars. From the air one could see troop trains at every switch. It was really a worthwhile target.

There are many things to be enthusiastic about in flying, and for a while I was much interested in bombing. It gave me a sinister pleasure to plaster our "friends" down below. I often went out twice a day on such flights. This day Manjewicze was the target. Each squadron made preparations to set out against the Russians.

The machines stood ready and each pilot tested his engine, for it is a painful thing to be forced to land on the wrong side of the Front, especially in Russia. The Russians are terrible to captured fliers. If they catch one they will certainly kill him. That is the one danger in Russia, for they have no fliers of their own, or as good as none at all. If a Russian flier appeared, he was sure to have bad luck and be shot down by his own men. The anti-aircraft guns in Russia are often quite good, but their number is not sufficient. Compared to the Western Front, in any case, flying on the Eastern Front is like a holiday.

The machines rolled with difficulty to the starting line. They were filled to capacity with bombs. Many times I hauled one-hundred-fifty-kilogram bombs with a normal C-type airplane. I have even had with me heavy observers, who had apparently not suffered from the meat shortage, as well as two machine guns, although I never got to try them out in Russia. It is a shame that there is not a Russian in my collection of victories. His cockade would look very picturesque on the wall. To get back to the main point, a flight with a heavily laden, clumsy machine is not easy, especially in the afternoon heat. On the take-off run, the planes sway very uncomfortably. They do not falter, of course; the one-hundred-fifty "horses" see to that. But it is not a pleasant feeling to have so much explosive material and gasoline along. At last one is in a calm sea of air, and gradually comes to enjoy the bombing flight. It is beautiful to fly straight ahead, with a definite target and firm orders. After a bombing flight one has the feeling he has accomplished something, whereas many times on a pursuit flight, when one has shot down nothing, you reproach yourself with the feeling that you could have done better. I liked dropping bombs. Gradually my observer had gotten the knack of flying perpendicular to the target, and, with the help of an aiming telescope, he waited for the right moment to lay his eggs.

The flight to Manjewicze was beautiful. I made it often. We flew over gigantic complexes of forests in which elk and lynx certainly must roam. To be sure, the villages looked as if only foxes could live in them. The only large village in the whole area was Manjewicze. Around the village countless tents were pitched, and by the train station were innumerable huts. We could not make out the sign of the Red Cross. A squadron had been there before us. One could determine this solely by the smoking houses and huts. They had not done badly. The one exit of the train station was obviously blocked by a lucky hit. The locomotive was still steaming. The engineer was probably hid in a dugout somewhere. On the other side of the town a locomotive was coming out at three-quarter speed. Of course, I could not resist to temptation to attack. We flew toward the engine and dropped a bomb a hundred metres in front of it. The desired result was obtained: the locomotive had stopped and could not move. We turned and neatly dropped bomb after bomb, finely aimed through the telescope sight, on the train station. We had plenty of time and no one bothered us. An enemy airfield was in the vicinity, but its pilots were not to be seen. Antiaircraft shells burst sporadically but in a different direction than where we were flying. We saved a bomb for use on the flight home. Then we saw an enemy flier as he started from his field. Did he plan to attack us? I don't think so. More than likely he sought security in the air, for during a bombing flight over an airfield the air is certainly the most comfortable place to be to avoid personal danger.

We took a roundabout way home and looked for troop encampments. It was special fun to harass the gentlemen below with our machine guns. Such half-civilized tribes as the Asiatics are more afraid of such things than the refined Englishmen. It is especially interesting to shoot at enemy cavalry. It causes an enormous commotion among the men. They rush off to all points of the compass. I would not like to be the commander of a Cossack squadron shot up by fliers with machine guns.

Soon we saw our lines again. Now it was time to get rid of our last bomb. We decided to present a bomb to a captive balloon, the only captive balloon the Russians had. We descended smoothly to a few hundred metres from the balloon. They had begun to reel it in with great haste, but as the bomb was falling, the reeling stopped. I do not believe I hit it but, rather, that the Russians in their panic had left their officer in the lurch up in the basket and had all run away.

We finally reached our own lines and, after arriving back home, were somewhat surprised to find that one of the wings showed a hit.

Another time we were in the same area preparing to attack the Russian troops about to cross the Stokhod River. We approached the dangerous place laden with bombs and plenty of ammunition for the machine guns. On arriving, we saw to our great astonishment that the enemy cavalry was already crossing the Stokhod. One single bridge served as the crossing point. It was clear that if this was hit, it would hurt the enemy advance tremendously. There was a thick mass of troops trundling over the narrow footbridge. We went down to the lowest possible altitude and observed that the enemy cavalry was crossing with great speed. The first bomb burst not far from them; the second and third followed directly after it. There was immediate confusion and disorder below. The bridge itself had not been hit; nevertheless, traffic was completely stopped and everything that had legs used them, taking off in all directions.

That was quite a successful attack, for it cost only three bombs; besides, another squadron was coming behind us. So we could proceed to other targets. My observer fired the machine gun continually at the chaps down below, and it was wild fun. How successful we were, I cannot say, of course. The Russians have not told me either. But I imagine that it was our plane alone that had repelled the Russian attack.

THE SOMME: A GERMAN SOLDIER WRITES HOME, 14 August 1916

Friedrich Steinbrecher, German Army

Steinbrecher was killed in action in 1917.

August 12th 1916

Somme. The whole history of the world cannot contain a more ghastly word! All the things I am now once more enjoying – bed, coffee, rest at night, water – seem unnatural and as if I had no right to them. And yet I was only there a week.

At the beginning of the month we left our old position. During the lorry and train journey we were still quite cheery. We knew what we were wanted for. Then came bivouacs, an "alarm", and we were rushed up through shell-shattered villages and barrage into the turmoil of war. The enemy was firing with 12-inch guns. There was a perfect torrent of shells. Sooner than we expected we were in the thick of it. First in the artillery position. Columns were tearing hither and thither as if possessed. The gunners could no longer see or hear. Very lights were going up along the whole Front, and there was a deafening noise: the cries of wounded, orders, reports.

At noon the gun-fire became even more intense, and then came the order: "The French have broken through. Counter-attack!"

We advanced through the shattered wood in a hail of shells. I don't know how I found the right way. Then across an expanse of shell craters, on and on. Falling down and getting up again. Machine-guns were firing. I had to cut across our own barrage and the enemy's. I am untouched.

At last we reach the front line. Frenchmen are forcing their way in. The tide of battle ebbs and flows. Then things get quieter. We have not fallen back a foot. Now one's eyes begin to see things. I want to keep running on – to stand still and look is horrible. "A wall of dead and wounded!" How often have I read that phrase! Now I know what it means.

I have witnessed scenes of horoism and of weakness. Men who can endure every privation. Being brave is not only a matter of will, it also requires strong nerves, though the will can do a great deal. A Divisional Commander dubbed us the "Iron Brigade" and said he had never seen anything like it. I wish it had all been only a dream, a bad dream. And yet it was a joy to see such heroes stand and fall. The bloody work cost us 177 men. We shall never forget Chaulmes and Vermandovillers.

PROVOCE, EASTERN FRONT: A GERMAN SOLDIER DREAMS OF HOME, 28 August 1916

Adolf Sturmer, German Army

Killed 23 October 1916.

August 28th, 1916.

I often think about Strassburg now. I got really to appreciate and love it for the first time during my last leave at home, in June. I realized for the first time what a beautiful city it is, and felt that it really was my home. I can't understand now how I have managed to ignore its beauties so long. I only knew the Cathedral and the old Kammerzell House. But this time I only needed to walk through the streets or along the Ill Straden to notice wonderful groups of houses, some timbered and covered with ancient carving, and some Gothic, with pointed arches, little towers, stepped gables, and steep roofs like those in Schwind's picture-books. The old black towers past which the Ill flows stand like a row of rugged giants, guarding the city. And then the splendid buildings of the French period! One could hardly keep count of the beautiful houses, as one after another appeared. The buildings in few towns of Germany can be richer in interesting associations, among which shine the names of Gottfried of Strassburg, Tauler and Fischart, Gutenberg, Master Erwin, and Goethe. Strassburg bears witness to the time of Germany's greatest and most beautiful productivity. Why is all that dead and forgotten? Directly we realize it, it seems to revive, and one's home, which was almost unknown before, appears beautiful and lovable. That is what I often dream of nowadays when I am on guard in the trenches or lying, as at this moment, in the camp under the birch-trees.

WESTERN FRONT: THE FIRST TANKS IN ACTION, THE SOMME, 15 September 1916

Bert Chaney, 7th London Territorial Battalion

The menacing rumble of a tank was heard for the first time in warfare when thirty-six British Mark Is were used in an attack on the Somme on 15 September 1916. The Mark I weighed 30 tons and was developed from the agricultural tractor of American engineer Benjamin Holt. Its top speed was 5mph.

We heard strange throbbing noises, and lumbering slowly towards us came three huge mechanical monsters such as we had never seen before. My first impression was that they looked ready to topple on their noses, but their tails and the two little wheels at the back held them down and kept them level. Big metal things they were with two sets of caterpillar wheels that went right round the body. There was a bulge on each side with a door in the bulging part, and machine-guns on swivels poked out from either side. The engine, a petrol engine of massive proportions, occupied practically all the inside space. Mounted behind each door was a motorcycle type of saddle seat and there was just about enough room left for the belts of ammunition and the drivers . . .

Instead of going on to the German lines the three tanks assigned to us straddled our front line, stopped and then opened up a murderous machine-gun fire, enfilading us left and right. There they sat, squat monstrous things, noses stuck up in the air, crushing the sides of our trench out of shape with their machine-guns swivelling around and firing like mad.

Everyone dived for cover, except the colonel. He jumped on top to the parapet, shouting at the top of his voice, "Runner, runner, go tell those tanks to stop firing at once. At once, I say." By now the enemy fire had risen to a crescendo but, giving no thought to his own personal safety as he saw the tanks firing on his own men, he ran forward and furiously rained blows with his cane on the side of one of the tanks in an endeavour to attract their attention.

Although, what with the sounds of the engines and the firing in such an enclosed space, no one in the tank could hear him, they finally realized they were on the wrong trench and moved on, frightening the Jerries out of their wits and making them scuttle like frightened rabbits.

One of the tanks got caught up on a tree stump and never reached their front line and a second had its rear steering wheels shot off and could not guide itself. The crew thought it more prudent to stop, so they told us afterwards, rather than to keep going as they felt they might go out of control and run on until they reached Berlin. The third tank went on and ran through Flers, flattening everything they thought should be flattened, pushing down walls and thoroughly enjoying themselves, our lads coming up behind them, taking over the village, or what was left of it, and digging in on the line prescribed for them before the attack. This was one of the rare occasions when they had passed through the enemy fire and they were enjoying themselves chasing and rounding up the Jerries, collecting thousands of prisoners and sending them back to our lines escorted only by Pioneers armed with shovels.

The four men in the tank that had got itself hung up dismounted, all in the heat of the battle, stretching themselves, scratching their heads, then slowly and deliberately walked round their vehicle inspecting it from every angle and appeared to hold a conference among themselves. After standing around for a few minutes, looking somewhat lost, they calmly took out from the inside of the tank a primus stove and, using the side of the tank as a cover from enemy fire, sat down on the ground and made themselves some tea. The battle was over as far as they were concerned.

WESTERN FRONT: A BLIGHTY ONE, HIGH WOOD, 15 September 1916

Bert Steward, British Army

It was the dream of many a combatant to be injured – not seriously, but seriously enough to be returned home. In the parlance of the British infantryman, such a wound was "a blighty one". Bert Steward received his at High Wood on the Somme.

Zero hour, and my corporal made a little gesture at me, and we got out of the ditch and started to walk. I never saw him again.

Imagine us then rather like overladen porters going slow over a shockingly ploughed field in a man-made thunder storm. Hailstones of a lethal kind zipped past our heads. From behind us the bombardment from our own guns, which I had seen massed wheel to wheel, went on. To left and right men were moving forward in uneven lines. My plan was to walk alone and not get bunched up with others. I kept away from them. I soon found this easier. On each side some had disappeared. I saw only one tank – in a ditch with a broken track, like a dying hippopotamus, with shells bursting round it. I kept walking. I walked about half a mile. I reached the shelter of an embankment. With this solid mass between me and the enemy I felt safe.

The next moment was the luckiest of my life. I had walked all the way through a hail of bullets. I had been a slowly-moving target for the machine guns. The bullets had all missed, though narrowly, for parts of my tunic were in ribbons. Then, just as I had reached safety, as I thought, what seemed like a hammer blow hit me on the top of my left shoulder. I opened my tunic. There was a clean round hole right through the shoulder. A bullet! But where from? Then I realised I was getting enfiladed by some machine-gunner to my right, on my side of the embankment. I threw myself down, but not before another bullet struck my right thigh.

In the embankment was the entrance to a dugout. I crawled into it. It was occupied by Germans. None of them spoke. They were all dead.

There was parcels from home strewn about, cigarettes, black bread, eatables, and one huge German, lying face downwards, made a good couch to sit on. Now I was joined by two friends, one less lucky, a young lad from Liverpool, with a bullet through the stomach.

Here we were, in front of our front line. About a hundred yards back I could see tin hats bobbing about. The remnants of the cast-irons were manning an improvised front line among the shellholes. Beyond them. I thought, was England, home and beauty.

I had taken High Wood, almost by myself, it seemed. I had no further territorial ambitions. Indeed, what I now had in mind was to go as quickly as possible in the opposite direction, as soon as possible. Leaving the dugout, I ran for it, zigzagging to escape bullets (two were enough) and so fast that I toppled head-first on top of a rifleman who was almost as scared as I was. After he had recovered he told me how I could work my way along the line of shellholes to a dressing station. I went, keeping my head down; I was taking no chances. I had two bullet holes. If they had been drilled by a surgeon they could not have been located more conveniently. I was incredibly lucky. But another might spoil everything. I crawled along.

The dressing station was a captured German underground hospital, with entrance big enough for an ambulance, built like a fortress, furnished with tiers of wooden bunks. It was crowded with wounded, now being sorted out by our adjutant.

"Those who can run follow me, nobody with a leg wound," he said. "We have to move fast," I was the first to follow. In and out of shellholes we went – a rough but rapid journey in the right direction – until we reached a sunken lane where a horse-drawn hooded cart waited to take a dozen of us an hour's trot nearer home . . .

The Canadian doctor looked like any other in his white coat. He turned out to be a saint. "You've been very lucky," he said in a kindly way. Then he explained that one bullet, almost incredibly, had found a narrow gap between collar-bone and shoulder-blade, and that neither of the two had touched muscle or bone. "How old are you and how long have you been in the trenches?" he asked and, when I told him, he wrote on a card and gave it to the nurse.

Later I looked up at the card pinned to the chart above my bed. It was marked with a big B. What did it mean? A nurse hurrying by answered my question. She smiled as she said – "It means Blighty."

THE RED BARON CLAIMS HIS FIRST KILL, WESTERN FRONT, 17 September 1916

Rittmeister Manfred von Richthofen, Imperial German Air Service

Von Richtofen was transferred in Summer 1916 from the Eastern Front to the fighter squadron in the West commanded by Oswald Boelcke, one of the pioneers of aerial combat. Von Richtofen's later conceit in painting his "bird" red earned him the soubriquet of "The Red Baron". He claimed 80 kills before his death on 21 April 1918, and was thus the highest-ranking ace of the First World War.

We were all at the butts trying our machine guns. On the previous day we had received our new aeroplanes and the next morning Boelcke was to fly with us. We were all beginners. None of us had had a success so far. Consequently everything that Boelcke told us was to us gospel truth. Every day, during the last few days, he had, as he said, shot one or two Englishmen for breakfast.

The next morning, the seventeenth of September, was a gloriously fine day. It was therefore only to be expected that the English would be very active. Before we started Boelcke repeated to us his instructions and for the first time we flew as a squadron commanded by the great man whom we followed blindly.

We had just arrived at the Front when we recognized a hostile flying squadron that was proceeding in the direction of Cambrai. Boelcke was of course the first to see it, for he saw a great deal more than ordinary mortals. Soon we understood the position and every one of us strove to follow Boelcke closely. It was clear to all of us that we should pass our first examination under the eyes of our beloved leader.

Slowly we approached the hostile squadron. It could not escape us. We had intercepted it, for we were between the Front and our opponents. If they wished to go back they had to pass us. We counted the hostile machines. They were seven in number.

We were only five. All the Englishmen flew large bomb-carrying two-seaters. In a few seconds the dance would begin.

Boelcke had come very near the first English machine but he did not yet shoot. I followed. Close to me were my comrades. The Englishman nearest to me was traveling in a large boat painted with dark colours. I did not reflect very long but took my aim and shot. He also fired and so did I, and both of us missed our aim. A struggle began and the great point for me was to get to the rear of the fellow because I could only shoot forward with my gun. He was differently placed for his machine gun was movable. It could fire in all directions.

Apparently he was no beginner, for he knew exactly that his last hour had arrived at the moment when I got at the back of him. At that time I had not yet the conviction "He must fall!" which I have now on such occasions, but on the contrary, I was curious to see whether he would fall. There is a great difference between the two feelings. When one has shot down one's first, second or third opponent, then one begins to find out how the trick is done.

My Englishman twisted and turned, going criss-cross. I did not think for a moment that the hostile squadron contained other Englishmen who conceivably might come to the aid of their comrade. I was animated by a single thought: "The man in front of me must come down, whatever happens." At last a favourable moment arrived. My opponent had apparently lost sight of me. Instead of twisting and turning he flew straight along. In a fraction of a second I was at his back with my excellent machine. I give a short series of shots with my machine gun. I had gone so close that I was afraid I might dash into the Englishman. Suddenly, I nearly yelled with joy for the propeller of the enemy machine had stopped turning. I had shot his engine to pieces; the enemy was compelled to land, for it was impossible for him to reach his own lines. The English machine was curiously swinging to and fro. Probably something had happened to the pilot. The observer was no longer visible. His machine gun was apparently deserted. Obviously I had hit the observer and he had fallen from his seat.

The Englishman landed close to the flying ground of one of our squadrons. I was so excited that I landed also and my eagerness was so great that I nearly smashed up my machine.

The English flying machine and my own stood close together. I rushed to the English machine and saw that a lot of soldiers were running towards my enemy. When I arrived I discovered that my assumption had been correct. I had shot the engine to pieces and both the pilot and observer were severely wounded. The observer died at once and the pilot while being transported to the nearest dressing station. I honoured the fallen enemy by placing a stone on his beautiful grave.

When I came home Boelcke and my other comrades were already at breakfast. They were surprised that I had not turned up. I reported proudly that I had shot down an Englishman. All were full of joy for I was not the only victor. As usual, Boelcke had shot down an opponent for breakfast and every one of the other men also had downed an enemy for the first time.

THE SOMME: THE BRITISH SECRETARY OF STATE FOR WAR SURVEYS THE BATTLEFIELD, 18–19 September 1916

David Lloyd George, Secretary of State for War

It is claimed that the battle of the Somme destroyed the old German Army by killing off its best officers and men. It killed off far more of our best and of the French best. The battle of the Somme was fought by the volunteer armies raised in 1914 and 1915. These contained the choicest and best of our young manhood. The officers were drawn mainly from our public schools and universities. Over 400,000 of our men fell in this bull-headed fight and the slaughter amongst our young officers was appalling . . .

Had it not been for the inexplicable stupidity of the Germans in provoking a quarrel with America and bringing that mighty people into the War against them just as they had succeeded in eliminating another powerful foe – Russia – the Somme would not have saved us from an inextricable stalemate . . .

Whilst the French generals and our own were reporting victory after victory against the German Army on the Western Front; whilst our Intelligence Departments at the front were assuring their Chiefs, and through them, their Governments at home, that five-sixths of the German divisions had been hammered to pulp and that the remaining divisions would soon be reduced to the same state, the German General Staff were detaching several divisions from the battle area in France and sending them to the Carpathians to join the Austrians and Bulgarians in an attack on Roumania. No one on the Allied side seemed to have anticipated this move – at least, no one made any plans to counter it, if and when it came. The whole mind of the western strategists was concentrated on one or other of the hamlets along the Somme. They exaggerated the effect of every slight advance, and worked themselves into a belief that the Germans were so pulvetized by these attacks that they had not the men, the guns, nor the spirit to fight anywhere much longer. They were only waiting, with hand cupped to ear, for the crack which would signify the final break of the German barrier, and they were massing cavalry immediately behind the French and British battle line in order to complete the rout of the tattered remains of the German Army. This is no exaggeration of their illusions. I saw them at this moment of exaltation.

When the battle of the Somme was being fought, I traversed the front from Verdun to Ypres. With M. Albert Thomas I visited General Haig at his Headquarters, and with him I drove to General Cavan's Headquarters to meet General Joffre. The latter and M. Thomas were anxious to secure a number of six-inch howitzers for the French Front. We had followed the advice given by the young French artillery officer at the Boulogne Conference and manufactured these howitzers on a great scale, with a view to concentrating a plunging fire to demolish the enemy trenches. The French had gone in more for the long-range gun, and they were short of howitzers.

When we reached General Cavan's quarters there was a heavy bombardment going on from our eight-inch howitzers assembled in the valley below, known to the soldiers as the Happy Valley. The roar of the guns beneath and the shrill "keen" of the shells overhead were deafening. We could hardly carry on a conversation. We found the noises were worse inside Lord Cavan's quarters than outside. After we had arranged the matter of the howitzers we got on to a general talk about the offensive. Both Generals – Joffre and Haig – were elated with the successes already achieved.

On my way to this rendezvous I had driven through squadrons of cavalry clattering proudly to the front. When I asked what they were for, Sir Douglas Haig explained that they were brought up as near the front line as possible, so as to be ready to charge through the gap which was to be made by the Guards in the coming attack. The cavalry were to exploit the anticipated success and finish the German rout.

The Guards could be seen marching in a long column through the valley on their way to the front line preparatory to the attack. Raymond Asquith was amongst them. Before I reached Ypres I heard that the attack had failed and that the brilliant son of the British Prime Minister was amongst the fallen. When I ventured to express to Generals Joffre and Haig my doubts as to whether cavalry could ever operate successfully on a front bristling for miles behind the enemy line with barbed wire and machine-guns, both Generals fell ecstatically on me, and Joffre in particular explained that he expected the French cavalry to ride through the broken German lines on his front the following morning. You could hear the distant racket of the massed guns of France which were at that moment tearing a breach for the French horsemen. Just then a Press photographer, of whose presence we were all unaware, snapped us.

The conversation gave me an idea of the exaltation produced in brave men by a battle. They were quite incapable of looking beyond and around or even through the struggle just in front of them . . .

"LIKE A RUINED STAR FALLING SLOWLY TO EARTH": THE END OF ZEPPELIN L31, LONDON, 1 October 1916

Michael MacDonagh

I saw last night what is probably the most appalling spectacle associated with the war which London is likely to provide – the bringing down in flames of a raiding Zeppelin.

I was late at the office, and leaving it just before midnight was crossing to Blackfriars Bridge to get a tramcar home, when my attention was attracted by frenzied cries of "Oh! Oh! She's hit!" from some wayfarers who were standing in the middle of the road gazing at the sky in a northern direction. Looking up the clear run of New Bridge Street and Farringdon Road I saw high in the sky a concentrated blaze of searchlights, and in its centre a ruddy glow which rapidly spread into the outline of a blazing airship. Then the searchlights were turned off and the Zeppelin drifted perpendicularly in the darkened sky, a gigantic pyramid of flames, red and orange, like a ruined star falling slowly to earth. Its glare lit up the streets and gave a ruddy tint even to the waters of the Thames.

The spectacle lasted two or three minutes. It was so horribly fascinating that I felt spellbound – almost suffocated with emotion, ready hysterically to laugh or cry. When at last the doomed airship vanished from sight there arose a shout the like of which I never heard in London before – a hoarse shout of mingled execration, triumph and joy; a swelling shout that appeared to be rising from all parts of the metropolis, ever increasing in force and intensity. It was London's *Te Deum* for another crowning deliverance. Four Zeppelins destroyed in a month! . . .

On getting to the office this morning I was ordered off to Potter's Bar, Middlesex, where the Zeppelin had been brought down, about thirteen miles from London. These days trains are infrequent and travel slowly as a war economy. The journey from King's Cross was particularly tedious. The train I caught was packed. My compartment had its twenty seats occupied and ten more passengers found standing room in it. The weather, too, was abominable. Rain fell persistently. We had to walk the two miles to the place where the Zeppelin fell, and over the miry roads and sodden fields hung a thick, clammy mist . . .

I got from a member of the Potter's Bar anti-aircraft battery an account of the bringing down of the Zeppelin. He said the airship was caught in the beams of three searchlights from stations miles apart, and was being fired at by three batteries also from distances widely separated. She turned and twisted, rose and fell, in vain attempts to escape to the shelter of the outer darkness. None of the shells reached her. Then an aeroplane appeared and dropped three flares – the signal to the ground batteries to cease firing as he was about to attack. The airman, flying about the Zeppelin, let go rounds of machine-gun fire at her without effect, until one round fired into her from beneath set her on fire, and down she came a blazing mass, roaring like a furnace, breaking as she fell into two parts which were held together by internal cables until they reached the ground.

The framework of the Zeppelin lay in the field in two enormous heaps, separated from each other by about a hundred yards. Most of the forepart hung suspended from a tree . . .

The crew numbered nineteen. One body was found in the field some distance from the wreckage. He must have jumped from the doomed airship from a considerable height. So great was the force with which he struck the ground that I saw the imprint of his body clearly defined in the stubbly grass. There was a round hole for the head, then deep impressions of the trunk, with outstretched arms, and finally the widely separated legs. Life was in him when he was picked up, but the spark soon went out. He was, in fact, the Commander, who had been in one of the gondolas hanging from the airship . . .

With another journalist I went to the barn where the bodies lay. As we approached we heard a woman say to the sergeant of the party of soldiers in charge, "May I go in? I would like to see a dead German." "No, madam, we cannot admit ladies," was the reply. Introducing myself as a newspaper reporter, I made the same request. The sergeant said to me, "If you particularly wish to go in you may. I would, however, advise you not to do so. If you do you will regret your curiosity." I persisted in my request . . .

Explaining to the sergeant that I particularly wanted to see the body of the Commander, I was allowed to go in. The sergeant removed the covering from one of the bodies which lay apart from the others. The only disfigurement was a slight distortion of the face. It was that of a young man, clean-shaven. He was heavily clad in a dark uniform and overcoat, with a thick muffler round his neck.

I knew who he was. At the office we had had official information of the identity of the Commander and the airship (though publication of both particulars was prohibited), and it was this knowledge that had determined me to see the body. The dead man was Heinrich Mathy, the most renowned of the

German airship commanders, and the perished airship was his redoubtable L31. Yes, there he lay in death at my feet, the bugaboo of the Zeppelin raids, the first and most ruthless of these Pirates of the Air bent on our destruction.

RUMANIA: THE MOUNTAIN WAR, October 1916

Hans Carossa, Rumanian Army Medical Corps

The flashy sucesses of the Russian Brusilov offensive encouraged Rumania to enter the war on the side of the Allies on 27th August 1916. Less than four months later, the poorly equipped – if vast – Rumanian army had been defeated by a hurricane of fast-moving, hard-hitting German arms.

Our road was now continuously uphill. The adjutant said it was only about ten miles to the trenches, but we heard no firing. The pine trees became sparser, and juniper, rich with violet-green berries, grew luxuriantly among the crags. We came on rows of graves which from the inscriptions could only have been five days old. Carp, a Roumanian lieutenant, was the name on one of the wooden crosses. Towards two o'clock we traversed a bare hollow streaked with mist, and saw a terrible and bewildering spectacle. Where a solitary house in the middle had been burned down, the embers were still smoking. The blackened walls were still standing, and one could see that they had been of the usual blue; but nothing was left of the roof save its charred ribs. Behind a wooden shed untouched by the fire lay two graves without crosses but decked with juniper; and a tall, very old woman, naked to the waist, with Magyar features, her grey hair wild and filthy, glided round and round the two hummocks talking confidentially to an invisible something. As we came nearer she drew herself up and made a forbidding gesture with her hand as if to warn us from the place; then she suddenly turned away and wrung her hands towards the east with a piercing wail. Trusting to his smattering of Hungarian, Lieutenant F. tried to speak to her, but she bent down, gathered a handful of earth from the nearest grave and flung it at him, more as an exorcism and a warning than as a hostile act. Half in vexation, half in horror, Lieutenant F. started back and returned to the column. None of the other officers or men halted. They did, indeed, wonder aloud what could have happened to the old woman; but most of them felt that here a tragedy had taken place which no facile sympathy could alleviate, and went on marching silently into the mists which soon blotted out the terrible grandeur of the scene.

The mountain we climbed was a mountain of blindness and death. From the eastern slope, where the battle was not yet decided, wild cries rang through the rattle of the musketry; and up here, in the position we had captured, the enemy were wreaking their vengeance on the conquerors. Like a swarm of hornets the shells dashed against the rocks, tearing the flesh from the limbs of the living and the dead. Sometimes German wounded called to us, sometimes Roumanian, who were now being mutilated for a second time by the fire of their comrades. Some of them suffered in silence; others twisted like wounded snakes. Through the zone of death we saw Germans lightly wounded descending the mountain, a few white and shaken, but others walking jauntily, dressed up as if for a fancy-dress ball in the gay-coloured belts, jackets and military decorations of their dead enemies. One had brought back a gramophone with him from the Roumanian lines; now an idea suddenly struck him, he placed it on a stone and set it going, the page in *Figaro* began to sing, and like the voice of a mad soul Mozart's music rose in a world of ruin. The despatch orderly Glavina was leaning against a granite block near the commander's dug-out; he was still breathing, but on his face was already the prescient look of the dead. We could see no trace of blood. Fighting down our sorrow and apprehension, we searched for the wound and found at last a tiny splinter driven into the nape of the neck. Soon his breathing ceased. A few closely written sheets of paper, which must have fallen out of his pocket, I took with me to hand over to the adjutant; but I noticed on the way back that they did not contain anything official, so I kept them beside me for the time being. We told the major that the Bosnian stretcher-bearers who had been arranged for had not yet come; he promised to communicate with the Division and sent us back to Hallesul.

Meanwhile the sky had darkened; snow began to fall. A flowing white veil shut off the guns from the targets they were firing at; one after another they fell silent, and we descended almost in safety. A Roumanian stretched between two birch trunks lay across my path; I thought he was dead and was stepping over him, when I heard a groan and felt a feeble but perceptible tug at my cloak. Turning round, I looked down on the dying face of a man of about thirty; his eyes were closed, his mouth terribly twisted with pain. His fingers still clutched the fast hem of my cloak. Through a grey cape which covered his breast a slight vapour was rising. R. threw it back; under his torn ribs his lungs and heart lay exposed, the heart beating sluggishly. A number of silver and copper medals of saints, which he had been wearing on a black ribbon round his neck, were driven deep into his flesh, some of them much bent. We covered him up again. The man half-opened his eyes, his lips moved. Simply for the sake of doing something I filled my morphia syringe, and then I saw that this was what he seemed to want: he pushed the cloak aside and tried to stretch out his arm to me in readiness – behaviour hard to account for in a man already almost dead! But perhaps there is an infinitely keen, infinitely poignant anguish which a man conscious of approaching death desires to be rid of at any price, because it holds him fast to life in burning pain and hinders a free and clean parting: who knows? After the injection he laid his head back against the birch almost in comfort and closed his eyes, in whose deep sockets large snowflakes were already beginning to fall.

At daybreak rifle-firing, which soon fell silent. After sunrise the overcast sky cleared; one could see behind a transparent veil of cloud the waning moon like an embryonic golden shape. The stretcher-bearers have come, and in relays all the wounded are being carried away. Pirkl must remain here; his pulse is almost imperceptible and he would most probably reach Oitóz as a corpse. His brother had obtained an hour's leave to visit him. As Pirkl cannot speak any longer his brother is employing his time in digging a grave for the still living man, and carving a cross, on which he is very carefully printing in blue pencil the name of the fallen.

"CITY OF BEAUTIFUL NONSENSE": A BRITISH JOURNALIST AT GENERAL HEADQUARTERS, FRANCE, 1916

Philip Gibbs, war correspondent

I came to know G.H.Q. more closely when it removed for fresher air to Montreuil, a fine old walled town, once within sight of the sea, which ebbed over the low-lying ground below its hill, but now looking across a wide vista of richly cultivated fields where many hamlets are scattered among clumps of trees. One came to G.H.Q. from journeys over the wild desert of the battle-fields, where men lived in ditches and "pill-boxes", muddy, miserable in all things but spirit, as to a place where the pageantry of war still maintained its old and dead tradition. It was like one of those pageants which used to be played in England before the War, picturesque, romantic, utterly unreal. It was as though men were playing at war here, while others, sixty miles away, were fighting and dying, in mud and gas-waves and explosive barrages.

An "Open Sesame", by means of a special pass, was needed to enter this City of Beautiful Nonsense. Below the gateway, up the steep hillside, sentries stood at white posts across the road, which lifted up on pulleys when the pass had been examined by a military policeman in a red cap. Then the sentries slapped their hands to their rifles to the occupants of any motor car, sure that more staff-officers were going in to perform those duties which no private soldier could attempt to understand, believing they belonged to such mysteries as those of God. Through the narrow streets walked elderly generals, middle-aged colonels and majors, youthful sub-alterns all wearing red hatbands, red tabs, and the blue-and-red armlet of G.H.Q., so that colour went with them on their way.

Often one saw the Commander-in-Chief [Douglas Haig] starting for an afternoon ride, a fine figure, nobly mounted, with two A.D.C.'s and an escort of Lancers. A pretty sight, with fluttering pennons and all their lances, and horses groomed to the last hair. It was prettier than the real thing up in the Salient or beyond the Somme, where dead bodies lay in upheaved earth among ruins and slaughtered trees. War at Montreuil was quite a pleasant occupation for elderly generals who liked their little stroll after lunch, and for young Regular officers, released from the painful necessity of dying for their country, who were glad to get a game of tennis down below the walls there, after strenuous office work in which they had written "Passed to you" on many "minutes", or had drawn the most comical caricatures of their immediate chief, and of his immediate chief, on blotting pads or writing-blocks.

It seemed at a mere glance, that all these military inhabitants of G.H.Q. were great and glorious soldiers. Some of the youngest of them had a row of decorations, from Montenegro, Serbia, Italy, Roumania, and other States, as recognition of gallant service in translating German letters (found in dug-outs by the fighting men), or arranging for visits of political personages to the back areas of war, or initialling requisitions for pink, blue, green, and yellow forms which in due course would find their way to battalion adjutants for immediate filling-up in the middle of an action. The oldest of them, those white-haired, bronze-faced, grey-eyed generals in the administrative side of war, had started their third row of ribbons well before the end of the Somme battles, and had flower borders on their breasts by the time the massacres had been accomplished in the fields of Flanders. I know an officer who was awarded the D.S.O. because he hindered the work of industrious men with the zeal of a hedge-sparrow in search of worms, and another who was the best decorated man in the army because he had presided over a visitors' château and entertained royalties, Members of Parliament, Mrs Humphry Ward, miners, Japanese, Russian revolutionaries, Portuguese ministers, Harry Lauder, Swedes, Danes, Norwegians, clergymen, Montenegrins, and the Editor of *John Bull*, at the Government's expense – and I am bound to say he deserved them all, being a man of infinite tact, many languages and a devastating sense of humour. There was always a Charlie Chaplin film between moving pictures of the Battles of the Somme. He brought the actualities of war to the vistiors' château, by sentry boxes outside the door, a toy tank in the front garden, and a collection of war trophies in the hall. He spoke to high personages with less deference than he showed to miners from Durham and Wales, and was master of them always, ordering them sternly to bed at ten o'clock (when he sat down to bridge with his junior officers), and with strict military discipline insisting upon their inspection of the bakeries at Boulogne, and boot-mending factories at Calais, as part of the glory of war which they had come out for to see.

So it was that there were brilliant colours in the streets of Montreuil and at every doorway a sentry slapped his hand to his rifle, with smart and untiring iteration, as the Brains of the Army, under brass hats and red bands, went hither and thither in the town, looking stern, as soldiers of grave responsibility, answering salutes absent-mindedly, staring haughtily at young battalion officers who passed through Montreuil and looked meekly for a chance of a lorry-ride at Boulogne, on seven days' leave from the lines.

The smart society of G.H.Q. was best seen at the Officers' Club in Montreuil, at dinner-time. It was as much like musical comedy as any stage setting of war at the Gaiety. A band played ragtime and light music while the warriors fed, and all these generals and staff officers, with their decorations and arm-bands and polished buttons, and crossed swords, were waited upon by little W.A.A.C.'s with the G.H.Q. colours tied up in bows on their hair. Such a chatter! such bursts of light-hearted laughter! such whisperings of secrets and intrigues and scandals in high places! such careless-hearted courage when British soldiers were being blown to bits, gassed, blinded, maimed and shell-shocked in places that were far – so very far – from G.H.Q.!

GHQ: A DEFENCE, 1916

Brigadier-General J. Charteris, General Headquarters Staff Officer

Here at G.H.Q. . . . nearly every one of the ramifications of civil law and life has its counterpart in the administration departments. Food supply, road and rail transport, law and order, engineering, medical work, the Church, education, postal service, even agriculture, and for a population bigger than any single unit of control (except London) in England. Can you imagine what it is to feed, administer, move about, look after the medical and spiritual requirements of a million men, even when they are not engaged in fighting, and not in a foreign country? . . . The work goes on continuously; office hours are far longer than of any civilian office in peacetime. There are few, if any, officers who do not do a fourteen-hour day, and who are not to be found at work far into the night.

RUSSIA: A DEMONSTRATION AGAINST THE ALLIES, 31 October 1916

Maurice Paleologue, French Ambassador to the Court of Nicholas II

War-weariness and food shortages caused disorders throughout many Russian cities in the autumn of 1916. They were the heralds of the Revolution of 1917.

For the last two days all the factories in Petrograd have been on strike. The workmen left the shops without giving any reason, and simply on an order issued by some mysterious committee . . .

Two French industrialists, Sicaut and Beaupied, were asking to see me. They are representatives of the "Louis Renault" motor-car house and in charge of a large factory in the Viborg quarter.

I received them at once. They said to me:

"*Monsieur l'Ambassadeur*, you know we've never had anything but praise for our workpeople, because they've never had anything but praise for us. So they've refused to join in the general strike. While work was in full swing this afternoon, a party of strikers from the Baranovsky works besieged our establishment, shouting: 'Down with the French! No more war!' Our engineers and foremen wanted to parley with them. They were received with stones and revolver shots. One French engineer and three French foremen were seriously wounded. The police had meanwhile arrived, and soon realized that they could not cope with the situation. A squad of gendarmes then succeeded in forcing a way through the crowd, and went to fetch two infantry regiments which are in barracks quite near. The two regiments appeared a few minutes later, but instead of raising the siege of our factory they fired on the police."

"On the police!"

"Yes, *Monsieur l'Ambassadeur*; you can see the bullet marks on our walls . . . A number of *gorodovoi* [*policemen*] and gendarmes were killed. A standup fight followed. At length we heard the gallop of the Cossacks, four regiments of them. They charged the infantrymen and drove them back to their barracks at the point of the lance. Order has now been restored."

LLOYD GEORGE BECOMES PRIME MINISTER, LONDON, 5–6 December 1916

Viscount Herbert Samuel, Home Secretary

Growing dissatisfaction over the British conduct of the war came to a head in December 1916 when the Asquith Government was replaced by one headed by Lloyd George. It was this government, one dedicated to a more vigorous war effort, which went on to win the conflict.

December 5th, 1916. Home Office, Whitehall, S.W.

On the evening of Monday, December 4th [1916], the Prime Minister [Asquith] asked me to come to Downing Street, where were also Grey, McKenna, Harcourt and Runciman. Henderson came in later. The P.M. explained Lloyd George's proposals, which were in effect that the War Committee of the Cabinet should consist of Ll.G., Bonar Law, Carson and Henderson, that the P.M. should see its agenda before its meetings, have a veto on its decisions, and, while not usually attending its sittings, have the right to be present when he wished. He asked me, when I came in, whether I thought his acceptance would be an abdication of his position and be inconsistent with his responsibilities. I said I thought it would. The others were all of the same opinion. I expressed the view that the country desired both the P.M. and Ll.G. to be in the Government, and that if the latter went, the Government would be greatly weakened in the eyes of the country and of the Allies. At the same time Ll.G.'s proposals were quite unacceptable. All the Liberal Ministers advised the P.M. that the right course would be for him to resign and throw upon Ll.G. the duty of forming an administration, the present position being intolerable, and a crisis sure to recur at short intervals. The P.M. expressed no final view, but said he feared that if a Ll.G.-Carson Government was formed Labour would break away, and the pacifist movement would become formidable. But he was not prepared to agree to terms which would lead to a demand for fresh surrenders. Grey and Runciman were strongly for immediate resignation, and the rest concurred. We were told that the Unionist members of the Cabinet had tendered their resignations the day before, but in no unfriendly spirit and in the belief that to put the possibility of a Ll.G. Government to the test was the only way to place matters on a sound footing.

At five on Tuesday, December 5th, all the Liberal members of the Cabinet met again – Asquith, Grey, McKenna, Buckmaster, Runciman, Harcourt, McKinnon Wood, Tennant, Montagu, H.S.; Henderson was also there. The P.M. read us the letter he had written the night before to Ll.G., refusing his terms, and Ll.G.'s letter of resignation received that afternoon. He also told us that Curzon, Austen Chamberlain and R. Cecil had been with him an hour that afternoon and had urged that the only course was the resignation of the whole Government. Later on a letter from Bonar Law was brought to us by Carson, to the effect that all the Unionist members of the Cabinet held that view, that they hoped the P.M. had arrived at the same conclusion, but that if not they desired their resignations to become effective. The P.M. had also read us correspondence with Balfour, who was ill, in which he resigned the office of First Lord of the Admiralty.

The P.M. said that he could not accept Ll.G.'s proposals for a War Committee, partly because the position suggested for himself was inconsistent with his tenure of the office of P.M., partly because the suggested personnel of the Committee would render it a most inefficient body, unless it was to be no more than a cloak for one-man control. He foresaw grave evils from a change of administration, because it would mean a divided nation at home, and because himself and Grey being so definitely identified with the war from the outset, the effect upon the Allies would be bad. (Grey did not concur in this, as Ll.G. equally personified the policy of carrying the war on to victory). He also foresaw that a general election might be the outcome, and this would be a great disaster. He evidently did not like the surrender to a minister in revolt that was involved by resignation. However, we were all strongly of opinion, from which he did not dissent, that there was no alternative. We could not in any case carry on without Ll.G. and without the Unionists, and ought not to give the appearance of wishing to do so. The resignation should take effect to-night. This was agreed, and Curzon who had come in at the end of the Conference was so informed.

December 6th, 1916. Home Office, Whitehall, S.W.

In the morning I went to see Asquith at 10 Downing Street to tell him that there was no foundation for the statement which had appeared in *The Times, Daily News* and *Manchester Guardian* that I would be willing to separate myself from him and my Liberal colleagues and take office under Bonar Law or Lloyd George. I said that in no circumstances would I serve under the latter and that if the former invited me to take office, I should like to consult him and others when the pros and cons would have to be considered. But I had heard no suggestion of anything of the kind from anyone and had discussed it with no one. I was at a loss to know how the paragraphs had originated. Asquith said that he would certainly not dissuade any of his colleagues from serving in a Coalition Govt. under a Unionist Prime Minister.

At 5.15 a conference was held at Downing St. of the Liberal members of the Cabinet. Henderson was also present. Asquith had been at the Palace where the King had made an attempt to reconcile differences. He had summoned Asquith, Bonar Law, Balfour, Lloyd George and Henderson to confer. The outcome was a suggestion that Law should form a Govt. and that Asquith should serve in it. He wanted our opinion on that. Henderson strongly supported it, but all the Liberals were definitely against it. In the first place, the Govt. would really be a Lloyd George Govt. and all the old difficulties would recur. It was much better that L.G. should be the ostensible as well as the real head of the Government, should have with him people who would trust him, and should show what he could do or not do. Secondly, if Asquith were absorbed as a unit in such a Govt. his influence would disappear. Outside it, his influence would remain. Under his leadership we should form a possible alternative Govt. which it was to the interest of the country to have.

Asquith took the same view and wrote to Bonar Law to decline his invitation.

THE POOR BLOODY INFANTRY: AN OFFICER'S VIEW, WESTERN FRONT, 14 December 1916

Captain Rowland Feilding, 3rd Battalion, Coldstream Guards

A letter to his wife.

December 14*th*, 1916.

I have for many weeks past been working to get some good company sergeant-majors out from home. One in particular, I have been trying for – a Sergeant-Major McGrath, reputed to have been the best at Kinsale. His commanding officer very kindly agreed to send him to me, although he wrote that he regretted parting with him. McGrath arrived the day after I returned from leave, and within half an hour of his reaching the fire-trench was lying dead, a heavy trench-mortar bomb having fallen upon him, killing him and two others, and wounding two more. Now, is not that a case of hard luck "chasing" a man, when you consider how long others of us last? I never even saw him alive.

I visited the fire-trench just after the bomb had fallen. It had dropped into the trench, and the sight was not a pleasant one. It was, moreover, aggravated by the figure of one of the dead, who had been blown out of the trench on to the parapet, and was silhouetted grotesquely against the then darkening sky.

But what I saw was inspiring, nevertheless. The sentries stood like statues. At the spot where the bomb had burst – within forty yards of the Germans – officers and men were already hard at work in the rain, quietly repairing the damage done to our trench, and clearing away the remains of the dead; all – to outward appearance – oblivious to the possibility – indeed the probability – of further trouble from the trench-mortar, trained upon this special bit of trench, that had fired the fatal round.

What wonderful people are our infantry! And what a joy it is to be with them! When I am here I feel – well, I can hardly describe it. I feel, if it were possible, that one should never go away from them: and I contrast that scene which I have described (at 1s. 1d. a day) with what I see and hear in England when I go on leave. My God! I can only say: "May the others be forgiven!" How it can be possible that these magnificent fellows, going home for a few days after ten months of this (and practically none get home in less), should be waylaid at Victoria Station, as they are, and exploited, and done out of the hard-earned money they have saved through being in the trenches, and with which they are so lavish, baffles my comprehension. It is unthinkable: and that, I think, is the opinion of most officers who go on leave.

I can never express in writing what I feel about the men in the trenches; and nobody who has not seen them can ever understand. According to the present routine, we stay in the front line eight days and nights; then go out for the same period. Each company spends four days and four nights in the fire-trench before being relieved. The men are practically without rest. They are wet through much of the time. They are shelled and trench-mortared. They may not be hit, but they are kept in a perpetual state of unrest and strain. They work all night and every night, and a good part of each day, digging and filling sandbags, and repairing the breeches in the breastworks; that is when they are not on sentry. The temperature is icy. They have not even a blanket. The last two days it has been snowing. They cannot move more than a few feet from their posts: therefore, except when they are actually digging, they cannot keep themselves warm by exercise; and when they try to sleep, they freeze. At present, they are getting a tablespoon of rum to console them, once in three days.

Think of these things, and compare them with what are considered serious hardships in normal life! Yet these men play their part uncomplainingly. That is to say, they never complain seriously. Freezing, or snowing, or drenching rain; always smothered with mud; you may ask any one of them, any moment of the day or night: "Are you cold?" or "Are you wet?" – and you will get but one answer. The Irishman will reply – always with a smile – "Not too cold, sir," or "Not too wet, sir." It makes me feel sick. It makes me think I never want to see the British Isles again so long as the War lasts. It makes one feel ashamed for these Irishmen, and also of those fellow-countrymen of our own, earning huge wages, yet for ever clamouring for more; striking, or threatening to strike; while the country is engaged upon this murderous struggle. Why, we ask here, has not the whole nation, civil as well as military, been conscripted?

The curious thing is that all seem so much more contented here than the people at home. The poor Tommy, shivering in the trenches, is happier than the beast who makes capital out of the War. Everybody laughs at everything here. It is the only way.

"THE DREGS OF ENGLAND": LIFE IN THE LABOUR CORPS, 1916–17

Captain Roger Pocock, 178th Labour Company

Created in late 1916 the Labour Corps of the British Army consisted of men unfit for combat who, by carrying out "garrison duties", released others for frontline service.

It was just after Christmas, 1916, that I was ordered to report at Taunton, where I found myself to be one of four platoon commanders, mobilizing a Labour Company. When we had worked our heads off for three days, the Officer Commanding turned up and was turned down. So I was given the command, my Captaincy, and France.

For young and able-bodied men it was their right to serve in the fighting line, but for us of the Labour Corps, the aged, the disabled, the wreckage of the army and of the nation, it was a privilege to be allowed within the danger areas. The coloured men of the Labour Corps were young, with thrice our strength, but they were not permitted as we were within the range of shells. Almost every man in my five hundred had been disabled, or claimed some mortal disease and gloried in it. We were an amazing mixture of volunteers up to seventy years of age, of conscripts drawn from sedentary life, of Jews from the slums, and gipsies from the highways, roughs, tramps, company directors, public entertainers, pavement artists, navvies, rich, poor, destitute, but all of us alike, rated unfit. Nobody as yet seems to have thought it worth while to tell the story of the dregs of England put to the test of war.

The parade was not so bad, the marching fairly good, the entraining free from muddle, there were no absentees. Crossing from Southampton to Boulogne, the weather being rather rough, men were perhaps too sea-sick to care about mines or torpedoes. We did not like the Base Wallahs at Boulogne, with plenty of decorations and no manners, but all went well in the night-train to Hazebrouck, and in the morning we marched about three miles to a couple of farms assigned to us as a billet. I think it would have been still nicer if the decorated Base Wallahs had mentioned to the Second Army that we might need food, fuel, blankets, while the snow drove through our barns before a yelling gale. In the morning we found two men dead.

On each highway I posted an officer, with orders to stop all army vehicles, plunder them, and turn them loose to report the robbery with the utmost possible speed. Meanwhile, I tramped through the drifts to Hazebrouck, found a telephone, and made its ears burn with the whole vocabulary of the Wild West. Would the Authorities send rations, or should I slaughter cows to feed my men? What with my perfect frankness and one or two highway robberies, we got fuel that morning, rations in the afternoon, indignant Staff Officers in the evening, and the next day a medical inspection which invalided a score of men to Blighty. Then transport arrived in force, and we were carried to the finest camp in Flanders. It was a prisoner-of-war camp evacuated in haste, because the German Government objected to its nationals being under shell-fire, and threatened reprisals upon British captives. We did not mind the shells which screamed overhead, addressed to Poperinghe, but we did like the hot baths, the comfortable stoves, the luxurious rations, and most of all the kindness of Captain Wallace, the Staff Officer in charge of our affairs. We had left behind us the areas of harsh discourtesy.

Our work was unloading trains, building light railways, or mending roads which shells had made untidy; and steadily our invalids gained in strength from outdoor living, good food, and moderate labour. I am told that under gusts of shell-fire the Chinese and Negro Companies had panicked so badly that they had to be withdrawn; but our men would walk to the nearest cover, smoke cigarettes, and watch the shelling with interest while they rested. The spell improved their work; but of much greater value was their interest in the drum-fire, in the movements of troops, in the aerial dog-fights overhead, in the burning of kite balloons and parachute descents, but most especially in the processions of German prisoners, to whom they would give the whole of their cigarettes. Interest in the army led to pride in the Service, eagerness to help, a sporting rivalry between platoons, and the discovery that the 178th Labour Company was not to be beaten by any sort of unit in the field.

When a strange Staff Officer came to inspect our camp with a view to taking it over for a General, I had grave misgivings, realised when I received a Movement Order. "At noon, your unit will move to M36b48, where a Guide will meet you at 2 p.m., conducting you to your destination. Acknowledge." The point of the joke was that the number of the map sheet was not mentioned, nor had I any maps, nor had the order arrived until three hours after my time of departure. I took that as a test, and sent off my three officers at the double to beg, to borrow, or if possible to steal maps while the men had their dinner. So that is how we found M36b48, and were conducted to Toronto Camp. The place was famous for rats. They went catting, and got my cat. They bit the sergeant-major's ear, an act of unheard-of insolence. The men tried poison gas, and smoked out the officers' mess while we sat at dinner. I used to ask all adjacent Staff Officers and even mere unit commanders, to my ratting parties. But that reminds me of the mess at dinner on an evening of steady downpour, when I heard a nightingale singing in the rain. That was unusual, but when a skylark followed I sent an officer to make inquiries about an event not foreshadowed in King's Regulations. In due course it was reported that Private So-and-so, who was So-and-so the eminent Bird Impersonator, was perched on a waggon, giving his entertaiment.

GERMANY: NEW YEAR'S MESSAGE TO THE ARMY AND NAVY, 31 December 1916

Emperor Wilhelm II

To My Army and My Navy!
Once more a war year lies behind us, replete with hard fighting and sacrifices, rich in successes and victories.

Our enemies' hopes for the year 1916 have been blasted. All their assaults in the East and West were broken to pieces through your bravery and devotion!

The latest triumphal march through Rumania has, by God's decree, again pinned imperishable laurels to your standards.

The greatest naval battle of this war, the Skager Rak victory, and the bold exploits of the U-boats have assured to My Navy glory and admiration for all time.

You are victorious on all theatres of war, ashore as well as afloat!

With unshaken trust and proud confidence the grateful Father-land regards you. The incomparable warlike spirit dwelling in your ranks, your tenacious, untiring will to victory, your love for the Fatherland are guarantees to Me that victory will remain with our colours in the new year also.

God will be with us further!

Main Headquarters, December 31, 1916.

Wilhelm.

Part Four

1917

To all U-boats – Sink on Sight

Kaiser Wilhelm, February 1917

INTRODUCTION

The First World War was definitely lost for Germany on the winter's day of 9 January 1917, when the Kaiser presided over a council that settled the question of the U-boat campaign. To that date, Germany's submarine warfare had been restricted; from 1 February U-boats were to attack all shipping, whatever national flag it had hoisted, "with the utmost energy". The aim was to starve Britain into surrender within six months; the result was to bring the USA into the war on the Allied side on 6 April. So enormous were America's resources that Allied victory was assured.

Provided, that was, the European Allies could hold out until America's might was mobilized. This was by no means certain, for Revolution in Russia in 1917 effectively removed Russia from the war, allowing Germany to switch divisions to the Western Front. And on the Western Front the Germans were seemingly impregnable; they badly mauled General Nivelle's "decisive" April offensive, which caused demoralization, even mutiny, amongst the *poilus*. Only cajoling by the venerated Pétain brought the French army to order. The British "big push" of 1917 on the Western Front fared no better than the rash Nivelle offensive; at Passchendaele, where the rain never seemed to cease and Tommies were forced to crawl into battle, the British sustained 400,000 casualties for five miles of mud. And then the British were dispirited too. Even at Cambrai in November, where the British imaginatively used massed tanks, they were too weak to exploit a potential war-winning breakthrough. Meanwhile, the Italian Front all but collapsed at Caporetto, in East Africa the German Comander, General von Lettow-Vorbeck tied down 100,000 men with a minuscule force of 15,000 soldiers, and in Palestine German-leavened Turkish forces beat back Sir Archibald Murray. (Not until Murray was replaced by Allenby did British fortunes change in the Middle East; by December 1917 Allenby was in Jerusalem.)

To most of its participants, the war at the end of 1917 seemed as deadlocked as it did at the start. Yet, in truth, time had run out for Germany. Thousands of American "doughboys" were arriving in Europe almost daily, whilst Germany had called its last reserves to the colours.

There was just one wild card left to play. At Mons on 11 November Ludendorff decided to launch an offensive in the Spring of 1918 to annihilate the British on the Western Front before the Americans became effective. Though Ludendorff did not know it, the war had exactly one year still to run.

WESTERN FRONT: A POET WRITES HOME, 4 January 1917

Lieutenant Wilfred Owen, British Fourth Army

Owen's poems, which helped shape subsequent public attitude to the Great War, included "Dulce et decorum est" and "Anthem for doomed youth". He was killed in action in 1918, a week before the armistice.

My own dear Mother,

I have joined the Regiment, who are just at the end of six weeks' rest.

I will not describe the awful vicissitudes of the journey here. I arrived at Folkestone, and put up at the best hotel. It was a place of luxury – inconceivable now – carpets as deep as the mud here – golden flunkeys; pages who must have been melted into their clothes and expanded since; even the porters had clean hands. Even the dogs that licked up the crumbs had clean teeth.

Since I set foot on Calais quays I have not had dry feet.

No one knew anything about us on this side, and we might have taken weeks to get here, and must have, but for fighting our way here.

I spent something like a pound in getting my baggage carried from trains to trains.

At the Base, as I said, it was not so bad. We were in the camp of Sir Percy Cunynghame, who had bagged for his Mess the Duke of Connaught's chef.

After those two days, we were let down, gently, into the real thing. Mud.

It has penetrated now into that Sanctuary my sleeping bag, and that holy of holies my pyjamas. For I sleep on a stone floor and the servant squashed mud on all my belongings; I suppose by way of baptism. We are 3 officers in this "Room"; the rest of the house is occupied by servants and the band; the roughest set of knaves I have ever been herded with. Even now their vile language is shaking the flimsy door between the rooms.

I chose a servant for myself yesterday, not for his profile, nor yet his clean hands, but for his excellence in bayonet work. For the servant is always at the side of his officer in the charge and is therefore worth a dozen nurses. Alas, he of the Bayonet is in the Bombing Section, and is against Regulations to employ such as a servant. I makeshift with another.

Everything is makeshift. The English seem to have fallen into the French unhappy-go-lucky non-system. There are scarcely any houses here. The men lie in Barns.

Our Mess Room is also an Ante and Orderly Room. We eat & drink out of old tins, some of which show traces of ancient enamel. We are never dry, and never "off duty".

On all the officers' faces there is a harassed look that I have never seen before, and which in England, never will be seen – out of jails. The men are just as Bairnsfather [British artist] has them – expressionless lumps.

We feel the weight of them hanging on us. I have found not a few of the old Fleetwood Musketry party here. They seemed glad to see me as far as the set doggedness of their features would admit.

I censored hundreds of letters yesterday, and the hope of peace was in every one. *The Daily Mail* map which appeared about Jan 2 will be of extreme interest to you.

We were stranded in a certain town one night and I saved the party of us by collaring an Orderly in the streets and making him take us to a Sergeants Mess. We were famishing, and a mug of beer did me more good than any meal I ever munched. The place was like a bit of Blighty, all hung with English Greetings and Mistletoe.

As I could I collected accoutrement, some here, some there, and almost complete: Steel Helmets, & Gas; improved Box Respirator, and etcetera.

The badge of the Regt is some red tabs on the shoulder thus I scarcely know any of the officers. The senior are old regulars. The younger are, several, Artists! In my room is an Artist of the same school as I passed. He is also a fine water-colour sketcher. I may have time to write again tomorrow. I *have* not of course had anything from you. I am perfectly well and strong, but unthinkably dirty and squalid. I scarcely dare to wash. Pass on as much of this happy news as may interest people. The favourite song of the men is

"The Roses round the door
Makes me love Mother more."

They sing this everlastingly.

I don't disagree.

Your very own *W.E.O. x*

AN AUSTRALIAN ON LEAVE IN LONDON, 27 January 1917

Corporal Francis Mack, AIF (Australian Imperial Force)

ENGLAND
27th January, 1917

Dear Mother and Father,

Just back from leave in London. I had a real roaring time. The time (4 days) was rather short. I managed to see most of the old ancient and historical sights. I was somehow disappointed in London after reading so much about it – really expected to see something more impressive than it is. Mind you, we see London now at its worst for everything is in darkness at 5 p.m. in the afternoon so the days were terribly short. I went to see the Tower of London, Buckingham Palace, Whitehall, The War Office, Westminster Abbey, St Paul's Cathedral, Trafalgar Square, Leicester Square, Piccadilly Circus, Bond Street and other places too numerous to mention. These sights are grand – there are no two ways about that but the rest, the business houses and eating places are only commonplace. The big difference between Sydney and London is the trans. London has no trams through the streets – they all run underground and are all privately owned. There are two classes of trams – the Tube and the Electric Line. The Tube is a way – it Billy O down – say 5 or 600 feet down while the Electric is only about 50 feet. They are very cheap and extra fast. On the streets run O'Buses (Motor) after the style of the trams. There are thousands – you can see them everywhere and these were very attractive to see. You wonder why. Well, firstly you can see London better from an omnibus than anything else and secondly but none the least important is that the conductor is a Girl. That's a thing which struck us as peculiar, girls doing all sorts of jobs, walk down the street and you see a window cleaner. I had seen photos of them in papers but had I not seen them I would not have believed it. But never the less they were there dressed in men's clothes of oilskin. Go a bit further and you see a girl page, girl done up in livery to put it plainly, girls are doing everything . . .

I'll answer all letters I receive so if anyone wants to hear from me direct it's up to them to write now and again. I am not too bad. I have had, and in fact I still have a very bad cold and terribly sore feet from walking over the hard frozen ground. Otherwise I am splendid. Well mother must close. Am sending you some views of London and the places I have visited together with some English papers.

Well goodbye mother and father, sisters and brothers. Fondest love to you all.

I remain yours, am luckily your loving son, Frank.

OBSERVATIONS OF A CENSOR, FRANCE, 4 February 1917

Lieutenant Eric Marchant, London Regiment

Calais, 4 February 1917

Dear Mother

. . . This morning I spent the whole time censoring letters. This is the first time I have had this job and though it is rather irksome after an hour or two I found the letters of absorbing interest.

I suppose there is no better way of getting an idea of the spirit of the men and I won't deny that I was surprised at the tone of practically all the letters. The percentage that showed a realization of religious truths and faith in God, was tremendously bigger than ever I suspected, and such phrases as "we must go on trusting in God" were in dozens of the letters I read. In particular I noticed one letter from a young fellow to his brother who was in the trenches and had evidently been out here some months and was getting badly "fed-up". The letter was worth printing if it had not been so sacred. The spelling was execrable and the writing almost illegible in parts but, strange to say, there was very little that could be called ungrammatical, and I am sure that the recipient will be cheered and helped beyond all measure when he gets it. In practically all the letters came the request "Write as often as you can" and nobody can doubt that the letters and parcels from "Blighty" keep up the spirits of the men as nothing else can.

You must remember that the men in this camp are of a very different class to the 7th London. There were not more than two or three letters in the whole bag addressed to London and the majority were going to little unheard of villages in Cambridgeshire and Suffolk. You would laugh at in the quaint spelling. Quite a number always spelt "here" as "hear" and one man spelt "used" as "Youst"! All express their firm conviction that the war was "nearly over" and one breezy optimist said that he thought "pece terms was already ben (being) arranged and shud (should) wake up one morning and find ourselfs (ourselves) orf to Blighty agen".

Altogether I found the duties of a Censor Officer most entertaining.

This afternoon it was too bitterly cold and slippery underfoot to go out so I stayed by the fire in the mess tent and read an extraordinary yarn by Max Pemberton called "Pro Patria" which I found more amusing than edifying. This evening I hope to go to a camp service if there is one. Everyone in the Mess seems to be contracting a "churchyarder cough" but so far I have kept clear of that and similar ills. The weather still continues extremely cold but dry and sunny, and I hope it will continue so, but the wind seems to be veering round to the west this afternoon so I suppose we must not be surprised if the rain comes into its own again, with its attending evils.

Well, I have no more news of interest at present so will close, give my love to all. Hoping to hear from someone shortly.

Your loving son, Eric.

HEIMATFRONT: THE FOOD CRISIS, LEIPZIG, GERMANY, 4 February 1917

Ethel Cooper

Cooper was an Australian who spent the duration of the war in Leipzig. The bad harvest of 1916, combined with the British blockade, caused the biggest food crisis in Germany for a century.

Coal has run out. The electric light is cut off in most houses (I have gas, thank Heaven!), the trams are not running, or only in the very early morning, all theatres, schools, the opera house, and cinemas are closed – neither potatoes nor turnips are to be had – they were our last resource – there is no fish – and

Germany has at last ceased to trumpet the fact that it can't be starved out. Added to that the thermometer outside my kitchen windows says 24 deg. Fahr. below zero. I have never seen that before.

THE *LACONIA* IS TORPEDOED, NORTH ATLANTIC, 25 February 1917

Floyd Gibbons, war correspondent Chicago Tribune

The U-boat peril was at its greatest in the spring and early summer of 1917 (with April the worst month for Allied losses). The victims included the *Laconia*, a British Cunard liner; among its passengers was the American journalist Floyd Gibbons, on his way to Europe to cover the war for the *Chicago Tribune*.

The first cabin passengers were gathered in the lounge Sunday evening, with the exception of the bridge fiends in the smoke room.

"Poor Butterfly" was dying wearily on the talking machine, and several couples were dancing.

About the tables in the smoke room the conversation was limited to the announcement of bids and orders to the stewards. Before the fireplace was a little gathering which had been dubbed the Hyde Park corner – an allusion I don't quite fully understand. This group had about exhausted available discussion when I projected a new bone of contention.

"What do you say are our chances of being torpedoed?" I asked.

"Well," drawled the deliberative Mr Henry Chetham, a London solicitor, "I should say four thousand to one."

Lucien J. Jerome, of the British diplomatic service, returning with an Ecuadorian valet from South America, interjected: "Considering the zone and the class of this ship, I should put it down at two hundred and fifty to one that we don't meet a sub."

At this moment the ship gave a sudden lurch sideways and forward. There was a muffled noise like the slamming of some large door at a good distance away. The slightness of the shock and the meekness of the report compared with my imagination were disappointing. Every man in the room was on his feet in an instant.

"We're hit!" shouted Mr Chetham.

"That's what we've been waiting for," said Mr Jerome.

"What a lousy torpedo!" said Mr Kirby in typical New Yorkese. "It must have been a fizzer."

I looked at my watch. It was 10:30 p.m.

Then came the five blasts on the whistle. We rushed down the corridor leading from the smoke room at the stern to the lounge, which was amidship. We were running, but there was no panic. The occupants of the lounge were just leaving by the forward doors as we entered . . .

The torpedo had hit us well astern on the starboard side and had missed the engines and the dynamos. I had not noticed the deck lights before. Throughout the voyage our decks had remained dark at night and all cabin portholes were clamped down and all windows covered with opaque paint . . .

Steam began to hiss somewhere from the giant grey funnels that towered above. Suddenly there was a roaring swish as a rocket soared upward from the captain's bridge, leaving a comet's tail of fire. I watched it as it described a graceful are in the black void overhead, and then, with an audible pop, it burst in a flare of brilliant colours.

There was a tilt to the deck. It was listing to starboard at just the angle that would make it necessary to reach for support to enable one to stand upright. In the meantime electric flood-lights – large white enamelled funnels containing clusters of bulbs – had been suspended from the promenade deck and illuminated the dark water that rose and fell on the slanting side of the ship . . .

A hatchet was thrust into my hand and I forwarded it to the bow. There was a flash of sparks as it crashed down on the holding pulley. One strand of the rope parted and down plunged the bow, too quick for the stern man. We came to a jerky stop with the stern in the air and the bow down, but the stern managed to lower away until the dangerous angle was eliminated.

Then both tried to lower together. The list of the ship's side became greater, but, instead of our boat sliding down it like a toboggan, the taffrail caught and was held. As the lowering continued, the other side dropped down and we found ourselves clinging on at a new angle and looking straight down on the water.

Many feet and hands pushed the boat from the side of the ship, and we sagged down again, this time smacking squarely on the pillowy top of a rising swell. It felt more solid than mid-air, at least. But we were far from being off. The pulleys stuck twice in their fastenings, bow and stern, and the one axe passed forward and back, and with it my flashlight, as the entangling ropes that held us to the sinking *Laconia* were cut away.

Some shout from that confusion of sound caused me to look up, and I really did so with the fear that one of the nearby boats was being lowered upon us . . .

As we pulled away from the side of the ship, its receding terrace of lights stretched upward. The ship was slowly turning over. We were opposite that part occupied by the engine rooms. There was a tangle of oars, spars, and rigging on the seat and considerable confusion before four of the big sweeps could be manned on either side of the boat . . .

We rested on our oars, with all eyes on the still lighted *Laconia*. The torpedo had struck at 10:30 p.m., according to our ship's time. It was thirty minutes afterward that another dull thud, which was accompanied by a noticeable drop in the hulk, told its story of the second torpedo that the submarine had dispatched through the engine room and the boat's vitals from a distance of two hundred yards.

We watched silently during the next minute, as the tiers of lights dimmed slowly from white to yellow, then to red, and nothing was left but the murky mourning of the night, which hung over all like a pall.

A mean, cheese-coloured crescent of a moon revealed one horn above a rag bundle of clouds in the distance. A rim of blackness settled around our little world, relieved only by general leering stars in the zenith, and where the *Laconia*'s lights had shone there remained only the dim outline of a blacker hulk standing out above the water like a jagged headland, silhouetted against overcast sky.

The ship sank rapidly at the stern until at last its nose stood straight up in the air. Then it slid silently down and out of sight like a piece of disappearing scenery in a panorama spectacle.

REVOLUTION IN RUSSIA: STREET FIGHTING IN PETROGRAD, 12 March 1917

Professor L.-H. Grandijs, correspondent for L'Illustration

At the beginning of 1917, after two years of military reverses and food shortages, the people of Russia were in discontented mood. It came as scant surprise to everybody outside the aloof imperial family when, after police fired on striking workers in St Petersburg, the country erupted in revolution; Tsar Nicholas's autocratic regime was promptly replaced by a moderate republican provisional government. Led by Alexander Kerensky, this government however committed an unwashable sin in the eyes of the Russian masses: it remained committed to the war. By the year's end, Kerensky too would be booted from power.

Monday, March 12th: Fights between soldiers broke out in the streets. The Lithuania and Volhynia Regiments went to the Arsenal. Its Director tried to address the men and persuade them to refrain from unruly behaviour, but he was killed by two bullets. The soldiers thereupon seized the Arsenal and set fire to the Palace of Justice . . .

At four o'clock in the afternoon, I went to the Nevsky Prospekt. I heard rifle shots everywhere. I was about to mount the stairs leading to the Anitschkov Bridge, when the crowd occupying it began to flee. Hardly had we bent our heads when a salvo burst out. The bullets whizzed over our heads, and I heard them hit the nearby houses.

The crowd remained strangely calm. As soon as the fusillade was over, people came back to the Nevsky Prospekt and looked around. The first to arrive there was an eighteen-year-old girl, who was as composed as if she were attending just any kind of show. Once the first moments of fear were gone, I heard people laugh all around me. More and more faces appeared from behind lamp-posts and gateways. To get a better view, small boys climbed upon the statues of horses placed on the bridge. Workers and bourgeois were watching events with the keenest interest . . .

At the junction of the Nevsky and Liteiny Prospekts, a group of about fifty soldiers commanded by an officer had formed a square facing the now empty main avenues of Petrograd. The soldiers had built a fire with the wooden pavement which they had torn loose. The officer was standing among his men who, with one knee on the ground, were aiming their rifles at the crowd as it began to reappear at some distance. He gave an order, whereupon the soldiers moved along the Nevsky Prospekt toward another group gathered further down. I was struck by the fact that a street lamp in the middle of the Liteiny Prospekt, quite close to the group that stood near the soldiers' square, had been hit by six bullets. The Imperial Guard must have fired over people's heads.

Two men, one killed and the other wounded, were carried by on stretchers. A Red Cross automobile was loudly cheered by the crowd as it drove by. A nurse was leaning out of it, wildly waving a red handkerchief. She was cheered all along the avenue.

The crowd was composed of workers, students belonging to the lower bourgeoisie, and a number of hoodlums, coming from God knows where, who were taking advantage of the disorder. There were also a few women, three or four girl-students and young women who, less virtuous than obliging, had been given Red Cross arm-badges and walked arm-in-arm with their boy-friends.

At some distance, orators were addressing the crowd from the statuos of the Anitschkov Bridge . . . Suddenly, rifle shots rang out again on the Liteiny Prospekt. The women began to run, and in a moment the street was deserted . . .

Huge flames were rising from the Palace of Justice, where so many brave and sincere young men, unafraid of expressing their opinion, had been sentenced to exile or jail by judges whose every action was closely watched by the Government . . .

The soldiers appearing on the Liteiny Prospekt looked tired and anxious, but also very determined, and were all armed with rifles. Then came youthful workers and students, armed with revolvers, bayonets, army rifles or hunting rifles. No one seemed to be in command, yet a certain order, stemming from a common purpose and the strength of their conviction, prevailed. I heard sounds of metal struck against wood: some hoodlums were trying to break down the door of a tobacco shop. Older workers, however, intervened and told them: "Don't do that, brothers! Get out of here, brothers!" I couldn't help admiring the sublime grandeur of the scene . . .

[*After a new fusillade.*] Some dead and wounded were carried past, as well as two machine guns and a great quantity of ammunition found at the home of two policemen who had just been killed. The private as well as the Red Cross automobiles, which in the soldiers' opinion were not needed as ambulances, have automatically been seized whenever they happened to enter this street . . . No one knew at one end of the street what was going on at the other end. There was no organization as yet, no liaison between the various rebel groups, no over-all command. Nevertheless, these men whom everybody had believed to be incapable of initiative and self-control, displayed amazing determination and moderation . . .

I followed the Neva quay, where few passers-by were walking hurriedly toward their homes . . . On the Parade Ground, another regiment was joining the revolutionary movement. Its soldiers, like those of other regiments, had been abandoned by their officers. All men were armed, and busily carrying cartridge boxes out of their barracks. They were tall, magnificent young fellows, who behaved like children. Since they had no tools to open the boxes, they simply kicked them about as if they were playing football. The boxes at last broke open, and every man filled his pockets with cartridges. Now and then, a soldier would fire in the air, thus provoking a panic. Such pranks, however, soon met with general reprobation . . .

All cafés have been closed since this morning. I went into a small popular tea-room on the Kazanskaia, and found it full of workers, soldiers and storekeepers who were all engrossed in discussing the day's events, but in a very moderate tone, as if their conversation was about the price of potatoes. Yet, they had participated in the revolt, and some of them had been in the thick of events! . . .

These men did not display any hatred of the Emperor, and they were ready to continue the war. But their hatred of the Germans was very strong, even among the humblest of them.

They also talked about hanging Protopopov [*Minister of the Interior*], whom many people compare to Rasputin. Immediate needs, rather than political ideas and systems, were uppermost in their minds. They all wanted more bread. They accused the Ministers of criminal neglect, and wanted them to be replaced. To them, the remedy lay in a change of Ministry, not in a new regime. The Social-Democrats have but little influence on these plain people, who are opposed to rigid systems and too vague ideals.

HOME FRONT: PARLIAMENT APPROVES WOMEN'S SUFFRAGE, BRITAIN 28 March 1917

Michael MacDonagh

The House of Commons yesterday [28 March] recognized the services of women to the State by approving, by 341 votes to 62, woman suffrage, which is included in a scheme of electoral reform to come into operation at the end of the War. The motion was moved by Asquith, who in a fine speech recanted the stout opposition which he gave to votes for women before the War. Women, he said, had worked out their own salvation in the War. The War could not have been carried on without them: and he felt it impossible to withhold from them the right of making their voice heard on the problems of the country's reconstruction when the War was over.

PRESIDENT WILSON ASKS CONGRESS TO DECLARE WAR, WASHINGTON DC, 2 April 1917

Anonymous correspondent, L'illustration

On that evening of April 2nd, 1917 – another historic date – the House was absolutely jammed. The public galleries had been courteously placed at the disposal of the ladies, and were tightly packed. Some wore pink blouses, others were in elegant evening dresses. The Press galleries, too, were overcrowded. Journalists had come from Texas and Alaska to witness the historic moment. Even the Senators' seats were crowded: some Congressmen, having been authorized to bring their youngest children, were holding them in their arms and on their knees in order that they, too, might witness the great event.

Everybody was seated when, at 8:39 p.m., the usher announced:

"The President of the United States!"

At once, in a spontaneous movement, everyone rose, and the room was filled with an immense acclamation, one of these strange American acclamations that include bravoes, howling, and whistles, the latter being not, as in our country, a sign of contempt, but on the contrary a mark of admiration. Slowly, the President entered the room and walked toward the rostrum. His pale face was impassive, his clear eyes looked straight ahead, his hands did not tremble. It was his walk, an imperceptible movement of his body, which betrayed his emotion. From an inner pocket of his tail-coat, he pulled a few small sheets of paper on which people in the galleries could distinguish a small handwriting through their opera glasses. From the beginning of his address till the end, the President assumed a military bearing: body erect, knees and heels together, his arms against his body, elbows resting on the rostrum's raised desk, hands holding the small sheets of paper. Then he began to read his address . . .

"The present German submarine warfare against commerce is a warfare against mankind. It is a war against all nations. American ships have been sunk, American lives taken, in which it has stirred us very deeply to learn of, but the ships and people of other neutral and friendly nations have been sunk and overwhelmed in the waters in the same way. There has been no discrimination. The challenge is to all mankind. Each nation must decide for itself how it will meet it . . ."

The President did not raise his voice, but made it clearer and more precise, and said: "There is one choice we cannot make, we are incapable of making; we will not choose the path of submission and suffer the most sacred rights of our nation and our people to be ignored or violated. The wrongs against which we now array ourselves are not common wrongs; they cut to the very roots of human life." The sentence was hardly ended when a formidable, unbelievable clamour rose from the absolutely quiet assembly . . . In the midst of the stormy ovation, not one muscle of the President's pale face quivered, and he went on reading his little sheets:

"With a profound sense of the solemn and even tragical character of the step I am taking and of the grave responsibilities which it involves, but in unhesitating obedience to what I deem my constitutional duty, I advise that the Congress declare the recent course of the Imperial German Government to be in fact nothing less than war against the Government and people of the United States; that it formally accept the status of belligerent which has thus been thrust upon it and that it take immediately steps not only to put the country in a more thorough state of defense, but also to exert all its power and employ all its resources to bring the Government of the German Empire to terms and end the war . . ."

The decisive words had now been pronounced . . . The whole assembly was on its feet. From its throats, an ardent and deep cry – similar to that uttered on August 3rd, 1914, by the French Chamber at the announcement of the German declaration of war – rose into the air . . . After that, every sentence of the presidential address was greeted by applause . . .

"We have no quarrel with the German people. We have no feeling toward them but one of sympathy and friendship. It was not upon their impulse that their Government acted in entering this war. It was not with their previous knowledge or approval . . .

"We have no selfish ends to serve. We desire no conquest, no domination. We seek no indemnities for ourselves, no material compensation for the sacrifices we shall freely make. We are but one of the champions of the rights of mankind. We shall be satisfied when those rights have been as secure as the faith and the freedom of the nations can make them. . . .

"We shall, happily, still have an opportunity to prove that friendship in our daily attitude and actions toward the millions of men and women of German birth and native sympathy who live among us and share our life, and we shall be proud to prove it toward all who are in fact loyal to their neighbours and to the Government in the hour of test.

"They are, most of them, as true and loyal Americans as if they had never known any other fealty or allegiance. They will be prompt to stand with us in rebuking and restraining the few who may be of a different mind and purpose . . ."

Then came these magnificent words:

"It is a fearful thing to lead this great, peaceful people into war – into the most terrible and disastrous of all wars, civilization itself seeming to be in the balance.

"But the right is more precious than peace, and we shall fight for the things which we have always carried nearest our hearts – for democracy, for the right of those who submit to authority to have a voice in their own government, for the rights and liberties of small nations, for a universal dominion of right by such a concert of free peoples as shall bring peace and safety to all nations and make the world itself at last free . . ."

And to say all these things, the President's voice never changed: it became neither more emphatic, nor more declamatory; it remained stern yet serene.

On 4 April the United States Senate voted in favour of war by 82 votes to 6; two days later the House of Representatives voted for war by 373 votes to 50.

WESTERN FRONT: LAST LETTER TO A SON, FRANCE, 1 p.m. 2 April 1917

Captain John Coull, 23rd Battalion, Royal Fusiliers

Coull was killed in action on 30 September 1918.

France 2.4. 17 1 p.m.

My dear boy Fred,

This is a letter you will never see unless your daddy falls in the field. It is his farewell words to you in case anything happens. My boy I love you dearly and would have greatly liked to get leave for a few days to kiss you and shake hands again, after a few months separation, but as this seems at the present moment unlikely, I drop you this few lines to say "God bless you" and keep you in the true brave manly upright course which I would like to see you follow.

You will understand better as you get older that your

daddy came out to France for your sakes and for our Empire's sake. If he died it was in a good cause and all I would ask of you dear boy, is that you will keep this note in memory of me, and throughout your life may all that is good attend you and influence you. May you be strong to withstand the temptations of life and when you come to the evening of your days may you be able to say with St Paul "I have fought the good fight".

Goodbye dear boy and if it is that we are not to meet again in this life, may it be certain that we shall meet in another life to come, which faith I trust you will hold on to and live up to.

I remain ever
Your loving Daddy
J.F. Coull

ALL QUIET ON THE EASTERN FRONT: PACIFISM IN THE RUSSIAN LINES, Spring 1917

Lieutenant General Anton Denikin, 4th Division, Russian Army

By Order Number 1 of the Petrograd Soviet, issued on 14 March 1917, control over all arms in the Russian army was entrusted to Soldiers' Soviets (ie councils), elected by the troops. With traditional military discipline broken, and most of its soldiers on an unofficial strike against "hostile" actions, the Russian war machine virtually came to a halt.

In a large, open field, as far as the eye can see, run endless lines of trenches, sometimes coming close up to each other, interlacing their barbed-wire fences, sometimes running far off and vanishing behind a verdant crest. The sun has risen long ago, but it is still as death in the field. The first to rise are the Germans. In one place and another their figures look out from the trenches; a few come out on to the parapet to hang their clothes, damp after the night, in the sun. A sentry in our front trench opens his sleepy eyes, lazily stretches himself, after looking indifferently at the enemy trenches. A soldier in a dirty shirt, bare-footed, with coat slung over his shoulders, cringing under the morning cold, comes out of his trench and plods towards the German positions, where, between the lines, stands a "post-box"; it contains a new number of the German paper, *The Russian Messenger*, and proposals for barter.

All is still. Not a single gun is to be heard. Last week the Regimental Committee issued a resolution against firing, even against distance firing; let the necessary distance be estimated by the map. A Lieutenant-Colonel of the gunners – a member of the Committee – gave his full approval to this resolution. When yesterday the Commander of a field battery began firing at a new enemy trench, our infantry opened rifle fire on our observation post and wounded the telephone operator. During the night the infantry lit a fire on the position being constructed for a newly arrived heavy battery.

Nine a.m. The first Company gradually begins to awaken. The trenches are incredibly defiled; in the narrow communication trenches and those of the second line the air is thick and close. The parapet is crumbling away. No one troubles to repair it; no one feels inclined to do so, and there are not enough men in the Company. There is a large number of deserters; more than fifty have been allowed to go. Old soldiers have been demobilized, others have gone on leave with the arbitrary permission of the Committee. Others, again, have been elected members of numerous Committees, or gone away as delegates; a while ago, for instance, the Division sent a numerous delegation to "Comrade" Kerensky to verify whether he had really given orders for advance. Finally, by threats and violence, the soldiers have so terrorized the regimental surgeons that the latter have been issuing medical certificates even to the "thoroughly fit".

In the trenches the hours pass slowly and wearily, in dullness and idleness. In one corner men are playing cards, in another a soldier returned from leave is lazily and listlessly telling a story; the air is full of obscene swearing. Someone reads aloud from the *Russian Messenger* the following:

"The English want the Russians to shed the last drop of their blood for the greater glory of England, who seeks her profit in everything . . . Dear soldiers, you must know that Russia would have concluded peace long ago had not England prevented her . . . We must turn away from her – the Russian people demand it; such is their sacred will."

Someone or other swears.

"Don't you wish for peace. *They* make peace, the —; we shall die here, without getting our freedom!"

Along the trenches came Lieutenant Albov, the Company Commander. He said to the group of soldiers, somewhat irresolutely and entreatingly:

"Comrades, get to work quickly. In three days we have not made a single communication trench to the firing line."

The card-players did not even look round; someone said in a low voice, "All right." The man reading the newspaper rose and reported, in a free and easy manner:

"The Company does not want to dig, because that would be preparation for an advance, and the Committee has resolved . . ."

"Look here, you understand nothing at all about it, and, moreover, why do you speak for the whole Company? Even if we remain on the defensive we are lost in case of an alarm; the whole Company cannot get out to the firing line along a single trench."

He said this, and with a gesture of despair went on his way. Matters were hopeless.

THE BATTLE OF ARRAS: THE VIEW FROM THE AIR, 9 April 1917

Billy Bishop, Royal Flying Corps

The British attack at Arras was intended to draw in German reserves, allowing the French general Nivelle to strike a decisive blow against the Hindenburg Line at Chemin des Dames.

Dawn was due at 5.30 o'clock on Easter Monday, and that was the exact hour set for the beginning of the Battle of Arras. We were up and had our machines out of the hangars while it was still night. The beautiful weather of a few hours before had vanished. A strong, chill wind was blowing from the east and dark, menacing clouds were scudding along low overhead.

We were detailed to fly at a low altitude over the advancing infantry, firing into the enemy trenches, and dispersing any groups of men or working troops we happened to see in the vicinity of the lines. Some phases of this work are known as "contact patrols", the machines keeping track always of the infantry advance, watching points where they may be held up, and returning from time to time to report just how the battle is going. Working with the infantry in a big attack is a most exciting experience. It means flying close to the ground and constantly passing through our own shells as well as those of the enemy.

The shell fire this morning was simply indescribable. The bombardment which had been going on all night gradually died down about 5 o'clock, and the Germans must have felt that the British had finished their nightly "strafing", were tired out and going to bed. For a time almost complete silence reigned over the battlefields. All along the German lines star-shells and rocket-lights were looping through the darkness. The old Boche is always suspicious and likes to have the country around him lit up as much as possible so he can see what the enemy is about.

The wind kept growing stiffer and stiffer and there was a distinct feel of rain in the air. Precisely at the moment that all the British guns roared out their first salvo of the battle, the skies opened and the rain fell in torrents. Gunfire may or may not have anything to do with rainmaking, but there was a strange coincidence between the shock of battle and the commencement of the downpour this morning. It was beastly luck, and we felt it keenly. But we carried on.

The storm had delayed the coming of day by several minutes, but as soon as there was light enough to make our presence worth while we were in the air and braving the untoward elements just as the troops were below us. Lashed by the gale, the wind cut our faces as we moved against the enemy. The ground seemed to be one mass of bursting shells. Farther back, where the guns were firing, the hot flames flashing from thousands of muzzles gave the impression of a long ribbon of incandescent light. The air seemed shaken and literally full of shells on their missions of death and destruction. Over and over again one felt a sudden jerk under a wing-tip, and the machine would heave quickly. This meant a shell had passed within a few feet of you. As the battle went on the work grew more terrifying, because reports came in that several of our machines had been hit by shells in flight and brought down. There was small wonder of this. The British barrage fire that morning was the most intense the war had ever known. There was a greater concentration of guns than at any time during the Somme. In fact, some of the German prisoners said afterward that the Somme seemed a Paradise compared to the bombardments we carried out at Arras. While the British fire was at its height the Germans set up a counter-barrage. This was not so intense, but every shell added to the shrieking chorus that filled the stormy air made the lot of the flying man just so much more difficult. Yet the risk was one we could not avoid; we had to endure it with the best spirit possible.

The waves of attacking infantry as they came out of their trenches and trudged forward behind the curtain of shells laid down by the artillery were an amazing sight. The men seemed to wander across No Man's Land, and into the enemy trenches, as if the battle was a great bore to them. From the air it looked as though they did not realize that they were at war and were taking it all entirely too quietly. That is the way with clockwork warfare. These troops had been drilled to move forward at a given pace. They had been timed over and over again in marching a certain distance, and from this timing the "creeping" or rolling barrage which moved in front of them had been mathematically worked out. And the battle, so calmly entered into, was one of the tensest, bitterest of the entire world war.

For days the battle continued, and it was hard work and no play for everybody concerned. The weather, instead of getting better, as spring weather should, gradually got worse. It was cold, windy, and wet. Every two or three hours sudden snowstorms would shut in, and flying in these squalls, which obliterated the landscape, was a very ticklish business.

On thc fourth day of the battle I happened to be flying about 500 feet above the trenches an hour after dawn. It had snowed during the night and the ground was covered with a new layer of white several inches thick. No marks of the battle of the day before were to be seen; the only blemishes in the snow mantle were the marks of shells which had fallen during the last hour. No Man's Land itself, so often a filthy litter, was this morning quite clean and white.

Suddenly over the top of our parapets a thin line of infantry crawled up and commenced to stroll casually toward the enemy. To me it seemed that they must soon wake up and run; that they were altogether too slow; that they could not realize the great danger they were in. Here and there a shell would burst as the line advanced or halted for a moment. Three or four men near the burst would topple over like so many tin soldiers. Two or three other men would then come running up to the spot from the rear with a stretcher, pick up the wounded and the dying, and slowly walk back with them. I could not get the idea out of my head that it was just a game they were playing at; it all seemed so unreal. Nor could I believe that the little brown figures moving about below me were really men – men going to the glory of victory or the glory of death. I could not make myself realize the full truth or meaning of it all. It seemed that I was in an entirely different world, looking down from another sphere on this strange, uncanny puppet-show.

Suddenly I heard the deadly rattle of a nest of machine guns under me, and saw that the line of our troops at one place was growing very thin, with many figures sprawling on the ground. For three or four minutes I could not make out the concealed position of the German gunners. Our men had halted, and were lying on the ground, evidently as much puzzled as I was. Then in a corner of a German trench I saw a group of about five men operating two machine guns. They were slightly to the flank of our line, and evidently had been doing a great amount of damage. The sight of these men thoroughly woke me up to the reality of the whole scene beneath me. I dived vertically at them with a burst of rapid fire. The smoking bullets from my gun flashed into the ground, and it was an easy matter to get an accurate aim on the German automatics, one of which turned its muzzle toward me.

But in a fraction of a second I had reached a height of only 30 feet above the Huns, so low I could make out every detail of their frightened faces. With hate in my heart I fired every bullet I could into the group as I swept over it, then turned my machine away. A few minutes later I had the satisfaction of seeing our line again advancing, and before the time had come for me to return from my patrol, our men had occupied all the

German positions they had set out to take. It was a wonderful sight and a wonderful experience. Although it had been so difficult to realize that men were dying and being maimed for life beneath me, I felt that at last I had seen something of that dogged determination that has carried British arms so far.

The next ten days were filled with incident. The enemy fighting machines would not come close to the lines, and there was very little doing in the way of aerial combats, especially as far as I was concerned, for I was devoting practically all of my time to flying low and helping the infantry. All of our pilots and observers were doing splendid work. Everywhere we were covering the forward movement of the infantry, keeping the troops advised of any enemy movements, and enabling the British artillery to shell every area where it appeared concentrations were taking place. Scores of counter-attacks were broken up before the Germans had fairly launched them. Our machines were everywhere behind the enemy lines. It was easy to tell when the Germans were massing for a counter-stroke. First of all our machines would fly low over the grey-clad troops, pouring machine-gun bullets into them or dropping high-explosive bombs in their midst. Then the exact location of the mobilization point would be signalled to the artillery, so that the moment the Germans moved our guns were on them. In General Orders commending the troops for their part in the battle, Field-Marshal Sir Douglas Haig declared that the work of the Flying Corps, "under the most difficult conditions," called for the highest praise.

We were acting, you might say, as air policemen.

MUD AND BLOOD: THE FLOUNDERING OF THE NIVELLE OFFENSIVE, 16 April 1917

Anonymous French Tank Officer

Launched by Nivelle with the words, "The hour has struck! Confidence! Courage! Vive la France!", his offensive of the wet, cold morning of 16 April threw thirty French divisions forward on a forty-mile front from the Montagne de Reims to the Oise. By evening the attack had become bogged down in mud and the guns and barbed wire of the Germans.

It was still raining, and the already soft ground was progressively turning into sticky mud. How were we going to fare in such terrain at the time of the attack?

Suddenly, a green star shell rose against the pale morning sky. It was followed by a second shell, but a red one. What was going on? I knew at once, for the same red shells rose all along the enemy positions. Obviously, it was a request for artillery barrage, and this meant that our men had begun the assault!

It was with deep emotion, in the dawn's early light, that we saw at some distance the wave of tiny blue-coats rushing up the slopes of Mont Cornillet, whose top was shrouded by numerous explosions. We were holding our breath. Poignant moment! Our men's wave, unbroken, a moment ago, presently moved on in echelons, spread out again, and then progressed in a zigzag motion. Here and there, the men would crowd together without advancing, having met some obstacle which we couldn't see, most likely one of these accursed, still intact barbed wire networks. Ah! If only we could be with them, to open a way for them!

On one side of the slope, our line of assault was extending and stretching out, and seemed to reach the top. Bravo, brave infantrymen! All around us, the guns were booming without interruption. At times, we could also hear the sharp rattle of machine guns. Many of our blue-coats fell under the deadly hail, but the others kept moving up and on, indomitable!

What emotion filled our hearts at this extraordinary sight! Tears filled our eyes . . . Suddenly, there was a burst of fire a short distance ahead of our group, on the other side of the road: a Schneider tank belonging to the group next to ours had been hit by a shell, and was burning like a huge torch.

Daylight slowly filled the gray sky. It was quite cold. Ahead of us, three batteries of 75's were firing as fast as they could . . . From the communication trenches large groups of soldiers came running, the first Boche prisoners, gray with chalk and wearing field-grey coats splattered with mud and blood. They were moving as fast as they could, and their terrified faces betrayed their desire to flee and get away from the storm of steel . . .

A snow squall swept our position. Our first wounded soldiers were coming in, men from the 83rd Infantry Regiment. We gathered round them, and learned from them, that the enemy positions were very strong, the resistance desperate. One battalion did reach the top of the Cornillet – probably the one whose gallant advance we had watched – but it was decimated by fire from intact machine gun positions, and was unable to withstand the enemy's counter-attack. One of the wounded men, his arm in a sling and patches of blood on his forehead, shouted while driving by:

"The Boches are still holding out in the Grille Wood, but we are attacking them with grenades."

A helmetless lieutenant, his clothes disarrayed and with a wound in his chest, walked slowly toward our group:

"Ah! If only you had been with us! We found nothing but intact barbed wire! If it hadn't been for that, we'd be far ahead now, instead of killing each other on the spot."

"We just couldn't keep moving," an alert corporal shouted, while using his rifle as a crutch. "Too many blasted machine guns, against which there was nothing doing!"

"The Boches certainly knew we were going to attack there," the lieutenant went on, "their trenches were jammed."

"Also, they keep getting reinforcements through the tunnel they have mined across the Cornillet!"

WESTERN FRONT: A TANK CHARGE, BULLECOURT, April 1917

Major W.H.L. Watson, Heavy Branch MGC

All the tanks, except Morris's had arrived without incident at the railway embankment. Morris ditched at the bank and was a little late. Haigh and Jumbo had gone on ahead of the tanks. They crawled out beyond the embankment into No Man's Land and marked out the starting-line. It was not too pleasant a job. The enemy machine-guns were active right through the night, and the neighbourhood of the embankment was shelled intermittently. Towards dawn this intermittent shelling became almost a bombardment, and it was feared that the tanks had been heard.

Skinner's tank failed on the embankment. The remainder crossed it successfully and lined up for the attack just before zero. By this time the shelling had become severe. The crews waited inside their tanks, wondering dully if they would be hit before they started. Already they were dead-tired, for they had had little sleep since their long painful trek of the night before.

Suddenly our bombardment began – it was more of a bombardment than a barrage – and the tanks crawled away into the darkness, followed closely by little bunches of Australians.

On the extreme right Morris and Puttock of Wyatt's section were met by tremendous machine-gun fire at the wire of the Hindenburg Line. They swung to the right, as they had been ordered, and glided along in front of the wire, sweeping the parapet with their fire. They received as good as they gave. Serious clutch trouble developed in Puttock's tank. It was impossible to stop since now the German guns were following them. A brave runner carried the news to Wyatt at the embankment. The tanks continued their course, though Puttock's tank was barely moving and by luck and good driving they returned to the railway, having kept the enemy most fully occupied in a quarter where he might have been uncommonly troublesome.

Morris passed a line to Skinner and towed him over the embankment. They both started for Bullecourt. Puttock pushed on back towards Noreuil. His clutch was slipping so badly that the tank would not move, and the shells were falling ominously near. He withdrew his crew from the tank into a trench, and a moment later the tank was hit again.

Of the remaining two tanks in this section we could hear nothing. Davies and Clarkson had disappeared. Perhaps they had gone through to Heudecourt. Yet the infantry of the right brigade, according to the reports we had received, were fighting most desperately to retain a precarious hold on the trenches they had entered.

In the centre Field's section of three tanks were stopped by the determined and accurate fire of forward field-guns before they entered the German trenches. The tanks were silhouetted against the snow, and the enemy gunners did not miss.

The first tank was hit in the track before it was well under way. The tank was evacuated, and in the dawning light it was hit again before the track could be repaired.

Money's tank reached the German wire. His men must have "missed their gears." For less than a minute the tank was motionless, then she burst into flames. A shell had exploded the petrol tanks, which in the old Mark I, were placed forward on either side of the officer's and driver's seats. A sergeant and two men escaped. Money, best of good fellows, must have been killed instantaneously by the shell.

Bernstein's tank was within reach of the German trenches when a shell hit the cab, decapitated the driver, and exploded in the body of the tank. The corporal was wounded in the arm, and Bernstein was stunned and temporarily blinded. The tank was filled with fumes. As the crew were crawling out, a second shell hit the tank on the roof. The men under the wounded corporal began stolidly to salve the tank's equipment, while Bernstein, scarcely knowing where he was, staggered back to the embankment. He was packed off to a dressing station, and an orderly was sent to recall the crew and found them still working stubbornly under direct fire.

Swears' section of four tanks on the left were slightly more fortunate.

Birkett went forward at top speed, and, escaping the shells, entered the German trenches, where his guns did great execution. The tank worked down the trenches towards Bullecourt followed by the Australians. She was hit twice, and all the crew were wounded, but Birkett went on fighting grimly until his ammunition was exhausted and he himself was badly wounded in the leg. Then at last he turned back, followed industriously by the German gunners. Near the embankment he stopped the tank to take his bearings. As he was climbing out, a shell burst against the side of the tank and wounded him again in the leg. The tank was evacuated. The crew salved what they could, and, helping each other, for they were all wounded, they made their way back painfully to the embankment. Birkett was brought back on a stretcher, and wounded a third time as he lay in the sunken road outside the dressing station. His tank was hit again and again. Finally it took fire, and was burnt out.

Skinner, after his tank had been towed over the railway embankment by Morris, made straight for Bullecourt, thinking that as the battle had now been in progress for more than two hours the Australians must have fought their way down the trenches into the village. Immediately he entered the village machine-guns played upon his tank, and several of his crew were slightly wounded by the little flakes of metal that fly about inside a Mk. I tank when it is subjected to really concentrated machine-gun fire. No Australians could be seen. Suddenly he came right to the edge of an enormous crater, and as suddenly stopped. He tried to reverse, but he could not change gear. The tank was absolutely motionless. He held out for some time, and then the Germans brought up a gun and began to shell the tank. Against field-guns in houses he was defenceless so long as his tank could not move. His ammunition was nearly exhausted. There were no signs of the Australians or of British troops. He decided quite properly to withdraw. With great skill he evacuated his crew, taking his guns with him and the little ammunition that remained. Slowly and carefully they worked their way back, and reached the railway embankment without further casualty.

The fourth tank of this section was hit on the roof just as it was coming into action. The engine stopped in sympathy, and the tank commander withdrew his crew from the tank.

Swears, the section commander, left the railway embankment, and with the utmost gallantry went forward into Bullecourt to look for Skinner. He never came back.

Such were the cheerful reports that I received in my little brick shelter by the cross-roads.

"TUBE 2, FIRE!": U-19 ATTACKS A CONVOY, NORTH ATLANTIC, 9 May 1917

Johannes Spiess, Commander U-19

At 7 p.m., we sighted a cloud of smoke. I immediately steered toward it and soon discovered that we were near a southward-bound convoy, which comprised eight ships coming from the Shetlands, probably from Lerwick. The ships were sailing in a perfect straight line, which we had always thought impossible for commercial vessels, the more so as they were of different sizes. Every ten minutes, the convoy changed course by about 20 degrees behind its leader. Four escort vessels fanned out before the convoy provided it with light, and two destroyers were zigzagging on both sides. The entire convoy gave the impression of a fleet of well-trained warships.

While we passed the trawlers in the van of the convoy, I had to use the periscope several times, in order to avoid collisions and observe the convoy's changes of course. For each observation, I stopped one of the engines and ordered the periscope to be hoisted. As soon as it reached the surface, I made a quick circular inspection of the waters. The navigator, who was standing before me, helped me swing it round faster, because it was very hard to turn. This exercise required a great deal of energy, and before every attack I perspired so abundantly that I had to change clothes, even though I always took off my heavy jacket beforehand. My nerves, too, were put to a severe test each time.

I had successfully passed the escort vessel line. All I had to do now was to get the *U19* into a favourable launching position while avoiding the destroyer protecting the convoy on our side. I was about to fire a torpedo when, suddenly, the convoy changed course and faced our forward tubes instead of our stern tubes. On the side of one of the largest steamers I could distinguish a name, painted in white letters, and next to it her national colors. At 9:04 p.m., I was no longer hindered by the destroyer and had the objective right in my sights. "Tube 2, fire!" I ordered, and immediately afterwards: "Quick, maximum depth!"

While the *U19* was obeying the hydroplanes, we were intently waiting for the detonation. But not a sound was heard. Damn it, I must have missed! But suddenly: Rrrboum! A powerful explosion shook and swayed our submarine.

BIG BANG: THE BLOWING OF THE MINES AT MESSINES, 3.10 a.m., 7 June 1917

Captain Oliver Woodward, 1st Australian Tunnelling Company, AIF

Messines, in Belgium, was a vantage point above the featureless Flanders plain. Held by the Germans from late 1914, it proved impervious to conventional Allied assault; consequently, it was decided to tunnel under Messines and detonate 19 huge mines, amounting to almost a million pounds of explosive. The detonation – which was felt as far away as southern England – was in the hands of Captain Oliver Woodward of the AIF (Australian Imperial Force).

At 2 a.m. all troops were withdrawn from the dugout and mine systems, and posted in their position for attack. At 2.25 a.m., I made the last resistance test, and then made the final connection for firing the mines. This was rather a nerve-racking task as one began to feel the strain, and wonder whether the leads were properly connected up. Just before 3 a.m. General Lambert took up his position in the firing dugout. It was his responsibility to give the order "FIRE". Watch in hand he stood there and in a silence that could almost be felt he said, "Five minutes to go". I again finally checked the leads, and Lieutenants Royle and Bowry stood with an exploder at their feet ready to fire should the dynamo fail. Then the General, in what seemed interminable periods, called out, "Three minutes to go, Two to go – One to go – 45 seconds to go – 20 seconds to go" – and then "9, 8, 7, 6, 5, 4, 3, 2, 1, – FIRE!!" Over went the firing switch and with a dull roar, accompanied by a heaving of the ground, the mines exploded. We had not failed in our duty.

Just prior to the actual firing of the mines, probably a second or two, we began to feel the earth tremors resulting from the firing of the other seventeen mines on the Army front. In those fractions of a second, arising from the variation in the synchronization of watches, I realized how quickly the mind functions, as I distinctly remember the feeling of envy of those officers similarly situated as I, who had brought their task to a successful conclusion, while mine had yet to be performed. I grabbed the handle firmly, and in throwing the switch over my hand came in contact with the terminals, so that I received a strong shock which threw me backward. For a fraction of a second I failed to realize what had happened, but there was soon joy in knowing that the Hill 60 Mines had done their work.

Lieutenant A.G. May, Machine-Gun Corps

The detonation was followed by artillery barrage and and all-out infantry attack.

When I heard the first deep rumble I turned to the men and shouted, "Come on, let's go." A fraction of a second later a terrific roar and the whole earth seemed to rock and sway. The concussion was terrible, several of the men and myself being blown down violently. It seemed to be several minutes before the earth stood still again though it may not really have been more than a few seconds. Flames rose to a great height – silhouetted against the flame I saw huge blocks of earth that seemed to be as big as houses falling back to the ground. Small chunks and dirt fell all around. I saw a man flung out from behind a huge block of debris silhouetted against the sheet of flame. Presumably some poor devil of a Boche. It was awful, a sort of inferno.

There was confusion on all sides, many men were lost to sight. While looking for my men to get them together again I came across Sgt Riddle and Private Davidson but where were the rest of them? Continuing to look around and futilely shouting I eventually found enough of my men to get together a gun team and sent them off. After waiting a few more minutes hoping some of the others would show up – none did – I decided that Riddle, Davidson and I would try to make up for a gun team. Riddle carried the gun and one box of ammo, Davidson a small chap carried three boxes of ammo and I carried five. We had no tripod but anyway ammo was more important.

At the same time the mines went off the artillery let loose, the heaviest group artillery firing ever known. The noise was impossible and it is impossible for anyone who was not there to imagine what it was like. Shells were bursting overhead and for no known reason I thought they were some of our shorts and then I realized the Boche was putting up a barrage on our front line and no man's land. I had forgotten it was not necessarily going to be all our own show. Not far in advance of our front parapet I saw a couple of our lads who had gone completely goofy, perhaps from the concussion. It was pitiful, one of them welcomed me like a long lost friend and asked me to give him his baby, I picked up a tin hat from the ground and gave it to him. He cradled the hat as if it were a child, smiling and laughing without a care in the world despite the fact that shells were exploding all around. I have no idea what happened to the poor chap but if he stayed there very long he must have been killed.

Crossing no man's land I had a narrow squeak. I was carrying two boxes of ammo in one hand and three in the other when a bit of shell went through one box and stopped in the next. Can't understand why the ammo did not go off but it did not. Would have lost my leg but for the boxes. Telling the others to wait I went back and got two more boxes and then rejoined the others. Surprisingly enough there in the middle of no man's land there was some green grass and I also saw one or two yellow iris though how these plants and grasses escaped destruction I cannot imagine.

From here on the ground was completely torn up, not a square inch left unturned by shells. The Boche wire was completely destroyed, only a few strands lying about. Their front line was utterly napoo, blown to bits and more or less filled with dirt from the mines. A bit further on and we had to rest for we were carrying heavy loads and dripping with sweat. It was just breaking dawn and the dust was still falling.

MESSINES: GASSED, 7 June 1917

Gunner William Pressey, Royal Artillery

We had been shooting most of the night and the Germans had been hitting back with shrapnel, high explosive and gas shells. With the terrific noise and blinding flashes of gunfire, if a lull occurred for only a few minutes and you were leaning against something, you had just to close your eyes and you were asleep. Nearing daylight we were told to rest. We dived into the dugout, I pulled off my tunic and boots and was asleep in no time at all.

I was awakened by a terrific crash. The roof came down on my chest and legs and I couldn't move anything but my head. I thought, "So this is it, then." I found I could hardly breathe. Then I heard voices. Other fellows with gas helmets on, looking very frightening in the half-light, were lifting timber off me and one was forcing a gas helmet on me. Even when you were all right, to wear a gas helmet was uncomfortable, your nose pinched, sucking air through a canister of chemicals. As I was already choking I remember fighting against having this helmet on.

The next thing I knew was being carried on a stretcher past our officers and some distance from the guns. I heard someone ask, "Who's that?" "Bombardier Pressey, sir." "Bloody hell." I was put into an ambulance and taken to the base, where we were placed on the stretchers side by side on the floor of a marquee, with about twelve inches in between. I suppose I resembled a kind of fish with my mouth open gasping for air. It seemed as if my lungs were gradually shutting up and my heart pounded away in my ears like the beat of a drum. On looking at the chap next to me I felt sick, for green stuff was oozing from the side of his mouth.

To get air into my lungs was real agony and the less I got the less the pain. I dozed off for short periods but seemed to wake in a sort of panic. To ease the pain in my chest I may subconsciously have stopped breathing, until the pounding of my heart woke me up. I was always surprised when I found myself awake, for I felt sure that I would die in my sleep. So little was known about treatment for various gases, that I never had treatment for phosgene, the type I was supposed to have had. And I'm sure that the gas some of the other poor fellows had swallowed was worse than phosgene. Now and then orderlies would carry out a stretcher.

CHEERS, ROSES, TEARS: PARIS WELCOMES GENERAL PERSHING, 13 June 1917

Floyd Gibbons, war correspondent

John Pershing was head of the American Expeditionary Force. Before heading to the Western Front, he visited Paris, where he was given an ecstatic welcome by its citizens.

The sooty girders of the Gare du Nord shook with cheers when the special train pulled in. The aisles of the great terminal were carpeted with red plush. A battalion of bearded poilus of the Two Hundred and Thirty-seventh Colonial Regiment was lined up on the platform like a wall of silent grey, bristling with bayonets and shiny trench helmets.

General Pershing stepped from his private car. Flashlights boomed and batteries of camera men manœuvred into positions for the lens barrage. The band of the Garde Républicaine blared forth the strains of the "Star Spangled Banner", bringing all the military to a halt and a long standing salute. It was followed by the "Marseillaise".

At the conclusion of the train-side greetings and introductions, Marshal Joffre and General Pershing walked down the platform together. The tops of the cars of every train in the station were crowded with workmen. As the tall, slender American commander stepped into view, the privileged observers on the cartops began to cheer.

A minute later, there was a terrific roar from beyond the walls of the station. The crowds outside had heard the cheering within. They took it up with thousands of throats. They made their welcome a ringing one. Paris took Pershing by storm . . .

Pershing's appearance in the open was the cue for wild, unstinted applause and cheering from the crowds which packed the streets and jammed the windows of the tall buildings opposite.

General Pershing and M. Painlevé, Minister of War, took seats in a large automobile. They were preceded by a motor containing United States Ambassador Sharp and former Premier Viviani . . . There were some fifty automobiles in the line, the rear of which was brought up by an enormous motor-bus load of the first American soldiers from the ranks to pass through the streets of Paris.

The crowds overflowed the sidewalks. They extended from the building walls out beyond the curbs and into the streets, leaving but a narrow lane through which the motors pressed their way slowly and with the exercise of much care. From the crowded balconies and windows overlooking the route, women and children tossed down showers of flowers and bits of coloured paper . . .

Old grey-haired fathers of French fighting men bared their heads and with tears streaming down their cheeks shouted greetings to the tall, thin, grey-moustached American commander who was leading new armies to the support of their sons. Women heaped armfuls of roses into the General's car and into the cars of other American officers that followed him . . .

American flags and red, white and blue bunting waved wherever the eye rested. English-speaking Frenchmen proudly explained to the uninformed that "Pershing" was pronounced "Peur-chigne" and not "Pair-shang". . . .

Occasionally there came from the crowds a good old genuine American whoop-em-up yell. This happened when the procession passed through groups of American ambulance workers and other sons of Uncle Sam, wearing the uniforms of the French, Canadian and English Corps.

They joined with Australians and South African soldiers on leave to cheer on the new-coming Americans with such spontaneous expressions as "Come on, you Yanks," "Now let's get 'em," and "Eat 'em up, Uncle Sam." . . .

The bus-load of enlisted men bringing up the rear received dozens of bouquets from the girls. The flowers were hurled at them from all directions. Every two hundred feet the French would organise a rousing shout, "*Vive l'Amérique!*" for them.

Being the passive recipients of this unusual adulation produced only embarrassment on the part of the regulars who simply had to sit there, smiling and taking it. Just to break the one-sided nature of the demonstrations, one of the enlisted men stood up in his seat and, addressing himself to his mates, shouted:

"Come on, fellows, let's give 'em a 'veever' ourselves. Now all together."

The bus-load rose to its feet like one man and shouted "Veever for France." Their "France" rhymed with "pants," so that none of the French understood it, but they did understand the sentiment behind the husky American lungs.

Through such scenes as these, the procession reached the great Place de la Concorde. In this wide, paved, open space an enormous crowd had assembled. As the autos appeared the cheering, the flower throwing, the tumultuous kiss-blowing began. It increased in intensity as the motors stopped in front of the Hôtel Crillon into which General Pershing disappeared, followed by his staff.

Immediately the cheering changed to a tremendous clamorous demand for the General's apperance on the balcony in front of his apartments.

"*Au balcon, au balcon,*" were the cries that filled the Place. The crowd would not be denied. General Pershing stepped forth on the balcony . . . looked down upon the sea of faces turned up toward him, and then it seemed that nature desired to play a part in the ceremony of that great day. A soft breeze from the Champs Elysées touched the cluster of flags on the General's right and from the Allied emblems fastened there it selected one flag.

The breeze tenderly caught the folds of this flag and wafted them across the balcony on which the General bowed. He saw and recognised that flag. He extended his hand, caught the flag in his fingers and pressed it to his lips. All France and all America represented in that vast throng that day cheered to the mighty echo when Pershing kissed the tri-colour of France.

It was a tremendous, unforgettable incident. It was exceeded by no other incident during those days of receptions and ceremonies.

ARABIA: GUERRILLA ATTACK ON A TURKISH OUTPOST, 2 July 1917

Lieutenant-Colonel T.E. Lawrence, attached Hejaz Expeditionary Force

After parlay with both his nominal Turkish overlords and the British, in June 1916 the grand sherif of Mecca, Hussein, proclaimed the independence of the Hejaz and urged all Muslims to wage war on the Ottoman Empire. The British liaison officer with the Arab insurgents was the 28-year-old T.E. Lawrence, an intelligence specialist and Arabist, who revealed himself to be an inspiring exponent of guerrilla warfare against the more numerous Turks.

We rode all night, and when dawn came were dismounting on the crest of the hills between Barra and Aba el Lissan, with a wonderful view westwards over the green and gold Guweira plain, and beyond it to the ruddy mountains hiding Akaba and the sea. Gasim Abu Dumeik, head of the Dhumaniyeh, was waiting anxiously for us, surrounded by his hard-bitten tribesmen, their grey strained faces flecked with the blood of the fighting yesterday. There was a deep greeting for Auda and Nasir. We made hurried plans, and scattered to the work, knowing we could not go forward to Akaba with this battalion in possession of the pass. Unless we dislodged it, our two months' hazard and effort would fail before yielding even first-fruits.

Fortunately the poor handling of the enemy gave us an unearned advantage. They slept on, in the valley, while we crowned the hills in wide circle about them unobserved. We began to snipe them steadily in their positions under the slopes and rock-faces by the water, hoping to provoke them out and up the hill in a charge against us. Meanwhile, Zaal rode away with our horsemen and cut the Maan telegraph and telephone in the plain.

This went on all day. It was terribly hot – hotter than ever before I had felt it in Arabia – and the anxiety and constant moving made it hard for us. Some even of the tough tribesmen broke down under the cruelty of the sun, and crawled or had to be thrown under rocks to recover in their shade. We ran up and down to supply our lack of numbers by mobility, ever looking over the long ranges of hill for a new spot from which to counter this or that Turkish effort. The hillsides were steep, and exhausted our breath, and the grasses twined like little hands about our ankles as we ran, and plucked us back. The sharp reefs of limestone which cropped out over the ridges tore our feet, and long before evening the more energetic men were leaving a rusty print upon the ground with every stride.

Our rifles grew so hot with sun and shooting that they seared our hands; and we had to be grudging of our rounds, considering every shot and spending great pains to make it sure. The rocks on which we flung ourselves for aim were burning, so that they scorched our breasts and arms, from which later the skin drew off in ragged sheets. The present smart made us thirst. Yet even water was rare with us; we could not afford men to fetch enough from Batra, and if all could not drink, it was better that none should.

We consoled ourselves with knowledge that the enemy's enclosed valley would be hotter than our open hills: also that they were Turks, men of white meat, little apt for warm weather. So we clung to them, and did not let them move or mass or sortie out against us cheaply. They could do nothing valid in return. We were no targets for their rifles, since we moved with speed, eccentrically. Also we were able to laugh at the little mountain guns which they fired up at us. The shells passed over our heads, to burst behind us in the air; and yet, of course, for all that they could see from their hollow place, fairly amongst us above the hostile summits of the hill.

Just after noon I had a heat-stroke, or so pretended, for I was dead weary of it all, and cared no longer how it went. So I crept into a hollow where there was a trickle of thick water in a muddy cup of the hills, to suck some moisture off its dirt through the filter of my sleeve. Nasir joined me, panting like a winded animal, with his cracked and bleeding lips shrunk apart in his distress: and old Auda appeared, striding powerfully, his eyes bloodshot and staring, his knotty face working with excitement.

He grinned with malice when he saw us lying there, spread out to find coolness under the bank, and croaked at me harshly, "Well, how is it with the Howeitat? All talk and no work?" "By God, indeed," spat I back again, for I was angry with everyone and with myself, "they shoot a lot and hit a little." Auda, almost pale with rage, and trembling, tore his head-cloth off and threw it on the ground beside me. Then he ran back up the hill like a madman, shouting to the men in his dreadful strained and rustling voice.

They came together to him, and after a moment scattered away downhill. I feared things were going wrong, and struggled to where he stood alone on the hill-top, glaring at the enemy: but all he would say to me was, "Get your camel if you want to see the old man's work". Nasir called for his camel and we mounted.

The Arabs passed before us into a little sunken place, which rose to a low crest; and we knew that the hill beyond went down in a facile slope to the main valley of Aba el Lissan, somewhat below the spring. All our four hundred camel men were here tightly collected, just out of sight of the enemy. We rode to their head, and asked the Shimt what it was and where the horsemen had gone.

He pointed over the ridge to the next valley above us, and said, "With Auda there": and as he spoke yells and shots poured up in a sudden torrent from beyond the crest. We kicked our camels furiously to the edge, to see our fifty horsemen coming down the last slope into the main valley, like a run-away, at full gallop, shooting from the saddle. As we watched, two or three went down, but the rest thundered forward at marvellous speed, and the Turkish infantry, huddled together under the cliff ready to cut their desperate way out towards Maan, in the first dusk began to sway in and out, and finally broke before the rush, adding their flight to Auda's charge.

Nasir screamed at me, "Come on," with his bloody mouth; and we plunged our camels madly over the hill, and down towards the head of the fleeing enemy. The slope was not too steep for a camel-gallop, but steep enough to make their pace terrific, and their course uncontrollable: yet the Arabs were able to extend to right and left and to shoot into the Turkish brown. The Turks had been too bound up in the terror of Auda's furious charge against their rear to notice us as we came over the eastward slope: so we also took them by surprise and in the flank; and a charge of ridden camels going nearly thirty miles an hour was irresistible.

My camel, the Sherari racer, Naama, stretched herself out, and hurled downhill with such might that we soon out-distanced the others. The Turks fired a few shots, but mostly only shrieked and turned to run: the bullets they did send at us were not very harmful, for it took much to bring a charging camel down in a dead heap.

I had got among the first of them, and was shooting, with a pistol of course, for only an expert could use a rifle from such plunging beasts; when suddenly my camel tripped and went down emptily upon her face, as though pole-axed. I was torn completely from the saddle, sailed grandly through the air for a great distance, and landed with a crash which seemed to drive all the power and feeling out of me. I lay there, passively waiting for the Turks to kill me, continuing to hum over the verses of a half-forgotten poem, whose rhythm something, perhaps the prolonged stride of the camel, had brought back to my memory as we leaped down the hill-side:

> For Lord I was free of all Thy flowers, but I chose the world's sad roses. And that is why my feet are torn and mine eyes are blind with sweat.

While another part of my mind thought what a squashed thing I should look when all that cataract of men and camels had poured over.

After a long time I finished my poem, and no Turks came, and no camel trod on me: a curtain seemed taken from my ears: there was a great noise in front. I sat up and saw the battle over, and our men driving together and cutting down the last remnants of the enemy. My camel's body had laid behind me like a rock and divided the charge into two streams; and in the back of its skull was the heavy bullet of the fifth shot I fired.

Mohammed brought Obeyd, my spare camel, and Nasir came back leading the Turkish commander, whom he had rescued, wounded, from Mohammed el Dheilan's wrath. The silly man had refused to surrender, and was trying to restore the day for his side with a pocket pistol. The Howeitat were very fierce, for the slaughter of their women on the day before had been a new and horrible side of warfare suddenly revealed to them. So there were only a hundred and sixty prisoners, many of them wounded; and three hundred dead and dying were scattered over the open valleys.

A few of the enemy got away, the gunners on their teams, and some mounted men and officers with their Jazi guides. Mohammed el Dheilan chased them for three miles into Mreigha, hurling insults as he rode, that they might know him and keep out of his way. The feud of Auda and his cousins had never applied to Mohammed, the political-minded, who showed friendship to all men of his tribe when he was alone to do so. Among the fugitives was Dhaif-Allah, who had done us the good turn about the King's Well at Jefer.

Auda came swinging up on foot, his eyes glazed over with the rapture of battle, and the words bubbling with incoherent speed from his mouth. "Work, work, where are words, work, bullets, Abu Tayi" . . . and he held up his shattered field-glasses, his pierced pistol-holster, and his leather sword-scabbard cut to ribbons. He had been the target of a volley which had killed his mare under him, but the six bullets through his clothes had left him scathless.

He told me later, in strict confidence, that thirteen years before he had bought an amulet Koran for one hundred and twenty pounds and had not since been wounded. Indeed, Death had avoided his face, and gone scurvily about killing brothers, sons and followers. The book was a Glasgow reproduction, costing eighteen pence; but Auda's deadliness did not let people laugh at his superstition.

He was wildly pleased with the fight, most of all because he had confounded me and shown what his tribe could do. Mohammed was wroth with us for a pair of fools, calling me worse than Auda, since I had insulted him by words like flung stones to provoke the folly which had nearly killed us all: though it had killed only two of us, one Rueili and one Sherari.

It was, of course, a pity to lose any one of our men, but time was of importance to us, and so imperative was the need of dominating Maan, to shock the little Turkish garrisons between us and the sea into surrender, that I would have willingly lost much more than two. On occasions like this Death justified himself and was cheap.

GOTHA AEROPLANES BOMB LONDON, 7 July 1917

Michael MacDonagh

The raid witnessed by MacDonagh was carried out by twenty-two Gothas; fifty-seven Londoners were killed.

I heard the weird swish of a bomb as it plunged downwards through the air and the roaring, rending explosion of its fall.

Instantly the scene in the streets was wholly transformed. The policeman standing near the monument of Queen Victoria worked himself into a state of excitement, shouting "Take cover! Take cover!" and wildly waving his arms. Everybody ran hither and thither for shelter. I joined the rush for the Blackfriars station of the Underground. We tumbled down the stairs to the platform of the trains going west, and ran along it to its end, some distance under the roadway. A second terrific explosion had given added swiftness to our feet. The girls of the Lyon's and ABC teashops at the station were in our wake, some of them being helped down, screaming hysterically. For my part, I felt that I had been plunged suddenly into a confused phantasmal state of being encompassed with dangers as in a nightmare. "The raiders have London at their mercy," I kept saying to myself; "there are no defences against them."

"WE DON'T GET MUCH MONEY, BUT WE DO SEE LIFE": LETTERS OF AN AIRMAN, 24 July–20 October 1917

Second Lieutenant H.G. Downing, Royal Flying Corps

Downing was posted missing in action in November 1917.

Castle Bromwich
Near Birmingham
July 24 1917

Dearest All,

I suppose I am exceeding the speed limit in letter writing, but daresay an extra letter will meet with your approval. I have been leading a most strenuous existence lately, and put in a tremendous amount of flying. Of course, unfortunately perhaps, it means going out to France sooner than expected but suppose pilots are wanted fairly badly.

I went on a cross country to a neighbouring aerodrome about 30 miles away this evening and had tea there. On my return journey I ran into a rain storm and got lost. When I came out I found I had wandered in a circle and was back at my original starting place. I thought I had just enough petrol, so continued my journey. When about 4 miles from this aerodrome, the engine started to misfire and finally stopped. I was a fair height up, about 1000 feet and just managed to make the aerodrome, missing some telegraph wires by a few inches, and finally stopping right in front of our mess door, without breaking anything. As you may guess it caused great excitement and everybody seems to think it is a good effort.

Ah! Well we don't get much money, but we do see life. I shall be going to Turnberry in Scotland for a aerial course on the 1st of August, for a fortnight. After that I shall be able to put up my wings if I do alright. In the meanwhile I had a very nice time last Saturday. Two charming members of the fair sex helped to look after this bashful young man and have now an invitation to the house, which I might say is *some* place. Oh! it is quite alright. I went and stunted over their house yesterday, and was pretty bucked to see an answering flutter of cambrio from the ground. Quite romantic. What! Well I suppose that is about all the news. Cheer oh! everybody.

BEF [France]
October 20, 1917

My dearest all,

I have been hoping for a letter, but so far the weekly budget has not turned up. I expect it takes some time nowadays.

Well, I am still in the land of the living and am enjoying myself no end. It is quite like old times. I had an exciting experience a day or two ago. You know how misty the weather is nowadays. Well we were flying about over the line, when a fellow and myself lost the rest of the patrol in a fog and we had not a bit of an idea where we were, so we came down to a few hundred feet from the ground. Presently we came to a large Town, which puzzled me immensely, and I circled round quite comically trying to locate it on the map. I thought, and so did the other fellow, that we were on our side of the lines. Imagine my amazement when I discovered it to be about 12 miles in Hun land. We were soon greeted with shells and machine gun fire. So of course we frightened everything we met on the roads, diving quite close to the ground and on to motor lorries etc and I bet we scared Huns out of their lives. When we eventually came home we noticed all the roads quite clear of men and lorries etc . . . so we were immensely bucked with ourselves and enjoyed a jolly good breakfast . . . Tonight I am dining with another squadron. I know a few fellows there and expect to have quite a cheery evening. Oh! Yes! I shall be quite good.

By the way I unfortunately smashed a machine the other day. I landed on my nose by mistake in the middle of the aerodrome. I didn't hurt myself though and my CO only laughed and suggested mildly that I should land on my wheels another time.

It was very funny because four more did exactly the same thing five minutes later. Well cheery oh! everybody.

PASSCHENDAELE: THE ADVANCE OF THE LANCASHIRE FUSILIERS, 31 July 1917

Lieutenant Thomas H. Floyd, Lancashire Fusiliers

On 31 July 1917 Haig launched his great assault against the Ypres salient. This third battle of Ypres – more often called Passchendaele – against strong German fortifications and almost incessant rain developed into a hell to outstrip even the Somme.

Our time was drawing near. At 8:30 we were to go over. At 8 we were all "standing to" behind the parapet waiting to go over. Colonel Best-Dunkley came walking along the line, his face lit up by smiles more pleasant than I have ever seen before. "Good morning, Floyd; best of luck!" was the greeting he accorded me as he passed; and I, of course, returned the good wishes. At about 8:20 Captain Andrews went past me and wished me good luck; and then he climbed over the parapet to reconnoitre. The minutes passed by. Everybody was wishing every-else good luck . . . Eventually, at 8:40, I got a signal . . . to go on. So forward we went, platoons in column of route. Could you possibly imagine what it was like? Shells were bursting everywhere. It was useless to take any notice where they were falling, because they were falling all round; they could not be dodged; one had to take one's chance: merely go forward and leave one's fate to destiny. Thus we advanced, amidst shot and shell, over fields, trenches, wire, fortifications, roads, ditches and streams which were simply churned out of all recognition by shell-fire. The field was strewn with wreckage, with the mangled remains of men and horses lying all over in a most ghastly fashion – just like any other battlefield I suppose. Many brave Scottish soldiers were to be seen dead in kneeling positions, killed just as they were firing on the enemy. Some German trenches were lined with German dead in that position. It was hell and slaughter. On we went. About a hundred yards on my right, slightly in front, I saw Colonel Best-Dunkley complacently advancing, with a walking stick in his hand, as calmly as if he were walking across a parade ground. He was still going strong last I heard of him.

We passed through the 166th Brigade. We left St Julien close on our left. Suddenly we were rained with bullets from rifles and machine guns. We extended. Men were being hit everywhere. My servant, Critchley, was the first in my platoon to be hit. We lay down flat for a while, as it was impossible for anyone to survive standing up. Then I determined to go forward. It was no use sticking here for ever, and we would be wanted further on; so we might as well try and dash through it. "Come along – advance!" I shouted, and leapt forward, I was just stepping over some barbed wire defences when the inevitable happened. I felt a sharp sting through my leg. I was hit by a bullet. So I dashed to the nearest shell-hole which, fortunately, was a very large one, and got my first field-dressing on.

BOMBS ON SOUTHEND: THE RECOLLECTIONS OF AN ELEVEN-YEAR-OLD, 12 August 1917

A.S. Hare

. . . the third bomb fell within ten feet; fortunately it fell in the flower bed and I was blown down and found myself with two others in the crater burnt by heat and coughing up cordite, one like me still alive. I got out and ran, unfortunately taking the same direction as the planes – the next one fell in front of the Technical School, and a Salvation Army girl and also a man trying to get protection along a low one-foot wall were both killed. The girl was mutilated beyond recognition. I was not so lucky this time getting a piece of shrapnel in my neck . . . The sights in the hospital (a small cottage type) were terrible to behold. Only two doctors, so the nurses had to operate ón the minor cases. Two ladies were helping in a third whose breasts were completely shot away, she was singing "Abide With Me". Australian soldiers billeted in the town brought in children in their arms with legs shattered, some with limbs missing. The sights in that hospital were terrible to behold.

AS ZERO HOUR APPROACHES: THE THOUGHTS AND FEARS OF AN INFANTRYMAN, PASSCHENDAELE, 15 August 1917

Arthur Lapointe, 22nd French-Canadian Battalion

4:15 a.m.: Only ten minutes now before Zero. The horizon shows a line of grey. Dawn is coming, and my heart is filled suddenly with bitterness when I realize that the day may be my last. In a few minutes we attack, and we shall need all our courage and skill to drive the enemy from his trenches. A shell bursts in our trench, breaking the leg of a man a few yards away. Stretcher-bearers apply a dressing and carry him to the rear. "There goes one man who won't die in the attack," remarks a soldier, almost enviously.

Our company commander, Capt. J. H. Roy, appears. "Ten rounds in your magazines and fix bayonets!" he orders. There is a click of steel on steel. Only two minutes now remain. Two minutes – in which a thousand thoughts mingle in my brain. The thought of the battlefield, where I may lie in a few moments weltering in blood; the sweet thought of our beloved land across the sea; and the thought of those I hold most dear. They do not know that in another moment I must face danger, even death. Yesterday, I believed I could die with something approaching indifference. Now I am aware of intense desire to live. I would give anything to know beyond doubt that I had even two whole days ahead of me. Yesterday, I had made all preparation for the voyage from which no traveller returns. But now I am unwilling to go. I see things – differently than I did yesterday.

SALONIKA: THE GREAT FIRE, 18 August 1917

Dr I. Emslie Hutton

The great fire of Salonika, which began on Saturday, August 18th, must certainly have been one of the most appalling fires of contemporary history. About five o'clock in the afternoon we noticed a thin lick of yellow flame just beyond the bazaar. Half an hour later it seemed to have grown bigger, and we all drew one another's attention to it, but none of us considered it was anything serious, and thought no more about it. The inhabitants must surely have realised the danger, but as they had no fire engines or methods of coping with it, nothing was done. The evening breeze arose and the flames licked along eastwards towards the principal parts of the town.

About 7 p.m. Dr McIlroy and I went into the town and walked up to the city walls; there below us was a belt of leaping, roaring fire that stretched almost from one end of the town to the other, and right across the middle part of it above the rue Ægnatia. This great ferocious monster ate up house after house with lightning speed, for the little evening breeze had developed into a mild Vardar wind, and now all the authorities saw that the situation was as bad as it could be, and that nothing could stop the progress of that roaring furnace. It was unforgettable; all the pictures of hell that were ever painted fall short of it in fearfulness, and its hungry roar, mingled with snarls and hisses and the crash of the falling ruins, was most awe-inspiring. The inhabitants ran about trying to save their possessions and not knowing where to take refuge. The progress of the flames was now so fast that the streets were thronged with the people carrying what they could, and the hamals were making a fortune carrying great loads of household goods for the highest bidder. A huge wardrobe, an enormous and hideous mirror or a piano would come blundering down one of the narrow streets, a hamal peeping out from under it, and it would sometimes meet a sewing-machine or a feather-bed going in the other direction and get jammed. Mothers and children scurried along with as much as they could carry, and bedridden grandmothers or invalids were half-dragged, half-carried along. All was confusion, grief and hopelessness.

We hurried back as soon as possible, for there seemed no reason why the fire should not spread along the line of houses both to our hospital, G.H.Q., and the other offices of the Allies.

By nine o'clock huge fire-balls were being blown right into our hospital and even beyond it, for the wind was still in the same direction, and there was great danger that our tents would catch fire, even if the fire itself did not reach us. Members of the staff, armed with brooms to beat out the flames, perched themselves on the ridge-poles of the high tents and stayed there till the wind changed and there was no more danger. "*Comme ces dames sont pratiques; les seestaires ont merveilleuses*," said our patients. "*Sont des garçons manqués*," grunted Danjou, the taciturn old *Médecin Chef* from next door.

Before midnight the entire town was a semicircle of fire, and it seemed as if nothing could escape; mercifully, after midnight the wind suddenly changed, and the flames, instead of licking further eastward, blazed straight southwards to the bay, setting fire to the barques that lay alongside the quay. These barques had been doing excellent work during the progress of the fire, and since the quay was till now untouched they had been able to save the inhabitants and some stores. Now moving out for safety, they spread the fire to other ships, and there was much confusion in the bay for a time. Nevertheless, the change of wind certainly saved the remainder of Salonika, and when daylight broke, though the fire had not stopped, and, indeed, continued to smoulder for days, the danger was over.

On all sides we heard praises of the British lorry-drivers, who worked most strenuously and considerately for all, especially the women and children. Of other Allies it was said that the drivers were not above taking tips and that much stealing went on (this is possible, for all the well-stocked shops were completely looted). It was said, too, that it was revolting to see the Russians lying in the gutters drinking the wine which flowed down from the burst barrels in the store-houses on the quay.

Olive Kelso King did splendid work in this fire, and was awarded the Gold Medal for bravery by the Serbian Headquarters for which she was now working.

A few days later we went down to see the town, which was still smouldering and hardly recognisable. All the quayside buildings were completely gutted, and nothing remained of Venizelos Street or the Bazaar but masses of masonry; every shop and hotel had been wiped out, the roads were blocked with smouldering debris, and the whole place was desolation. The Turkish quarter, however, nestled on the hillside as cheerfully as ever, and the old walls and the mosques rose dignified among the desolation, save the beautiful Church of St. Demetrius, which was almost completely destroyed. Many Salonicians were heavily insured with British Insurance Companies, who paid up the full amounts at once, much to the amazement of the inhabitants, who thought it a wonderful and noble act of generosity.

Salonika was soon in working order again, though no attempt was made to rebuild it. The inhabitants went back into the skeletons of their shops, raised tarpaulins and corrugated iron, and carried on as brisk a trade as before. Great fires must have occurred many times there during the previous centuries, and the inhabitants seemed to take it all as a matter of course, and hardly ever alluded to it. There was great discussion as to whether it was caused by enemy incendiarism, and since Salonika was full of spies this would not have been a difficult matter; on the previous day Monastir had been evacuated because of a fire caused by incendiary bombs, and Florina had likewise suffered. Be that as it may, the official opinion seemed to be that it was accidental, and was caused by a careless housewife upsetting some boiling fat on the fire.

TRENCH LIFE: A DAY IN THE LIFE OF AN OFFICER, WESTERN FRONT, 3 September 1917

Captain Geoffrey Bowen, 2nd Battalion Lancashire Fusiliers

8 p.m. Started.
9.30 p.m. Arrived.

11 p.m. Company arrived.
11 p.m. – 3 a.m. Round the line.
3.15 a.m. – 4.15 a.m. Sleep.
4.15 a.m. – 6 a.m. Stand to.
6 a.m. – 9. Sleep.
9 a.m. – 9.30 a.m. Breakfast: bacon, eggs, tinned sausage.
9.30 a.m. – 10.10. Round line.
10.10 a.m. – 12. Reports etc.
12.30 p.m. Lunch: Steak, potatoes, beans, sweet omelette.
1.45 p.m. – 2.15. Daylight patrol.
2.15 p.m. – 2.30 Sleep.
2.30 p.m. 3.40. Gup [chat] with C.O.
4. pm. Tea, bread, jam.
4.30 p.m. – 4.35. Sleep.
4.35 p.m. – 5.10. Entertain "Bowes".
5.10 p.m. – 5.15. Sleep.
5.15 p.m. – 5.25. Trench Mortar Officer reports.
5.25 p.m. – 6.15. Sleep.
6.15 p.m. – 6.35. Entertain Brain and Padre.
6.35 p.m. – 7.30. Sleep.
7.30 p.m. – 8. Round line.
8 p.m. – 8.15 Dinner: Steak, potatoes, tinned fruit and custard.
8.15 p.m. – 9. Round line.
11.30 p.m. – 12.30 a.m. Sleep.
12.30 – 2.30 a.m. Intensive sniping.
2.30–5 a.m. Sleep.

THE LAST LETTER OF A NAVAL MUTINEER, BERLIN, 11 September 1917

Able Seaman Albin Kobes, Imperial German Navy

From late summer 1917 the German navy was affected by mutinies, which culminated in 1918 in the wholesale rebellion of sailors at Kiel and the hoisting of the red flag.

My Dear Parents

I have been sentenced to death today, September 11th, 1917. Only myself and another comrade; the others have been let off with fifteen years' imprisonment. You will have heard why this has happened to me. I am a sacrifice of the longing for peace, others are going to follow. I cannot stop it now, it is six o'clock in the morning, I am being taken to Cologne at 6.30, and on Wednesday September 12th at 9 o'clock in the morning I am going to be sacrificed to military justice. I would have liked to press your hands once more to say goodbye, but I will do it silently. Console Paula and my little Fritz. I don't like dying so young, but I die with a curse on the German-militarist state. These are my last words. I hope that some day you and mother will be able to read them.

Always
Your Son.
Albin Köbes

ARABIA: BLOWING UP A TRAIN ON THE HEJAZ RAILWAY, 19 September 1917

Lieutenant-Colonel T.E. Lawrence, attached Hejaz Expeditionary Force

Much of the activity of T.E. Lawrence in the desert consisted of disrupting the Hejaz railway, the Turks' main supply line.

Next morning we returned on our tracks to let a fold of the plain hide us from the railway, and then marched south across the sandy flat; seeing tracks of gazelle, oryx and ostrich; with, in one spot, stale padmarks of leopard. We were making for the low hills bounding the far side, intending to blow up a train; for Zaal said that where these touched the railway was such a curve as we needed for mine-laying, and that the spurs commanding it would give us ambush and a field of fire for our machine-guns.

So we turned east in the southern ridges till within half a mile of the line. There the party halted in a thirty-foot valley, while a few of us walked down to the line, which bent a little eastward to avoid the point of higher ground under our feet. The point ended in a flat table fifty feet above the track, facing north across the valley.

The metals crossed the hollow on a high bank, pierced by a

two-arched bridge for the passage of rain-water. This seemed an ideal spot to lay the charge. It was our first try at electric mining and we had no idea what would happen; but it stood to our reason that the job would be more sure with an arch under the explosive because, whatever the effect on the locomotive, the bridge would go, and the succeeding coaches be inevitably derailed.

The ledge would make an admirable position for Stokes. For the automatics, it was rather high; but the enfilade would be masterful whether the train was going up or down the line. So we determined to put up with the disadvantages of plunging fire. It was good to have my two British responsibilities in one place, safe from surprise and with an independent retreat into the rough: for to-day Stokes was in pain with dysentery. Probably the Mudowwara water had upset his stomach. So few Englishmen seemed to have been endowed by their upbringing with any organic resistance to disease.

Back with our camels, we dumped the loads, and sent the animals to safe pasture near some undercut rocks from which the Arabs scraped salt. The freedmen carried down the Stokes gun with its shells; the Lewis guns; and the gelatine with its insulated wire, magneto and tools to the chosen place. The sergeants set up their toys on a terrace, while we went down to the bridge to dig a bed between the ends of two steel sleepers, wherein to hide my fifty pounds of gelatine. We had stripped off the paper wrapping of the individual explosive plugs and kneaded them together by help of the sun-heat into a shaking jelly in a sand-bag.

The burying of it was not easy. The embankment was steep, and in the sheltered pocket between it and the hill-side was a wind-laid bank of sand. No one crossed this but myself, stepping carefully; yet I left unavoidable great prints over its smoothness. The ballast dug out from the track I had to gather in my cloak for carriage in repeated journeys to the culvert, whence it could be tipped naturally over the shingle bed of the watercourse.

It took me nearly two hours to dig in and cover the charge: then came the difficult job of unrolling the heavy wires from the detonator to the hills whence we would fire the mine. The top sand was crusted and had to be broken through in burying the wires. They were stiff wires, which scarred the wind-rippled surface with long lines like the belly marks of preposterously narrow and heavy snakes. When pressed down in one place they rose into the air in another. At last they had to be weighted down with rocks which, in turn, had to be buried at the cost of great disturbance of the ground.

Afterwards it was necessary, with a sand-bag, to stipple the marks into a wavy surface; and, finally, with a bellows and long fanning sweeps of my cloak, to simulate the smooth laying of the wind. The whole job took five hours to finish; but then it was well finished: neither myself nor any of us could see where the charge lay, or that double wires led out underground from it to the firing point two hundred yards off, behind the ridge marked for our riflemen.

The wires were just long enough to cross from this ridge into a depression. There we brought up the two ends and connected them with the electric exploder. It was an ideal place both for it and for the man who fired it, except that the bridge was not visible thence.

However, this only meant that someone would have to press the handle at a signal from a point fifty yards ahead, commanding the bridge and the ends of the wires alike. Salem, Feisal's best slave, asked for this task of honour, and was yielded it by acclamation. The end of the afternoon was spent in showing him (on the disconnected exploder) what to do, till he was act-perfect and banged down the ratchet precisely as I raised my hand with an imaginary engine on the bridge.

We walked back to camp, leaving one man on watch by the line. Our baggage was deserted, and we stared about in a puzzle for the rest, till we saw them suddenly sitting against the golden light of sunset along a high ridge. We yelled to them to lie down or come down, but they persisted up there on their perch like a school of hooded crows, in full view of north and south.

At last we ran up and threw them off the skyline, too late. The Turks in a little hill-post by Hallat Ammar, four miles south of us, had seen them, and opened fire in their alarm upon the long shadows which the declining sun was pushing gradually up the slopes towards the post. Beduin were past masters in the art of using country, but in their abiding contempt for the stupidity of the Turks they would take no care to fight them. This ridge was visible at once from Mudowwara and Hallat Ammar, and they had frightened both places by their sudden ominous expectant watch.

However, the dark closed on us, and we knew we must sleep away the night patiently in hope of the morrow. Perhaps the Turks would reckon us gone if our place looked deserted in the morning. So we lit fires in a deep hollow, baked bread and were comfortable. The common tasks had made us one party, and the hill-top folly shamed everyone into agreement that Zaal should be our leader.

Day broke quietly, and for hours we watched the empty railway with its peaceful camps. The constant care of Zaal and of his lame cousin Howeimil, kept us hidden, though with difficulty, because for the insatiate restlessness of the Beduin, who would never sit down for ten minutes, but must fidget and do or say something. This defect made them very inferior to the stolid English for the long, tedious strain of a waiting war. Also it partly accounted for their uncertain stomachs in defence. Today they made us very angry.

Perhaps, after all, the Turks saw us, for at nine o'clock some forty men came out of the tents on the hill-top by Hallat Ammar to the south and advanced in open order. If we left them alone, they would turn us off our mine in an hour; if we opposed them with our superior strength and drove them back, the railway would take notice, and traffic be held up. It was a quandary, which eventually we tried to solve by sending thirty men to check the enemy patrol gradually; and, if possible, to draw them lightly aside into the broken hills. This might hide our main position and reassure them as to our insignificant strength and purpose.

For some hours it worked as we had hoped; the firing grew desultory and distant. A permanent patrol came confidently up from the south and walked past our hill, over our mine and on towards Mudowwara without noticing us. There were eight soldiers and a stout corporal, who mopped his brow against the heat, for it was now after eleven o'clock and really warm. When he had passed us by a mile or two the fatigue of the tramp became too much for him. He marched his party into the shade of a long culvert, under whose arches a cool draught from the east was gently flowing, and there in comfort they lay on the soft sand, drank water from their bottles, smoked, and at last slept. We presumed that this was the noon-day rest which every solid Turk in the hot summer of Arabia took as a matter of principle, and that their allowing themselves the pause showed that we were disproved or ignored. However, we were in error.

Noon brought fresh care. Through my powerful glasses we saw a hundred Turkish soldiers issue from Mudowwara Station and make straight across the sandy plain towards our place. They were coming very slowly, and no doubt unwillingly, for sorrow at losing their beloved midday sleep: but at their very worst marching and temper they could hardly take more than two hours before they reached us.

We began to pack up, preparatory to moving off, having decided to leave the mine and its leads in place on chance that the Turks might not find them, and we be able to return and take advantage of all the careful work. We sent a messenger to our covering party on the south, that they should meet us farther up, near those scarred rocks which served as screen for our pasturing camels.

Just as he had gone, the watchman cried out that smoke in clouds was rising from Hallat Ammar. Zaal and I rushed uphill and saw by its shape and volume that indeed there must be a train waiting in that station. As we were trying to see it over the hill, suddenly it moved out in our direction. We yelled to the Arabs to get into position as quick as possible, and there came a wild scramble over sand and rock. Stokes and Lewis, being booted, could not win the race; but they came well up, their pains and dysentery forgotten.

The men with rifles posted themselves in a long line behind the spur running from the guns past the exploder to the mouth of the valley. From it they would fire directly into the derailed carriages at less than one hundred and fifty yards, whereas the ranges for the Stokes and Lewis guns were about three hundred yards. An Arab stood up on high behind the guns and shouted to us what the train was doing – a necessary precaution, for if it carried troops and detrained them behind our ridge we should have to face about like a flash and retire fighting up the valley for our lives. Fortunately it held on at all the speed the two locomotives could make on wood fuel.

It drew near where we had been reported, and opened random fire into the desert. I could hear the racket coming, as I sat on my hillock by the bridge to give the signal to Salem, who danced round the exploder on his knees, crying with excitement, and calling urgently on God to make him fruitful. The Turkish fire sounded heavy, and I wondered with how many men we were going to have affair, and if the mine would be advantage enough for our eighty fellows to equal them. It would have been better if the first electrical experiment had been simpler.

However, at that moment the engines, looking very big, rocked with screaming whistles into view around the bend. Behind them followed ten box-waggons, crowded with rifle-muzzles at the windows and doors; and in little sand-bag nests on the roofs Turks precariously held on, to shoot at us. I had not thought of two engines, and on the moment decided to fire the charge under the second, so that however little the mine's effect, the uninjured engine should not be able to uncouple and drag the carriages away.

Accordingly, when the front "driver" of the second engine was on the bridge, I raised my hand to Salem. There followed a terrific roar, and the line vanished from sight behind a spouting column of black dust and smoke a hundred feet high and wide. Out of the darkness came shattering crashes and long, loud metallic clangings of ripped steel, with many lumps of iron and plate; while one entire wheel of a locomotive whirled up suddenly black out of the cloud against the sky, and sailed musically over our heads to fall slowly and heavily into the desert behind. Except for the flight of these, there succeeded a deathly silence, with no cry of men or rifle-shot, as the now grey mist of the explosion drifted from the line towards us, and over our ridge until it was lost in the hills.

In the lull, I ran southward to join the sergeants. Salem picked up his rifle and charged out into the murk. Before I had climbed to the guns the hollow was alive with shots, and with the brown figures of the Beduin leaping forward to grips with the enemy. I looked round to see what was happening so quickly, and saw the train stationary and dismembered along the track, with its waggon sides jumping under the bullets which riddled them, while Turks were falling out from the far doors to gain the shelter of the railway embankment.

As I watched, our machine-guns chattered out over my head, and the long rows of Turks on the carriage roofs rolled over, and were swept off the top like bales of cotton before the furious shower of bullets which stormed along the roofs and splashed clouds of yellow chips from the planking. The dominant position of the guns had been an advantage to us so far.

When I reached Stokes and Lewis the engagement had taken another turn. The remaining Turks had got behind the bank, here about eleven feet high, and from cover of the wheels were firing point-blank at the Beduin twenty yards away across the sand-filled dip. The enemy in the crescent of the curving line were secure from the machine-guns; but Stokes slipped in his first shell, and after a few seconds there came a crash as it burst beyond the train in the desert.

He touched the elevating screw, and his second shot fell just by the trucks in the deep hollow below the bridge where the Turks were taking refuge. It made a shambles of the place. The survivors of the group broke out in a panic across the desert, throwing away their rifles and equipment as they ran. This was the opportunity of the Lewis gunners. The sergeant grimly traversed with drum after drum, till the open sand was littered with bodies. Mushagraf, the Sherari boy behind the second gun, saw the battle over, threw aside his weapon with a yell, and dashed down at speed with his rifle to join the others who were beginning, like wild beasts, to tear open the carriages and fall to plunder. It had taken nearly ten minutes.

I looked up-line through my glasses and saw the Mudowwara patrol breaking back uncertainly towards the railway to meet the train-fugitives running their fastest northward. I looked south, to see our thirty men cantering their camels neck and neck in our direction to share the spoils. The Turks there, seeing them go, began to move after them with infinite precaution, firing volleys. Evidently we had a half hour respite, and then a double threat against us.

I ran down to the ruins to see what the mine had done. The bridge was gone; and into its gap was fallen the front waggon, which had been filled with sick. The smash had killed all but three or four and had rolled dead and dying into a bleeding heap against the splintered end. One of those yet alive deliriously cried out the word typhus. So I wedged shut the door, and left them there, alone.

Succeeding waggons were derailed and smashed: some had frames irreparably buckled. The second engine was a blanched pile of smoking iron. Its driving wheels had been blown upward, taking away the side of the fire-box. Cab and tender were twisted into strips, among the piled stones of the bridge abutment. It would never run again. The front engine had got off better: though heavily derailed and lying halfover, with the cab burst, yet its steam was at pressure, and driving-gear intact.

Our greatest object was to destroy locomotives, and I had kept in my arms a box of gun-cotton with fuse and detonator ready fixed, to make sure such a case. I now put them in position on the outside cylinder. On the boiler would have been better, but the sizzling steam made me fear a general explosion which would sweep across my men (swarming like ants over the booty) with a blast of jagged fragments. Yet they would not finish their looting before the Turks came. So I lit the fuse, and in the half-minute of its burning drove the plunderers a little back, with difficulty. Then the charge burst, blowing the cylinder to smithers, and the axle too. At the moment I was distressed with uncertainty whether the damage were enough; but the Turks later found the engine beyond use and broke it up.

The valley was a weird sight. The Arabs, gone raving mad, were rushing about at top speed bareheaded and half-naked, screaming, shooting into the air, clawing one another nail and fist, while they burst open trucks and staggered back and forward with immense bales, which they ripped by the railside, and tossed through, smashing what they did not want. The train had been packed with refugees and sick men, volunteers for boat-service on the Euphrates, and families of Turkish officers returning to Damascus.

There were scores of carpets spread about; dozens of mattresses and flowered quilts, blankets in heaps, clothes for men and women in full variety; clocks, cooking-pots, food, ornaments and weapons. To one side stood thirty or forty hysterical women, unveiled, tearing their clothes and hair; shrieking themselves distracted. The Arabs without regard to them went on wrecking the household goods; looting their absolute fill. Camels had become common property. Each man frantically loaded the nearest with what it could carry and shooed it westward into the void, while he turned to his next fancy.

Seeing me tolerably unemployed, the women rushed, and caught at me with howls for mercy. I assured them that all was going well: but they would not get away till some husbands delivered me. These knocked their wives off and seized my feet in a very agony of terror of instant death. A Turk so broken down was a nasty spectacle: I kicked them off as well as I could with bare feet, and finally broke free.

Next a group of Austrians, officers and non-commissioned officers, appealed to me quietly in Turkish for quarter. I replied with my halting German; whereupon one, in English, begged a doctor for his wounds. We had none: not that it mattered, for he was mortally hurt and dying. I told them the Turks would return in an hour and care for them. But he was dead before that, as were most of the others (instructors in the new Skoda mountain howitzers supplied to Turkey for the Hejaz war), because some dispute broke out between them and my own bodyguard, and one of them fired a pistol shot at young Rahail. My infuriated men cut them down, all but two or three, before I could return to interfere.

DEATH OF AN ACE: THE SHOOTING DOWN OF WERNER VOSS, WESTERN FRONT, 23 September 1917

Flight-Commander James McCudden VC, 56 Squadron Royal Flying Corps

With 48 "kills", the German fighter pilot Werner Voss was one of the undisputed aces of the World War; he was finally downed by Rhys-Davids from 56 Squadron RFC, in what many considered the classic dogfight of the First World War. McCudden, the Flight-Commander of 56 Squadron, died on 9 July 1918, with 57 kills to his tally.

On the evening of the 23rd I led my patrol from the aerodrome and crossed the lines at Bixschoote at 8,000 feet as there was a very thick wall of clouds up at 9,000 feet. As soon as we crossed over Hunland I noted abnormal enemy activity, and indeed there seemed to be a great many machines of both sides about. This was because every machine that was up was between 9,000 feet and the ground instead of as usual from 20,000 feet downwards.

We flew south from Houthoulst Forest, and although there were many Huns about they were all well over. Archie was at his best this evening, for he had us all silhouetted against a leaden sky, and we were flying mostly at 7,000 feet. When over Gheluvelt, I saw a two-seater coming north near Houthem. I dived, followed by my patrol, and opened fire from above and behind the D.F.W., whose occupants had not seen me, having been engrossed in artillery registration. I fired a good burst from both guns, a stream of water came from the D.F.W.'s centre-section, and then the machine went down in a vertical dive and crashed to nothing, north-east of Houthem.

We went north, climbing at about 6,000 feet. A heavy layer of grey clouds hung at 9,000 feet, and although the visibility was poor for observation, the atmosphere was fairly clear in a horizontal direction. Away to the east one could see clusters of little black specks, all moving swiftly, first in one direction and then another. Farther north we could see formations of our own machines, Camels, Pups, S.E.'s, Spads and Bristols, and lower down in the haze our artillery R.E.8's.

We were just on the point of engaging six Albatros Scouts away to our right, when we saw ahead of us, just above Poelcappelle, an S.E. half spinning down closely pursued by a silvery blue German triplane at very close range. The S.E. certainly looked very unhappy, so we changed our minds about attacking the six V-strutters, and went to the rescue of the unfortunate S.E.

The Hun triplane was practically underneath our formation now, and so down we dived at a colossal speed. I went to the right, Rhys-Davids to the left, and we got behind the triplane together. The German pilot saw us and turned in a most disconcertingly quick manner, not a climbing nor Immelmann turn, but a sort of flat half spin. By now the German triplane was in the middle of our formation, and its handling was wonderful to behold. The pilot seemed to be firing at all of us simultaneously, and although I got behind him a second time, I could hardly stay there for a second. His movements were so quick and uncertain that none of us could hold him in sight at all for any decisive time.

I now got a good opportunity as he was coming towards me nose on, and slightly underneath, and had apparently not seen me. I dropped my nose, got him well in my sight, and pressed both triggers. As soon as I fired up came his nose at me, and I heard clack-clack-clack-clack, as his bullets passed close to me and through my wings. I distinctly noticed the red-yellow flashes from his parallel Spandau guns. As he flashed by me I caught a glimpse of a black head in the triplane with no hat on at all.

By this time a red-nosed Albatros Scout had arrived, and was apparently doing its best to guard the triplane's tail, and it was well handled too. The formation of six Albatros Scouts which we were going to attack at first stayed above us, and were prevented from diving on us by the arrival of a formation of Spads, whose leader apparently appreciated our position, and kept the six Albatroses otherwise engaged.

The triplane was still circling round in the midst of six S.E.'s, who were all firing at it as opportunity offered, and at one time I noted the triplane in the apex of a cone of tracer bullets from at least five machines simultaneously, and each machine had two guns. By now the fighting was very low, and the red-nosed Albatros had gone down and out, but the triplane still remained. I had temporarily lost sight of the triplane whilst changing a drum of my Lewis gun, and when I next saw him he was very low, still being engaged by an S.E. marked I, the pilot being Rhys-Davids. I noticed that the triplane's movements were very erratic, and then I saw him go into a fairly steep dive and so I continued to watch, and then saw the triplane hit the ground and disappear into a thousand fragments, for it seemed to me that it literally went to powder.

Strange to say, I was the only pilot who witnessed the triplane crash, for even Rhys-Davids, who finally shot it down, did not see its end.

It was now quite late, so we flew home to the aerodrome, and as long as I live I shall never forget my admiration for that German pilot, who single-handed fought seven of us for ten minutes, and also put some bullets through all of our machines. His flying was wonderful, his courage magnificent, and in my opinion he is the bravest German airman whom it has been my privilege to see fight.

We arrived back at the mess, and at dinner the main topic was the wonderful fight. We all conjectured that the enemy pilot must be one of the enemy's best, and we debated as to whether it was Richthofen or Wolff or Voss. The tri-plane fell in our lines, and the next morning we had a wire from the Wing saying that the dead pilot was found wearing the Boelcke collar and his name was Werner Voss. He had the "Ordre Pour le Mérite."

Rhys-Davids came in for a shower of congratulations, and no one deserved them better, but as the boy himself said to me, "Oh, if I could only have brought him down alive," and his remark was in agreement with my own thoughts.

MATA HARI IS EXECUTED, FRANCE, 18 October 1917

Henry G. Wales, war correspondent

Born in 1876, Mata Hari was a double agent, whose main loyalty was to the Germans.

Mata Hari, which is Javanese for Eye-of-the-Morning, is dead. She was shot as a spy by a firing squad of Zouaves at the Vincennes Barracks. She died facing death literally, for she refused to be blindfolded.

Gertrud Margarete Zelle, for that was the real name of the beautiful Dutch-Javanese dancer, did appeal to President Poincare for a reprieve, but he refused to intervene.

The first intimation she received that her plea had been denied was when she was led at daybreak from her cell in the Saint-Lazare prison to a waiting automobile and then rushed to the barracks where the firing squad awaited her.

Never once had the iron will of the beautiful woman failed her. Father Arbaux, accompanied by two sisters of charity, Captain Bouchardon, and Maître Clunet, her lawyer, entered her cell, where she was still sleeping – a calm, untroubled sleep, it was remarked by the turnkeys and trusties.

The sisters gently shook her. She arose and was told that her hour had come.

"May I write two letters?" was all she asked.

Consent was given immediately by Captain Bouchardon, and pen, ink, paper, and envelopes were given to her.

She seated herself at the edge of the bed and wrote the letters with feverish haste. She handed them over to the custody of her lawyer.

Then she drew on her stockings, black, silken, filmy things, grotesque in the circumstances. She placed her high-heeled slippers on her feet and tied the silken ribbons over her insteps.

Shc arose and took the long black velvet cloak, edged around the bottom with fur and with a huge square fur collar hanging down the back, from a hook over the head of her bed. She placed this cloak over the heavy silk kimono which she had been wearing over her nightdress.

Her wealth of black hair was still coiled about her head in braids. She put on a large, flapping black felt hat with a black silk ribbon and bow. Slowly and indifferently, it seemed, she pulled on a pair of black kid gloves. Then she said calmly:

"I am ready."

The party slowly filed out of her cell to the waiting automobile.

The car sped through the heart of the sleeping city. It was scarcely half past five in the morning and the sun was not yet fully up.

Clear across Paris the car whirled to the Caserne de Vincennes, the barracks of the old fort which the Germans stormed in 1870.

The troops were already drawn up for the execution. The

twelve Zouaves, forming the firing squad, stood in line, their rifles at ease. A subofficer stood behind them, sword drawn.

The automobile stopped, and the party descended, Mata Hari last. The party walked straight to the spot, where a little hummock of earth reared itself seven or eight feet high and afforded a background for such bullets as might miss the human target.

As Father Arbaux spoke with the condemned woman, a French officer approached, carrying a white cloth.

"The blindfold," he whispered to the nuns who stood there and handed it to them.

"Must I wear that?" asked Mata Hari, turning to her lawyer, as her eyes glimpsed the blindfold.

Maître Clunet turned interrogatively to the French officer.

"If Madame prefers not, it makes no difference," replied the officer, hurriedly turning away.

Mata Hari was not bound and she was not blindfolded. She stood gazing steadfastly at her executioners, when the priest, the nuns, and her lawyer stepped away from her.

The officer in command of the firing squad, who had been watching his men like a hawk that none might examine his rifle and try to find out whether he was destined to fire the blank cartridge which was in the breech of one rifle, seemed relieved that the business would soon be over.

A sharp, crackling command, and the file of twelve men assumed rigid positions at attention. Another command, and their rifles were at their shoulders; each man gazed down his barrel at the breast of the woman which was the target.

She did not move a muscle.

The underofficer in charge had moved to a position where from the corners of their eyes they could see him. His sword was extended in the air.

It dropped. The sun – by this time up – flashed on the burnished blade as it described an arc in falling. Simultaneously the sound of the volley rang out. Flame and a tiny puff of greyish smoke issued from the muzzle of each rifle. Automatically the men dropped their arms.

At the report Mata Hari fell. She did not die as actors and moving-picture stars would have us believe that people die when they are shot. She did not throw up her hands nor did she plunge straight forward or straight back.

Instead she seemed to collapse. Slowly, inertly, she settled to her knees, her head up always, and without the slightest change of expression on her face. For the fraction of a second it seemed she tottered there, on her knees, gazing directly at those who had taken her life. Then she fell backward, bending at the waist, with her legs doubled up beneath her. She lay prone, motionless, with her face turned towards the sky.

A non-commissioned officer, who accompanied a lieutenant, drew his revolver from the big, black holster strapped about his waist. Bending over, he placed the muzzle of the revolver almost – but not quite – against the left temple of the spy. He pulled the trigger, and the bullet tore into the brain of the woman.

Mata Hari was surely dead.

CAPORETTO: ROMMEL BEHIND THE ITALIAN LINES, 25 October 1917

Leutnant Erwin Rommel, Wurtemberg Mountain Battalion, Alpine Corps

In the Caporetto region of the Alps, the Italian and Austrian armies had fought a chain of inconclusive battles since 1915. On 24 October 1917 the Austrians launched yet another offensive, but this time with German reinforcements, notably the Alpine Corps. The result was one of the most spectacular Central Power's victories of the entire war, one which allowed them to within shelling distance of Venice. For his part in infiltrating the Italian lines, Erwin Rommel was awarded the *Pour le Merite*. As Rommel recounts below, the appearance of his troops deep in Italian territory so dismayed Italian units that they simply surrendered on sight.

On the Lucio-Savogna road

. . . single soldiers and vehicles came unsuspectingly toward us. They were politely received at the sharp curves of the road by a few mountain soldiers and taken prisoner. Everyone was having fun and there was no shooting. Great care was taken that the movement of the vehicles did not slacken on the curves. While a few mountain troops took care of the drivers and escorts, others seized the reins of the horses or mules and drove the teams to a previously designated parking place . . . Business was booming . . . The contents of the various vehicles offered us starved warriors unexpected delicacies. Chocolate, eggs, preserves, grapes, wine and white bread were unpacked and distributed . . . Morale two miles behind the enemy front was wonderful!

Later on the slops of Mount Mataju, Rommel walked up to a large Italian unit and asked it to surrender

I came to within 150 yards of the enemy! Suddenly the mass began to move and, in the ensuing panic, swept its resisting officers along downhill. Most of the soldiers threw their weapons away and hundreds hurried to me. In an instant I was surrounded and hoisted on Italian soldiers. "*Evviva Germania!*" sounded from a thousand throats. An Italian officer who hesitated to surrender was shot down by his own troops. For the Italians on Mrzli peak the war was over. They shouted with joy.

"SO TERRIBLE A PURGATORY": SCENES FROM PASSCHENDAELE, 2–6 November 1917

Major C.E.L. Lyne, Royal Field Artillery

Shortly after the scenes described by Lyne below, Haig called off the Passchendaele offensive. Some 400,000 Allied casualties attested to the success of the German defensive line.

2 November 1917

The events of the last week have succeeded each other with such rapidity that I am absolutely dazed. I can't remember how long it is since I wrote you on what I was doing at that time. I think I did tell you we had been sent hurriedly upwards, and how we battered mightily with mud and other discomforts and various treks to and fro. Well anyway, here we are, in absolutely *the* most unholy spot from the North Sea to the Mediterranean, when I say it's about the most lively spot on the map, you'll know where to look for me.

I'll forgo description till I'm feeling a bit more optimistic, they say first thoughts are best, but I know darn well they couldn't be worse, anyway I'm dead tired, so –

4 November 1917

I'm feeling a bit tired and muzzy in the nut, so not much in the way of a letter. Shall be glad of that new shirt, have lived in the present one for the last three weeks, have had *one* hot bath since last leave and at present moment am saturated in mud and dirt. Had your letter containing budget on psychical research today, a subject which cuts no ice with us at the present moment as materialistic matters count just nineteen to the dozen. We are properly up against it here, we've struck the liveliest spot on the Front. I've never yet struck a proposition which filled me with less enthusiasm than the present stunt. The conditions are awful, beyond description, nothing we've had yet has come up to it, the whole trouble is the weather which daily gets worse. One's admiration goes out to the infantry who attack and gain ground under these conditions. Had I a descriptive pen I could picture to you the squalour and wretchedness of it all and through it the wonder of the men who carry on. Figure to yourself a desolate wilderness of water filled with shell craters, and crater after crater whose lips form narrow peninsulas along which one can at best pick but a slow and precarious way. Here a shattered tree trunk, there a wrecked "pill-box", sole remaining evidence that this was once a human and inhabited land. Dante would never have condemned lost souls to wander in so terrible a purgatory. Here a shattered wagon, there a gun mired to the muzzle in mud which grips like glue, even the birds and rats have forsaken so unnatural a spot. Mile after mile of the same unending dreariness, landmarks are gone, of whole villages hardly a pile of bricks amongst the mud marks the site. You see it at its best under a leaden sky with a chill drizzle falling, each hour an eternity, each dragging step a nightmare. How weirdly it recalls some half formed horror of childish nightmare, one would flee, but whither? – one would cry aloud but there comes no blessed awakening. Surely the God of Battles has deserted a spot where only devils can reign. Think what it means, weeks of it, weeks which are eternities, when the days are terrible but the nights beyond belief. Through it all the horror of continual shell fire, rain and mud. Gas is one of the most potent components of this particular inferno. Nights are absolutely without rest, and gas at night is the crowning limit of horrors. The Battery that occupied the position before we came was practically wiped out by it, and had to be relieved at short notice, and the battery that relieved them lost 37 men on the way in. You can imagine how bucked I was when they handed me out these spicy bits of gossip on the way up. I daren't risk more than three men per gun up here at the same time and only 2 officers besides myself, at the moment they are rather sorry for themselves after last night's gas stunt, and doing unhelpful things to their eyes with various drops and washes. I've got a throat like raw beef and a voice like a crow.

They shot us up in style last night, hardly got 30 minutes sleep and I was dead tired. We've got a dugout for our mess with 4 inches of concrete on top, last night there were our 3 selves, our servants, a stray officer and his servant and one of my wounded men. I kept on telling them the roof would not stop a splinter, but no one seemed inclined to go elsewhere.

6 November 1917

Very troublous days, particular hell all day, shells of many calibres have descended upon us, aussi rain. I lost a corporal, killed, also a bombardier and best gunner wounded. I thought the war was over when a shell burst 5 yards away and projected a 12 feet beam on to me. Two guns out of action. Altogether what you'd call a rosy-hued outlook. We're up against it here, more than any place I've struck yet. Up firing most of last night, a very disjointed and hand to mouth existence on the whole. What price Xmas dinner in peace! Had to send C off down to wagon line, he was quite bad from the gas, and would have gone to pieces with another night like the last few, and he's a real tough nut as a rule. Great days these.

RUSSIA IN REVOLUTION: THE BOLSHEVIKS SEIZE POWER, 6–7 November 1917

Leon Trotsky

When the moderate government of Kerensky proved unwilling to extract Russia for the First World War, it was rapidly overtaken in prestige and popularity among Russian workers by the revolutionary Bolshevik party of V.I. Lenin. On the evening of 27 October (6 November in the Western calendar) the Bolsheviks seized power in Petrograd (St Petersburg). Leon Trotsky was Lenin's chief comrade-in-arms and the main overseer of the coup, which was organized via the Bolshevik-dominated Military Revolutionary Committee. The Committee's headquarters were the Smolny building, where Trotsky spent the fateful night.

On the night of the 24th the members of the Revolutionary Committee went out into the various districts, and I was left alone. Later on Kamenev came in. He was opposed to the uprising, but he had come to spend that deciding night with me, and together we stayed in the tiny corner room on the third floor, so like the captain's bridge on that deciding night of the revolution.

There is a telephone booth in the large empty room adjoining us, and the bell rings incessantly about important things and trifles. Each ring heightens the alertness of the silence. One can readily picture the deserted streets of Petrograd, dimly lit, and whipped by the autumn winds from the sea; the bourgeois and officials cowering in their beds, trying to guess what is going on in those dangerous and mysterious streets; the workers' quarters quiet with the tense sleep of a war-camp. Commissions and conferences of the government parties are exhausting themselves in impotence in the Tsar's palaces, where the living ghosts of democracy rub shoulders with the still hovering ghosts of the monarchy. Now and again the silks and gildings of the halls are plunged into darkness – the supplies of coal have run short. In the various districts detachments of workers, soldiers, and sailors are keeping watch. The young proletarians have rifles and machine-gun belts across their shoulders. Street pickets are warming themselves at fires in the streets. The life of the capital, thrusting its head from one epoch into another on this autumn night, is concentrated about a group of telephones.

Reports from all the districts, suburbs, and approaches to the capital are focused in the room on the third floor. It seems that everything has been foreseen; the leaders are in their places; the contacts are assured; nothing seems to have been forgotten.

Once more, let us go over it in our minds. This night decides. Only this evening in my report to the delegates of the second congress of the Soviets, I said with conviction: "If you stand firm, there will be no civil war, our enemies will capitulate at once, and you will take the place that belongs to you by right. There can be no doubt about victory; it is as assured as the victory of any uprising can be". And yet these hours are still tense and full of alarm, for the coming night decides. The government while mobilizing cadets yesterday, gave orders to the cruiser *Aurora* to steam out of the Neva. They were the same Bolshevik sailors whom Skobelev, coming hat in hand, in August begged to protect the Winter Palace from Kornilov. The sailors referred to the Military-Revolutionary Committee for instructions, and consequently the *Aurora* is standing tonight where she was yesterday. A telephone call from Pavlovsk informs me that the government is bringing up from there a detachment of artillery, a battalion of shock troops from Tsarskoye Syelo, and student officers from the Peterhof military school. Into the Winter Palace Kerensky has drawn military students, officers, and the women shock troops. I order the commissaries to place dependable military defences along the approaches to Petrograd and to send agitators to meet the detachments called out by the government. All our instructions and reports are sent by telephone and the government agents are in a position to intercept them. Can they still control our communications?

"If you fail to stop them with words, use arms. You will answer for this with your life."

I repeat this sentence time and time again. But I do not believe in the force of my order. The revolution is still too trusting, too generous, optimistic and light-hearted. It prefers to threaten with arms rather than really use them. It still hopes that all questions can be solved by words, and so far it has been successful in this – hostile elements evaporate before its breath. Earlier in the day (the 24th) an order was issued to use arms and to stop at nothing at the first sign of pogroms. Our enemies don't even dare think of the streets; they have gone into hiding. The streets are ours; our commissaries are watching all the approaches to Petrograd. The officers' school and the gunners have not responded to the call of the government. Only a section of the Oraniembaum military students have succeeded in making their way through our defences, but I have been watching their movements by telephone. They end by sending envoys to the Smolny. The government has been seeking support in vain. The ground is slipping from under its feet.

The outer guard of the Smolny has been reinforced by a new machine-gun detachment. The contact with all sections of the garrison is uninterrupted. The companies on duty are on watch in all the regiments. The commissaries are in their places. Delegations from each garrison unit are in the Smolny, at the disposal of the Military-Revolutionary Committee, to be used in case the contact with that unit should be broken off. Armed detachments from the districts march along the streets, ring the bells at the gates or open the gates without ringing, and take possession of one institution after another. Nearly everywhere these detachments are met by friends who have been waiting impatiently for them. At the railway terminals, specially appointed commissaries are watching the incoming and outgoing trains, and in particular the movement of troops. No disturbing news comes from there. All the more important points in the city are given over into our hands almost without resistance, without fighting, without casualties. The telephone alone informs us: "We are here!"

All is well. It could not have gone better. Now I may leave the telephone. I sit down on the couch. The nervous tension lessens. A dull sensation of fatigue comes over me.

"Give me a cigarette," I say to Kamenev. (In those years I still smoked, but only spasmodically.) I take one or two puffs, but suddenly with the words, "Only this was lacking!" I faint. (I inherited from my mother a certain susceptibility to fainting spells when suffering from physical pain or illness. That was why some American physician described me as an epileptic.) As

I come to, I see Kamenev's frightened face bending over me. "Shall I get some medicine?" he asks.

"It would be much better," I answer after a moment's reflection, "if you got something to eat." I try to remember when I last had food, but I can't. At all events it was not yesterday.

RUSSIA IN REVOLUTION: THE STORMING OF THE WINTER PALACE, PETROGRAD, November 1917

John Reed

The radical American journalist John Reed reported the Russian Revolution for several publications, particularly the *Liberator*. Reed died in the Soviet Union of typhus in 1920. He was later immortalized in the Hollywood biopic *Reds*.

When we came into the chill night, all the front of Smolny was one huge park of arriving and departing automobiles, above the sound of which could be heard the far-off slow beat of the cannon. A great motor-truck stood there, shaking to the roar of its engine. Men were tossing bundles into it, and others receiving them, with guns beside them.

"Where are you going?" I shouted.

"Down-town – all over – everywhere!" answered a little workman, grinning, with a large exultant gesture.

We showed our passes. "Come along!" they invited. "But there'll probably be shooting –" We climbed in: the clutch slid home with a raking jar, the great car jerked forward, we all toppled backward on top of those who were climbing in; past the huge fire by the gate, and then the fire by the outer gate, glowing red on the faces of the workmen with rifles who squatted around it, and went bumping at top speed down the Suvorovsky Prospect, swaying from side to side . . . One man tore the wrapping from a bundle and began to hurl handfuls of papers into the air. We imitated him, plunging down through the dark street with a tail of white papers floating and eddying out behind. The late passer-by stooped to pick them up; the patrols around bonfires on the corners ran out with uplifted arms to catch them. Sometimes armed men loomed up ahead, crying "*Stoi!*" and raising their guns, but our chauffeur only yelled something unintelligible and we hurtled on . . .

I picked up a copy of the paper, and under a fleeting streetlight read:

To the Citizens of Russia!

The Provisional Government is deposed. The State Power has passed into the hands of the organ of the Petrograd Soviet of Workers' and Soldiers' Deputies, the Military Revolutionary Committee, which stands at the head of the Petrograd proletariat and garrison.

The cause for which the people were fighting: immediate proposal of a democratic peace, abolition of landlord property-rights over the land, labour control over production, creation of a Soviet Government – that cause is securely achieved.

LONG LIVE THE REVOLUTION OF WORKMEN, SOLDIERS, AND PEASANTS!

Military Revolutionary Committee
Petrograd Soviet of Worker's and Soldiers' Deputies

A slant-eyed, Mongolian faced man who sat beside me, dressed in a goatskin of Caucasian cape, snapped, "Look out! Here the provocators always shoot from the windows!" We turned into Znamensky Square, dark and almost deserted, careened around Trubetskoy's brutal statue and swung down the wide Nevsky, three men standing up with rifles ready, peering at the windows. Behind us the street was alive with people running and stooping. We could no longer hear the cannon, and the nearer we drew to the Winter Palace end of the city the quieter and more deserted were the streets. The City Duma was all brightly lighted. Beyond that we made out a dark mass of people, and a line of sailors, who yelled furiously at us to stop. The machine slowed down, and we climbed out.

It was an astonishing scene. Just at the corner of the Ekaterina Canal, under an arc-light, a cordon of armed sailors was drawn across the Nevsky, blocking the way to a crowd of people in column of fours. There were about three or four hundred of them, men in frock coats, well-dressed women, officers – all sorts and conditions of people. Among them we recognized many of the delegates from the Congress, leaders of the Mensheviki and Socialist Revolutionaries; Avksentiev, the lean, red-bearded president of the Peasants' Soviets, Sarokin, Kerensky's spokesman, Khinchuk, Abramovich; and at the head white-bearded old Schreider, Mayor of Petrograd, and Prokopovich, Minister of Supplies in the Provisional Government, arrested that morning and relcased. I caught sight of Malkin, reporter for the *Russian Daily News*. "Going to die in the Winter Palace," he shouted cheerfully. The procession stood still, but from the front of it came loud argument. Schreider and Prokopovich were bellowing at the big sailor who seemed in command.

"We demand to pass!" they cried. "See, these comrades come from the Congress of Soviets! Look at their tickets! We are going to the Winter Palace!"

The sailor was plainly puzzled. He scratched his head with an enormous hand, frowning. "I have orders from the Committee not to let anybody go to the Winter Palace," he grumbled. "But I will send a comrade to telephone to Smolny . . ."

"We insist upon passing! We are unarmed! We will march on whether you permit us or not!" cried old Schreider, very much excited.

"I have orders –" repeated the sailor sullenly.

"Shoot us if you want to! We will pass! Forward!" came from all sides. "We are ready to die, if you have the heart to fire on Russians and comrades! We bare our breasts to your guns!"

"No," said the sailor, looking stubborn, "I can't allow you to pass."

"What will you do if we go forward? Will you shoot?"

"No, I'm not going to shoot people who haven't any guns. We won't shoot unarmed Russian people . . ."

"We will go forward! What can you do?"

"We will do something!" replied the sailor, evidently at a loss.

"We can't let you pass. We will do something."

"What will you do? What will you do?"

Another sailor came up, very much irritated. "We will spank you!" he cried energetically. "And if necessary we will shoot you too. Go home how, and leave us in peace!"

At this there was a great clamour of anger and resentment. Prokopovich had mounted some sort of box, and waving his umbrella, he made a speech:

"Comrades and citizens!" he said. "Force is being used against us! We cannot have our innocent blood upon the hands of these ignorant men! It is beneath our dignity to be shot down here in the streets by switchmen –" (What he meant by "switchmen" I never discovered.) "Let us return to the Duma and discuss the best means of saving the country and the Revolution!"

Whereupon, in dignified silence, the procession marched around and back up the Nevsky, always in column of fours. And taking advantage of the diversion we slipped past the guards and set off in the direction of the Winter Palace.

Here it was absolutely dark, and nothing moved but pickets of soldiers and Red Guards grimly intent. In front of the Kazan Cathedral a three-inch field-gun lay in the middle of the street, slewed sideways from the recoil of its last shot over the roofs. Soldiers were standing in every doorway talking in loud tones and peering down towards the Police Bridge. I heard one voice saying: "It is possible that we have done wrong . . ." At the corners patrols stopped all passers-by – and the composition of these patrols was interesting, for in command of the regular troops was invariably a Red Guard . . . The shooting had ceased.

Just as we came to the Morskaya somebody was shouting: "The *yunkers* have sent word that they want us to go and get them out!" Voices began to give commands, and in the thick gloom we made out a dark mass moving forward, silent but for the shuffle of feet and the clinking of arms. We fell in with the first ranks.

Like a black river, filling all the street, without song or cheer we poured through the Red Arch, where the man just ahead of me said in a low voice: "Look out, comrades! Don't trust them. They will fire, surely!" In the open we began to run, stooping low and bunching together, and jammed up suddenly behind the pedestal of the Alexander Column.

"How many of you did they kill?" I asked.

"I don't know. About ten . . ."

After a few minutes huddling there, some hundreds of men, the Army seemed reassured and without any orders suddenly began again to flow forward. By this time, in the light that streamed out of all the Winter Palace windows, I could see that the first two or three hundred men were Red Guards, with only a few scattered soldiers. Over the barricade of fire-wood we clambered, and leaping down inside gave a triumphant shout as we stumbled on a heap of rifles thrown down by the *yunkers* who had stood there. On both sides of the main gateway the doors stood wide open, light streamed out, and from the huge pile came not the slightest sound.

Carried along by the eager wave of men we were swept into the right-hand entrance, opening into a great bare vaulted room, the cellar of the east wing, from which issued a maze of corridors and staircases. A number of huge packing cases stood about, and upon these the Red Guards and soldiers fell furiously, battering them open with the butts of their rifles, and pulling out carpets, curtains, linen, porcelain, plates, glass-ware . . . One man went strutting around with a bronze clock perched on his shoulder; another found a plume of ostrich feathers, which he stuck in his hat. The looting was just beginning when somebody cried, "Comrades! Don't take anything. This is the property of the People!" Immediately twenty voices were crying, "Stop! Put everything back! Don't take anything! Property of the People!" Many hands dragged the spoilers down. Damask and tapestry were snatched from the arms of those who had them; two men took away the bronze clock. Roughly and hastily the things were crammed back in their cases, and self-appointed sentinels stood guard. It was all utterly spontaneous. Through corridors and up staircases the cry could be heard growing fainter and fainter in the distance, "Revolutionary discipline! Property of the People . . ."

We crossed back over to the left entrance, in the west wing. There order was also being established. "Clear the Palace!" bawled a Red Guard, sticking his head through an inner door.

"Come, comrades, let's show that we're not thieves and bandits. Everybody out of the Palace except the Commissars, until we get sentries posted."

Two Red Guards, a soldier and an officer, stood with revolvers in their hands. Another soldier sat at a table behind them, with pen and paper. Shouts of "All out! All out!" were heard far and near within, and the Army began to pour through the door, jostling, expostulating, arguing. As each man appeared he was seized by the self-appointed committee, who went through his pockets and looked under his coat. Everything that was plainly not his property was taken away, the man at the table noted it on his paper, and it was carried into a little room. The most amazing assortment of objects were thus confiscated; statuettes, bottles of ink, bed-spreads worked with the Imperial monogram, candles, a small oil-painting, desk blotters, gold-handled swords, cakes of soap, clothes of every description, blankets. One Red Guard carried three rifles, two of which he had taken away from *yunkers*; another had four portfolios bulging with written documents. The culprits either sullenly surrendered or pleaded like children. All talking at once the committee explained that stealing was not worthy of the people's champions; often those who had been caught turned around and began to help go through the rest of the comrades.

Yunkers came out in bunches of three or four. The committee seized upon them with an excess of zeal, accompanying the search with remarks like, "Ah, Provocators! Kornilovists! Counter-revolutionists! Murderers of the People!" But there was no violence done, although the *yunkers* were terrified. They too had their pockets full of small plunder. It was carefully noted down by the scribe, and piled in the little room . . . The *yunkers* were disarmed. "Now, will you take up arms against the People any more?" demanded clamouring voices.

"No," answered the *yunkers*, one by one. Whereupon they were allowed to go free.

We asked if we might go inside. The committee was doubtful, but the big Red Guard answered firmly that it was forbidden. "Who are you anyway?" he asked. "How do I know that you are not all Kerenskys?" (There were five of us, two women.)

"*Pazhal'st*", *tovarishchi*! Way, Comrades!" A soldier and a Red Guard appeared in the door, waving the crowd aside, and other guards with fixed bayonets. After them followed single file half a dozen men in civilian dress – the members of the Provisional Goverment. First came Kishkin, his face drawn and pale, then Rutenberg, looking sullenly at the floor; Tereshchenko was next, glancing sharply around; he stared at us with cold fixity . . . They passed in silence; the victorious insurrectionists crowded to see, but there were only a few angry mutterings. It was only later that we learned how the people in the street wanted to lynch them, and shots were fired – but the sailors brought them safely to Peter-Paul . . .

In the meanwhile unrebuked we walked into the Palace. There was still a great deal of coming and going, of exploring new-found apartments in the vast edifice, of searching for hidden garrisons of *yunkers* which did not exist. We went upstairs and wandered through room after room. This part of the Palace had been entered also by other detachments from the side of the Neva. The paintings, statues, tapestries, and rugs of the great state apartments were unharmed; in the offices, however, every desk and cabinet had been ransacked, the papers scattered over the floor, and in the living-rooms beds had been stripped of their coverings and wardrobes wrenched open. The most highly prized loot was clothing, which the working people needed. In a room where furniture was stored we came upon two soldiers ripping the elaborate Spanish leather upholstery from chairs. They explained it was to make boots with . . .

The old Palace servants in their blue and red and gold uniforms stood nervously about, from force of habit repeating, "You can't go in there, *barin*! It is forbidden –" We penetrated at length to the gold and malachite chamber with crimson brocade hangings where the Ministers had been in session all that day and night, and where the *shveitzari* had betrayed them to the Red Guards. The long table covered with green baize was just as they had left it, under arrest. Before each empty seat was pen, ink, and paper; the papers were scribbled over with beginnings of plans of action, rough drafts of proclamations and manifestoes. Most of these were scratched out, as their futility became evident, and the rest of the sheet covered with absent-minded geometrical designs, as the writers sat despondently listening while Minister after Minister proposed chimerical schemes. I took one of these scribbled pages, in the handwriting of Konovalov, which read, "The Provisional Government appeals to all classes to support the Provisional Government –"

All this time, it must be remembered, although the Winter Palace was surrounded, the Government was in constant communication with the front and with provincial Russia. The Bolsheviki had captured the Ministry of War early in the morning, but they did not know of the military telegraph office in the attic, nor of the private telephone line connecting it with the Winter Palace. In that attic a young officer sat all day, pouring out over the country a flood of appeals and proclamations; and when he heard the Palace had fallen, put on his hat and walked calmly out of the building . . .

Interested as we were, for a considerable time we didn't notice a change in the attitude of the soldiers and Red Guards around us. As we strolled from room to room a small group followed us, until by the time we reached the great picture-gallery where we had spent the afternoon with the *yunkers*, about a hundred men surged in upon us. One giant of a soldier stood in our path, his face dark with sullen suspicion.

"Who are you?" he growled. "What are you doing here?" The others massed slowly around, staring and beginning to mutter. "*Provocatori*!" I heard somebody say, "Looters!" I produced our passes from the Military Revolutionary Committee. The soldier took them gingerly, turned them upside down and looked at them without comprehension. Evidently he could not read. He handed them back and spat on the floor. "*Bumagi!* Papers!" said he with contempt. The mass slowly began to close in, like wild cattle around a cow-puncher on foot. Over their heads I caught sight of an officer, looking helpless, and shouted to him. He made for us, shouldering his way through.

"I'm the Commissar," he said to me. "Who are you? What is it?" The others held back, waiting. I produced the papers.

"You are foreigners?" he rapidly asked in French. "It is very dangerous . . ." Then he turned to the mob, holding up our documents. "Comrades!" he cried, "These people are foreign comrades – from America. They have come here to be able to tell their countrymen about the bravery and the revolutionary discipline of the proletarian army!"

"How do you know that?" replied the big soldier. "I tell you they are provocators! They say they came here to observe the revolutionary discipline of the proletarian army, but they have been wandering freely through the Palace, and how do we know they haven't their pockets full of loot?"

"*Pravilno!*" snarled the others, pressing forward.

"Comrades! Comrades!" appealed the officer, sweat standing out on his forehead. "I am Commissar of the Military Revolutionary Committee. Do you trust me? Well, I tell you that these passes are signed with the same names that are signed to my pass!"

He led us down through the Palace and out through a door opening on to the Neva quay, before which stood the usual committee going through pockets . . . "You have narrowly escaped," he kept muttering, wiping his face.

"What happened to the Women's Battalion?" we asked.

"Oh – the women!" He laughed. "They were all huddled up in a back room. We had a terrible time deciding what to do with them – many were in hysterics, and so on. So finally we marched them up to the Finland Station and put them on a train to Levashovo, where they have a camp . . ."

We came out into the cold, nervous night, murmurous with obscure armies on the move, electric with patrols. From across the river, where loomed the darker mass of Peter-Paul came a hoarse shout . . . Underfoot the sidewalk was littered with broken stucco, from the cornice of the Palace where two shells from the battleship *Avrora* had struck; that was the only damage done by the bombardment.

It was now after three in the morning. On the Nevsky all the street-lights were again shining, the cannon gone, and the only signs of war were Red Guards and soldiers squatting around fires. The city was quiet – probably never so quiet in its history; on that night not a single hold-up occurred, not a single robbery.

CLEMENCEAU IS CALLED TO BE PREMIER, PARIS, 15 November 1917

Raymond Poincaré, President of the Republic

Almost everywhere in November 1917 war-weariness was taking its toll, France included. There the rudderless government of Painlevé was ejected by the Chamber of Deputies, and Georges Clemenceau was once again called to the office of Premier. Bad-tempered and ruthless, Clemenceau was known to all as "the Tiger". In his first speech as Premier he called for "only war, nothing but war".

I informed Clemenceau, through an officer, that I wished to see him at the Elysée at 3 o'clock in the afternoon.

Jules Roche came quite spontaneously to see me at 11:30 a.m., to tell me that he favored a Clemenceau Cabinet. He also told me that already in 1909, William II considered Clemenceau a formidable enemy. Franklin-Bouillon, too, came to see me of his own initiative, but he insisted that a Clemenceau Cabinet would mean civil war, and he added: "It will be your fault," to which I replied, "No responsible person will be able to reproach me with having made a personal choice. The choice, in fact, is between Caillaux and Clemenceau. I have made up my mind."

Clemenceau arrived at 3 o'clock, somewhat breathless and with a cold, but otherwise good-humoured and full of vitality. I at once told him: "After all the consultations of the past few days, I have reached the decision that I should ask you to form the new Cabinet. My personal wish and suggestion is that there be no secret between us. I shall tell you all I know and all I think. I won't be sparing with my advice, and it will be your responsibility to heed or disregard it. To begin with, I shall inform you of the consultations I have had during the past few days." I told him about the talks, but his reply was that he would form his Cabinet without taking the political groups into account. He had no desire to court the Socialists. He thanked me for having tried to win Thomas to the idea of Socialist co-operation . . .

He explained his views quite spontaneously, and concluded by saying: "I shall never make any decision without previously asking your advice." I replied that I would make my observations to him personally, for which he thanked me. He confided that there were times when he was under the impression that I was behind the attacks of the *Action Française* against him, as he was told so. He added, "You may count on me. . . . When Briand was Premier, he told everybody that you were talking too much during the Council of Ministers. Personally, I believe that one should talk as little as possible." "It's my opinion too." "I'd rather talk to you personally." "It's agreed!" . . .

The *Figaro*, the *Echo de Paris*, and the *Gaulois* have but praises for my choice, and approve of the Clemenceau Ministry. The *Matin*, which for some weeks now has been reconciled with Clemenceau, is also in agreement. *Le Rappel* is blowing hot and cold. Maurras has some reservations to make, but in a moderate tone.

I am well aware of the risks involved. But how could I oppose the nearly unanimous choice of all true patriots, who believe that the new team will offer the best guarantees? I am, of course, aware of Clemenceau's grave shortcomings, his immense pride, his all too rapid changes of mind and lack of depth, but I really did not see any one else who, in the present circumstances, could have taken over.

A PORTRAIT OF CLEMENCEAU, November 1917

David Lloyd George, British Prime Minister

One resolutely war-minded premier on another.

There was only one man left [*for the post of Premier*], and it is not too much to say that no one wanted him. The President, Poincaré, disliked him. He had insulted every prominent politician in France and conciliated none. He had no party or group attached to him. He was the Ishmael of French politics. I once said of him that he loved France but hated all Frenchmen. That is a substantially fair account of his personal attitude throughout his career. He was nevertheless much the most arresting and powerful personality in the arena of French politics during the Third Republic. He was a deadly controversialist who had brought down one Minister after another, with his piercing and pertinacious sword . . . I never heard him speak with respect of any French politician except Jaurès, the great Socialist leader, and he was dead . . . When you asked his opinion, as I often did, of some one or other of them, he concentrated his reply either into a contemptuous ejaculation (not always publishable) or into a fierce snort. In his estimation they were just flabby and flashy Parliamentarians and nothing more . . .

Clemenceau was a master of words. No orator of his day had a more perfect command and choice of word and phrase. But he was pre-eminently a man of action. His scorn was for the man who thought words a substitute for deeds and not a stimulus to deeds. He was not always fair even to doers whom he personally disliked . . .

During the whole of the War, he had criticized and condemned everybody and everything. His newspaper had been suppressed. He started another. It had no circulation – except in the quarters that mattered to him. Deputies and Senators read every word of it. He made a few speeches, but in parliamentary Committees he was a terror not so much to evildoers as to those who, in my opinion, are worse in an emergency – the non-doers. For three years no one thought of him as a possible War Premier. He was a growler, and an old growler at that. He was 78 years of age . . .

Then all of a sudden there came a cry from the lobbies of the Chamber of Deputies. "Why not give the Tiger a turn? If he fails, as he probably will, it will stop his snarling, and we can then try someone else, and we can silence him by an allusion to his own failure." . . . At 78 Clemenceau began the most notable episode in his strenuous and stormy career. As he exerted such an influence on the course of events I should like here to give my personal impression of this remarkable man.

The first time I ever met M. Clemenceau was at Carlsbad in 1910 . . . M. Clemenceau was known to be taking his annual cure, and I was anxious to meet him. T.P. arranged a meeting. Soon after I arrived there bustled into the room a short, broad-shouldered and full-chested man, with an aggressive and rather truculent countenance, illuminated by a pair of brilliant and fierce eyes set deeply under overhanging eyebrows. The size and hardness of his great head struck me. It seemed enormous, but there was no dome of benevolence, reverence, or kindliness. It was an abnormally large head with all the sympathetic qualities flattened out . . . He looked the part of the Tiger – the man-eating Tiger who had hunted down Ministry after Ministry, and rent them with his terrible claws. He came into the room with short, quick steps. He was then seventy years of age, and his greatest days were to come seven or eight years later.

We were introduced and he greeted me none too genially. I was then Chancellor of the Exchequer, and was doing my utmost to urge an understanding with Germany on the question of naval construction. I feared war was inevitable, unless such an understanding could be reached. M. Clemenceau referred to my efforts with scornful disapproval. His hatred of Germany had a concentrated ferocity which I had never seen before, not even among the most violent of our British Germanophobes. Their hostility to Germany always seemed to be calculated and histrionic – his was of the blood. Later on I understood it better.

My first interview with M. Clemenceau was not a success. He made it clear that he thoroughly disapproved of me. Had I never seen him again, I should have recalled him as a powerful but a disagreeable and rather bad-tempered old savage. It was years – eventful years – after this meeting that I discovered his real fascination: his wit, his playfulness, the hypnotic interest of his arresting and compelling personality . . .

He possessed restless energy, indomitable courage and a gift of infecting others with his own combativeness and confidence . . . By conviction and temperament he was an inexorable cynic. He had no belief in the ultimate victory of right. His essential creed – if he had any – was that history demonstrated clearly that in the end might invariably triumphed over abstract justice. His faith was in organized and well-directed force . . . One of the most piquant passages of arms between himself and President Wilson was one in which he reminded the American idealist that the United States of America would never have come into existence without force, and that but for force it would have fallen to pieces half a century ago . . .

M. Clemenceau was the greatest French statesman – if not the greatest Frenchman – of his day. He was in every fibre of his being a Frenchman. He had no real interest in humanity as a whole. His sole concern was for France. As long as France was humbled he cared not what a people were exalted. As long as France was victorious he did not worry in the least about the tribulations of any other country. To him France was all in all. When he began his public life he found his beloved country humiliated to the dust. When he ended his career he left France the most powerful State on the Continent of Europe – largely through his exertions.

TANKS AT CAMBRAI, WESTERN FRONT, 19 November 1917

Major W.H.L. Watson, Heavy Branch MGC

Cambrai was the first time in warfare that tanks (324 of them) led the main assault.

Until the 17th, the enemy apparently suspected nothing at all; but on the night of the 17th–18th he raided and captured some prisoners, who fortunately knew little. He gathered from them that we were ourselves preparing a substantial raid, and he brought into the line additional companies of machine-gunners and a few extra field-guns.

The 19th came with its almost unbearable suspense. We did not know what the Germans had discovered from their prisoners. We could not believe that the attack could be really a surprise. Perhaps the enemy, unknown to us, had concentrated sufficient guns to blow us to pieces. We looked up for the German aeroplanes, which surely would fly low over the wood and discover its contents. Incredibly, nothing happened. The morning passed and the afternoon – a day was never so long – and at last it was dusk.

At 8.45 p.m. my tanks began to move cautiously out of the wood and formed into column. At 9.30 p.m., with engines barely turning over, they glided imperceptibly and almost without noise towards the trenches. Standing in front of my own tanks, I could not hear them at two hundred yards.

By midnight we had reached our rendezvous behind the reserve trenches and below the crest of the slope. There we waited for an hour. The Colonel arrived, and took me with him to pay a final visit to the headquarters of the battalions with which we were operating. The trenches were packed with Highlanders, and it was with difficulty that we made our way through them.

Cooper led the tanks for the last half of the journey. They stopped at the support trenches, for they were early, and the men were given hot breakfast. The enemy began some shelling on the left, but no damage was done.

At 6.10 a.m. the tanks were in their allotted positions, clearly marked out by tapes which Jumbo had laid earlier in the night . . .

I was standing on the parados of a trench. The movement at my feet had ceased. The Highlanders were ready with fixed bayonets. Not a gun was firing, but there was a curious murmur in the air. To right of me and to left of me in the dim light were tanks – tanks lined up in front of the wire, tanks swinging into position, and one or two belated tanks climbing over the trenches.

I hurried back to the Colonel of the 6th Black Watch, and I was with him in his dug-out at 6.20 a.m. when the guns began. I climbed on to the parapet and looked.

In front of the wire, tanks in a ragged line were surging forward inexorably over the short down grass. Above and around them hung the blue-grey smoke of their exhausts. Each tank was followed by a bunch of Highlanders, some running forward from cover to cover, but most of them tramping steadily behind their tanks. They disappeared into the valley. To the right the tanks were moving over the crest of the shoulder of the hill. To the left there were no tanks in sight. They were already in among the enemy.

Beyond the enemy trenches the slopes, from which the German gunners might have observed the advancing tanks, were already enveloped in thick, white smoke. The smoke shells burst with a sheet of vivid red flame, pouring out blinding, suffocating clouds. It was as if flaring bonfires were burning behind a bank of white fog. Over all, innumerable aeroplanes were flying steadily to and fro.

The enemy made little reply. A solitary field-gun was endeavouring pathetically to put down a barrage. A shell would burst every few minutes on the same bay of the same trench. There were no other enemy shells that we could see. A machine-gun or two were still trained on our trenches, and an occasional vicious burst would bring the venturesome spectator scrambling down into the trench.

Odd bunches of men were making their way across what had been No-Man's Land. A few, ridiculously few, wounded were coming back. Germans, in twos and threes, elderly men for the most part, were wandering confusedly towards us without escort, putting up their hands in tragic and amazed resignation, whenever they saw a Highlander.

The news was magnificent. Our confidence had been justified. Everywhere we had overrun the first system and were pressing on.

A column of tanks, equipped with a strange apparatus, passed across our front to clear a lane through the wire for the cavalry.

On our left another column of tanks had already disappeared into the valley on their way to Flesquteres. It was Ward's company, but Ward was not with them. A chance bullet had killed him instantly at the head of his tanks. When we heard of his death later, the joy of victory died away . . .

TANKS: THE VIEW OF A DEMORALIZED ENEMY, November 1917

Field Marshal Paul von Hindenburg, Chief of the German General Staff

As the Flanders battle was drawing to a close, a fierce conflict unexpectedly blazed up at a part of the line which had hitherto been relatively inactive. On November 20th we were suddenly surprised by the English near Cambrai. The attack at this point was against a portion of the Siegfried Line which was certainly very strong from the point of view of technical construction, but was held by few troops and those exhausted in previous battles. With the help of their tanks, the enemy broke through our series of obstacles and positions which had been entirely undamaged.

English cavalry appeared on the outskirts of Cambrai. At the end of the year, therefore, a breach in our line appeared to be a certainty. At this point a catastrophe was averted by German divisions which had arrived from the East, and were more or less worn out by fighting and the long journey. Moreover, after a murderous defensive action lasting several days we succeeded in quickly bringing up comparatively fresh troops, taking the enemy salient in flank by a counter-attack, and almost completely restoring the original situation at very heavy cost to the enemy. Not only the Army Headquarters on the spot, but the troops themselves and our railways had performed one of the most brilliant feats of the war . . .

The English attack at Cambrai for the first time revealed the possibilities of a great surprise attack with tanks. We had had previous experience of this weapon in the spring offensive, when it had not made any particular impression. However, the fact that the tanks had now been raised to such a pitch of technical perfection that they could cross our undamaged trenches and obstacles did not fail to have a marked effect on our troops. The physical effects of fire from machine-guns and light ordnance with which the steel Colossus was provided were far less destructive than the moral effect of its comparative invulnerability. The infantryman felt that he could do practically nothing against its armoured sides. As soon as the machine broke through our trenchlines, the defender felt himself threatened in the rear and left his post.

CAMBRAI: A CAVALRY CHARGE, 20 November 1917

Private Chris Knight, 2nd Dragoon Guards

The great offensive was to begin on the 20th. Meanwhile, officers and N.C.O.'s were being given instructions. New maps were issued to section leaders; the types of aeroplanes that were going to work with us were explained, and the streamers and the colour of the Verey lights. On the night of the 19th we moved off at a walk. It was pitch dark and approaching midnight. "March at ease, but no smoking" was the order, and later on, "No talking." All that could be heard was the clip-clop of horses' feet, creaking of saddlery and champing of bits. Now and again the sound of a muffled cough. Fins was the rendezvous. We got there about 3 a.m., and off-saddled.

Zero hour was 6 a.m.

I was detailed for fodder fatigue. To get to the limbers we had to go through the lines of several regiments, and here I saw men with whom I had been training in 1914 in barracks in England. All our cavalry in France was concentrated at this rendezvous. I had never seen so many horses and men together at one parade. It was an awe-inspiring sight. Dragoons, Lancers, Hussars – they were all there, as well as Indian mounted troops. The "saddle-up" went for an Indian brigade first. By this time the bombardment was heavy. Tanks and infantry were well on their way to the Hindenburg Line, the supposed impregnable trench. Rumours had already reached us that this trench was taken. The Indian brigade disappeared over the Ridge in column of troop. Prisoners were coming towards us. A good sign. Everybody seemed in high spirits.

Saddle-up came for our brigade next. We moved off in column of troop. We crossed the Hindenburg Line fairly early in the morning. Many tanks had got across, but several had been put out of action and were lying derelict.

Seemingly we marched for hours, without a sign of the enemy, except for prisoners. We went through captured villages two abreast. In the afternoon we received a check, but no Germans were in sight. Only their artillery was in evidence. We took cover behind a battered hedge. Our troop lost a couple of horses there. They had to be destroyed after being wounded.

All the afternon we moved about, trotting here, galloping there, scarcely knowing in what direction the enemy was by this time. Towards dusk we halted and dismounted on the borders of a village. There were many prisoners here, looking at us with fixed gaze. Some had a cynical smile upon their faces, some looked dejected, while others simply grinned. Later, we moved off at a walk, and, coming to an open field by the roadside, we again dismounted. It was raining. A dismal rain. Real November stuff that gradually wetted us through until eventually we could feel it trickling through our puttees. For hours we stood by our horses. Then, at midnight, we were told to off-saddle and peg down for the night. The prospect was by no means a cheerful one, but we lay down behind the horses to get what little sleep we could.

Two or three hours later I was aroused by a savage dig in the ribs. My section corporal had been told to get in some ammunition that had been dumped by the roadside, so, with several others, I was kicked into a state of somnambulism, and we trudged down the road for about half a mile in one of the blackest nights that I can remember. We sweated, we grumbled, and we cursed. But the job had to be done. Our Hotchkiss gun team would need this ammunition tomorrow. To-morrow came. It was still raining.

At daybreak we went on fodder fatigue, replenished nose-bags, had a bully-beef and biscuit breakfast, and went forward once more. Early in the afternoon our regiment lined up in a sunken road in front of a small village. The enemy was there. We were to drive him out. Enemy 'planes had spotted us though. Enemy shells were plentiful. Lieutenant T. galloped along the rear, at the same time shouting, "See that your swords are loose."

We sat tense in our saddles, waiting for the order to go forward. Everybody was "keyed up". Would the order ever come? Now, after the lapse of a dozen years, I try to recall some of my thoughts and emotions during those moments. I was young then, very young indeed to be a cavalryman. Barely twenty, and there were men in my troop who had campaigned in South Africa. There I sat astride a powerful bay, wondering whether he would keep his feet in the plunge that was to come, or whether he would fall in the morass; whether we should both come back triumphant or whether I should come back carrying my saddle. It never occurred to me that *I* should not come back.

At last the orders came: "Half-sections right, walk march! Form sections! Head, left wheel! Draw swords! Trot! Form troop! Form column of half squadron! Gallop!"

The village lay about three-quarters of a mile away. We galloped fiercely to the outskirts, rapidly formed sections and got on to the road, numbers 1 and 2 troops cantering into the village first. Donelly, the Irishman, went raving mad, cutting and thrusting wildly at retreating Germans.

Indescribable scenes followed.

The order came to dismount. Germans emerged from dug-outs in all directions, some giving themselves up, others making a fight of it with a few bombs. No. I troops received the bombs in its midst. The bomb-throwers were accounted for with rifle and revolver.

We took many prisoners, but the major portion of the garrison holding the village had cleared out before we arrived. Very soon their machine guns were in action again, and shells were dropping in and behind the village. I, being No. 3 of a section, was a horse-holder and had to take four horses to the rear. All except No. 3's manned the trenches. Then followed a night of anguish. A week in the front-line trenches is better than one night as a horse-holder under shell-fire. What can one man do with four terrified horses? Nothing, except keep them together as much as possible. If shells burst behind they lunge forward. If shells burst ahead they go back on their haunches, nearly pulling your arms out of their sockets.

PALESTINE: THE FALL OF JERUSALEM, 11 December 1917

General Edmund Allenby, Commander-in-Chief, British Expeditionary Force, Egypt

Appointed Commander-in-Chief of the British Expeditionary Force against the Turks in July 1917, Allenby succeeded with a smaller force in rolling back the Turkish armies towards Jerusalem in a series of fierce, highly mobile actions. On 9 December, the Turks abandoned the Holy City without a fight, leaving Allenby to enter on the 11th unopposed. Herewith is his own account of his official entry, as cabled to London:

(1) At noon to-day I officially entered this City with a few of my staff, the commanders of the French and Italian detachments, the heads of the Picot Mission, and the Military Attachés of France, Italy, and the United States of America.

The procession was all on foot.

I was received by Guards representing England, Scotland, Ireland, Wales, Australia, India, New Zealand, France, and Italy at the Jaffa Gate.

(2) I was well received by the population.

(3) The Holy Places have had Guards placed over them.

(4) My Military Governor is in touch with the Acting Custos of Latins and the Greek representative has been detailed to supervise Christian Holy Places.

(5) The Mosque of Omar and the area round it has been placed under Moslem control and a military cordon composed of Indian Mahomedan officers and soldiers has been established round the Mosque. Orders have been issued that without permission of the Military Governor and the Moslem in charge of the Mosque no non-Moslem is to pass this cordon.

(6) The proclamation has been posted on the walls, and from the steps of the Citadel was read in my presence to the population in Arabic, Hebrew, English, French, Italian, Greek and Russian.

(7) Guardians have been established at Bethlehem and on Rachel's Tomb. The Tomb of Hebron has been placed under exclusive Moslem control.

(8) The hereditary custodians of the Wakfs at the Gates of the Holy Sepulchre have been requested to take up their accustomed duties in remembrance of the magnanimous act of the Caliph Omar who protected that Church.

The Proclamation read from the steps of David's Tower on the occasion of the Commander-in-Chief's Official Entry into Jerusalem was in these terms:

To the inhabitants of Jerusalem the Blessed and the people dwelling in its vicinity:

The defeat inflicted upon the Turks by the troops under my command has resulted in the occupation of your City by my forces. I therefore here and now proclaim it to be under martial law, under which form of administration it will remain as long as military considerations make it necessary.

However, lest any of you should be alarmed by reason of your experiences at the hands of the enemy who has retired, I hereby inform you that it is my desire that every person should pursue his lawful business without fear of interruption. Furthermore, since your City is regarded with affection by the adherents of three of the great religions of mankind, and its soil has become consecrated by the prayers and pilgrimages of multitudes of devout people of those three religions for many centuries, therefore do I make it known to you that every sacred building, monument, holy spot, shrine, traditional site, endowment, pious bequest, or customary place of prayer, of whatsoever form of the three religions, will be maintained and protected according to the existing customs and beliefs of those to whose faiths they are sacred.

TRENCH LIFE: CHRISTMAS AT PASSCHENDAELE, December 1917

Rifleman B.F. Eccles, 7th (S) Battalion, the Rifle Brigade

France,
28 December 1917

Dearest Mother, Dad and kids,

This letter will be posted by a chap on leave so here goes: Before I begin. I am quite well, alive and kicking, happy and "grateful for life". So by that you can bet I have had the most exciting run of my existence. Christmas on the Passchendaele Ridge. Yes, and take it from me it is not a nice place to spend one's Christmas Vacation. Fortunately winter had come and everything was ice-bound which banished the mud.

I was on a bombing post with six others in a shell hole about eight yards long. We were out of touch with the rest, but Fritz did not know exactly where we were. We were so near him we could hear him talking and coughing. It was trying work as we had to be so vigilant. On the night of the 24th I was warned to report to a pillbox (Company Headquarters) as guide. The snow was thick and being moonlight I had several times to throw myself down to avoid the machine-gun bullets, for as you know there are no trenches. Five of us had to find the track to Battalion HQ, which was not too easy seeing the snow had obliterated many landmarks. On our return we were rewarded by a decent tot of rum. On Xmas night, we five had again to set out and report to a place known as "so-and-so" farm and stay till Boxing night to guide up our relief, a battalion of the Worcesters.

We were not sorry to get out of it for a day, although the journey is so risky. For the cold was pretty keen, and jolly hard to bear especially in a shell hole, where to stand up by day means a bullet through the napper.

More snow on Boxing Day and a brilliant moon. How we cursed that moon.

Consider it. A full moon on a vast waste of snow six inches to a foot deep. And to take a battalion of men over open country in full sight of the enemy. All went well until we had gone two kilos, and appeared on the last ridge, within 600 yards of what is left of Passchendaele. Then we were spotted by Fritz and he opened on us with machine-guns on three sides (the salient is like a horse-shoe). We carried on until it became too hot and fellows were drooping over too thickly. Two of my platoon (I mean the platoon I was guiding) were knocked over besides others, so we dropped on the track, and rolled into shell holes. Bullets were whizzing over us a hundred to the minute. We tried to move forward again from shell hole to shell hole, when the platoon behind shouted they had lost their guide. I cried to them to follow me. We were so massed that Fritz properly got the breeze up. He fully thought that we were extending to make an attack, so up went his SOS signal. It was what I had dreaded, for immediately his artillery opened a terrific barrage. Talk about a big slice of Hell! I yelled to the chaps to get flat. I went forward on my hands and knees in the snow and dropped into a shell hole with Ravenhill my fellow Guide, and for fully half an hour we lay with our faces in the snow, while shells did everything but hit us, even though they seemed to burst on the edge of the shell holes. It was the worst half hour I have ever spent. Casualties were heavy and many were the cries of wounded men. In one place no less than four men had their heads blown off.

Then – thank the Lord – our artillery got the wire and they put up such an avalanche of shells on Jerry's lines that he closed up like a wet sack. Then came a respite and a bit of mist arose. I went forward to our lines and we made the relief as well as possible although so many were missing. I met an officer, told him we had got the men up, and he said, "Grease out of it", which I did. I closed up with some of my old platoon, and we did that three miles out of the danger zone in double quick time.

We had one more narrow escape after, being nearly gassed when a shell hit the track within a few yards of us.

Then at last we reached a zone of safety. Exhausted after living on biscuits, bully etc. for four days, but happy as lords, for after twenty-four days in the Ypres sector our Division had been relieved. We were met by Brigade Officers near St Jean, and a Canteen by the roadside provided hot tea and rum, biscuits and cigs. Then to a camp under canvas until morning. On the 27th, we arose and got the thickest of five days beard off. Then a train journey to our present place sixty miles behind the line near St Omer.

The snow is thick and the frosts are keen, but what matters is we are away from it all again. So we can sing and shout once more.

I may be wrong in telling you all this, but the reason I do is that it is some record of exciting adventure which I never dreamed of.

But here I am, I am not worrying so you need not. I am in the pink, barring being a bit stiff and bruised.

But believe me anything is preferable to that Hell upon earth, Passchendaele Ridge.

So dear people you can play the piano when you read this, and make your minds easy for a bit.

The weather is severe, but we get hardened. We are having our Xmas feed on Sunday, a big pay day. I have plenty of fags, and a fine pipe so I am très bon.

Meanwhile we are nearer the end of the war. I have seen no paper lately but shall get my chance now. I will write Emilla as soon as possible. Tel! her she is a dear for sending me such a jolly fine pipe. Meanwhile, the best of wishes for 1918.

May next Christmas be quieter for me. Bank Holidays seem to be Helldays. So Cheero Mother, darling, I enjoyed the Butter-scotch within forty yards of Fritz. The socks and gloves reached me just in time.

Fondest love,
Burton.

EAST AFRICA: THE BITTER GUERRILLA WAR OF VON LETTOW-VORBECK, Winter 1917

General Paul von Lettow-Vorbeck

With never more than 15,000 soldiers von Lettow-Vorbeck had no chance of defeating Allied forces in East Africa; however his continued resistance forced the Allies to commit vital troops and resources. Not until the armistice was signed in Europe did von Lettow-Vorbeck's guerrilla army surrender.

So there was nothing for it but to seek to attain our object by means of small detachments, or patrols. To these patrols we afterwards attached great importance. Starting from the Engare-Nairobi, small detachments of eight to ten men, Europeans and Askari, rode round the rear of the enemy's camps, which had been pushed up as far as the Longido, and attacked their communications. They made use of telephones we had captured at Tanga, tapping in on the English telephone-lines; then they waited for large or small hostile detachments or columns of ox-wagons to pass. From their ambush they opened fire on the enemy at thirty yards' range, captured prisoners and booty, and then disappeared again in the boundless desert. Thus, at that time, we captured rifles ammunition, and war material of all kinds. One of these patrols had observed near Erok Mountain that the enemy sent his riding-horses to water at a certain time. Ten of our horsemen at once started out, and, after a two-days' ride through the desert, camped close to the enemy. Six men went back with the horses; the four others each took a saddle, and crept at a distance of a few paces past the enemy's sentries, close up to the watering-place, which lay behind the camp. An English soldier was driving the horses, when suddenly two of our men confronted him out of the bush and, covering him with their rifles, ordered "Hands up!" In his surprise he dropped his clay pipe out of his mouth. At once he was asked: "Where are the missing four horses?" for our conscientious patrol had noticed that there were only fifty-seven, whereas the day before they had counted sixty-one! The four needed light treatment and had been left in camp. The leading horse and a few others were quickly saddled, mounted, and off they went at a gallop round the enemy's camp towards the German lines. Even in the captured Englishman, who had to take part in this *safari* on a bare horse, without much comfort, the innate sporting instinct of his nation came out. With great humour he shouted: "I should just like to see my captain's face now!" and when the animals had arrived safely in the German camp, he remarked: "It was a damned good piece of work."

This capture, increased by a number of other horses and mules we had picked up, enabled us to form a second mounted company. We now had two mounted companies, composed of Askari and Europeans mixed, an organisation which proved successful. They provided us with the means of sweeping the extensive desert north of Kilima Njaro with strong patrols who went out for several days at a time; they penetrated even as far as the Uganda and Magad Railways, destroyed bridges, surprised guards posted on the railways, mined the permanent way and carried out raids of all kinds on the land communications between the railways and the enemy's camps. In these enterprises our own people did not get off scot-free. One patrol had brilliantly surprised two companies of Indians by rifle-fire, but had then lost their horses, which had been left behind in hiding, by the fire of the enemy; they had to make their way back across the desert on foot, which took four days, and they had no food. Luckily they found milk and cattle in a Masai kraal, and later on saved themselves from starvation by killing an elephant. But success whetted the spirit of adventure, and the requests to be sent on patrol, mounted or on foot, increased.

The patrols that went out from the Kilima Njaro in a more easterly direction were of a different character. They had to work on foot through the dense bush for days on end. The patrols sent out to destroy the railway were mostly weak: one or two Europeans, two to four Askari, and five to seven carriers. They had to worm their way through the enemy's pickets and were often betrayed by native scouts. In spite of this they mostly reached their objective and were sometimes away for more than a fortnight. For such a small party a bit of game or a small quantity of booty afforded a considerable reserve of rations. But the fatigue and thirst in the burning sun were so great that several men died of thirst, and even Europeans drank urine. It was a bad business when anyone fell ill or was wounded, with the best will in the world it was often impossible to bring him along. To carry a severely wounded man from the Uganda Railway right across the desert to the German camps, as was occasionally done, is a tremendous performance. Even the blacks understood that, and cases did occur in which a wounded Askari, well knowing that he was lost without hope, and a prey to the numerous lions, did not complain when he had to be left in the bush, but of his own accord gave his comrades his rifle and ammunition, so that they at least might be saved.

Part Five

1918

There is no other course open to us but to fight it out. Every position must be held to the last man.

– Field Marshal Douglas Haig, 11 April 1918

INTRODUCTION

And so Imperial Germany determined to play its last card, an all-out offensive in the West before the mass of American troops reached the war zone. Two hundred German divisions were gathered at the front by trains running night and day, while special attack soldiers were trained at Valenciennes and Sedan. The air-force was increased to over 2,500 planes and artillery was beefed up (with, not least, pieces robbed from the Russians in the great German advance before the Bolsheviks signed the treaty of Brest-Litovsk of 3 March).

Then, at 4 a.m. on 21 March, more than 6,500 guns and 3,500 trench mortars announced the opening of "Operation Michael". The objective of Ludendorff's storm of steel against the Allies on the Western Front was to drive the French from the Aisne and the British from the Somme. Seventy German divisions hurled themselves against twenty-six British divisions positioned between Arras and Noyon. Within days the BEF had been forced back 40 miles, despite a stout resistance in which some regiments fought literally to the last man. Only the hasty summoning up of ten French divisions to "plug the gap" prevented a collapse of the front line between the French and British armies.

It would be an exaggeration to say that Ludendorff came within an ace of victory in March 1918. There were some important cards missing in the German pack. They had few tanks – ten indeed – and, more serious still, no strategic plan. In the event, after the brilliant victories of the first days, Ludendorff allowed the German attack to fan out – and thus weaken itself. By 27 March the offensive had degenerated into the old position warfare.

Undaunted, Ludendorff moved the focus of the campagn to Flanders, striking the British on the Lys. Again the Germans made spectacular progress; Haig was even forced to issue on 12 April a reminder to British troops that they had their "backs to the wall". Yet, within two weeks the British had stabilized the front.

Once more, Ludendorff attempted a break-through. On 27 May the Germans attacked the French 6th Army on the Aisne, and by early June delirious German soldiers were in the same positions they had reached in September 1914. From Crepy, modified 21-cm Krupp naval guns – Big Berthas – shelled Paris. But the march against Paris was halted just outside its gates by an Allied counter-offensive, which included the American 2nd and 3rd Divisions, on 11 June. Having lost 209, 345 men in June alone, the German army was badly bloodied. But not quite unbowed. In mid-July Ludendorff mounted an abortive assault on the Marne.

It was now that run of play in the last game of the war changed. On the Italian front, the Austro-Hapsburg army had already raced to disaster on the Piave river, losing men to death and desertion by the tens of thousand per day. Meanwhile, the Allies under Marshal Foch counter-attacked on the Western Front – and there was little the exhausted Germans could do but fight the retreat. There was no hope of victory any more, for the Germans had run out of men. Over a million were listed as sick, and almost a million were listed as casualties. The Allies had superior numbers in men, artillery, tanks and planes, and so Foch struck the Germans in a wide series of harrying blows. Behind the retreating frontline, German morale sunk, which was only exacerbated by Allied victories in Bulgaria and Syria.

By 8 August, when the Allies mounted a major offensive on the Somme, Ludendorff realized that the game was up. German frontline troops were not showing the spirit of before. Reinforcements were jeered as "war-prolongers". Defeat followed defeat. There were mutinies. The retreat became a rout.

In late October the German war effort collapsed spectacularly. To avoid dismissal, Ludendorff resigned on 27 October. Germany's allies, Turkey and Austria, signed separate peace treaties on 30 October and 3 November respectively. The Kaiser abdicated on 9 November. Two days later, in the forest of Compiègne, the Germans signed an unconditional surrender.

The Great War was over. As bells of rejoicing rang out, the bodies of fourteen million men and women lay still in battlefields from Flanders to Africa.

STORM OF STEEL: FACING THE MICHAEL OFFENSIVE, 22 March 1918

Private R.G. Bultitude, 1st Battalion Artists Rifles

Ludendorff's last gamble on the Western Front, the Michael Offensive, opened at 4 a.m. on 21 March.

In the early hours of the morning of 22 March, 1918, our own front-line troops retired through us. At the time we were occupying a shallow trench forming the support line before Marcoing, in the Cambrai salient, and a little later we also withdrew.

Our first halt was on the slope of a hill. We could not see the attackers, but their artillery plastered the hillside with shrapnel, and we were not sorry to get orders to move again. During the halt one of our officers handed me a bottle of whisky to "look after" for him. I did not see him again, but the whisky came in useful.

My company was leading, and we were under fairly heavy shell-fire for some time. As we passed through one village, evidently some sort of headquarters, the mixed assortment of clerks, storekeepers, and other oddments were making a hurried exit. A hundred yards or so ahead of us, a two-horsed wagon, containing stores and half a dozen men, had just started off when a shell burst, apparently immediately over it. We made a detour round the mangled remains of horses and men.

Although our latest spell in the trenches had only been the normal one of eight days, we had been relieved, had marched back to the reserve line, a distance of about eight miles, had immediately been exposed to a protracted shelling, with gas, and then, without food or rest, had returned to the line.

During the spell of trench life, too, there had been considerable activity; it had been difficult to get rations up when we were in the front line, and there had been no rest during our four days in support. The infantry-man is a soldier by day and a navvy by night. Sleep is a luxury in which he is allowed to indulge only on rare occasions, and then for very brief periods.

We did not start on our long trek any too fresh. We marched all day, with very few and very short halts. A little after dark we came to some cross-roads, went straight across them, and very shortly after, walked plump into the arms of the enemy!

For several hours we had been marching at ease in apparent security, and were therefore taken completely by surprise on the first challenge in a foreign tongue.

We scattered in open order on to the fields on either side of the road, and lay flat awaiting developments. A sergeant shouted out that he knew the place as the site of an Indian Labour Corps encampment.

An officer and one or two men went forward, calling out that we were English, and were promptly shot.

The fight that followed remains in my recollection as a confused medley of bursting bombs, rifle and machine-gun fire.

I found a shallow hole in the ground, and from its shelter fired point-blank at forms just seen in the darkness under the unmistakable squarish German helmets, until my ammunition gave out.

A form appeared, and Johnson's voice said, "I've got one in the thigh, old man." I felt the wet blood on his trouser-leg, but by the time I had fumbled for and found my first-aid outfit he had wandered off again. I heard afterwards that he acted as orderly in a German War Hospital.

Among the confusion of shouts, groans, curses, and the detonation of bursting bombs, I thought I recognized a voice calling for help as that of a company stretcher bearer and one of my pals. He was known as "Blanco", from which anyone acquainted with Army humour will at once realize that he had coal-black hair and a swarthy complexion.

I crawled towards the voice, and found its owner in a shell hole with five wounded whom he had collected by the exercise of I don't know what powers of sight and physical exertion. He bandaged their wounds in the darkness with my unskilful assistance.

Loud commands in German, and a sudden intensification of firing apparently from all sides told us that we were almost if not quite surrounded. The only chance seemed to be the road; obviously if the enemy were behind us there we were completely ringed round; if not, there might be an avenue of escape by the way we had come.

By the time we had got our wounded companions on to the road (I have no idea how), the enemy were pretty fully occupied in guarding and disposing of their captives. Luck favoured us, and we got clear. A few others, possibly a dozen, also escaped, as we found out eventually.

We had, of course, no idea as to the whereabouts of the remainder of our battalion, and when we reached the cross-roads any direction seemed as likely as another to lead us into trouble again.

Providence, sheer chance, or a sense of direction led us to turn left.

During the rest of that night, and, I think, the whole of the next day we struggled along. By good fortune we all escaped being hit by splinters from a huge ammunition dump which had been fired by our engineers, and from which a shower of red-hot metal rained, down over a large area of the road and its surroundings.

The noise of the explosions completely shattered the nerves of the most seriously hurt of our comrades, and it was almost impossible to control him. We got him past the blazing dump somehow, and I then remembered the officer's whisky. We all had a swig, and we poured a very generous quantity of the neat spirit down the delirious man's throat. We had practically to carry him, after that, but he became quite quiet. He died an hour or two later, and we were able to leave him by the roadside.

The other four needed more and more support as time went on, and our progress became a crawl.

I retained a few small personal belongings, my haversack and rifle, but had to discard the rest of my equipment.

At last in the distance we saw a group of huts, but now also we came under sporadic machine-gun fire. It was not very heavy in our direction, and we got safely into one of the buildings. In a field a little further on British troops were digging themselves in, but the space between them and ourselves was swept by bullets and it would have been suicidal to attempt to reach them.

THE MICHAEL OFFENSIVE: TAKEN PRISONER, LA FRERE, 22 March 1918

Private Alfred Grosch, Post Office Rifles

Lieutenant W. calls for volunteers to go to Headquarters for help. I set off, and take a boy with me who is badly hit in the head.

The area we cross is swept by rifle and machine-gun fire; we crawl and escape it. The boy is in pain and crying. Presently he jumps up. "Here they come!" he cries. I pull him down. "Who?" I ask. "Jerry," he says. I look cautiously up. There he is right enough, the first wave almost on top of us.

"Leave it to me, boy; we're done; we're prisoners now. Do whatever I tell you." I wait a second, then "Up!" I say, "and take your helmet off." We do so. The German in front of me says, "Ach!" raises his rifle and takes aim. I mutter to myself, "I hope to God he won't pull that trigger." For ten seconds we remain so, then he lowers his rifle, and says what I take to be "Wounded?" I nod, and say, "Yes, yes." He beckons, and we approach. We still have our equipment on, and the Germans utter shouts, pointing to it. "Slip it off!" I cry to the boy, doing so myself.

The German has spared us. Would we have spared him under the circumstances? God knows! Perhaps not.

We go back, through our own barrage, to the rear of the German line, passing through successive waves of troops going forward.

Only one thought now: to get out of this hell, and as far back as possible. But the Germans in charge of us do not know the country. More prisoners join us, little groups of dead are here and there where they have fallen, English and German together. It is very hard, many are only boys.

One of our officers from "A" company is lying on a stretcher badly wounded in the stomach. He is delirious with pain. It hurts to see him writhe, and hear him call his N.C.O.'s one by one. I know each one he mentions, and wonder whether they are living or dead.

We carry this officer about for some hours, until we reach a German casualty clearing station, where we leave him. He has grown much quieter, and I think his end is near. But oh, for a sleep; my head is fit to burst.

Relentlessly onward we go. Back, back, right clear of the battlefield, moving all night.

Morning comes, we reach a camp where the remnants of my company are already assembled, having travelled by a quicker route. I greet them, and am glad to meet the survivors. But I go off to sleep, and am oblivious to everything. I get just an hour. We are off again, no stopping here. What a crowd: hundreds, perhaps thousands, French and English – a long column stretches down the road before and behind us. We are escorted by Uhlans, not bad fellows. They rest us frequently, and after each rest I am shaken vigorously before I come round. They send a horseman in advance, we go through a village, the inhabitants line the road with pails of water, we drink as we pass. The women wring their hands at the sight of us, and when they can pass us a piece of bread quickly, so that our guards cannot see the action. We go to Guise; the castle on the hill is visible some way off.

We enter the town, which, though in German occupation, is still full of French inhabitants. They rush into the ranks, push tobacco, bread, and food into our hands. One woman braves the guards, and rushes to me with a can of hot coffee, then she is gone. The men throw their caps to those who are without. Tears are in all eyes.

We stay here the night. We who are wounded are taken to a dressing station, they give us bread and jam to eat, with weak coffee to drink. The place is full of German wounded. Some are terrible; a man is near me with half his jaw blown off; they are trying to feed him with a little teapot. The sight is ghastly. Poor fellow. He is only one. The whole place is overflowing. They come in one long stream all night and all day. The push is costing them dear.

We must go away next day; there is no room for us, others are on the way. Down to the railway we go. A huge train is waiting. From many trucks come cries of men in mortal agony. What a load; whither are we going? Sixty of us, all wounded, all packed in one truck. We pass Le Cateau. At Diedenhofen, a German says, "Here you get hot eat." We do, and it is good.

The Jerries scrounge an issue of cigars and cigarettes for us. We are at Trier West, and change from trucks to carriages. On we go into Germany. Adventure is at an end; henceforth we are prisoners.

TRENCH LIFE: SHELL SHOCK, 1918

Arthur Osborn, British Army

It was a depressing experience. The shelter we were in had only been a temporary one, constructed for the crews of the German artillery before they had been driven back. So the side facing their line was naturally quite unprotected from their fire. Long abandoned and out of repair, a single hit would have undoubtedly brought the half-rotten "roof" and tons of bricks and rubble down on top of us. We literally cowered in the mud, feeling quite helpless. Suddenly three men of the Brigade Signals appeared in the entrance carrying or rather dragging a Staff Officer. Breathlessly they flung him inside and, shouting something about "the General's orders," bolted out again. There was no chance of getting further explanations, for the piece of ground that lay between our shelter and the ladder leading underground to the good German dug-out which Brigade Headquarters had annexed was being well plastered with shell.

The Staff Officer, a biggish man, somewhere between twenty-five and thirty, lay moaning on the ground. We could find no wound. In the din I tried to question him, thinking he had been seized with a fit or with acute internal pain. But he only moaned and jibbered and shook his head, grovelling on the ground at my feet with his face pressed to the muddy floor. While I questioned him we were suddenly assailed by a more than usually heavy burst of shelling. A perfect hurricane of whizz-bangs, skimming just over the roof and bursting on a bank only about ten yards away, the splinters rattling on the roof or flying back through the entrance.

The grovelling object appeared now to be suddenly seized with a fresh access of terror. Wildly and incoherently he made efforts to conceal himself between the remains of a broken chair and the mud wall of the shelter. Then suddenly, spasmodically, he began to dig furiously with his fingers. The huddled men, mostly stretcher-bearers of the R.A.M.C., stared at him in amazement, the pink tabs on his collar, and a decoration on his smart uniform, seemed strangely inconsistent with this extraordinary behaviour. It was a case of complete loss of nerve and self-control. Driven mad with terror, slobbering and moaning, he clawed and scrabbled violently in the mud, his head under the chair. It was like a terrified and overrun fox going to ground, trying to dig his way back to safety through the very bowels of the earth. His behaviour was simply less than human. Extreme terror had driven him back through a thousand generations to some pre-human form of life. I suppose some cringing prehistoric half-human thing, making futile efforts to escape from rending beak and steely claw of hovering pterodactyl, may once have burrowed and behaved thus. Not wishing to have my men, who were in any case not enjoying the shelling, demoralized by this exhibition of terror from an officer, who had himself passed orders on to me, I made renewed attempts to quiet him. Above the roar of shelling I shouted in his ear:

"You're all right – safe here! Keep still – be quiet! In a moment, as soon as this shelling stops we'll carry you to an ambulance! Quite close! You'll go back – straight to the Base – Home – and have a long rest! Try and sit up and swallow some brandy."

But one might as well have spoken to a mad dog. At last, the shelling abating a little, I got three of the biggest men I had with me to lay hold of this pathetic, scrabbling incoherent animal that had once been a British Staff Officer, and we tried to drag him, or carry him out. He resisted violently.

At last after several efforts we got rid of him. Halfway to the ambulance that would carry him to safety he tried to bolt back to us! The three men had to risk their lives to get him across the hundred and fifty yards of comparatively open ground and across a road into an old gun-pit where I had had a Ford motor-ambulance concealed. I do not know what became of him; possibly he never reached home alive, or perhaps he is in an asylum. Perhaps, recovered, he shoots partridges now in Norfolk, dines at Claridges, hunts with the North Cotswold, or keeps a chicken farm in Surrey. But when one thinks of how we treated this Staff Officer, and how, on the other hand, some poor, half-educated, blubbering ploughboy, whose nerves had likewise given way, and who was not much more than half this Staff Officer's age, was sent back to face the enemy or be shot for cowardice . . . But that is war. It must often be luck; it can never mean justice.

"BIG BERTHAS" FIRE ON PARIS, 23 March 1918

William Graves Sharp, American Ambassador to France

Named after the daughter of manufacturer Alfred Krupp, "Big Berthas" were German long-range guns.

The most beautiful moonlight nights . . . came to be looked upon with a feeling of the gravest concern. Rarely, if ever, were such nights free from the aerial raids of the enemy. Time and again I have seen, from the large windows of my sleeping apartment facing the north-east, the most brilliant pyrotechnic display from exploding shells of the barrage fire from a hundred guns, accompanied by the signal light of our Allied machines, rivalling at times in brilliancy an electric headlight of a railway locomotive . . . But great as was this method of destruction by night, by far the gravest concern, if not the most real danger, was caused by the shells of the long range guns – or "Big Berthas," as they came to be called.

Clearly one of the most unique incidents which occurred, during a war so crammed full of strange situations, was the sudden appearance in the midst of the Parisians of this new instrument of death, even if it did not lead to any considerable events from a military point of view. Very much as though some strange visitation from the planet Mars, bringing death in its pathway, had suddenly intruded upon the streets of the city, fell the first shell of this great German gun. People were stupefied at what, in its very suddenness and the terror of its work, only differed from some horrible apparition in that it could not be seen. By those who later at different times happened to be very near the places where these shells fell, it was stated that there was not the slightest sound made by them in passing through the air. They simply dropped from space like some huge meteorite, without its warning trail of light, which had been charged with the highest explosives that the science of man could invent . . . The shell . . . had a much-elongated funnelled nose, equal in length to half of that of the entire shell.

On that momentous twenty-third of March, explosions as of bombs of unusual size were heard in Paris at frequent and fairly regular intervals, from about eight o'clock in the morning until about the middle of the afternoon. Certain lines of the tramways stopped and many stores were closed. The general explanation was that German air-raids were in progress over Paris by day-light, for the first time since the beginning of the war. The bombs dropped in different parts of the city were reckoned at thirty at least, there being a number of killed and wounded . . .

There were many who believed, for some hours after those shells first began to fall, that they came from cunningly concealed positions of the enemy at no more than twenty or twenty-five miles from the city. Indeed, in a conversation with me at dinner, the night of the first day of this new kind of bombardment, one French gentleman, who had been entrusted by the Government with important duties connected with the "camouflage" service, ridiculed the idea that it could come from guns located upwards of seventy-five miles away. "Such a thing is impossible!" he exclaimed with much vehemence . . .

Another belief, quite as current as it was unfounded, was that invisible aeroplanes or other aircraft had dropped bombs upon the city from a great height . . . And yet the skies were unusually clear that day, and no semblance of any aircraft was seen . . .

Of course, as was to be expected, there were not those lacking to come forward almost immediately and assert that, after all, there was nothing in this achievement beyond the possibilities already known to science . . . an assurance, under the circumstances, more enlightening than comforting.

WESTERN FRONT: THE MOOD OF THE TOMMIES, April 1918

British Army Censor

To divine the mood of the Army in the wake of the German offensive, GHQ surveyed soldiers' letters home.

You will probably have seen a few bits about us in the newspapers (Glorious Deeds!). If you ever hear anybody say that the troops are in excellent spirits just refer them to this battery. The sooner one side wins the better and we know who will win (*not us*).

It is no use being pessimistic Clara for I tell you we are bound to win with the men we have got. I have just seen a battalion of them going into the trenches. They look into the gates of Hell and laugh, this every day and night, and I tell you the boys of Britain cannot be beat.

Any one reading the papers can see that our Government is full of corruption, that is what has made a chap sick of the whole business out here, there are a good many out here my dear like myself fed up and don't care a damn which side wins. After four years and now we are being pushed back and no end in sight.

The night previous to our departure from the billet for the trenches we were all singing and a chap just remarked "You would think we were going home instead of going into the arena", but this is where we beat Fritz; in dark days or bright, we don't lose heart, "Jerry" may give us a smack today, but he will get a harder one tomorrow. Really I am so proud to be a

British soldier and to be able to fight to the bitter end for British interest and it is the same with us all here.

THE BATTLE OF LYS: THE PORTUGUESE ARE DRIVEN BACK, 9 April 1918

Captain R.C.G. Dartford, attached 2nd Division Portuguese Expeditionary Force

On 9 April the Germans struck further north in the Michael Offensive. At one point in the line four German divisions attacked a single Portuguese division; 6000 Portuguese prisoners were taken.

9 April Tues: Woke at 4.10 a.m. very heavy shelling. Guessed from the start it meant an attack. Phoned to brigade – every communication cut already. Dressed hurriedly and set out for brigade. The Rue de la Gare was dangerous for shells were falling in it. Smelt gas and put on my respirator, dodging into doors as shells fell. Reached bde dugout. Next 3 hours we could do nothing, but nearly got asphyxiated by lack of oxygen owing to having to keep gas blankets down. Runner from battalions came nearly dead with fatigue, but their message was nothing more than SOS. Heavy fog on and everybody seemed isolated from others.

About 9 a.m. a shell hit the corner of the dugout and wounded Branco the signals officer in the face. I had my gumboots off at the time and later found my left foot had several small cuts probably pieces of brick. We then all made for the Aid Post cellar. Gas was not hanging about then but the road was a pretty sight – houses down and fog and dust. I persuaded the others to go to the mission cellar. There three civilians were saying prayers in a corner and odd wounded were being treated in another and the rest of us wondering what to do. Impossible to send messages forward. We kept sending mounted orderlies or cyclists back to division but it appears few ever got there.

I think the Boche must have taken our front line about 8.30 and the B line 8.45 and was up to batt H.Q. by 9.15 or so. One message from X. de Costa (CO 29th Batt.) said he no longer had any command and that it was now a question of individuals fighting out. He was killed we learnt after. So was Captain Montenegro, OC 20th Batt. (right) and nothing is known of Montalvao (left) and Woodrow and Sgt Ransdale.

Stragglers passed thro' Laventie but most of them chose the open fields and wisely. We got hold of one and he said "Everyone was running from the B line so I did too", though he hadn't seen the Boche. We put 2 sgts to try and collect stragglers but they soon came back saying it was impossible to stop them and that officers were getting away too. Was very surprised to see Captain Valle CO 3rd Batt. come in, all of a tremble and nearly fainting. He said his batt. was all out of hand. M.-Gs were reported playing on roads leading S. out of Laventie so we decided that we should move to avoid capture and to try and get in touch with division. Meanwhile I had put on my high boots and Sam Browne and got my stationery box down into the cellar. Tore up most secret things and took my diaries and cheque book out of my writing case. The rest was left.

"WITH OUR BACKS TO THE WALL . . .": HAIG ASKS THE BEF TO FIGHT TO THE LAST MAN, 11 April 1918

Brigadier-General John Charteris, Staff Officer, GHQ

The news from the battle is not good. The Germans are making a big effort, and the French are doing nothing. Foch said two days ago that he had at last made up his mind that the big German attack was against the British Army, and that he would send a large French force to take part in the battle, but so far nothing has happened. It looks as if we should have to fight out this battle alone, and we have no reserves. It will decide the War. God grant the decision is not against us! Everything else fades into insignificance. We are paying in blood for the follies of professional politicians. I pray that our payment in the lives of the army may suffice and that the whole nation be not strangled.

D.H. has issued a finely worded appeal to the army to fight to the last, saying that French troops are hurrying to our assistance. I wish they were. It is all so like 1914 when we told the 1st Corps the French were coming, and they did not come. Yet then we won alone, and I believe we shall now. All the same I wish D.H. had *not* issued his order. It will immensely hearten the Germans when they hear of it, as they must. I do not think our own men needed it to make them fight it out. If the French are really hurrying to our assistance, they should be here in a few days, almost as soon as the order will reach the front-line troops. If they are not, it may have a really bad effect to raise false hopes in the troops' minds.

Although the position is serious, I do not think this attack can possibly get through. It will outrun its supplies and come to the end of its momentum just as the March attack did. So far there is no sign of a check. Our men are fighting well, but are hopelessly outnumbered, and practically untrained owing to the enormous front we have had to hold all winter, when the divisions should have been training. Our losses are huge, and we are still being steadily pushed back. It is all so sad.

Recriminations are useless. After all, the real judges are those of history, and the army has little cause to fear the verdict.

This northern attack was, of course, a gigantic strategic surprise. Probably it was meant to be the real effort of the Germans, to have followed immediately after the first March attack. The success in the early days then tempted the Germans to develop it, and now they have not enough men left to drive this one through. The Channel Ports are, of course, the vital point to the British Army, and the Germans know it very well. If the French act, there should not be the least possibility of the Germans driving us back to the coast. Even if the French do nothing, I still think the German man-power will be exhausted before the enemy succeeds in driving us back to the coast – but that is not a certainty.

The text of Haig's appeal of 11 April:

To All Ranks of the British Forces in France
Three weeks ago to-day the enemy began his terrific attacks upon us on a fifty-mile front. His objects are to separate us from the French, to take the Channel Ports, and destroy the British Army.

In spite of throwing already 106 divisions into battle, and enduring the most reckless sacrifice of human life, he has as yet made little progress towards his goals.

We owe this to the determined fighting and self-sacrifice of our troops. Words fail me to express the admiration which I feel for the splendid resistance offered by all ranks of our army under most trying circumstances.

Many among us now are tired. To those I would say that Victory belongs to the side which holds out longest. The French Army is moving rapidly and in great force to our support.

There is no other course open to us but to fight it out! Every position must be held to the last man. With our backs to the wall and believing in the justice of our cause, each one of us must fight on to the end. The safety of our Homes and the Freedom of Mankind alike depend upon the conduct of each one of us at this critical moment.

D. M. Haig,
F.M.

Thursday,
11*th April*, 1918.

RAID ON ZEEBRUGGE, BELGIUM, 22–23 April 1918

Vice-Admiral Roger Keyes, Royal Navy

The Zeebrugge canal was a main base for U-boat attacks on Allied shipping in the North Sea. After the submarine pens revealed themselves impervious to air attack, the Royal Navy devised a plan to sink blockships at the sea entrance to the canal. Whatever the practical limitations of the valiant raid – it only managed to halt German operations from Zeebrugge for three weeks – its effect on Allied morale was high.

In accordance with the time-table for the 22–23 April, the Swin Force got under way at 1 p.m. and joined the vessels from Dover at "A" buoy, in time for the whole force to form up punctually in their cruising order by 5 p.m., when the expedition set out once again for the Belgian coast.

The force immediately under my flag, that night consisted of 76 vessels organised in 26 units, each distinguished by a letter and each of which had definite instructions for its conduct.

On the previous occasions the *Warwick* took up a position well ahead of the *Vindictive*; this time she took station ahead of the starboard wing column, which was led by the *Phoebe*, as I wished to keep the boarding ship and blockship column under observation.

Before night fell, remembering my wife's last words, I made a general signal by semaphore, "St. George for England," and Carpenter signalled back: "May we give the dragon's tail a damned good twist," which was very apt and to the point, but did not fit in with my mood at the moment.

After the twilight had faded, the full moon made it almost as bright as day – at least so it seemed to me, for I was very alive to the risks I had added by attempting the enterprise with a full moon, and the visibility appeared to be at least eight to ten miles. When I remarked on this, Tomkinson said drily: "Well, even if the enemy expect us, they will never think we are such damned fools as to try and do it in bright moonlight." Soon after this it became misty; later it commenced to drizzle and the visibility was reduced to less than a mile.

On arriving at "D" buoy, the whole force stopped to enable the surplus steaming parties in the blockships to be disembarked; some of them could not be found; in fact several men stowed away in the *Iphigenia*, determined not to be deprived of the honour of taking part in the expedition. An admirable spirit, but it added to the difficulties of the rescue work. The *Intrepid*'s M.L. broke down and failed to go alongside, with the result that she carried a crew of 84 instead of 54 as intended.

All the C.M.B.'s having been slipped, we got under way again, with the *Iris*, *Daffodil* and submarines still in tow, in time to pass "G" buoy at 10.30 p.m., precisely the programme time. Commodore Boyle had kept me well informed – through his destroyers – as to the state of the wind, which was still satisfactory when we passed the *Attentive*; a misty rain was blowing lightly but steadily from the north-east.

The *Brilliant*, *Sirius*, two destroyers and two C.M.B.s then parted company, bound for Ostend, while we continued on our way to Zeebrugge.

There was no sign of the air attack, which should have

commenced an hour earlier, and we concluded that it had been held up by the rain.

After passing "G" buoy, the *Warwick*, followed by the *Phoebe* and *North Star* (L Unit), the *Whirlwind* and *Myngs* (F Unit) on her port beam, drew out a mile ahead of the main force to drive off any enemy vessels that might be out on patrol. L Unit was charged with the duty of protecting the boarding ships, and the approach of the blockships, from possible destroyer attacks, and I decided to remain with them, because it seemed almost incredible that the enemy's destroyers – several of whom were known normally to lie alongside the Mole – would not come out to seek action and at least attempt to torpedo the *Vindictive* after she arrived alongside; this was the only way she could be attacked, since all her vitals would then be protected from gunfire by the Mole, if she berthed anywhere near her proper position.

The bombardment by the *Erebus* and *Terror* should have commenced at 40 minutes after "X", but was also delayed; we learnt later that it was on account of the low visibility, but fortunately they were able to pick up the Oost gas light and whistle buoy marking the limit of the Dutch territorial waters which Douglas knew to be accurately charted, and they commenced firing 15 minutes later than the programme time. Captain Wills of the *Erebus*, who was in command of that unit, had orders to continue the bombardment at intervals throughout the operation, until ordered by wireless to cease fire; but in any case he was to get out of range of Knocke Battery by daylight.

Three C.M.B.s (Units A and B) went ahead at full speed at 40 minutes after "X" to lay smoke-waves across our front, behind which the whole force was to advance. Another C.M.B. (Unit C) also went off ten minutes later to lay a smoke-float off Blankenberghe and renew it every 20 minutes. This she did very effectively, but owing to engine trouble was a little behind her time-table; anyhow, no enemy fast motor-boats appear to have emerged.

At 11.30 the *Warwick* passed an occulting light buoy, five miles N. 30° W. from Zeebrugge Mole, the correct charted position of the Blankenberghe buoy. In the meantime the other

C.M.B.s were overtaking us, and the M.L.s closing up, to carry out their appointed tasks in compliance with their special instructions.

Fifty minutes after passing "X", one C.M.B. (Unit D) proceeded towards the Mole at high speed to lay smoke-floats in the western section, for screening in a north-easterly wind. She was then to patrol this line, making smoke, until relieved by eight M.L.s (Unit G).

Another C.M.B. (Unit E) proceeded at the same time to lay smoke-floats and patrol the eastern section until relieved by eight M.L.s (Unit I).

Two C.M.B.s (Unit H) proceeded at full speed, to fire their torpedoes at the enemy destroyers secured to the inner side of the Mole, and then run to the eastward making smoke, about a mile from the shore, to blank off the heavy batteries to the eastward of the canal entrance.

Two C.M.B.s (Unit V), 70 minutes after "X", proceeded at full speed direct for the end of the Mole, to lay their smoke-floats under the seaward side of the lighthouse extension, within 50 yards of the Mole if possible; the object being to mask the guns on the lighthouse extension, during the near approach of the boarding vessels. These floats had their baffle plates removed, so that the flame emanating from them would indicate the approximate position of the Mole end.

At the same time, the *Whirlwind* and *Myngs* altered course to port to patrol the eastern area; the *Warwick*, *Phoebe* and *North Star* stood on for a few minutes towards the Mole, and then reduced speed and hauled a little to starboard, to allow the boarding vessels to overtake them.

The smoke-screens appeared to be excellent, and they were entirely responsible for enabling the whole force to close unseen. It was not until about 11.50 p.m. – about ten minutes before the *Vindictive* was due alongside the Mole – that the enemy appear to have heard the C.M.B.s, and then the star-shells burst in the sky, making it as light as day, some well to seaward of us: one actually fell on the deck of the *Myngs*, three miles from the Mole. As they descended the lights were blanked out by the pall of smoke, which at that time rose to a good height above the sea level. Shortly after this, just before midnight, the enemy appeared to be thoroughly alarmed and with a roar like express trains, great shells passed over our heads, and a heavy barrage from the coast batteries was put down two or three miles outside us. It was an intense relief to me to know, that the battle was now joined and there would be no more turning back.

I had been deploring the absence of our aircraft's flare parachutes, but the enemy's star-shells provided all the illumination we required throughout the action . . .

ZEEBRUGGE: THE VIEW FROM HMS *VINDICTIVE*, 22–23 April 1918

Captain A.F.B. Carpenter, HMS Vindictive

Soon after passing the Blankenberghe light-buoy the enemy appeared to suspect that something more than a bombardment was afoot. Star shells were fired to seaward and searchlights were switched on. That was exactly what we had hoped for. If only they would continue to illuminate the atmosphere our navigational difficulties would be enormously reduced. The star shells were extraordinary. They burst with a loud report just overhead and lit up our surroundings to the maximum of the then visibility. Much to our surprise no enemy vessels were encountered or even seen; presumably the enemy set the greater dependence on their mines.

To the southward, that is, between us and the shore, our smoke-screeners had laid down a "pea-soup" fog. Nothing was to be seen in that direction except the glare of searchlights and of gun flashes, the latter being presumably directed against the fast motor boats which had run into the anchorage behind the Mole for the purpose of torpedoing vessels secured alongside. At this stage the wind died away completely and the rain was heavier than ever . . .

A few seconds before the schedule time for the last alteration of course – designed to take us alongside the outer wall – the smoke screen, which had been drifting northwards before the new wind, suddenly cleared. Barely three hundred yards distant, dead ahead of us, appeared a long low dark object which was immediately recognised as the Mole itself with the lighthouse at its extremity. We had turned up heading direct for the six-gun battery exactly as arranged in the plan . . . Course was altered immediately to the southwestward and speed was increased to the utmost.

The Mole battery opened fire at once; our own guns, under the direction of Commander E. O. B. S. Osborne, replied with the utmost promptitude. The estimated distance at which we passed the Mole battery was two hundred and fifty yards off the western gun. It was a truly wonderful sight. The noise was terrific and the flashes of the Mole guns seemed to be within arm's length. Of course it was, to all intents and purposes, impossible for the Mole guns to miss their target. They literally poured projectiles into us. In about five minutes we had reached the Mole, but not before the ship had suffered a great amount of damage to both *matériel* and personnel . . . To my mind the chief reasons for our successful running of the gauntlet were twofold, firstly, the fact that we were so close, and secondly, the splendid manner in which our guns' crews stuck to their work . . . The petty officer at one of our six-inch guns, when asked afterwards what ranges he fired at, said that he reckoned he opened fire at about two hundred yards and he continued till close to the Mole. "How close?" he was asked. "Reckoning from the gun muzzle," he replied, "I should say it was about three feet!" . . .

The material damage was very great, but, though it may sound paradoxical, of not much importance . . . The damage to the personnel was exceedingly serious . . . Captain Halahan, commanding the naval storming forces, who had repeatedly told me this was to be his last fight, was shot down and killed at the outset. Commander Edwards, standing near him on the gangway deck, was also shot down and completely incapacitated. Colonel Elliot, commanding the Marine storming forces, and his second-in-command, Major Corner, were killed on the bridge, where they had taken up a commanding position in full view of the gangway deck. Many others were killed or wounded. The death of so many brave men was a terrible blow . . .

At one minute past midnight the ship actually arrived alongside the Mole, one minute late on schedule time, having steamed alongside at sixteen knots speed. The engines were immediately reversed at full speed and the ship bumped the Mole very gently on the specially constructed fender fitted on the port bow . . .

After we had been struggling against our difficulties alongside for about five minutes *Daffodil* suddenly appeared steaming straight for our foremast in a direction perpendicular to the Mole. Campbell [*Commander of the* Daffodil] pushed her nose against us, hawsers were passed to his vessel, and he shoved us bodily alongside the Mole, exactly in accordance with the Plan. Really he might have been an old stager at tug-master's work, pursuing his vocation in one of our own harbours, judging by the cool manner in which he carried out his instructions to the letter.

Immediately the two foremost gangways reached the wall they were lowered until they rested on it. No other gangways were then available. The order was at once passed to "Storm the Mole." . . .

The only two gangways which could reach the Mole were, to say the least of it, very unsteady platforms. Their inboard ends were rising and falling several feet as the ship rolled; the outer ends were see-sawing and sliding backwards and forwards on the top of the wall . . . the run across these narrow gangways with a thirty-foot drop beneath to certain death was not altogether inviting.

The first act of the advance party, in accordance with the instructions, was to secure the ship to the wall by means of the grappling anchors. A great struggle to do this was undertaken. The foremost grappling anchors only just reached the Mole. Some men sat on the top of the wall and endeavoured to pull the grapnels over the top as they were lowered from the ship. These grapnels, by virtue of the use for which they were designed, were heavy. That fact, combined with the continuous rolling of the ship, made it exceedingly difficult to control them. Rosoman and a party of men on board joined in the struggle, but a heavy lurch of the ship broke up the davit on which the foremost grappling iron was slung and the latter fell between the ship and the wall . . .

Campbell had been shot in the face, but such a trifle as that did not appear to have worried him, and he continued to push the *Vindictive* alongside from the moment of his arrival until the whole hour and five minutes had elapsed before we left the Mole . . .

The high wall, towering above our upper deck, was now protecting the hull of the ship from gun-fire; no vital damage could be sustained in that way so long as we remained alongside . . . Our guns in the fighting-top were directing a murderous fire into [*the German*] special targets . . . the heavy gun battery at the end of the broad part of the Mole and the lighter battery on the lighthouse extension . . .

A few minutes after the storming of the Mole had commenced a terrific explosion was seen away to the westward, and we guessed that the submarine party had attacked the viaduct . . . The explosion presented a wonderful spectacle. The flames shot up to a great height – one mentally considered it at least a mile . . . At about 12:15 a.m. the blockships were expected to be close to the Mole, and a momentary glimpse of them was obtained as they passed close to the lighthouse on their way to the canal entrance. So far so good . . . Our further tasks were firstly that of continuing the diversion until the crews of the blockships had had a reasonable chance of being rescued subsequent to sinking their vessels in the canal, secondly of re-embarking our storming parties and withdrawing to seaward, and thirdly of carrying out demolition work on the Mole during our stay alongside . . .

Every available space on the mess deck was occupied by casualties. Those who could do so were sitting on the mess stools awaiting their turn for medical attention. Many were stretched at full length on the deck, the majority being severely wounded. Some had already collapsed and were in a state of coma; I fear that many had already passed away. It was a sad spectacle indeed. Somehow, amidst all the crashing and smashing on deck, one had not realized the sacrifice that was taking place . . .

The work of [Staff-Surgeon) McCutcheon and his confrères was beyond all praise; untiring energy, consummate care and withal real brotherly bearing characterised their actions . . .

It is not possible to say how many of the storming parties reached the Mole – the loss of officers and men and the resulting temporary disorganization naturally prevented the collection of definite information. Suffice it to say that a large number stormed the Mole in furtherance of our diversion, and that the latter was undoubtedly successful in that we attained our primary object of assisting the blockships to pass an all-important obstacle in the Mole batteries . . .

Undoubtedly the assault would be difficult enough. But what of the retirement? The bodies of any men who were killed or disabled on the Mole could only be re-embarked by way of the vertical ladders against the wall. It would be bad enough to descend them in the first place, but a herculean task to carry a body twenty feet up a vertical ladder under incessant shell and machine-gun fire. Yet – and I think this fact sums up the splendid gallantry of these men – of the large number of men who stormed the Mole, many of whom were killed or completely disabled, the total number left on the Mole after the retirement, including both dead and wounded, amounted to little more than a *dozen* . . .

Shortly after 12:50 a.m. the order was given to make the retirement signal. *Vindictive*'s sirens had both been shot away. The starboard searchlight had received a direct hit from a projectile and had been hurled off the bridge down to the upper deck. The port searchlight had also been put out of action. An order was passed to *Daffodil* to make the retirement signal on her siren. The latter spluttered and gurgled whilst emitting a veritable shower bath, but presently began to show signs of being useful. A low groan developed into a growling note which in turn travelled gradually up the scale until loud enough to be heard at a distance . . . The storming parties commenced to return to the ship almost at once . . . One Marine carried a disabled man on board, placed his charge on the deck, kissed him on both cheeks and was heard to remark, "I wasn't going to leave you, Bill." . . .

We steamed away to the northwestward at utmost speed. The flames were pouring through the holes in the funnels; the ship had the appearance of being heavily on fire . . . we had the sensation of the ship jumping at irregular but frequent intervals. This may have been due to the concussion of heavy shell striking the water near the ship. Whether any shell hit us or not during the retirement is unlikely to be known . . . The ship had already been hit so often that any further damage of the same description would hardly have been noticed.

RICHTHOFEN: THE END, WESTERN FRONT, 23 April 1918

General John Monash, Australian Infantry Force

Richthofen's Flight was seen travelling at a considerable height overhead, probably 7,000 feet, and engaged a formation of our own machines . . . Some fighting took place in the air, and then suddenly one of our R.E. 8s made a quick dive to within 150 feet of the ground, followed by Richthofen in a fast plane, which rapidly overhauled our machine, and we could see him pumping tracer bullets after our machine. All the Lewis-gunners in the neighbourhood immediately opened fire and made an awful row. Suddenly Richthofen's machine was seen to stagger, but recovered itself and made as if to fly off. In turning it flew directly over one of General Hobbs's batteries in the vicinity . . . A lucky stream of bullets got the machine fair and square; it turned over, came down with a crash, and was completely wrecked.

Before the machine could be approached the enemy artillery, which, like us, had seen the aeroplane come down and had marked the spot, put down a circle of sharpnel all around it and maintained their fire for about half an hour, while Richthofen's Flight circled round overhead four or five times and then majestically flew away. Such was the requiem of this doughty and chivalrous warrior. When our people could get near the aeroplane they found that Richthofen had been shot through the head and heart by bullets, and the papers on the body left no doubt as to his identity.

Our Royal Air Force was soon on the ground; the wrecked machine and the body of Richthofen were brought in, and late in the day buried with military honours. His personal effects were afterwards taken over the German lines and dropped with a message of condolence from the Royal Air Force.

RICHTHOFEN: A GERMAN SOLDIER MOURNS A HERO, 24 April 1918

Herbert Sulzbach, German Army

Richthofen has really been killed in action! I am completely shattered by the news. No words will suffice to do justice to his deeds, or to describe the grief which every German feels at the loss of this national hero; it is just impossible to grasp; he has been buried by the British with the highest military honours, for he crashed the British lines. Six British flying officers bore his coffin, and a British chaplain presented the sermon and sang his praises as an enemy hero, a British plane with mourning pennants circled the burial ground during the funeral, and showed the highest honour to this fallen enemy. The British are indeed truly chivalrous, and we must thank them all for honouring our great airman.

WESTERN FRONT: TANK VS TANK, 24 VILLERS-BRETONNEUX, 24 April 1918

Lieutenant F. Mitchell, Tank Corps

Just before dawn on April 24th a tremendous bombardment deluged the wood. I was aroused in the dark by someone shaking me violently. "Gas, sir, gas!" I struggled up, half awake, inhaled a foul odour and quickly slipped on my mask. My eyes were running, I could not see, my breath came with difficulty. I could hear the trees crashing to the ground near me.

For a moment I was stricken with panic, then, suddenly, a thought sped through my confused mind, "If you are going to die, why not die decently?" I listened to that inner voice and pulled myself together, only to discover that I had omitted to attach my nose clip!

Holding hands with my section commander and the orderly who had aroused us, we groped our way to the open. It was pitch dark, save where, away on the edge of the wood, the rising sum showed blood red.

As we stumbled forward, tree trunks, unseen in that infernal gloom, separated our joined hands and we were tripped up by bushes and brambles. Suddenly a hoarse cry came from the orderly, "My mouthpiece is broken, sir!" "Run like hell for the open!" shouted the section commander. There was a gasp, and then we heard him crashing away through the undergrowth like a hunted beast.

Soon I found my tank covered with its tarpaulin. The small oblong doors were open, but the interior was empty. On the ground, in the wrappings of the tarpaulin, however, I felt something warm and fleshy. It was one of the crew lying full length, wearing his mask, but dazed by gas.

Behind the trenches a battery of artillery was blazing away, the gunners in their gas masks feverishly loading and unloading like creatures of a nightmare. Meanwhile, as the shelling grew in intensity, a few wounded men and some stragglers came into sight. Their report was depressing, Villers-Bretonneux had been captured and with it many of our own men. The Boche had almost broken through.

By this time two of my crew had developed nasty gas symptoms, spitting, coughing, and getting purple in the face. They were led away to the rear, one sprawling limply in a wheelbarrow found in the wood. We waited till an infantry brigadier appeared on the scene with two orderlies. He was unaware of the exact position ahead and, accompanied by our section captain and the runners, he went forward to investigate. In ten minutes one of the runners came back, limping badly, hit in the leg. In another ten minutes the second returned, his left arm torn by shrapnel, then, twenty minutes after that, walking, unhurt and serene, through the barrage came the brigadier and our captain. The news was grave. We had suffered heavy losses and lost ground, but some infantry were still holding out in the switch-line between Cachy and Villers-Bretonneux. If this line were over-whelmed the Boche would obtain possession of the high ground dominating Amiens and would, perhaps, force us to evacuate that city and drive a wedge between the French and British armies.

A serious consultation was held and the order came, "Proceed to the Cachy switch-line and hold it at all costs."

We put on our masks once more and plunged, like divers, into the gas-laden wood. As we strove to crank up, one of the three men, turning the huge handle, collapsed. We put him against a tree, gave him some tablets of ammonia to sniff, and then, as he did not seem to be coming round, we left him, for time was pressing. Out of a crew of seven, four men, with red-rimmed, bulging eyes, only remained.

The three tanks, one male, armed with two six-pounder guns and machine guns, and two females, armed with machine guns only, crawled out of the wood and set off over the open ground towards Cachy.

Ahead, the German barrage stood like a wall of fire in our path. There was no break in it anywhere. It seemed impossible that we could pass through that deadly area unhit. I decided to attempt a zigzag course, as somehow it seemed safer.

Luck was with us; going at top speed, we went safely through the danger zone and soon reached the Cachy lines, but there was no sign of our infantry.

Suddenly, out of the ground 10 yards away, an infantryman rose, waving his rifle furiously. We stopped. He ran forward and shouted through the flap, "Look out! Jerry tanks about!" and then as swiftly disappeared into the trench again.

I informed the crew, and a great thrill ran through us all. Opening the loophole, I looked out. There, some 300 yards away, a round, squat-looking monster was advancing. Behind it came waves of infantry and further away to left and right crawled two more of these armed tortoises.

So we had met our rivals at last! For the first time in history tank was encountering tank!

The 6-pounder gunners crouching on the floor, their backs against the engine cover, loaded their guns expectantly.

We still kept on a zigzag course, threading the gaps between the lines of hastily dug trenches, and coming near the small protecting belt of wire, we turned left and the right gunner, peering through his narrow slit, made a sighting shot. The shell burst some distance beyond the leading enemy tank. No reply came. A second shot boomed out, landing just to the right, but again no reply.

Suddenly, against our steel wall, a hurricane of hail pattered, and the interior was filled with myriads of sparks and flying splinters. Something rattled against the steel helmet of the driver sitting next to me and my face was stung with minute fragments of steel. The crew flung themselves flat on the floor. The driver ducked his head and drove straight on.

Above the roar of our engine could be heard the staccato rat-tat-tat-tat of machine guns and another furious jet of bullets sprayed our steel side, the splinters clanging viciously against the engine cover.

The Jerry tank had treated us to a broadside of armour-piercing bullets!

Taking advantage of a dip in the ground, we got beyond range and then turning, we manœuvred to get the left gunner on to the moving target. Owing to our gas casualties the gunner was working single-handed and his right eye being too swollen with gas he aimed with the left. In addition, as the ground was heavily scarred with shell holes we kept going up and down like a ship in a heavy sea, making accurate shooting difficult.

His first shot fell some 30 yards in front and the next went beyond.

Nearing the village of Cachy, I saw to my astonishment that the two female tanks were slowly limping away to the rear. They had both been hit by shells almost immediately on their arrival and had great holes in their sides. As their Lewis guns were useless against the heavy armour-plate of the enemy and their gaping sides no longer afforded them any defence against machine-gun bullets, they had nothing to do but withdraw from action.

We still were lucky enough to dodge the enemy shelling, although the twisting and turning once or twice almost brought us on top of our own trenches.

Whilst we were ranging on the leading German tank, our own infantry were standing in their trenches watching the duel with tense interest, like spectators in the pit of a theatre.

Looking down on one occasion I saw to my horror that we were going straight down into a trench full of men who, huddled together, were yelling at the tops of their voices to attract our attention. A quick signal to the gears-man seated in the rear of the tank and we turned swiftly, avoiding catastrophe by a second.

Another raking broadside of armour-piercing bullets gave us

our first casualty, a bullet passing through the fleshy part of both legs of the Lewis gunner at the rear after piercing the side of the tank!

We had no time to put on more than a temporary dressing and he lay on the floor, bleeding and groaning, whilst the 6-pounder boomed over his head and the empty shell cases clattered all round him.

The roar of our engine, the nerve-racking rat-tat-tat of our machine guns blazing at the Boche infantry, and the thunderous boom of the 6-pounders, all bottled up in that narrow space, filled our ears with tumult. Added to this we were half-stifled by the fumes of petrol and cordite.

Again we turned and proceeded at a slower pace; the left gunner, registering carefully, hit the ground right in front of the Jerry tank. I took a risk and stopped the tank for a moment.

The pause was justified; a carefully aimed shot hit the turret of the German tank, bringing it to a standstill. Another roar and yet another white puff at the front of the tank denoted a second hit! Peering with swollen eyes through his narrow slit the elated gunner shouted words of triumph that were drowned by the roaring of the engine.

Then once more with great deliberation he aimed and hit for the third time. Through a loophole I saw the tank heel over to one side and then a door opened and out ran the crew. We had knocked the monster out!

Quickly I signed to the machine-gunner, and he poured volley after volley into the retreating figures.

My nearest enemy being now out of action, I turned to look at the other two, who were coming forward slowly. As the German infantry were still advancing, the 6-pounder gunner sent round after round of case shot in their direction which, scattering like the charge of a shot gun, spread havoc in their ranks.

Now, I thought, we shall not last very long. The two great tanks were creeping forward relentlessly; if they both concentrated their fire on us at once we would be finished. We sprinkled the neighbourhood of one of them with a few sighting shells, when to my intense joy and amazement, I saw it go slowly backwards. Its companion did likewise and in a few minutes they both had disappeared from sight, leaving our tank the sole possessor of the field.

A BRITISH PACIFIST WRITES FROM PRISON, 3 June 1918

Bertrand Russell

Brixton

To my brother Frank

Existence here is not disagreeable, but for the fact that one can't see one's friends. The one fact does make it, to me, very disagreeable – but if I were devoid of affection, like many middle-aged men. I should find nothing to dislike. One has no responsibilities, and infinite leisure. My time passes very fruitfully. In a normal day, I do four hours' philosophical writing, four hours' philosophical reading, and four hours' general reading – so you can understand my wanting a lot of books. I have been reading Madame Roland's memoirs and have come to the conclusion that she was a very over-rated woman: snobbish, vain, sentimental, envious – rather German type. Her last days before her execution were spent in chronicling petty social snubs or triumphs of many years back. She was a democrat chiefly from envy of the noblesse. Prisons in her day were more cheerful than now: she says if she were not writing her memoirs she would be painting flowers or playing an air. Pianos are not provided in Brixton. On the other hand, one is not guillotined on leaving, which is in some ways an advantage. – During my two hours' exercise I reflect upon all manner of things. It is good to have a time of leisure for reflection and altogether it is a godsend being here. But I don't want too much godsend!

I am quite happy and my mind is very active. I enjoy the sense that the time is fruitful – after giving out all these last years, reading almost nothing and writing very little and having no opportunity for anything civilized, it is a real delight to get back to a civilized existence. But oh I shall be glad when it is over! I have given up the bad habit of imagining the war may be over some day. One must compare the time with that of the Barbarian invasion. I feel like Apollinaris Sidonius – The best one could be would be to be like St Augustine. For the next 1,000 years people will look back to the time before 1914 as they did in the Dark Ages to the time before the Gauls sacked Rome. Queer animal, Man!

Your loving brother
Bertrand Russell

RUSSIA IN REVOLUTION: TSAR NICHOLAS II AND THE ROYAL FAMILY ARE SHOT, EKATERINBURG, 16 July 1918

Pavel Medvedev

In the evening of 16 July, between seven and eight p.m., when the time for my duty had just begun, Commandant Yurovsky [the head of the guard] ordered me to take all the Nagan revolvers from the guards and to bring them to him. I took twelve revolvers from the sentries as well as from some other of the guards, and brought them to the commandant's office. Yurovsky said to me, "We must shoot *them all* tonight, so notify the guards not to be alarmed if they hear shots." I understood, therefore, that Yurovsky had it in his mind to shoot the whole of the Tsar's family, as well as the doctor and the servants who lived with them, but I did not ask him where or by whom the decision had been made. I must tell you that in accordance with Yurovsky's order the boy who assisted the cook was transferred in the morning to the guardroom (in the Popov house). The lower floor of Ipatiev's house was occupied by the Letts from the Letts Commune, who had taken up their quarters there after Yurovsky was made commandant. They were ten in number. At about ten o'clock in the evening, in accordance with Yurovsky's order, I informed the guards not to be alarmed if they should hear firing. About midnight Yurovsky woke up the Tsar's family. I do not know if he told them the reason they had been awakened and where they were to be taken, but I positively affirm that it was Yurovsky who entered the rooms occupied by the Tsar's family. Yurovsky had not ordered me or Dobrynin to awaken the family. In about an hour the whole of the family, the doctor, the maid and the waiters got up, washed and dressed themselves. Just before Yurovsky went to awaken the family, two members of the Extraordinary Commission [of the Ekaterinburg Soviet] arrived at Ipatiev's house. Shortly after one o'clock a.m., the Tsar, the Tsaritsa, their four daughters, the maid, the doctor, the cook and the waiters left their rooms. The Tsar carried the heir in his arms. The Emperor and the heir were dressed in *gimnasterkas* [soldiers' shirts] and wore caps. The Empress and her daughters were dressed but their heads were uncovered. The Emperor, carrying the heir, preceded them. The Empress, her daughters and the others followed him. Yurovsky, his assistant and the two abovementioned members of the Extraordinary Commission accompanied them. I was also present. During my presence none of the Tsar's family asked any questions. They did not weep or cry. Having descended the stairs to the first floor, we went out into the court, and from there by the second door (counting from the gate) we entered the ground floor of the house. When the room (which adjoins the store room with a sealed door) was reached, Yurovsky ordered chairs to be brought, and his assistant brought three chairs. One chair was given to the Emperor, one to the Empress, and the third to the heir. The Empress sat by the wall by the window, near the black pillar of the arch. Behind her stood three of her daughters (I knew their faces very well, because I had seen them every day when they walked in the garden, but I didn't know their names). The heir and the Emperor sat side by side almost in the middle of the room. Doctor Botkin stood behind the heir. The maid, a very tall woman, stood at the left of the door leading to the store room; by her side stood one of the Tsar's daughters (the fourth). Two servants stood against the wall on the left from the entrance of the room.

The maid carried a pillow. The Tsar's daughters also brought small pillows with them. One pillow was put on the Empress's chair; another on the heir's chair. It seemed as if all of them guessed their fate, but not one of them uttered a single sound. At this moment eleven men entered the room: Yurovsky, his assistant, two members of the Extraordinary Commission, and seven Letts. Yurovsky ordered me to leave, saying, "Go on to the street, see if there is anybody there, and wait to see whether the shots have been heard." I went out to the court, which was enclosed by a fence, but before I got to the street I heard the firing. I returned to the house immediately (only two or three minutes having elapsed) and upon entering the room where the execution had taken place, I saw that all the members of the Tsar's family were lying on the floor with many wounds in their bodies. The blood was running in streams. The doctor, the maid and two waiters had also been shot. When I entered the heir was still alive and moaned a little. Yurovsky went up and fired two or three more times at him. Then the heir was still.

CASUALTIES OF WAR: SCENES FROM A MILITARY HOSPITAL, FRANCE, July 1918

Robert C. Hoffman, US 28th Division, American Expeditionary Force

There were constant operations in this part of the hospital. But most sinister of all, and perhaps most important of all, was a small room, which contained a few beds, in which the very worst patients were placed. Many called this the morgue, the "dead room," or the "dying room". Men were dying every day in spite of the fact that the more seriously wounded usually died before they reached a base hospital. In spite of all medical skill, tetanus – lockjaw – would set in; gangrene could not always be prevented. Some of these men had lost a great amount of blood, and many of them, even during the summer season, already had contracted Flu, which in their weakened state was fatal.

When a man was dying they would move him out. It was bad enough for him to die without his comrades, who did not know when their own turn might come, having to watch him die. Some of the men went out screaming when they were moved. The nurses would try to ease their going by telling them that they were only going to the operating room for minor treatment or to the dressing room, to have their bandages changed. The fellows soon learned to observe whether the little bag which held their personal belongings – sometimes a helmet or a coat – came with them. If it remained behind they could expect to come back; but if it too was moved, then they were sure that worse was in store for them. Some begged to be left there to die with their friends around them, not to be placed with a lot of near corpses who were complete strangers.

The more pitifully wounded did not wish to live. They constantly begged doctors and nurses, sometimes at the top of their voices, to put an end to them. Some made attempts to end their lives with a knife or fork. It became necessary to feed these wounded and never leave a knife or fork with them. One of the orderlies told me that a blinded man who was suffering greatly and did not wish to live had killed himself at one time with a fork. It was hard to drive it deep enough through his chest to end his life, and he kept hitting it with his clenched fist to drive it deeper.

There was a limit to how many pain tablets could be given to any man – how many his heart would stand. But most of them begged for another tablet the minute they recovered sufficiently from the former tablets and once again felt severe pain.

Most of the nurses back at the base were older women. I am sure the long hours they had to work and the demands of their patients shortened their lives considerably. The younger and stronger girls were up nearer the front, where even more labour and more difficult duties were encountered. It was interesting, although somewhat gruesome, to stand in the lobbies and watch the traffic going by: wheeled carts containing men who were going up into wards such as mine; men who were hurt worse than they had expected and were going downstairs in the ward with the worst cases; many men expecting to die being moved to the living morgue and men who had died being taken out for burial. Some of them were better off; at least I would rather be dead than as horribly crippled as many – a lifelong dependant upon others – living dead. I have always felt that life would not be worth living if constant pain and suffering, being confined to pain-ridden beds and wheel chairs, was to be one's lot until death. But humans cling to life. They want to see loved ones, their home, the sun rise the next day, see the spring again. They seem willing to live in spite of all suffering. It is a good old world, after all. So we may change our minds if we must face the stern realization that death is finally at hand.

Five or six men a day were dying. They were taken right out in the fields back of the hospital and buried. Bugles sounding taps, and the firing of guns, as each man was buried with military honours, became familiar sounds. Normal death is not so bad. I've seen a lot of death of one sort and another. I've really died several times myself – by drowning, unconscious four days after an automobile accident, knocked to unconsciousness in the Argonne; not a bit different than actual death as far as one's feelings are concerned. The difference is the fact that in real death one never wakes up, never opens his eyes to the light of the world again. But I was brought back each time to life. I am sure that I experienced real death at one time; although in my prime, my life before me, everything to live for, I had absolutely no desire to live. I felt this way when I first became conscious four days after an auto accident in which I was involved. Dying under those circumstances could not be so bad. And dying of old age must not be so bad either. Under those circumstances one has lived his or her life. There is a slow losing of the faculties, a dulling of the mind; finally one has no realization of whether he is alive or not. That would be a nice way to die. Some of my relatives died that way, really of old age. But others died horrible deaths from cancer, Bright's disease, dropsy, or diabetes. Sudden death from heart trouble would be quick – like a bullet that ends things.

But many of these men were doomed to a life of slow and painful death. The doctors and nurses, of course, told them that they would become completely cured in time, but the fellows talked among themselves and didn't quite believe it. I admired their courage, for many of them were smiling and calm under the circumstances. I wondered if they were not more deserving of medals for bravery than was I. It is one thing to be brave when one's body is whole, one's comrades around, and a stirring fight is in progress; but still another thing to be torn to pieces, in pain, little more than half a man lying in a hard bed, in dark and miserable surroundings, without one's friends and loved ones nearby. But I suppose it is worse to die, as so many died, in the mud, in front of our lines, unable to get medical attention as so many were to die a bit later in our part of the war.

These brave young fellows, like the young German I had seen in the field hospital, knew that they must die, were soon to leave this world, friends, hopes, prospects, many of them never having had the opportunity to live. They had been studying, working, training, striving for better things to come. But there were to be no better things for some. Their lives were all but ended, their candle of life had all but burned away.

Far from pleasant moments I spent in this ward below ours. It was bad enough in our section, and I could tell even the most sorely wounded of the men whose beds were around mine how lucky they were. It is hard to feel lucky when a rifle or machine gun bullet has gone through the bones of the shin; when it has gone entirely through the huge muscles of the thigh (for there it is difficult to heal. It must be kept open, forced to heal from the centre first. Drainage tubes must be constantly kept in it, so that it will remain clean within and not become infected in any manner. It was necessary to reopen so many of these hastily cared for wounds that had grown shut while not quite clean inside); a shot through the elbow or the knee, a wound that would usually leave the bone stiff for the remainder of life; or through the hand or the foot. Such wounds might take years to heal. The men who merely had a hole in an arm or a shoulder were lucky enough.

And I was so lucky that I was ashamed to be in the hospital with men who were really hurt. But the doctors had insisted that I go there. They must have know whether it was necessary or not. I believe that they thought some of the bits of iron, sand, and gravel, which had made my face so terrible to look at, might have penetrated the flesh or even the skull to a point where they would be removed some time later. But it turned out that my wounds were only superficial. You can be sure I was pleased when I saw what the doctor was doing to other men around me. I was lucky.

It is not pleasant to lie on one's back with a leg suspended in the air high above one's head – perhaps to have it enclosed in splints for long weeks and months; or to have closed eyes, as so many hundreds in that hospital had, from gas; to lie there in absolute darkness, having no idea whether they would be able to see again or not. There were no radios in those days – nothing to do but lie there in darkness until the doctor and the nurse made one of their two trips a day; until the orderly brought a bed pan or one of the meals.

And speaking about meals – they were mighty poor in this hospital. They may have sufficed for a small man who was sorely wounded; but I was perpetually hungry. I became a pest in the kitchen – until my pajamas were commandeered. Then my only redress was to complain orally. During the entire war I wondered what became of the food that was sent to France. The people at home were doing without it so that the men who were doing the fighting would have it. The men in the rear didn't have it; they said it was at the front. It wasn't at the front; we had just enough to exist on; it wasn't at the big camps. Where could it be? I often wondered. Later I was to learn that much of it was at the base ports. The marine guards at those ports, even the coloured stevedores, lived royally – it not being unusual to have roast beef and chicken, five or six kinds of vegetables, one or two desserts besides ice cream – and not on Christmas either. That's where the food was – in the hands of the men who took it off the ship. The more desirable portions stayed there; we at the front got only what was left.

The days dragged along. I helped where I could – talking to the more seriously wounded, helping the orderlies feed a badly wounded man, even aiding the nurses in making beds. I wasn't a pretty sight as I went around in my pajamas and with slippers of the Oriental type. With my head shaved in front, with my face still swollen and bloated, I looked like an accident that had happened or at least a cross between a Chinaman and a misspent life.

THE BLACK DAY OF THE GERMAN ARMY, 8 August 1918

General Erich von Ludendorff

August 8th was the black day of the German Army in the history of this War. This was the worst experience that I had to go through, except for the events that, from 15 September onwards, took place on the Bulgarian Front and sealed the fate of the Quadruple Alliance.

Early on 8 August, in a dense fog, rendered still thicker by artificial means, the English, mainly with Australian and Canadian divisions, and the French attacked between Albert and Moreuil with strong squadrons of tanks, but otherwise in no great superiority. Between the Somme and the Luce they penetrated deep into our positions. The divisions in line at that point allowed themselves to be completely overwhelmed. Divisional staffs were surprised in their headquarters by enemy tanks. The breach very soon extended across the Luce stream; the troops that were still gallantly resisting at Moreuil were rolled up. To the northward the Somme imposed a halt. Our troops in action north of the river had successfully parried a similar assault. The exhausted divisions that had been relieved a few days earlier and were now resting in the region south-west of Peronne, were immediately warned and set in motion by the commander of the Second Army. At the same time he brought forward into the breach all other available troops. The Rupprecht Army Group dispatched reserves thither by train. The Eighteenth Army threw its own reserves directly into the battle from the south-east, and pushed other forces forward in the region north-west of Roye. On an order from me, the Ninth Army too, although itself in danger, had to contribute. Days, of course, elapsed before the troops from more distant areas could reach the spot. For their conveyance the most extensive use was made of motor lorries.

By the early hours of the forenoon of 8 August I had already gained a complete impression of the situation. It was a very gloomy one. I immediately dispatched a General Staff officer to the battlefield, in order to obtain an idea of the condition of the troops.

The losses of the Second Army had been very heavy. Heavy demands had also been made on its reserves to fill up the gaps. The infantry of some divisions had had to go into action straight off the lorries, whilst their artillery had been sent to some other part of the line. Units were badly mixed up. It could be foreseen that a number of additional divisions would become necessary in order to strengthen the Second Army, even if the enemy continued the offensive, and that was not certain. Besides, our losses in prisoners had been so heavy that GHQ was again faced with the necessity of breaking up more divisions to form reserves. Our reserves dwindled. The losses of the enemy, on the other hand, had been extraordinarily small. The balance of numbers had moved heavily against us; it was bound to become increasingly unfavourable as more American troops came in. There was no hope of materially improving our position by a counter-attack. Our only course, therefore, was to hold on.

We had to resign ourselves now to the prospect of a continuation of the enemy's offensive. Their success had been too easily gained. Their wireless was jubilant, and announced – and with truth – that the morale of the German Army was no longer what it had been. The enemy had also captured many documents of inestimable value to them. The Entente must have gained a clear idea of our difficulty in finding reserves, a further reason why they should pursue the offensive without respite.

The report of the Staff Officer I had sent to the battlefield as to the condition of those divisions which had met the first shock of the attack on the 8th, perturbed me deeply. I summoned divisional commanders and officers from the line to Avesnes to discuss events with them in detail. I was told of deeds of glorious valour, but also of behaviour which, I openly confess, I should not have thought possible in the German Army; whole bodies of our men had surrendered to single troopers, or isolated squadrons. Retiring troops, meeting a fresh division going bravely into action, had shouted out things like "Blackleg," and "You're prolonging the War," expressions that were to be heard again later. The officers in many places had lost their influence and allowed themselves to be swept along with the rest. At a meeting of Prince Max's War Cabinet in October, Secretary Scheidemann called my attention to a Divisional

Report on the occurrences of 8 August, which contained similar unhappy stories. I was not acquainted with this report, but was able to verify it from my own knowledge. A battalion commander from the front, who came out with a draft from home shortly before 8 August, attributed this to the spirit of insubordination and the atmosphere which the men brought back with them from home. Everything I had feared, and of which I had so often given warning, had here, in one place, become a reality. Our war machine was no longer efficient. Our fighting power had suffered, even though the great majority of divisions still fought heroically.

The 8th of August put the decline of that fighting power beyond all doubt, and in such a situation as regards reserves, I had no hope of finding a strategic expedient whereby to turn the situation to our advantage. On the contrary, I became convinced that we were now without that safe foundation for the plans of GHQ, on which I had hitherto been able to build, at least so far as this is possible in war. Leadership now assumed, as I then stated, the character of an irresponsible game of chance, a thing I have always considered fatal. The fate of the German people was, for me, too high a stake.

AUGUST 8: THE BRITISH COMMANDER'S VIEW, 8 August 1918

Field Marshal Douglas Haig, Commander-in-Chief, British Expeditionary Force

Thursday, August 8. Glass steady. Fine night and morning – a slight mist in the valley. An autumn feel in the morning air. 7 a.m. Fourth Army reported, "Generally quiet night until zero, 4.20 a.m. We attacked from southern boundary (S. of Domart en Luce) to Morlancourt (near Ancre) in conjunction with French on right. Attack apparently complete surprise and is progressing satisfactorily."

Soon after 12 noon I motored to Flexicourt with General Davidson and saw Sir H. Rawlinson. Some hard fighting was then going on near Morlancourt (South of the Somme). But Butler, Commanding 3rd Corps, was fully alive to the situation, and had an adequate number of troops to deal with the situation.

Everywhere else the situation had developed more favourably for us than I, optimist though I am, had dared to hope! *The enemy were completely surprised*, two reliefs of Divisions were in progress, very little resistance was offered, and our troops got their objectives quickly with very little loss.

AUGUST 8: THE VIEW OF THE BRITISH MINISTER OF MUNITIONS, 8 August 1918

Winston Churchill MP

At 4.20 a.m. on August 8, in the half light of a misty dawn, the British tanks rolled forward into No Man's Land, and simultaneously the Allied artillery opened fire. Four Canadian, four Australian and two British divisions, followed by three more in reserve and the Cavalry Corps, advanced on the British front. Eight French divisions co-operated later in *échelon* on their right. All along the line, but especially in the centre where the Canadians and Australians fought, victory declared itself forthwith. Ludendorff had taken special measures to strengthen the German line. "In this storm-centre," he writes, "the divisional fronts were narrow, artillery was plentiful, and the trench system was organized in depth. All experience gained on the 18th July had been acted upon." It was of no avail. The Germans were unable to resist the tanks. "Six battle-worthy divisions" collapsed almost immediately before forces scarcely superior in numbers. In less than two hours 16,000 prisoners and more than 200 guns were taken by the British, and by noon tanks and armoured motor cars, followed by cavalry, were scouring the country 14 kilometres behind the German front. The French, who attacked without tanks, advanced about half as far. But the British advance enabled Chaulnes junction to be brought under close fire and consequently destroyed the German communications on which their whole front from Montdidier to Lassigny depended. This was decisive. Two days later, when Humbert's army joined the battle, the high ground near Lassigny was found abandoned; and the advance of the Allies was general along a front of 120 kilometres.

ALLIED BREAK-OUT: FIGHTING BRITISH TANKS, 8 August 1918

Anonymous soldier, German 58th Artillery Regiment

After the rolling barrage had moved beyond our battery, the gunnery officer, Sergeant-Major Reese, ordered his men to push the two guns still in action towards the crest, so that they might fire at sight. On the nearby road, we could already hear the roar of armored cars racing toward our rear one behind another. Our two guns, however, had no time to fire at them: ahead of us, the khaki lines of British infantry were emerging from the ravine. "Look out, buddies, or else we are lost!" somebody shouted. We began firing time shells. The enemy wave slowed down, swayed, and dispersed . . . Suddenly Sergeant Niermann, commander of one of our two remaining guns, shouted: "A tank, straight ahead!" A light tank was roaring toward us with great speed, plunging into craters and climbing over trenches, while his machine guns kept firing at our battery. Bullets were whizzing all around us. Our men feverishly set the sights and fired one, two shells in rapid succession. Before us, there was a shattering roar followed by a dark cloud the size of a house: the tank had been destroyed. But this was only the beginning. Two large tanks emerged from the ruins of Lamotte, flames flashing from their steel turrets. Their projectiles were exploding around our battery. Our pointers aimed at them hurriedly, fired a few shells, and disposed of the two tanks as rapidly as they had wiped out the first. But three new tanks were approaching in single file through the high grass on our right, and had arrived within several hundred yards. We could clearly see their occupants' flat helmets above the turrets. Their guns opened fire on us, and again four men of our battery were badly wounded. Yet our team, under its resolute leader, fought bravely on. Each of us knew that a life and death struggle was raging!

As we had only two guns, we first fired at the tank on the left, then on that on the right. The order, "Fire at will!" was followed by a desperate cannonade. Our left gun, commanded by Wessel, destroyed its tank almost at once. Its fuel tank exploded with a blinding flash and a big black cloud, tossing pieces of iron and human remains high into the air. The tank in the middle, which had approached to within three hundred yards, was destroyed in a few seconds. The tank on the right had a broken tread, and kept turning round and round . . . During the short respite, we prepared the material to be blown up, burned maps and plans, and gathered our essential belongings. In Bayonvillers, a village behind the front, we heard the tumult of battle. Our situation was becoming critical, as we risked being cut off. Suddenly, one more warning cry rang out: "Tank on the right!" A large male tank, the seventh in a matter of minutes, came speeding straight toward us and opened a murderous fire when only two hundred yards distant. Sergeant Wessel's gun was disabled while being trained on this new enemy. Its commander was badly wounded, its crew either wounded too, or killed. Our last gun's shield and sights were seriously damaged in the attack, but its crew did not give up the fight. Crouched behind the steel shield, under a hail of bullets, they turned the gun-carriage. The cool-headed pointer took aim and, at the very instant the tank plunged into the sunken path ahead of us, the fatal shell crashed through its side. Nothing other than dense smoke and flying pieces of iron could be seen. The tank's destruction was our last-minute salvation. Now it was high time to fall back. The British assault troops behind the tanks, were surging in small groups from all directions. Machine guns began rattling, our bullets whizzed all around us. We dashed from shell-hole to shell-hole. Some of our survivors strayed too far to the right, and were made prisoners near Bayonvillers. Others, whom we had believed dead, returned exhausted to the battery after two days.

THE SIGHTS AND SMELLS OF DEATH: CORPSES ON A BATTLEFIELD, WESTERN FRONT, August 1918

Robert C. Hoffman, US 28th Division, American Expeditionary Force

Our organization lost men heavily from gas near here for they had two rather unpleasant assignments to perform. One was the burying of the dead soldiers who had lain for two or three weeks under the July sun, and the other was the digging up of dead Germans to remove their identification tags.

In a woods nearby the soldiers were still lying who had helped stop the German advance toward Paris. They had sold their lives dearly in many cases, for a great many Germans had died too. Three weeks these men had lain in the sun and our troops set out to bury them. Americans and Germans alike were put under the sod. There were horses too and they were a problem. Horses are huge when they become bloated, swell to twice their normal size. Their legs are thrust out like steel posts and it requires a hole about ten feet square and six feet deep to put a horse under. If the legs were off, a hole hardly more than half that size is required. At times we succeeded in using an axe and saw to cut off the horses' legs. It was a hard task and an unpleasant one, but it had to be done.

Finally the fields were cleared but there was still another gruesome task to perform. It is a law of war that the names of enemy dead be sent back through a neutral country to their homeland. The identification tags had been taken from the dead Americans but the Germans had been buried just as they were. There was the task to dig them up again – enough to remove half of their oval-shaped identification tags. That was a much more disagreeable job than the first. Gas came over and owing to the terrific odour even the powerful-smelling mustard gas could not be detected. Our men were working hard in the mid-July heat, perspiring, just in the right condition for mustard gas. Nearly half the remainder of our company, sixty-seven in all, were gassed badly enough to be sent to the hospital. Many of them died; most of them were out for the duration of the war – all reasons why I never saw any of the men who made the attack on Hill 204 at the front again.

Did you ever smell a dead mouse? This will give you about as much idea of what a group of long dead soldiers smell like as will one grain of sand give you an idea of Atlantic City's beaches. A group of men were sent to Hill 204 to make a reconnaissance, to report on conditions there as well as to bury the dead. The story was a very pathetic one. The men were still lying there nearly two weeks later just as they had fallen. I knew all of these men intimately and it was indeed painful to learn of their condition. Some had apparently lived for some time, had tried to dress their own wounds, or their comrades had dressed them; but later they had died there. I was especially pleased that the capture of the German soldiers had made it possible to bring back all the wounded in our sector. Many of the men had been pumped full of machine gun bullets – shot almost beyond recognition. A hundred or so bullets, even in a dead man's body, is not a pretty sight. One of our men was lying with a German bayonet through him – not unlike a pin through a large beetle. Bayonets are hard to remove when once they have been caught between the ribs, especially the saw-tooth bayonets many of the Germans carried. To dislodge them it is usually necessary to shoot once or more to loosen the bayonet. This German had not waited, but had left his gun and passed on. The little Italian boy was still lying on the barbed wire, his eyes open and his helmet hanging back on his head. There had been much shrapnel and some of the bodies were torn almost beyond recognition. This was the first experience at handling and burying the dead for many of our men. It was a trying experience as I was to personally find somewhat later. The identification tags removed from the dead were corroded white, and had become imbedded in the putrid flesh. Even after the burial, when these tags were brought back to the company, they smelled so horribly that some of the officers became extremely sick. One huge man – a giant of a man – who was shot cleanly between the eyes was lying among a group of dead Americans and Germans (that must have been Corporal Graves); and a middle-aged sergeant, who must have been Sergeant George Amole. There is nothing much more pitiful than a battlefield after a battle.

There are two chief reasons why a soldier feels fear: first, that he will not get home to see his loved ones again; but, most of all, picturing himself in the same position as some of the dead men we saw. They lay there face up, usually in the rain, their eyes open, their faces pale and chalk-like, their gold teeth showing. That is in the beginning. After that they are usually too horrible to think about. We buried them as fast as we could – Germans, French and Americans alike. Get them out of sight, but not out of memory. I can remember hundreds and hundreds of dead men. I would know them now if I were to meet them in a hereafter. I could tell them where they were lying and how they were killed – whether with shell fire, gas, machine gun or bayonet. In the town of Varennes there were scores of dead Germans lying around. They had held their positions until the last moment. Many of them had been killed by the tremendous bombardment as they tried to leave. Others had been killed by our advance troops. I spent three days in this town as our battalion was in reserve and I came to know all the dead Germans as I walked around. Later perhaps a hundred of them were laid out for burial. I saw them lying there and I am sure that I could have taken every one of them back to the point where he had died and put him in the exact position in which he had lain.

In the beginning we had a fear of the dead. We hated to touch them. Some of the hardest experiences of my life were taking the identification tags from my dead friends. The first dead man I touched was Philip Beketich, an Austrian baker who was with our company. He was wounded in the battle of Fismes. I had tried to save his life by carrying him through the heavy enemy fire and putting him in one of the cellars of the French houses. He was shot in my arms as I carried him. A few hours later I found time to go round and find how he was. He was dead – stiff and cold. He had quite a splendid development of the pectoral muscles – the big muscles of the chest. Working as a baker had apparently been responsible for that. I had to remove his identification tags, and they had slipped down between his collar bones and the flesh of his chest. They were held there, and it took an effort to get them out. I thrilled and chilled with horror as I touched him. Just a bit later I had to touch my very good friend Lester Michaels, a fine young fellow who had been a star football player on our company team, and a good piano player who entertained us when such an instrument was available. He had been walking past me in Fismes, bent well over. "Keep down, Mike," I said. "There's a sniper shooting through here." Just then Mike fell, with a look of astonishment on his face. "What's the matter, Mike?" I asked. He replied, "They've got me," shook a few times and lay dead upon his face with his legs spread apart – shot through the heart. He lay there for more than a day. There was a terrific battle on and we had no chance to help the wounded – certainly not the dead. I was running short of ammunition and I needed the cartridges in Mike's belt. I tried to unfasten his belt, but I could not reach it. Finally I had to turn him completely over. It was quite an effort owing to the spread-eagle manner in which he lay. His body was hard and cold, and I saw his dead face – difficult to describe the feeling I had. But necessity demanded that I unloosen his belt and take his ammunition and still later his identification tag. After the war I heard from his relatives who wanted to know exactly how he had died.

There are many people who sought this information. They liked to know whether the soldier was killed by shell fire, whether while fighting hand to hand, while running to the attack, or in some phase of defensive work. It was hard to touch these dead men at first. My people at home, hearing of what I was passing through, expected me to come back hard, brutal, callous, careless. But I didn't even want to take a dead mouse out of a trap when I was home. Yet over there I buried seventy-eight men one morning. I didn't dig the holes for them, of course, but I did take their personal belongings from them to return to their people – their rings, trinkets, letters and identification tags. They were shot up in a great variety of ways, and it was not pleasant, but I managed to eat my quota of bread and meat when it came up with no opportunity to wash my hands.

ONE MAN'S WAR: CORPORAL ELMER SHERWOOD ON THE WESTERN FRONT, 9 September–8 November 1918

Corporal Elmer Sherwood, American Expeditionary Force

September 9

This will be the first battle of the war in which the participating troops of our side are to be commanded by Pershing personally, according to the snow [gossip] and it will be the first big all-American drive.

The command may be endeavouring to keep the plans secret. If so, it has not altogether succeeded, because it seems to me everybody in France surmises that we are going to fight to flatten the St Mihiel salient. Even the French peasants spoke of it as we came up to the front.

This projection of the battlefront is popularly known as the "hernia of St Mihiel," and it has existed for almost four years. In 1914 the German horde forced its way to this point, which has been held by the enemy ever since.

The salient has an area of some 150 square miles, almost the size of the former Chateau-Thierry salient, and among other things, it contains a very important railway junction. It is a grand and glorious feeling to know that it is the American army which will carry on this operation.

These fellows have so much confidence that they swear they will capture Metz if ordered to, or die in the attempt.

September 11

We are all set for the party. Unlike the Champagne front, we do not have any reserve positions picked out in case of retreat on this front. Evidently Pershing feels that there is no doubt but that this battle will go our way.

September 12

The zero hour was 1:05 a.m., the heavy artillery starting it off. The earth seemed to give way when the rest of our guns joined in the stupendous and fierce barrage. The roar was so loud that we could scarcely distinguish the deep intonation of our own howitzers from the reports of the 75s.

For four hours the deafening roar continued as our messengers of death were hurled into enemy territory. Then at 5:00 our infantry preceded by tanks went over the top, making a picture of dash and activity.

Not content with ordinary progress the boys of our division leaped ahead of the clumsy tanks and pressed forward in irresistible waves to the German trenches.

The enemy artillery reply was feeble, though the infantry machine-gun and rifle fire was more menacing.

Our artillery fire in the first place demoralized enemy resistance, and the Boche are surrendering in droves. Surely they must regret giving up these luxurious dugouts and trenches which they have lived in for four years. Many of them even have electric lights and good furniture "requisitioned" from nearby French villages.

We must have slipped up on the enemy because they left a great deal of equipment, ammunition and food. Before we left the battery on detail work, two or three hundred prisoners passed our position. Up here in the advance we pass prisoners in droves of from ten to a hundred with a doughboy in the rear prodding the laggards with a bayonet whenever necessary.

A good many of the Germans are being utilized to carry back wounded. A sedate-looking officer wearing white gloves had to bow his back in the work just as his men did. It seemed to do these enemy enlisted men good to see their officers thus reduced to their own plane. Most of them became quite cheerful after they found that they weren't going to be scalped as they had been led to believe these aboriginal Americans were wont to do.

The condition of the roads is very bad and No Man's Land is a mess of shellholes and mud. A good many enemy dead are lying about and a few of our own men are lying where they were struck down by enemy fire this morning.

The doughboys are still advancing swiftly. In the air we are supreme. We are not in the position of the rat in the cage, as we were at Chateau-Thierry when enemy planes swooped down upon us and threw streams of machine-gun bullets into our ranks. This time the tables are turned. We see our aviators flying over the retreating enemy, dropping bombs and creating havoc.

September 13
No rest for the weary last night. By inches we progressed to Seicheprey, the town which saw such terrific fighting between the 26th division and the Germans late last winter.

October 3
We are now hiking up to the line over newly captured territory. For four years this land had been in German hands.

A doughboy who was under fire for the first time Thursday was on the way back today on some detail. He told me that half of his company was wiped out by gas attack. These fellows, without actual battle experience, didn't detect gas in time, and the officers gave no command to put on masks. By the time they did get their masks on, if indeed they got them on at all, half of them were casualties; many of them died.

I feel sure that we are going to suffer heavy casualties in this drive, due to the nature of the German defence – enemy machine guns scattered through the forests in front of us like snakes in the grass.

October 8
This morning Cliff Schwartz awakened us and I rolled out of my blankets hungry and thirsty. Our little signal detail is located in a trench to the left of the battery, just at the bottom of the hill on which the village of Montfaucon stands.

Cliff had obtained a paper from a passing Red Cross worker, and I read the German peace appeal which the enemy had made to President Wilson.

Art Long interrupted me with, "These whiz-bangs Fritz is putting over don't sound like peace to me, any more than the steel we are dousing him with."

"Well, any way you take it, boys, we've got him licked, and I believe that all of us who are lucky enough to live through this battle will get back home," replied Danny Slentz.

I stopped the discussion by announcing that I was going to get some mess.

"You're crazy, Doc," Cliff remarked. "A big H.E. [high explosive shell] will pounce on you and leave nothing but a grease spot. Better wait for a while right here in the trench until things clear up a bit."

Two of our fellows had already been wounded by an explosion near our kitchen this morning, but I was determined to go back for some mess because I was so confounded hungry. Besides, shells seemed to be landing everywhere and one place seemed about as safe as another (or as dangerous), so I climbed out of the trench and made my way carefully back to the clump of bushes where our kitchen was concealed.

I had just got a panful of slum and started eating when I saw part of the temporary trench which I had left screened by an exploding shell. I thought it had come over the trench, but no – just then Smithy and Netterfield jumped out calling for stretchers.

I dropped my mess and ran to the trench and looked in. Poor Art was dead, one arm completely severed from his body. Danny had a hole in his stomach and we placed him on a stretcher and sent him back to the first aid station.

Dan Slentz looked at me with a smile on his face as we loaded him into the ambulance. I gave him a word of cheer and he said, "I don't know, Doc old boy. I've got a pretty bad wound in my stomach. You boys give 'em hell for me." [He died that day.]

I have seen many die, but none have been so close to me as these fellows. I have worked with them and fought beside them every day since I joined the outfit, and they have been my best pals. But we must carry on, whatever happens.

October 30

Last night Fritz put on a whale of a bombardment, and I don't see how any of us escaped to tell the story. In the thick of it our communications were knocked out and I was detailed to repair the telephone line. How kind they are to me! Well, I thought of all the mean things I'd done in my life, breathed a little prayer, climbed out of my foxhole, and darted out into the inferno.

Flashes of exploding artillery at intervals lighted up the blackness of the night. Explosions of enemy shells on every hand and the scream of big ones going overhead to back areas added to the thunderous uproar so that I could not have heard my own voice had I dared to speak. Boy! I was glad when I came to that break in the line. I was splicing the wire when – Shriek! Bang! A ton of steel came over me. Just as I finished the job – hell's bells! – another hit knocked the line out in another place.

For once I lost my cocky self-assurance, and I wasn't so certain that I would ever see home and Mother again. But finally, after stumbling over the body of a dead German, I came upon the next break and spliced it in a hurry. Then I raced back to my hole after reporting communications in order.

Jack Skull has just been sent back to the hospital suffering from shellshock. No wonder nerves give way and normal men go crazy.

November 8 (Advancing Toward Sedan)
The battle has changed from a slow, bloody, inch-by-inch fight to a mad chase. The enemy is in full retreat.

AMERICAN SOLDIERS: LETTERS HOME, WESTERN FRONT, September 1918

Lieutenant Phelps Harding and Rudolph Bowman

Lieutenant Phelps Harding, 306th Infantry Regiment, 77th Division, American Expeditionary Force

10 September 1918

Dear Christine,

The last time I wrote you I was in Paris, having received my Commission and about ready to start for my new Division. Since then I have covered a lot of territory, both in lorries and on foot, and I have passed over a battlefield that has but recently been the scene of some mighty hard fighting – some that my new Division and people of New York will long remember.

My orders took me first to Château Thierry. You have probably read about the fighting in that city. The place is pretty badly banged up from shell fire, but not as badly as most of the smaller villages beyond it. The Huns tore things up in great shape – statues, ornaments and pictures in homes were broken and cut up as if by a band of plundering outlaws. From Château Thierry my trail led toward the Ourcq River, which our men had to cross under heavy machine-gun fire and artillery shelling. Beyond was open country. You will see what a tough proposition it was when you read the casualty list for the few days when the Boche were retreating. They retreated, but they put up a stiff resistance with machine-guns, artillery and planes – and taking machine-gun nests is a real man's job.

I found my Division by the Ourcq, having been relieved, and spent three days in camp with it. The men were pretty tired, and of course they felt the loss of their comrades. I realized this latter point best when censoring their letters. It is mighty hard for a boy to write home to his mother and tell her that his brother has been killed. I read two such letters in the first batch I censored. Each writer tried to tell how painless the death was, and how bravely the brother met it – but in each case I imagine the mother will think only of her loss, and not of the fact that her boy died a true American.

22 September, 1918

Dear Christine,

My last letter was written just before we commenced the St Mihiel offensive, which began September 12th. I am writing this letter in what was then German occupied territory, sixteen kilometres from our original front line.

When the Division left the Chateau Thierry front we thought we were bound for a rest camp, for the organisation was badly in need of both rest and replacements. Then the order came to move. We marched by night and slept in the daytime, arriving at our position back of the front line after several nights of pretty hard going – hard because the rain fell almost continuously, the roads were bad, the traffic heavy. Our stopping places at the end of each march were thick woods. It is no fun moving into thick, wet woods in the dark, and trying to find places to sleep.

The last night the rain and wind were fierce – I had to be careful not to lose my platoon, the night was so dark and the marching conditions so bad. We moved to within about a kilometre of our line, my battalion being in support of the regiment, and took cover in an old drainage ditch. Wet? Rather!

At exactly 1 a.m., the artillery cut loose. It seemed as if all the artillery in France had suddenly opened up. The sky was red with big flashes, the air seemed full of Empire State Expresses, and the explosion of the heavier shells made the ground tremble. It was a wonderful and awe-inspiring sight.

At 5 a.m., the assault troops went over the top. We followed in the third wave. First we passed batteries that had been shoved right up to our lines – 75s firing like six-shooters. Ahead of us French tanks were ploughing along like big bugs, standing on their beam ends at times as they crossed the trenches or unusually bad ground. Our first line went too fast for them, but they did a lot of good work in breaking up machine-gun nests and in taking villages. Our boys in front just couldn't wait for them, even to smash the wire.

Before we had gone far prisoners began to come in first by twos and threes, then by platoons and companies. We took 13,000 Boche that day. We passed dead men of both armies, but many more Boche than Americans. I was surprised at the indifference I felt toward dead Americans – they seemed a perfectly natural thing to come across, and I felt absolutely no shudder go down my back as I would have had I seen the same thing a year ago.

We kept on going forward until we reached the crest of a hill, and here the shelling became so heavy that we made ourselves as small as possible in ditches and holes. Shells were striking all around us, and too close for comfort. A big "dud" – a shell that failed to explode – landed in the middle of my platoon and hit a man from the Engineers on the thigh, practically taking his leg off and tearing him up pretty badly. He died in a short time. The company at our right had sixteen casualties from this shell fire, but we, apparently being better duckers, came out without a scratch except for the Engineer who had happened to take cover with us.

After taking the shelling for possibly twenty minutes our artillery spotted the Boche batteries, which were either destroyed or withdrew, permitting us to move forward again. After this the Boche did not make much of a stand. His artillery was apparently too busy moving homeward to bother about fighting.

The first day we covered nearly sixteen kilometres, reaching our objective on scheduled time. It was pretty hard work, for the going was often bad, even after leaving the front line area. It was up and down hill, and at a fairly fast pace. That night we slept on a hillside, and since then we have been moving around slightly, digging in each time, and acting as a reserve for the troops ahead who, with Engineers, are making a line of trenches and putting up wire, placing machine-guns and doing everything necessary to give the Boche a warm reception if he attempts a counter-attack.

In this recent drive, our artillery moved almost as rapidly as our Infantry – sometimes faster than our kitchens and wagon trains – and a Boche battery would hardly open up before a plane would go over it, signal the battery location, and presto! American shells would drop on it. The Boche may not have had much respect for the American Army a few months ago, but from what prisoners say now, we are about as welcome as the proverbial skunk at a lawn party!

Just one more item before I end this letter and go to inspect my platoon. We had expected to be relieved before now, but yesterday news arrived that changed all our plans. Probably my battalion will go into the new line in a day or so, possibly to stay there for a fairly long period. We may even move forward again – no one knows definitely. Anyway, you may not hear from me for a couple of weeks or so – longer, if we push on toward Berlin.

Rudolph Bowman, Headquarters Troop, 89th Division, American Expeditionary Force

Bowman writes to his wife, Gertrude, and children.

[In German envelope]
France, September 20th 1918

My Darling Wife and Loved Ones:

Has it been ten years since I wrote? Ten years have passed for me. This letter will sound like I am drunk, but I'm not – just tired. This is the synopsis of a long long story.

On Sept 10th I was sent to a village ½ Kilometre behind the front line, for final instructions in enemy observation. Our O.P. (observation post) was shelled that night because an ammunition truck had gotten stuck near it. (Now, all thru this everything seemed natural and I thought nothing of it.) Shrapnel struck our building (the only one with a roof on it in town) but we got no direct hit. The next day we (three other observers & I) went up to the front line trench to take over an advance O.P. Rain-Rain-Rain-Mud-Mud-Mud-Wet to the skin. Well – two of us were on our post at 1:00 a.m. Thurs. Sept 12th when all our big guns broke loose at once.

I can't describe it – it was awful – and wonderful – glorious – hideous – hellish, to think what one shell will do – then to think what 6,000 to 8,000 guns will do all firing as fast as they can, all sizes – well we stayed on till 3:00 and our relief came – went back to dug out for a last rest, for we had decided to go "Over the Top" with the doughboys ("God Bless Them") on the big drive.

Well we went over in the second wave, its all confused to me – I saw many dead men (mostly Boche) many of our boys wounded, men fell all around us, we were shot at by snipers, machine guns, Boche avions, and went thru our own barrage twice – those guns kept up that fire till about 9:30, then the light artillery tried to move up with us but could not keep up, all I could shoot at was mach. gun nests (I can only hope I got *one* Boche for I got no fair shot) but I saw boys throw grenades in dugouts full of Huns, and was glad, – we advanced all day, first with one company & another, everybody was lost; late in the afternoon we reached our objective, but we could not find where we were to stay, we kept going till 4:30 a.m. Fri, then we came back to this village – and I dropped on the floor with my saddle pockets (I hung on to them) over my shoulder and slept – and my pal could not wake me to make me eat. We'd had no sleep since Sun. night, except an hour at a time.

So we established an O.P. about a Kilometre behind the present line, we can see all the action for six Kilometres, there's not much doing except artillery fire, constantly from both sides, I've been under shell fire almost constantly for ten days – the closest one came within twenty feet, I wouldn't tell this now, but I'm going to send a wire home as soon as we are relieved, which will be soon. I got enough souvinirs too. Expect to get a chance to go to Paris for a week now. I want to come home, but this will be over soon I think. I got six letters from you sweetheart and about six from home yesterday. I'll answer them all when I can. Phone Mother when you get this. I can only write one letter now. I'll have some tales to tell Dear, but the one I want to tell most is the story of my love for my wonderful little wife. You & Mother and the rest must not worry about me, I'll be relieved long before you get this. Now I can come home satisfied to *stay* and *love*. Your Own Loving

Soldier Boy X X
R.M. Bowman
Hq. Troop, 89th Division
American E.F., A.P.O. 761

(I pray always before I sleep, for my wonderful Mother & Wife and the rest, and for our early reunion.)

Heard from Johnnie

ST MIHIEL: THE AMERICANS GO IT ALONE, 12–13 September 1918

General John Pershing, Commander, American Expeditionary Force

At St Mihiel in Lorraine the AEF undertook, for the first time, a large-scale action alone.

The attack on the southern face of the salient started at 5:00 o'clock on the morning of the 12th, and before that hour I went with several staff officers to old Fort Gironville, situated on a commanding height overlooking the battlefield from the south. The secondary attack on the west was launched at 8:00 a.m. as an element of surprise and in order to give more time for artillery preparation there.

A drizzling rain and mist prevented us from getting a clear view, but the progress of our troops could be followed by the barrage which preceded them. Notwithstanding a heavy rainfall on the night of the 11th–12th, the weather gave us an advantage, as the mist partially screened our movements from the enemy . . . The sky over the battlefield, both before and after dawn, aflame with exploding shells, star signals, burning supply dumps and villages, presented a scene at once picturesque and terrible. The exultation in our minds that here, at last, after seventeen months of effort, an American army was fighting under its own flag was tempered by the realization of the sacrifice of life on both sides, and yet fate had willed it thus and we must carry through. Confidence in our troops dispelled every doubt of ultimate victory.

As we returned from Gironville, groups of prisoners were already being marched to stockades in the rear. About 9 o'clock reports began to come in to army headquarters at Ligny from all portions of the twenty-five mile front that everything was going well, with losses light . . .

Thanks to the thorough preparations beforehand, the wire entanglements were more easily overcome than we expected. Trained teams of pioneers and engineers, with Bangalore torpedoes, wire cutters and axes, assisted in opening gaps in the masses of barbed wire protecting the German positions. The leading troops themselves carried along rolls of chicken wire which was thrown across entanglements here and there, forming a kind of bridge for the infantry . . . The fact that we had smothered the enemy artillery was an advantage, as it enabled the leading waves deliberately to do their work without serious loss.

The quick passage through these entanglements by our troops excited no little surprise among the French, who sent a large number of officers and noncommissioned officers to St Mihiel several days later to see how it had been done. One of these officers, after his reconnaissance, remarked in all seriousness that the Americans had the advantage over Frenchmen because of their long legs and large feet . . .

The entire operation was carried through with dash and precision. By afternoon the troops had pushed beyond their scheduled objectives and by evening had reached the second day's objective on most of the southern front. The divisions of the IV Corps and those on the left of the I Corps overwhelmed the hostile garrisons and quickly overran their positions, carrying the fighting into the open. The German resistance on this part of the front was disorganized by the rapidity of our advance and was soon overcome . . .

On the western face of the salient progress was not so satisfactory. The 26th Division, in its attempt to make a deep advance toward Vigneulles, met with considerable resistance and except for a battalion sent from the divisional reserve had not reached the day's objective . . .

On the afternoon of the 12th, learning that the roads leading out of the salient between the two attacks were filled with retreating enemy troops, with their trains and artillery, I gave orders to the commanders of the IV and V Corps to push forward without delay. Using the telephone myself, I directed the commander of the V Corps to send at least one regiment of the 26th Division toward Vigneulles with all possible speed. That evening, a strong force from the 51st Brigade pushed boldly forward and reached Vigneulles at 2:15 a.m. on the 13th. It immediately made dispositions that effectively closed the roads leading out of the salient west of that point. In the IV Corps the 2nd Brigade of the 1st Division advanced in force about dawn of the 13th, its leading elements reaching Vigneulles by 6:00 a.m. The salient was closed and our troops were masters of the field.

The troops continued to advance on the 13th, when the line was established approximately along the final objectives set for this offensive . . . Reports received during the 13th and 14th indicated that the enemy was retreating in considerable disorder. Without doubt, an immediate continuation of the advance would have carried us well beyond the Hindenburg Line and possibly into Metz, and the temptation to press on was very great, but we would probably have become involved and delayed the greater Meuse-Argonne operation, to which we were wholly committed . . . Nearly 16,000 prisoners were taken and some 540 enemy guns had fallen into our hands. Our casualties numbered about 7,000.

THE ROAD TO DAMASCUS: A TURKISH COLUMN IS MASSACRED, 24 September 1918

Lieutenant-Colonel T.E. Lawrence

The Arabs told us that the Turkish column – Jemal Pasha's lancer regiment – was already entering Tafas. When we got within sight, we found they had taken the village (from which sounded an occasional shot) and were halted about it. Small pyres of smoke were going up from between the houses. On the rising ground to this side, knee deep in the thistles, stood a remnant of old men, women and children, telling terrible stories of what had happened when the Turks rushed in an hour before.

We lay on watch, and saw the enemy force march away from their assembly ground behind the houses. They headed in good order toward Miskin, the lancers in front and rear, composite formations of infantry disposed in column with machine-gun support as flank guards, guns and a mass of transport in the centre. We opened fire on the head of their line when it showed itself beyond the houses. They turned two field guns upon us, for reply. The shrapnel was as usual over-fused, and passed safely above our heads.

Nuri came with Pisani. Before their ranks rode Auda abu

Tayi, expectant, and Tallal, nearly frantic with the tales his people poured out of the sufferings of the village. The last Turks were now quitting it. We slipped down behind them to end Tallal's suspense, while our infantry took position and fired strongly with the Hotchkiss; Pisani advanced his half-battery among them; so that the French high explosive threw the rearguard into confusion.

The village lay stilly under its slow wreaths of white smoke, as we rode near, on our guard. Some grey heaps seemed to hide in the long grass, embracing the ground in the close way of corpses. We looked away from these, knowing they were dead; but from one a little figure tottered off, as if to escape us. It was a child, three or four years old, whose dirty smock was stained red over one shoulder and side, with blood from a large half-fibrous wound, perhaps a lance thrust, just where neck and body joined.

The child ran a few steps, then stood and cried to us in a tone of astonishing strength (all else being very silent), "Don't hit me, Baba." Abd el Aziz, choking out something – this was his village, and she might be of his family – flung himself off his camel, and stumbled, kneeling, in the grass beside the child. His suddenness frightened her, for she threw up her arms and tried to scream; but, instead, dropped in a little heap, while the blood rushed out again over her clothes; then, I think, she died.

We rode past the other bodies of men and women and four more dead babies, looking very soiled in the daylight, towards the village; whose loneliness we now knew meant death and horror. By the outskirts were low mud walls, sheepfolds, and on one something red and white. I looked close and saw the body of a woman folded across it, bottom upwards, nailed there by a saw bayonet whose haft stuck hideously into the air from between her naked legs. About her lay others, perhaps twenty in all, variously killed.

The Zaagi burst into wild peals of laughter, the more desolate for the warm sunshine and clear air of this upland afternoon. I said, "The best of you bring me the most Turkish dead," and we turned after the fading enemy, on our way shooting down those who had fallen out by the roadside and came imploring our pity. One wounded Turk, half naked, not able to stand, sat and wept to us. Abdulla turned away his camel's head, but the Zaagi, with curses, crossed his track and whipped three bullets from his automatic through the man's bare chest. The blood came out with his heart beats, throb, throb, throb, slower and slower.

Tallal had seen what we had seen. He gave one moan like a hurt animal; then rode to the upper ground and sat there a while on his mare, shivering and looking fixedly after the Turks. I moved near to speak to him, but Auda caught my rein and stayed me. Very slowly Tallal drew his headcloth about his face; and then he seemed suddenly to take hold of himself, for he dashed his stirrups into the mare's flanks and galloped headlong, bending low and swaying in the saddle, right at the main body of the enemy.

It was a long ride down a gentle slope and across a hollow. We sat there like stone while he rushed forward, the drumming of his hoofs unnaturally loud in our ears, for we had stopped shooting, and the Turks had stopped. Both armies waited for him; and he rocked on in the hushed evening till only a few lengths from the enemy. Then he sat up in the saddle and cried his war cry, "Tallal, Tallal," twice in a tremendous shout. Instantly their rifles and machine-guns crashed out, and he and his mare riddled through and through with bullets, fell dead among the lance points.

Auda looked very cold and grim. "God give him mercy; we will take his price." He shook his rein and moved slowly after the enemy. We called up the peasants, now drunk with fear and blood, and sent them from this side and that against the retreating column. The old lion of battle waked in Auda's heart, and made him again our natural, inevitable leader. By a skilful turn he drove the Turks into bad ground and split their formation into three parts.

The third part, the smallest, was mostly made up of German and Austrian machine-gunners grouped round three motor cars and a handful of mounted officers or troopers. They fought magnificently and repulsed us time and again despite our hardiness. The Arabs were fighting like devils, the sweat blurring their eyes, dust parching their throats; while the flame of cruelty and revenge which was burning in their bodies so twisted them that their hands could hardly shoot. By my order we took no prisoners, for the only time in our war.

At last we left this stern section behind, and pursued the faster two. They were in panic; and by sunset we had destroyed all but the smallest pieces of them, gaining as and by what they lost. Parties of peasants flowed in on our advance. At first there were five or six to a weapon: then one would win a bayonet, another a sword, a third a pistol. An hour later those who had been on foot would be on donkeys. Afterwards every man had a rifle and a captured horse. By nightfall the horses were laden, and the rich plain was scattered over with dead men and animals. In a madness born of the horror of Tafas we killed and killed, even blowing in the heads of the fallen and of the animals; as though their death and running blood could slake our agony.

SERBIA: THE ALLIES ENTER USKUB, 29 September 1918

Anonymous French cavalry officer

Bulgaria was the first central power to collapse. She did so after a 700,000-strong Allied offensive was launched on 15 September from Albania to the Struma River. Uskub, occupied by the Bulgarians, was the capital of Old Serbia.

At 8 a.m., as if to celebrate our victorious advance, a bright sun broke through the fog in which our squadrons were manoeuvring like shadows . . . Its rays lit the red roofs, the handsome mosques, and elegant minarets of Uskub. More austere-looking buildings, probably orthodox churches, seemed to be smiling too.

There were clouds, however, which did not follow the rising fog. They were smoke clouds caused by fires burning in the city's Turkish district, in the Greek district, in the Serbian, and even in the Bulgarian district . . . Cypresses, set ablaze by the flames from nearby houses, were burning like giant torches. Ammunition dumps were exploding, shooting up huge red and black flames. The railroad station was aflame too. As expected, our attack fully surprised the enemy, whose troops were retreating in disorder and kept shooting in a haphazard manner from the northern and western ridges.

Our advance continued uninterrupted. Our cavalry was progressing in infantry formation, each company having two squadrons in first line and two in reserve. Spirits were very high. The Moroccans were splendid. Nothing could stop them. Our advance sections reached the city's southern and south-eastern outskirts at 8 a.m. We were able to save from certain destruction almost all of a great variety of supplies which the surprised enemy was in the process of looting.

A strong patrol, under Second-Lieutenant Guérin, advanced to the station and fired on the Germans still there, as well as on the armored train. The disorganized enemy was hurriedly endeavouring to send off the last trains loaded with all sorts of material and supplies. Our patrol was forced back by an attack of German pioneers, but brought back precious information concerning the surprise caused by our rapid attack.

8:30 a.m. The 4th Light Infantry entered the capital of Old Serbia, and crossed it rapidly in order to attack the northern hills. Behind them, the city was full of fleeing and exhausted enemies, unable to fight . . . Uskub has been captured. The city's leader met us at the entrance, behind a white flag and accompanied by French and Italian soldiers. The latter had escaped from Bulgarian prisoner camps, and had been hidden and fed by the local population. Both the Serbian notables and the soldiers were shouting enthusiastically. The population's emotion was deeply moving: the women kept kissing our hands while crying with joy . . .

At 10 a.m. a French plane, the first we saw since Florina, flew over the battlefield. By means of panels, we gave the flier the conventional signs that enabled him to recognize us and get acquainted with our exact situation and needs. The High Command would thus be informed of our decisive action and its probable results.

Two more planes flew over the city at 2 p.m. We signalled the news of our victory to them, and soon they turned back toward General Headquarters. The news of the capture of Uskub, in fact, enabled General Franchet d'Esperey to impose upon Bulgaria, on this very day September 29, an armistice which was a complete capitulation.

ALLIED BREAK-OUT: LIEUTENANT G. HARVARD THOMAS WINS THE MC, ST QUENTIN CANAL, 30 September–6 October 1918

Lieutenant G. Harvard Thomas, 8th Sherwood Foresters

30 September
The big attack went off yesterday morning and we advanced with great success. My company alone captured one Boche colonel and another 100 other ranks. We had a few casualties but not half what I expected. A great mist arose in the early morning and together with the smoke made direction very difficult, but with the aid of compasses I led my crowd to the right places. We had to cross a very large canal and the first waves had life-belts on, like going on leave. My colonel has recommended me for the Military Cross. I hope they give it to me.

6 October
I daresay you have read in the papers of the deeds of the 46th North Midland Div., how we stormed the St Quentin Canal and the whole of the Hindenburg system capturing 4000 prisoners. 3 days after we were again hurled at Fritz at a moment's notice and again we gave him Hell. This time we captured all our objectives and broke right through into new country behind where French inhabitants welcomed us as deliverers.

LAWRENCE OF ARABIA ENTERS DAMASCUS, 1 October 1918

Lieutenant-Colonel T.E. Lawrence

Our war was ended – even though we slept that night in Kiswe, for the Arabs told us the roads were dangerous, and we had no wish to die stupidly in the dark at the gate of Damascus . . . I wanted to sleep, for my work was coming on the morrow; but I could not. Damascus was the climax of our two years' uncertainty, and my mind was distracted by tags of all the ideas which had been used or rejected in that time. Also Kiswe was stifling with the exhalations of too many trees, too many plants, too many human beings: a microcosm of the crowded world in front of us.

As the Germans left Damascus they fired the dumps and ammunition stores, so that every few minutes we were jangled by explosions, whose first shock set the sky white with flame. At each such roar the earth seemed to shake; we would lift our eyes to the north and see the pale sky prick out suddenly in sheaves of yellow points, as the shells thrown to terrific heights from each bursting magazine, in their turn burst like clustered rockets. I turned to Stirling and muttered "Damascus is burning," sick to think of the great town in ashes as the price of freedom.

When dawn came we drove to the head of the ridge, which stood over the oasis of the city, afraid to look north for the ruins we expected: but, instead of ruins, the silent gardens stood blurred green with river mist, in whose setting shimmered the city, beautiful as ever, like a pearl in the morning sun. The uproar of the night had shrunk to a stiff tall column of smoke, which rose in sullen blackness from the store-yard by Kadem, terminus of the Hejaz line.

We drove down the straight banked road through the watered fields, in which the peasants were just beginning their day's work. A galloping horseman checked at our head-cloths in the car, with a merry salutation, holding out a bunch of yellow grapes. "Good news! Damascus salutes you." He came from Shukri.

Nasir was just beyond us: to him we carried the tidings, that he might have the honourable entry, a privilege of his fifty battles. With Nuri Shaalan beside him, he asked a final gallop from his horse, and vanished down the long road in a cloud of dust, which hung reluctantly in the air between the water splashes. To give him a fair start, Stirling and I found a little stream, cool in the depths of a deep channel. By it we stopped to wash and shave.

Some Indian troopers peered at us and our car and its ragged driver's army shorts and tunic. I was in pure Arab dress; Stirling but for his head covering, was all British staff officer. Their N.C.O., an obtuse and bad-tempered person, thought he had taken prisoners. When delivered from his arrest we judged we might go after Nazir.

Quite quietly we drove up the long street to the Government buildings on the bank of the Barada. The way was packed with people, lined solid on the side-walks, in the road, at the windows and on the balconies or house-tops. Many were crying, a few cheered faintly, some bolder ones cried our names: but mostly they looked and looked, joy shining in their eyes. A movement, like a long sigh from gate to heart of the city, marked our course . . .

When we came in there had been some miles of people greeting us: now there were thousands for every hundred of them. Every man, woman and child in this city of a quarter-million souls seemed in the streets, waiting only the spark of our appearance to ignite their spirits. Damascus went mad with joy. The men tossed up their tarbushes to cheer, the women tore off their veils. Householders threw flowers, hangings, carpets, into the road before us: their wives leaned, screaming with laughter, through the lattices and splashed us with bath-dippers of scent.

DOGFIGHTS, AMBUSHES & PEACE: RICKENBACKER ON THE WESTERN FRONT, October–November 1918

Eddie V. Rickenbacker

With 26 kills Rickenbacker was the "ace of aces" of the US Air Service in France in World War I.

Those were hectic days. I put in six or seven hours of flying time each day. I would come down, gulp a couple of cups of coffee while the mechanics refueled the plane and patched the bullet holes and take off again. I caught an unguarded balloon while returning from a night mission, and Reed Chambers and I together brought down a Hanover. With the dead pilot at the controls, it glided to a perfect landing two miles within our own lines. We hurried to claim it and had it hauled back to our own field. Then Reed and I each dropped a Fokker in the same dogfight. I shot down a German plane so far behind the lines that the victory was never confirmed. Our 94th squadron pulled out well ahead of the 27th, and after that our lead was never threatened.

In my 134 air battles, my narrowest escape came at a time when I was fretting over the lack of action. I was out alone one afternoon, looking for anything to shoot at. There was a thick haze over the valley of the Meuse, however, and the Germans had pulled down their balloons. To the south the weather seemed a little better; the American balloons were still up. German planes rarely came over late in the afternoon, and everyone had relaxed his vigilance. As I was flying toward the nearest Allied balloon, I saw it burst into flames. A German plane had obviously made a successful attack. Because of the bend in the lines of the front at that point, I saw that I could cut off the Boche on his return to his own territory. I had the altitude on him and, consequently, a superior position. I headed confidently to our rendezvous.

Guns began barking behind me, and sizzling tracers zipped by my head. I was taken completely by surprise. At least two planes were on my tail. They had me cold. They had probably been watching me for several minutes and planning this whole thing.

They would expect me to dive. Instead I twisted upward in a corkscrew path called a "chandelle". I guessed right. As I went up, my two attackers came down, near enough for me to see their faces. I also saw the red noses on those Fokkers. I was up against the Flying Circus again.

I had outwitted them. Two more red noses were sitting above me on the chance that I might just do the unexpected.

Any time one plane is up against four and the four are flown by pilots of such caliber, the smart thing to do is to get away from there. There is an old saying that it's no disgrace to run if you are scared.

I zigzagged and sideslipped, but the two planes on top of me hung on, and the two underneath remained there. They were daring me to attack, in which case the two above would be on my tail in seconds. They were blocking me from making a dash for home. I was easy meat sandwiched between two pairs of experts. Sooner or later one would spot an opening and close in.

For a split second one of the Fokkers beneath me became

vulnerable. I instantly tipped over, pulled back the throttle and dived on him. As my nose came down I fired a burst ahead of him. Perhaps he did not see the string of bullets. At any rate, he flew right into them. Several must have passed through his body. An incendiary hit his gas tank, and in seconds a flaming Fokker was earthbound.

If I had been either of the two Fokkers above me in such a situation, I would have been on my tail at that very moment. I pulled the stick back in a loop and came over in a renversement, and there they were. Before I could come close enough to shoot, they turned and fled. I suppose that the sight of that blazing plane took some of the fight out of them.

It did not take any fight out of me. I started chasing all three of them back into Germany. We were already three miles behind the lines, but I was annoyed – with them and with myself.

My Spad was faster. One Fokker began to fall behind. He tried a shallow dive to gain speed, but I continued to close in. We were only about a thousand feet up. He began stunting, but I stuck with him and fired a burst of about two hundred shots. He nosed over and crashed. I watched him hit.

All around the crashed plane, I saw flashes of fire and smoke. I was only about five hundred feet above the deck, and the Germans on the ground were shooting at me with all the weapons they had. I could see their white faces above the flashes. The air around me must have been full of flying objects. I got out of there fast and went home to report that I had blundered into a trap and had come out of it with two victories. I now had nineteen.

During the month of October the fortunes of war shifted both on the ground and in the air. From the air we could see the German ground forces retreating, sometimes in complete disorganization. Our bombers were carrying the fight into Germany, and large numbers of German fighters were pulled back from the front in an effort to protect the civilian population.

All along the lines the feeling was growing that the war was coming to an end. I took a three-day leave in Paris and, for the first time, found the streets illuminated at night and unrestrained gaiety.

During the month of October, I shot down fourteen enemy aircraft. On the 30th I got my twenty-fifth and twenty-sixth victories, my last of the war. My title "American Ace of Aces" was undisputed. The last victory for the 94th Squadron came on November 10. The Hat-in-the-Ring Squadron downed sixty-nine Boche planes, more than any other American unit.

On the night of the 10th a group of us was discussing the next day's mission when the phone rang. An almost hysterical voice shouted the news in my ear: at 11:00 the following morning, the war would end. Our mission was called off. For us the war ended at that moment.

I dropped the phone and turned to face my pilots. Everyone sensed the importance of that phone call. There was total silence in the room.

"The war is over!" I shouted. At that moment the anti-aircraft battalion that ringed our field fired off a salvo that rocked the building. We all went a little mad. Shouting and screaming like crazy men, we ran to get whatever firearms we had, including flare pistols, and began blasting up into the sky. It was already bright up there. As far as we could see the sky was filled with exploding shells and rockets, star shells, parachute flares, streams of Very lights and searchlights tracing crazy patterns. Machine guns hammered; big guns boomed. What a night!

A group of men came out of the hangar, rolling barrels of gasoline in front of them. Perhaps I should have made an effort to stop them, but instead I ran over and helped. We dumped them in an open place, and I struck the match myself. Up roared a bonfire that could be seen for miles. We danced around that blazing pyre screaming, shouting and beating one another on the back. One pilot kept shouting over and over and over. "I've lived through the war, I've lived through the war!"

Somebody emptied every bottle of liquor he could find into a huge kettle, and the orderlies served it in coffee cups, including themselves in. For months these twenty combat pilots had been living at the peak of nervous energy, the total meaning of their lives to kill or be killed. Now this tension exploded like the guns blasting around us.

We all ran over to the 95th Squadron. They had a piano, and

somebody sat down and began banging the keys. We began dancing or simply jumping up and down. Somebody slipped and fell, and everyone else fell on him, piling up in a pyramid. A volunteer band started playing in the area outside. We ran outside again to continue our dancing and jumping and shrieking under the canopy of bursting rockets. Again somebody went down, and again we all piled on and made a human pyramid, this time bigger and better and muddier, a monument to the incredible fact that we had lived until now and were going to live again tomorrow.

In the morning orders came down that all pilots should stay on the ground. It was a muggy, foggy day. About 10:00 I sauntered out to the hanger and casually told my mechanics to take the plane out on the line and warm it up to test the engines. Without announcing my plans to anyone, I climbed into the plane and took off. Under the low ceiling I hedgehopped towards the front. I arrived over Verdun at 10:45 and proceeded on toward Conflans, flying over no-man's-land. I was at less than five hundred feet. I could see both Germans and Americans crouching in their trenches, peering over with every intention of killing any man who revealed himself on the other side. From time to time ahead of me on the German side I saw a burst of flame, and I knew that they were firing at me. Back at the field later I found bullet holes in my ship.

I glanced at my watch. One minute to 11:00, thirty seconds, fifteen. And then it was 11:00 a.m., the eleventh hour of the eleventh day of the eleventh month. I was the only audience for the greatest show ever presented. On both sides of no-man's-land, the trenches erupted. Brown-uniformed men poured out of the American trenches, gray-green uniforms out of the German. From my observer's seat overhead, I watched them throw their helmets in the air, discard their guns, wave their hands. Then all up and down the front, the two groups of men began edging toward each other across no-man's-land. Seconds before they had been willing to shoot each other; now they came forward. Hesitantly at first, then more quickly, each group approached the other.

Suddenly grey uniforms mixed with brown. I could see them hugging each other, dancing, jumping. Americans were passing out cigarettes and chocolate. I flew up to the French sector. There it was even more incredible. After four years of slaughter and hatred, they were not only hugging each other but kissing each other on both cheeks as well.

Star shells, rockets and flares began to go up, and I turned my ship toward the field. The war was over.

HEIMAT FRONT: REVOLUTION IN MUNICH, 7 November 1918

Rainer Maria Rilke

In the last few days, Munich has lost some of its nothingness and stillness, the tensions of this time are evident even here . . . Everywhere, vast assemblies in beer-halls nearly every evening, speakers everywhere, of whom Professor Jaffé is evidently excellent, and where halls are inadequate, gatherings in thousands under the open sky. I also was one of the thousands on Monday night in the rooms of the Hotel Wagner. Professor Max Weber of Heidelberg was speaking, a political economist rated one of the best of intellects and a fine orator, and then, discussing the anarchy and the fatiguing strain, more students, fellows from four years at the front – all so simple and frank, "men of the people". And though we sat round the beer-tables and between them so that the waitresses could only penetrate the dense human mass like weevils – it was not at all oppressive, not even for the breath; the fumes of beer and smoke and bodies did not seem oppressive, we barely noticed, so important was it and so obvious that things could be uttered whose time had at last arrived, and that the simplest and truest of these, in as much as they were presented more or less intelligently, were taken up by the huge crowd with heavy, massive acclamation. Suddenly a pale young worker stood up, spoke quite simply. "Have you or you or you, have any of you offered an armistice? And yet we are those who should have done so, not these gentlemen at the top; if we could take over a radio station and speak as common folk to the common folk on the other side, peace would come immediately."

I cannot say it half as well as he did, but suddenly when he had spoken this, a difficulty occurred to him, and with a moving gesture at Weber, Quidde and the other professors standing on the stage beside him, he went on: "Here, these professor chaps, they know French, they'll help us say it right, as we mean it." Such moments are marvellous, there have been all too few in Germany, where only intransigence found voice, or submission, itself in its own way only a participation in violence by the under-dogs . . . We have a remarkable night behind us. Here also a council of soldiers, peasants and workers has been established with Kurt Eisner as the first President . . . the Bavarian Republic declares that the people are promised Peace and Security . . . It only remains to be hoped that this extraordinary upheaval will provoke reflection in people's minds and not a fatal intoxication once all is over.

THE GERMANS REQUEST AN ARMISTICE, FOREST OF COMPIÈGNE, FRANCE, 9 November 1918

Marshal Ferdinand Foch, Commander-in-Chief, Allied Armies

Places were now taken at the conference table.

Marshal Foch asked the German delegates the purpose of their visit.

Herr Erzberger replied that the German delegation had come to receive the proposals of the Allied Powers looking to an armistice on land, on sea and in the air, on all the fronts and in the colonies.

Marshal Foch replied that he had no proposals to make.

Count Oberndorff asked the Marshal in what form he desired that they should express themselves. He did not stand on form; he was ready to say that the German delegation asked the conditions of the armistice.

Marshal Foch replied that he had no conditions to offer.

Herr Erzberger read the text of President Wilson's last note, stating that Marshal Foch is authorized to make known the armistice conditions.

Marshal Foch replied that he was authorized to make these known if the German delegates asked for an armistice.

"Do you ask for an armistice? If you do, I can inform you of the conditions subject to which it can be obtained."

Herr Erzberger and Count Oberndorff declared that they asked for an armistice.

Marshal Foch then announced that the armistice conditions would be read; as the text was rather long, only the principal paragraphs would be read for the present; later on the complete text would be communicated to the plenipotentiaries.

General Weygand read the principal clauses of the armistice conditions (text agreed upon at Versailles on November 4th).

The reading terminated, and Herr Erzberger requested that military operations be immediately suspended. He gave as a reason the disorganization and lack of discipline which reigned in the German Army, and the spirit of revolution that was spreading through Germany as a consequence of the people's sufferings. He described the difficulties which he and his fellow delegates had encountered in passing through the German Armies and in crossing their lines, where even the order to cease fire was executed only after considerable trouble. All these circumstances led him to fear that Germany might soon fall into the grip of Bolshevism, and once Central Europe was invaded by this scourge, Western Europe, he said, would find the greatest difficulty in escaping it. Nothing but the cessation of Allied attacks would make it possible to re-establish discipline in the German Army and, through the restoration of order, save the country.

I immediately answered: "At the moment when negotiations for the signing of an armistice are just being opened, it is impossible to stop military operations until the German delegation has accepted and signed the conditions which are the very consequence of those operations. As for the situation described by Herr Erzberger as existing among the German troops and the danger he fears of Bolshevism spreading in Germany, the one is the usual disease prevailing in beaten armies, the other is symptomatic of a nation completely worn out by war. Western Europe will find means of defending itself against the danger."

When I had finished my statement regarding the impossibility of my acquiescence to the verbal request of Herr Erzberger, General von Winterfeldt asked to be heard. He had a special mission to fulfil on behalf of the German Supreme Command and the German Government.

He read the following statement, prepared in advance:

> "The Armistice terms which have just been brought to our knowledge require careful examination by us. As it is our intention to come to a decision, this examination will be made as promptly as possible. Nevertheless, it will require a certain amount of time, especially as it will be necessary to consult our Government and the military Supreme Command.
>
> "During this time the struggle between our Armies will continue and it will result, both among soldiers and civilians, in numerous victims who will die in vain at the last minute, and who might be preserved to their families.
>
> "Therefore, the German Government and the German Supreme Command have the honour to revert to the proposal made by them in their wireless message of the day before yesterday, viz. that Marshal Foch be kind enough to consent to an immediate suspension of hostilities on the entire front, to begin to-day at a certain fixed hour, the very simple details of which could be decided upon without loss of time."

To this Marshal Foch replied:

> "I am the Commander-in-Chief of the Allied Armies and representative of the Allied Governments. These Governments have decided upon their terms. Hostilities cannot cease before the signing of the Armistice. I am likewise desirous of reaching a conclusion and therefore I shall help you as far as is possible toward this end. But hostilities cannot cease before the signing of the Armistice."

General Order.

"Officers, non-commissioned officers and soldiers of the Allied Armies:

"After resolutely repulsing the enemy for months, you confidently attacked him with an untiring energy.

"You have won the greatest battle in History and rescued the most sacred of all causes, the Liberty of the World.

"You have full right to be proud, for you have crowned your standards with immortal glory and won the gratitude of posterity.

"F. Foch,
"Marshal of France,
"Commander-in-Chief of the Allied Armies."

The armistice was signed at 5.10 on the morning of 11 November. Hostilities were terminated at 11 a.m. on that day. The war was over.

ARMISTICE, 11 a.m., 11 November 1918

Philip Gibbs, war correspondent

On the morning of 11 November 1918 I was on the way to Mons, where for us the war had begun. Our guns and transport were still moving forward along the roads. Bodies of our men – the poor old foot-sloggers – were trudging on, with wet capes and muddy boots, and sweat dripping below their tin hats. It was a dank morning with white mist lying on the fields. At an advanced headquarters an officer came out and spoke to us.

"Hostilities will cease at eleven o'clock."

A young staff officer was excited.

"The end of the war!" he cried. "And not too soon for me."

He did a little dance in the road.

We knew it was coming. For several days there had been talk of a German surrender. They had asked for terms. Now it had come, and it seemed unbelievable. Peace? Could it be possible? No more blood! No more casualties! No more mutilated, blinded and shell-shocked men. No more sacrifice of boys, too young to die. Peace! . . . How marvellous! How incredible! How miraculous!

Civilians were coming back our way already, mostly young men. They carried little flags, though heaven alone knows how they found them. They were some of the young men who had been sent behind the German lines, and now were straggling homewards to Liège and Lille.

I followed behind our transport wagons on the way to Mons. We looked at our wrist-watches – 11 a.m.

Through the white woolly mist a bugle sounded. It was the Cease Fire to a world war. The transport went on. The guns went on. The infantry slogged on with wet capes and sweat under their steel hats.

I went as far as Mons where the Canadian cavalry had been fighting the night before . . .

The Retreat from Mons . . . How long ago it seemed – like a lifetime ago. Now we were back again, and it was the end of the war after rivers of blood. It was – at last – Peace!

"Last night" (I wrote in my despatch from the war zone) "for the first time since August in the first year of the war, there was no light of gunfire in the sky. No sudden stabs of flame through the darkness, no long spreading glow above the black trees, where, for four years of nights, human beings were being smashed to death. The fires of hell had been put out. It was silent all along the front, with the beautiful silence of the nights of peace . . . On the way back from Mons I listened to this silence which followed the going down of the sun, and heard the rustling of the russet leaves, and the little sounds of night in peace, and it seemed as though God gave a benediction to the wounded soul of the world."

Vera Brittain, VAD

When the sound of victorious guns burst over London at 11 a.m. on November 11th, 1918, the men and women who looked incredulously into each other's faces did not cry jubilantly: "We've won the War!" They only said: "The War is over."

From Millbank I heard the maroons crash with terrifying clearness, and, like a sleeper who is determined to go on dreaming after being told to wake up, I went on automatically washing the dressing bowls in the annex outside my hut. Deeply buried beneath my consciousness there stirred the vague memory of a letter that I had written to Roland in those legendary days when I was still at Oxford, and could spend my Sundays in thinking of him while the organ echoed grandly through New College Chapel. It had been a warm May evening, when all the city was sweet with the scent of wallflowers and lilac, and I had walked back to Micklem Hall after hearing an Occasional Oratorio by Handel, which described the mustering of troops for battle, the lament for the fallen and the triumphant return of the victors.

"As I listened," I told him, "to the organ swelling forth into a final triumphant burst in the song of victory, after the solemn and mournful dirge over the dead, I thought with what mockery and irony the jubilant celebrations which will hail the coming of peace will fall upon the ears of those to whom their best will never return, upon whose sorrow victory is built, who have paid with their mourning for the others' joy. I wonder if I shall be one of those who take a happy part in the triumph – or if I shall listen to the merriment with a heart that breaks and ears that try to keep out the mirthful sounds."

And as I dried the bowls I thought: "It's come too late for me. Somehow I knew, even at Oxford, that it would. Why couldn't it have ended rationally, as it might have ended, in 1916, instead of all that trumpet-blowing against a negotiated peace, and the ferocious talk of secure civilians about marching to Berlin? It's come five months too late – or is it three years? It might have ended last June, and let Edward, at least, be saved! Only five months – it's such a little time, when Roland died nearly three years ago."

But on Armistice Day not even a lonely survivor drowning in black waves of memory could be left alone with her thoughts. A moment after the guns had subsided into sudden, palpitating silence, the other V.A.D. from my ward dashed excitedly into the annex.

"Brittain! Brittain! Did you hear the maroons? It's over – it's all over! Do let's come out and see what's happening!"

Mechanically I followed her into the road. As I stood there, stupidly rigid, long after the triumphant explosions from Westminster had turned into a distant crescendo of shouting, I saw a taxicab turn swiftly in from the Embankment towards the hospital. The next moment there was a cry for doctors and nurses from passers-by, for in rounding the corner the taxi had knocked down a small elderly woman who in listening, like myself, to the wild noise of a world released from nightmare, had failed to observe its approach.

As I hurried to her side I realized that she was all but dead and already past speech. Like Victor in the mortuary chapel, she seemed to have shrunk to the dimensions of a child with the sharp features of age, but on the tiny chalk-white face an expression of shocked surprise still lingered, and she stared hard at me as Geoffrey had stared at his orderly in those last moments of conscious silence beside the Scarpe. Had she been thinking, I wondered, when the taxi struck her, of her sons at the front, now safe? The next moment a medical officer and some orderlies came up, and I went back to my ward.

But I remembered her at intervals throughout that afternoon, during which, with a half-masochistic notion of "seeing the sights," I made a circular tour to Kensington by way of the intoxicated West End. With aching persistence my thoughts went back to the dead and the strange irony of their fates – to Roland, gifted, ardent, ambitious, who had died without glory in the conscientious performance of a routine job; to Victor and Geoffrey, gentle and diffident, who, conquering nature by resolution, had each gone down bravely in a big "show"; and finally to Edward, musical, serene, a lover of peace, who had fought courageously through so many battles and at last had been killed while leading a vital counter-attack in one of the few decisive actions of the War. As I struggled through the waving, shrieking crowds in Piccadilly and Regent Street on the overloaded top of a 'bus, some witty enthusiast for contemporary history symbolically turned upside down the signboard "Seven Kings."

Late that evening, when supper was over, a group of elated V.A.D.s who were anxious to walk through Westminster and Whitehall to Buckingham Palace prevailed upon me to join them. Outside the Admiralty a crazy group of convalescent Tommies were collecting specimens of different uniforms and bundling their wearers into flag-strewn taxis; with a shout they seized two of my companions and disappeared into the clamorous crowd, waving flags and shaking rattles. Wherever we went a burst of enthusiastic cheering greeted our Red Cross uniform, and complete strangers adorned with wound stripes rushed up and shook me warmly by the hand. After the long, long blackness, it seemed like a fairy-tale to see the street lamps shining through the chill November gloom.

I detached myself from the others and walked slowly up Whitehall, with my heart sinking in a sudden cold dismay. Already this was a different world from the one that I had known during four life-long years, a world in which people would be light-hearted and forgetful, in which themselves and their careers and their amusements would blot out political ideals and great national issues. And in that brightly lit, alien world I should have no part. All those with whom I had really been intimate were gone; not one remained to share with me the heights and the depths of my memories. As the years went by and youth departed and remembrance grew dim, a deeper and ever deeper darkness would cover the young men who were once my contemporaries.

For the first time I realized, with all that full realization meant, how completely everything that had hitherto made up my life had vanished with Edward and Roland, with Victor and Geoffrey. The War was over, a new age was beginning, but the dead were dead and would never return.

Ernest Read Cooper, Town Clerk, Southwold

11 Nov. I went to the office and at 11 was rung up by the County Adjutant who told me that the Armistice had been signed and that guns were firing and bells ringing at Ipswich. I did not take it in at first and could hear him shouting "War is over" at the other end. I hurried down to the Mayor and found he had just received the news and in a few minutes a car came in from the Covehithe Air Station full of mad Officers, cheering, waving flags and blowing trumpets. Flags soon came out, the Bells began to ring and a few of us adjourned to the Mayor's house and cracked some bottles of Fizz. An impromptu Meeting was called and the Mayor read the official Telegram from the Swan

Balcony, some soldiers came up on a waggon with the Kaiser in effigy, which they tied to the Town Pump and burnt amidst cheers.

At 12.45 we went to a short thanksgiving service at the Church and nearly all work was knocked off for the day but the Town took it very quietly on the whole. The Band played at the Mess in the evening and there were some squibs and cheering on the Green etc. The Town Pump and a few other lamps were lit up, also the Lighthouse which I do not think has been alight half a dozen times since the War, the fun finished soon after ten.

Winston Churchill MP, Minister for Munitions

It was a few minutes before the eleventh hour of the eleventh day of the eleventh month. I stood at the window of my room looking up Northumberland Avenue towards Trafalgar Square, waiting for Big Ben to tell that the War was over. My mind strayed back across the scarring years to the scene and emotions of the night at the Admiralty when I listened for these same chimes in order to give the signal of war against Germany to our Fleets and squadrons across the world. And now all was over! The unarmed and untrained island nation, who with no defence but its Navy had faced unquestioningly the strongest manifestation of military power in human record, had completed its task. Our country had emerged from the ordeal alive and safe, its vast possessions intact, its war effort still waxing, its institutions unshaken, its people and Empire united as never before. Victory had come after all the hazards and heartbreaks in an absolute and unlimited form. All the Kings and Emperors with whom we had warred were in flight or exile. All their Armies and Fleets were destroyed or subdued. In this Britain had borne a notable part, and done her best from first to last.

The minutes passed. I was conscious of reaction rather than elation. The material purposes on which one's work had been centred, every process of thought on which one had lived, crumbled into nothing. The whole vast business of supply, the growing outputs, the careful hoards, the secret future plans – but yesterday the whole duty of life – all at a stroke vanished like a nightmare dream, leaving a void behind. My mind mechanically persisted in exploring the problems of demobilization. What was to happen to our three million Munition workers? What would they make now? How would the roaring factories be converted? How in fact are swords beaten into ploughshares? How long would it take to bring the Armies home? What would they do when they got home? We had of course a demobilization plan for the Ministry of Munitions. It had been carefully worked out, but it had played no part in our thoughts. Now it must be put into operation. The levers must be pulled – *Full Steam Astern.* The Munitions Council must meet without delay.

And then suddenly the first stroke of the chime. I looked again at the broad street beneath me. It was deserted. From the portals of one of the large hotels absorbed by Government Departments darted the slight figure of a girl clerk, distractedly gesticulating while another stroke resounded. Then from all sides men and women came scurrying into the street. Streams of people poured out of all the buildings. The bells of London began to clash. Northumberland Avenue was now crowded with people in hundreds, nay, thousands, rushing hither and thither in a frantic manner, shouting and screaming with joy. I could see that Trafalgar Square was already swarming. Around me in our very headquarters, in the Hotel Metropole, disorder had broken out. Doors banged. Feet clattered down corridors. Everyone rose from the desk and cast aside pen and paper. All bounds were broken. The tumult grew. It grew like a gale, but from all sides simultaneously. The street was now a seething mass of humanity. Flags appeared as if by magic. Streams of men and women flowed from the Embankment. They mingled with torrents pouring down the Strand on their way to acclaim the King. Almost before the last stroke of the clock had died away, the strict, war-straitened, regulated streets of London had become a triumphant pandemonium. At any rate it was clear that no more work would be done that day. Yes, the chains which had held the world were broken. Links of imperative need, links of discipline, links of brute force, links of self-sacrifice links of terror, links of honour which had held our nation, nay, the greater part of mankind, to grinding toil, to a compulsive cause – every one had snapped upon a few strokes of the clock. Safety, freedom, peace, home, the dear one back at the fireside – all after fifty-two months of gaunt distortion. After fifty-two months of making burdens grievous to be borne and binding them on men's backs, at last, all at once, suddenly and everywhere the burdens were cast down. At least so for the moment it seemed.

My wife arrived, and we decided to go and offer our congratulations to the Prime Minister, on whom the central impact of the home struggle had fallen, in his hour of recompense. But no sooner had we entered our car than twenty people mounted upon it, and in the midst of a wildly cheering multitude we were impelled slowly forward through Whitehall. We had driven together the opposite way along the same road on the afternoon of the ultimatum. There had been the same crowd and almost the same enthusiasm. It was with feelings which do not lend themselves to words that I heard the cheers of the brave people who had borne so much and given all, who had never wavered, who had never lost faith in their country or its destiny, and who could be indulgent to the faults of their servants when the hour of deliverance had come . . .

Captain Llewellyn Evans, Royal Welsh Fusiliers

November 11th. There had been so much talk of an armistice that a Brigade message in the morning telling us of its having been signed at 8 o'clock, and that hostilities were to cease at 11, fell somewhat flat. The event was anticlimax relieved by some spasmodic cheering when the news got about, by a general atmosphere of "slacking off for the day", and by the notes of a lively band in the late afternoon. The men betook themselves to their own devices. There was a voluntary Service of Thanksgiving in the cinema which the Germans had built; the spacious building was quite full. The local civilians were over-joyed. They dug out some *drapeaux des Alliées* in astonishingly quick time. And they were hospitable with their poor means. They brewed an awful decoction of baked ground oats in place of coffee which had been unobtainable for a long time. To me the most remarkable feature of that day and night was the uncanny silence that prevailed. No rumbling of guns, no staccato of machine-guns, nor did the roar of exploding dumps break into the night as it had so often done. The War was over.

Part Six

1919

FEATURES OF THE WAR

Sir Douglas Haig (1861–1928) was appointed Commander in Chief of the British Expeditionary Force in December 1915, and was the main architect of the Somme and Passchendaele battles. A cavalryman, he disliked the new war's weaponry – he said famously of the machine gun that it was "much overated" – and many have claimed that he had no real tactical ability, and even less regard for the lives of his men. Haig's defenders, meanwhile, have argued that the Somme was, strictly speaking a victory, and that Haig's hand on the Western Front was repeatedly forced by the French. What can be said with certainty, is that Haig had an unique influence on the Great War; below is his own assessment of its course.

FEATURES OF THE WAR

Field Marshal Sir Douglas Haig
The London Gazette, 8 April 1919

In this, my final dispatch, I think it desirable to comment briefly upon certain general features which concern the whole series of operations carried out under my command. I am urged thereto by the conviction that neither the course of the war itself nor the military lessons to be drawn therefrom can properly, be comprehended, unless the long succession of battles commenced on the Somme in 1916 and ended in November of last year on the Sambre are viewed as forming part of one great and continuous engagement.

To direct attention to any single phase of that stupendous and incessant struggle and seek in it the explanation of our success, to the exclusion or neglect of other phases possibly less striking in their immediate or obvious consequences is, in my opinion, to risk the formation of unsound doctrines regarding the character and requirements of modern war.

If the operations of the past four and a half years are regarded as a single continuous campaign, there can be recognized in them the same general features and the same necessary stages which between forces of approximately equal strength have marked all the conclusive battles of history. There is in the first instance the preliminary stage of the campaign in which the opposing forces seek to deploy and manoeuver for position, endeavouring while doing so to gain some early advantage which might be pushed home to quick decision. This phase came to an end in the present war with the creation of continuous trench lines from the Swiss frontier to the sea.

Battle having been joined, there follows the period of real struggle in which the main forces of the two belligerent armies are pitted against each other in close and costly combat. Each commander seeks to wear down the power of resistance of his opponent and to pin him to his position, while preserving or accumulating in his own hands a powerful reserve force with which he can manoeuver, and when signs, of the enemy becoming morally and physically weakened are observed, deliver the decisive attack. The greatest possible pressure against the enemy's whole front must be maintained, especially when the crisis of the battle approaches. Then every man, horse, and gun is required to cooperate, so as to complete the enemy's overthrow and exploit success.

In the stage of the wearing out struggle, losses will necessarily be heavy on both sides, for in it the price of victory is paid. If the opposing forces are approximately equal in numbers, in courage, in morale, and in equipment, there is no way of avoiding payment of the price or of eliminating this phase of the struggle.

In former battles this stage of the conflict has rarely lasted more than a few days, and has often been completed in a few hours. When armies of millions are engaged, with the resources of great Empires behind them, it will inevitably be long. It will include violent crises of fighting which, when viewed separately and apart from the general perspective, will appear individually as great indecisive battles. To this stage belong the great engagements of 1916 and 1917 which wore down the strength of the German armies.

Finally, whether from the superior fighting ability and leadership of one of the belligerents, as the result of greater resources or tenacity, or by reason of higher morale, or from a combination of all these causes, the time will come when the other side will begin to weaken and the climax of the battle is reached. Then the commander of the weaker side must choose whether he will break off the engagement, if he can, while there is yet time, or stake on a supreme effort what reserves remain to him. The launching and destruction of Napoleon's last reserves at Waterloo was a matter of minutes. In this World War the great sortie of the beleaguered German armies commenced on March 21 1918, and lasted for four months, yet it represents a corresponding stage in a single colossal battle.

The breaking down of such a supreme effort will be the signal for the commander of the successful side to develop his greatest strength and seek to turn to immediate account the loss in material and morale which their failure must inevitably produce among his opponent's troops. In a battle joined and decided in the course of a few days or hours, there is no risk that the lay observer will seek to distinguish the culminating operations by which victory is seized and exploited from the preceding stages by which it has been made possible and determined. If the whole operations of the present war are regarded in correct perspective, the victories of the summer and autumn of 1918 will be seen to be as directly dependent upon the two years of stubborn fighting that preceded them.

If the causes which determined the length of the recent contest are examined in the light of the accepted principles of war, it will be seen that the duration of the struggle was governed by and bore a direct relation to certain definite factors which are enumerated below.

In the first place, we were unprepared for war, or at any rate for a war of such magnitude. We were deficient in both trained men and military material, and, what was more important, had no machinery ready by which either men or material could be produced in anything approaching the requisite quantities. The consequences were twofold. Firstly, the necessary machinery had to be improvised hurriedly, and improvisation is never economical and seldom satisfactory. In this case the high-water mark of our fighting strength in infantry was only reached after two and a half years of conflict, by which time heavy casualties had already been incurred. In consequence, the full man power of the Empire was never developed in the field at any period of the war.

As regards material, it was not until midsummer 1916 that the artillery situation became even approximately adequate to the conduct of major operations. Throughout the Somme Battle the expenditure of artillery ammunition had to be watched with the greatest care. During the battles of 1917 ammunition was plentiful, but the gun situation was a source of constant anxiety. Only in 1918 was it possible to conduct artillery operations independently of any limiting consideration other than that of transport.

The second consequence of our unpreparedness was that our armies were unable to intervene either at the outset of the war or until nearly two years had elapsed, in sufficient strength adequately to assist our Allies. The enemy was able to gain a notable initial advantage by establishing himself in Belgium and northern France, and throughout the early stages of the war was free to concentrate in undue proportion of his effectives against France and Russia. The excessive burden thrown upon the gallant army of France during this period caused them losses, the effect of which has been felt all through the war and directly influenced its length. Just as at no time were we as an Empire able to put our own full strength into the field, so at no time were the Allies as a whole able completely to develop and obtain the full effect from their greatly superior man power. What might have been the effect of British intervention on a larger scale in the earlier stages of the war is shown by what was actually achieved by our original expeditionary force.

It is interesting to note that in previous campaigns the side which has been fully prepared for war has almost invariably gained a rapid and complete success over its less well prepared opponent. In 1866 and 1870, Austria, and then France, were overwhelmed at the outset by means of superior preparation. The initial advantages derived therefrom were followed up by such vigorous and ruthless action, regardless of loss, that there was no time to recover from the first stunning blows. The German plan of campaign in the present war was undoubtedly based on similar principles. The margin by which the German onrush in 1914 was stemmed was so narrow and the subsequent struggle so severe that the word "miraculous" is hardly too strong a term to describe the recovery and ultimate victory of the Allies.

A further cause adversely influencing the duration of the war on the western front during its later stages, and one following indirectly from that just stated, was the situation in other theaters. The military strength of Russia broke down in 1917 at a critical period, when, had she been able to carry out her military engagements, the war might have been shortened by a year. At a later date, the military situation in Italy in the autumn of 1917 necessitated the transfer of five British divisions from France to Italy, at a time when their presence in France might have had far-reaching effects.

Thirdly, the Allies were handicapped in their task and the war thereby lengthened by the inherent difficulties always associated with the combined action of armies of separate nationalities differing in speech and temperament, and, not least important, in military organization, equipment, and supply.

Finally, as indicated in the opening paragraph of this part of my dispatch, the huge numbers of men engaged on either side, whereby a continuous battle front was rapidly established from Switzerland to the sea, outflanking was made, impossible and manoeuver very difficult, necessitated the delivery of frontal attacks. This factor, combined with the strength of the defensive under modern conditions, rendered a protracted wearing-out battle unavoidable before the enemy's power of resistance could be overcome. So long as the opposing forces are at the outset approximately equal in numbers and morale and there are no flanks to turn, a long struggle for supremacy is inevitable.

Obviously the greater the length of a war the higher is likely to be the number of casualties incurred in it on either side. The same causes therefore, which served to protract the recent struggle are largely responsible for the extent of our casualties. There can be no question that to our general unpreparedness must be attributed the loss of many thousands of brave men whose sacrifice we deeply deplore, while we regard their splendid gallantry and self-devotion with unstinted admiration and gratitude.

Given, however, the military situation existing in August 1914, our total losses in the war have been no larger than were to be expected. Neither do they compare unfavorably with those of any other of the belligerent nations, so far as figures are available, from which comparison can be made. The total British casualties in all theaters of war, killed, wounded, missing, and prisoners, including native troops, are approximately three million (3,076,388). Of this total some two and a half million (2,568,834) were incurred on the western front. The total French losses, killed, missing, and prisoners, but exclusive of wounded, have been given officially as approximately 1,831,000. If an estimate for wounded is added, the total can scarcely be less than 4,800,000, and of this total it is fair to assume that over four million were incurred on the western front. The published figures for Italy killed and wounded only, exclusive of prisoners, amount to 1,400,060, of which practically the whole were incurred in the western theater of war.

Figures have also been published for Germany and Austria. The total German casualties, killed, wounded, missing, and prisoners, are given at approximately six and a half million (6,485,000), of which the vastly greater proportion must have been incurred on the western front, where the bulk of the German forces were concentrated and the hardest fighting took place. In view of the fact, however that the number of German prisoners is definitely known to be considerably understated, these figures must be accepted with reserve. The losses of Austria-Hungary in killed, missing, and prisoners are given as approximately two and three-quarter million (2,772,000). An estimate of wounded would give a total of over four and a half million.

The extent of our casualties, like the duration of the war was dependent on certain definite factors which can be stated shortly.

In the first place, the military situation compelled us, particularly during the first portion of the war to make great efforts before we had developed our full strength in the field or properly equipped and trained our armies. These efforts were wasteful of men, but in the circumstances they could not be avoided. The only alternative was to do nothing and see our French Allies overwhelmed by the enemy's superior numbers.

During the second half of the war, and that part embracing the critical and costly period of the wearing-out battle, the losses previously suffered by our Allies laid upon the British armies in France an increasing share in the burden of attack. From the opening of the Somme Battle in 1916 to the termination of hostilities the British armies were subjected to a strain of the utmost severity which never ceased, and consequently had little or no opportunity for the rest and training they so greatly needed.

In addition to these particular considerations, certain general factors peculiar to modern war made for the inflation of losses. The great strength of modern field defenses and the power and precision of modern weapons, the multiplication of machine guns, trench mortars, and artillery of all natures, the employment of gas, and the rapid development of the aeroplane as a formidable agent of destruction against both men and material, all combined to increase the price to be paid for victory.

If only for these reasons, no comparisons can usefully be made between the relative losses incurred in this war and any previous war. There is, however, the further consideration that the issues involved in this stupendous struggle were far greater than those concerned in any other war in recent history. Our existence as an Empire and civilization itself, as it is understood by the free western nations, were at stake. Men fought as they have never fought before in masses.

Despite our own particular handicaps and the foregoing general considerations, it is satisfactory to note that, as the result of the courage and determination of our troops, and the high level of leadership generally maintained, our losses even in attack over the whole period of the battle compare favourably with those inflicted on our opponents. The approximate total of our battle casualties in all arms, and including overseas troops, from the commencement of the Somme Battle in 1916 to the conclusion of the armistice is 2,140,000. The calculation of German losses is obviously a matter of great difficulty. It is estimated, however, that the number of casualtics inflicted on the enemy by British troops during the above period exceeds two and a half million. It is of interest, moreover, in the light of the paragraph next following, that more than half the total casualties incurred by us in the fighting of 1918 were occasioned during the five months, March–July, when our armies were on the defensive.

Closely connected with the question of casualties is that of the relative values of attack and defense. It is a view often expressed that the attack is more expensive than defense. This is only a half statement of the truth. Unquestionably, unsuccessful attack is generally more expensive than defense, particularly if the attack is pressed home with courage and resolution. On the other hand, attack so pressed home, if skillfully conducted, is rarely unsuccessful, whereas in its later stages especially, unsuccessful defense is far more costly than attack.

Moreover, the object of all war is victory, and a purely defensive attitude can never bring about a successful decision, either in a battle or in a campaign. The idea that a war can be won by standing on the defensive and waiting for the enemy to attack is a dangerous fallacy, which owes its inception to the desire to evade the price of victory. It is an axiom that decisive success in battle can be gained only by a vigorous offensive. The principle here stated has long been recognized as being fundamental and is based on the universal teaching of military history in all ages. The course of the present war has proved it to be correct.

To pass for a moment from the general to the particular, and consider in the light of the present war the facts upon which this axiom is based.

A defensive role sooner or later brings about a distinct lowering of the morale of the troops, who imagine that the enemy must be the better man, or at least more numerous, better equipped with and better served by artillery or other mechanical aids to victory. Once the mass of the defending infantry become possessed of such ideas, the battle is as good as lost. An army fighting on enemy soil, especially if its standard of discipline is high, may maintain a successful defense for a protracted period, in the hope that victory may be gained elsewhere or that the enemy may tire or weaken in his resolution and accept a compromise. The resistance of the German Armies was undoubtedly prolonged in this fashion, but in the end the persistence of our troops had its natural effect.

Further, a defensive policy involves the loss of the initiative, with all the consequent disadvantages to the defender. The enemy is able to choose at his own convenience the time and place of his attacks. Not being influenced himself by the threat of attack from his opponent, he can afford to take risks, and by greatly weakening his front in some places can concentrate an overwhelming force elsewhere with which to attack. The defender, on the other hand, becomes almost entirely ignorant of the dispositions and plans of his opponent, who is thus in a position to effect a surprise. This was clearly exemplified during the fighting of 1918. As long as the enemy was attacking, he obtained fairly full information regarding our dispositions. Captured documents show that, as soon as he was thrown once more on the defensive and the initiative returned to the Allies, he was kept in comparative ignorance of our plans and dispositions. The consequence was that the Allies were able to effect many surprises, both strategic and tactical.

As a further effect of the loss of the initiative and ignorance of his opponent's intentions, the defender finds it difficult to avoid a certain dispersal of his forces. Though for a variety of reasons, including the fact that we had lately been on the offensive, we were by no means entirely ignorant of the enemy's intentions in the spring of 1918, the unavoidable uncertainty resulting from a temporary loss of the initiative did have the effect of preventing a complete concentration of our reserves behind the point of the enemy's attack.

An additional reason, peculiar to the circumstances of the present war, which in itself compelled me to refuse to adopt a purely defensive attitude, so long as any other was open to me, is to be found in the geographical position of our armies. For reasons stated by me in my dispatch of July 20 1918, we could not afford to give much ground on any part of our front. The experience of the war has shown that if the defense is to be maintained successfully, even for a limited time, it must be flexible.

If the views set out by me in the preceding paragraphs are accepted, it will be recognized that the war did not follow any unprecedented course, and that its end was neither sudden nor should it have been unexpected. The rapid collapse of Germany's military powers in the latter half of 1918 was the logical outcome of the fighting of the previous two years. It would not have taken place but for that period of ceaseless attrition which used up the reserves of the German Armies while the constant and growing pressure of the blockade sapped with more deadly insistence from year to year at the strength and resolution of the German people. It is in the great battles of 1916 and 1917 that we have to seek for the secret of our victory in 1918.

Doubtless, the end might have come sooner had we been able to develop the military resources of our Empire more rapidly and with a higher degree of concentration or had not the defection of Russia in 1917 given our enemies a new lease of life.

So far as the military situation is concerned, in spite of the great accession of strength which Germany received as the result of the defection of Russia, the battles of 1916 and 1917 had so far weakened her armies that the effort they made in 1918 was insufficient to secure victory. Moreover, the effect of the battles of 1916 and 1917 was not confined to loss of German man power. The moral effects of those battles were enormous, both in the German Army and in Germany. By their means our soldiers established over the German soldier a moral superiority which they held in an ever-increasing degree until the end of the war, even in the difficult days of March and April, 1918.

From time to time as the war of position dragged on and the enemy's trench systems remained unbroken, while questions of man power and the shortage of shipping became acute, the wisdom or necessity of maintaining any large force of mounted men was freely discussed. In the light of the full experience of the war the decision to preserve the cavalry corps has been completely justified. It has been proved that cavalry, whether used for shock effect under suitable conditions or as mobile infantry, have still an indispensable part to play in modern war. Moreover, it can not safely be assumed that in all future wars the flanks of the opposing forces will rest on neutral states or impassable obstacles. Whenever such a condition does not obtain, opportunities for the use of cavalry must arise frequently.

Throughout the great retirement in 1914 our cavalry covered the retirement and protected the flanks of our columns against the onrush of the enemy, and on frequent occasions prevented our infantry from being overrun by the enemy's cavalry. Later in the same year at Ypres their mobility multiplied their value as a reserve, enabling them rapidly to reinforce threatened portions of our line.

During the critical period of position warfare, when the trial of strength between the opposing forces took place, the absence of room to manoeuver made the importance of cavalry less apparent. Even under such conditions however, valuable results may be expected from the employment of a strong force of cavalry when, after there has been severe fighting on one or more fronts, a surprise attack is made on another front. Such an occasion arose in the operations before Cambrai at the close of 1917, when the cavalry were of the greatest service, while throughout the whole period of trench fighting they constituted an important mobile reserve.

At a later date, when circumstances found us operating once more in comparatively open country, cavalry proved themselves of value in their true role. During the German offensive in March 1918, the superior mobility of cavalry fully justified their existence. At the commencement of the battle cavalry were used under the fifth army over wide fronts. So great, indeed, became the need for mounted men that certain units which had but recently been dismounted were hurriedly provided with horses and did splendid service. Frequently, when it was impossible to move forward other troops in time, our mounted troops were able to fill gaps in our line and restore the situation. The absence of hostile cavalry at this period was a marked feature of the battle. Had the German command had at their disposal even two or three well-trained cavalry divisions, a wedge might have been driven between the French and British armies. Their presence could not have failed to have added greatly to the difficulties of our task.

In the actions already referred to east of Amiens, the cavalry were again able to demonstrate the great advantage which their power of rapid concentration gives them in a surprise attack. Operating in close concert with both armoured cars and infantry, they pushed ahead of the latter and by anticipating the arrival of German reserves assisted materially in our success. In the battle of October 8 they were responsible for saving the Cambrai-Le Cateau-St Quentin Railway from complete destruction. Finally, during the culminating operations of the war when the German armies were falling back in disorganized masses a new situation arose which demanded the use of mounted troops. Then our cavalry, pressing hard upon the enemy's heels, hastened his retreat and threw him into worse confusion. At such a time the moral effect of cavalry is overwhelming and is in itself a sufficient reason for the retention of that arm.

On the morning of the armistice, two British cavalry divisions were on the march east of the Scheldt, and before the orders to stop reached them they had already gained a line 10 miles in front of our infantry outposts. There is no doubt that, had the advance of the cavalry been allowed to continue, the enemy's disorganized retreat would have been turned into a rout.

A remarkable feature of the present war has been the number and variety of mechanical contrivances to which it has given birth or has brought to a higher state of perfection.

Besides the great increase in mobility made possible by the development of motor transport, heavy artillery, trench mortars, machine guns, aeroplanes, tanks, gas, and barbed wire have in their several spheres of action played very prominent parts in operations, and as a whole have given a greater driving power to war. The belligerent possessing a preponderance of such mechanical contrivances has found himself in a very favourable position as compared with his less well provided opponent. The general superiority of the Allies in this direction during the concluding stages of the recent struggle undoubtedly contributed powerfully to their success. In this respect the army owes a great debt to science and to the distinguished scientific men who placed their learning, and skill at the disposal of their country.

It should never be forgotten, however, that weapons of this character are incapable of effective independent action. They do not in themselves possess the power to obtain a decision, their real function being to assist the infantry to get to grips with their opponents. To place in them a reliance out of proportion to their real utility, to imagine, for example, that tanks, and aeroplanes can take the place of infantry and artillery, would be to do a disservice to those who have the future of these new weapons most at heart by robbing them of the power to use them to their best effect.

Every mechanical device so far produced is dependent for its most effective upon the closest possible association with other arms, and in particular with infantry and artillery. Aeroplanes must rely upon infantry to prevent the enemy from overrunning their aerodromes, and, despite their increasing range and versatility of action, are clearly incapable in themselves of bringing about a decision. Tanks require the closest artillery support to enable them to reach their objectives without falling victims to the enemy's artillery, and are dependent upon the infantry to hold the position they have won.

As an instance of the interdependence of artillery and tanks we may take the actions fought east of Amiens on August 8 1918, and following days. A very large number of tanks were employed in these operations, and they carried out their tasks in the most brilliant manner. Yet a scrutiny of the artillery ammunition returns for this period discloses the fact that in no action of similar dimensions had the expenditure of ammunition been so great.

Immense as the influence of mechanical devices may be, they can not by themselves decide a campaign. Their true role is that of assisting the infantryman, which they have done in a most admirable manner. They can not replace him. Only by the rifle and bayonet of the infantryman can the decisive victory be won.

This war has given no new principles; but the different mechanical appliances above mentioned and in particular the rapid improvement and multiplication of aeroplanes, the use of immense numbers of machine guns and Lewis guns, the employment of vast quantities of barbed wire as effective obstacles, the enormous expansion of artillery, and the provision of great masses of motor transport have introduced new problems of considerable complexity concerning the effective cooperation of the different arms and services. Much thought has had to be bestowed upon determining how new devices could be combined in the best manner with the machinery already working.

The development of the air service is a matter of general knowledge, and figures showing something of the work done by our airmen were included in my last dispatch. The combining of their operations with those of the other arms, and particularly of the artillery, has been the subject of constant study and experiment, giving results of the very highest value. As regards machine guns, from a proportion of 1 gun to approximately 500 infantrymen in 1914, our establishment of machine guns and Lewis guns had risen at the end of 1918 to 1 machine gun or Lewis gun to approximately 20 infantrymen. This great expansion was necessarily accompanied by a modification of training and methods both for attack and defense, and resulted ultimately in the establishment of the machine-gun corps under an inspector general.

During the same period, the growth of our artillery was even more remarkable, its numbers and power increasing out of all proportion to the experience of previous wars. The 486 pieces of light and medium artillery with which we took the field in August 1914, were represented at the date of the armistice by 6,437 guns and howitzers of all natures, including pieces of the heaviest calibre.

This vast increase so profoundly influenced the employment of artillery and was accompanied by so intimate an association with other arms and services that it merits special comment.

In the first place, big changes were required in artillery organization, as well as important decisions concerning the proportions in which the different natures of artillery and artillery ammunition should be manufactured. These changes and decisions were made during 1916, and resulted in the existing artillery organization of the British armies in France.

In order to gain the elasticity essential to the quick concentration of guns at the decisive point, to enable the best use to be made of them, and to facilitate ammunition supply and fire control, artillery commanders, acting under army and corps commanders, were introduced, and staffs provided for them. This enabled the large concentrations of guns required for our offensives to be quickly absorbed and efficiently directed. The proportions required of guns to howitzers and of the lighter to the heavier natures were determined by certain factors, namely the problem of siting in the comparatively limited areas available the great numbers of pieces required for an offensive; the "lives" of the different types of guns and howitzers, that is the number of rounds which can be fired from them before they become unserviceable from wear, and questions of relative accuracy and fire effect upon particular kinds of targets.

The results attained by the organization established in 1916 is in itself strong evidence of the soundness of the principles upon which it was based. It made possible a high degree of elasticity, and by the full and successful exploitation of all the means placed it its disposal by science and experience, insured that the continuous artillery battle which began on the Somme should culminate, as it did, in the defeat of the enemy's guns.

The great development of air photography, sound ranging, flash spotting, air-burst ranging, and aerial observation brought counterbattery work and harassing fire both by day and night to a high state of perfection. Special progress was made in the art of engaging moving targets with fire controlled by observation from aeroplanes and balloons. The work of the field survey sections in the location of hostile battery positions by resection and the employment of accurate maps was brought into extended use. In combination with the work of the calibration sections in the accurate calibration of guns and by careful calculation of corrections of range required to compensate for weather conditions it became possible to a large extent to dispense with registration, whereby the chance of effecting surprise was greatly increased. In the operations east of Amiens on August 8 1918, in which over 2,000 guns were employed, practically the whole of the batteries concentrated for the purpose of the attack opened fire for the first time, on the actual morning of the assault.

The use of smoke shell for covering the advance of our infantry and masking the enemy's positions was introduced and employed with increasing frequency and effect. New forms of gas shell were made available, and their combination with the infantry attack carefully studied. The invention of a new fuse known as "106," which was first used in the Battle of Arras, 1917, enabled wire entanglements to be easily and quickly destroyed, and so modified our methods of attacking organized positions. By bursting the shell the instant it touched the ground and before it had become buried, the destructive effect of the explosion was greatly increased. It became possible to cut wire with a far less expenditure of time and ammunition, and the factor of surprise was given a larger part in operations.

Great attention was paid to the training of personnel and in particular the Chapperton Down Artillery School, Salisbury Plain, was formed for training artillery brigade commanders and battery commanders, while artillery schools in France were organized for the training of subalterns and noncommissioned officers.

A short examination of our principal attacks will give a good idea of the increasing importance of artillery. On the first day of the Somme Battle of 1916 the number of artillery personnel engaged was equal to about half the infantry strength of the attacking divisions. On this one day a total of nearly 13,000 tons of artillery ammunition was fired by us on the western front. Our attacks at Arras and Messines, on April 9 and June 7 1917, saw the total expenditure of artillery ammunition nearly doubled on the first days of those battles, while the proportion of artillery personnel to infantry steadily grew.

During the period following the opening of the Somme Battle, the predominance of our artillery over that of the enemy gradually increased, till at the time of the Arras Battle it had reached a maximum. In the course of the summer and autumn of 1917, however, the enemy constantly reinforced his artillery on our front, being enabled to do so owing to the relaxation of pressure elsewhere.

The Battle of Ypres in the autumn of 1917 was one of intense struggle for artillery supremacy. By dint of reducing his artillery strength on other parts of the western front, and by bringing guns from the east, the enemy definitely challenged the predominance of our artillery. In this battle, therefore, the proportion of our artillery to infantry strength was particularly large. In the opening attack on July 31 our artillery personnel amounted to over 80 per cent of the infantry engaged in the principal attack on our front, and our total expenditure of artillery ammunition on this day exceeded 23,000 tons. During the succeeding weeks the battle of the rival artilleries became ever more violent. On the two days, September 20 and 21, about 42,000 tons of artillery ammunition were expended by us, and in the successful attack of October 4, which gave us the main ridge about Broodseinde, our artillery personnel amounted to 85 per cent of the infantry engaged in the assault.

During the winter of 1917–18 the enemy so greatly added to his artillery strength by batteries brought from the Russian front that in his spring offensive he was able temporarily to effect a definite local artillery superiority. This state of affairs was short-lived. Even before the breakdown of the German offensive, our guns had regained the upper hand. In the battles later in the year the superiority of our batteries once more grew rapidly, until the defeat of the German artillery became an accomplished fact. From the commencement of our offensive in August 1918, to the conclusion of the armistice, some 700,000 tons, of artillery ammunition were expended by the British armies on the western front. For the fortnight from August 21 to September 3 our average daily expenditure exceeded 11,000 tons, while for the three days of crucial battle on the 27th, 28th, and 29th of September nearly 65,000 tons of ammunition were fired by our artillery.

The tremendous growth of our artillery strength above described followed inevitably from the character of the wearing out battle upon which we were engaged. The restricted opportunities for manoeuver and the necessity for frontal attacks made the employment of great masses of artillery essential.

The massing of the guns alone, however, could not have secured success without the closest possible combination between our batteries and the infantry they were called upon to support, as well as with the other arms. The expansion was accompanied, therefore, by a constant endeavour to improve the knowledge of all ranks of both artillery and infantry and the air service concerning the work and possibilities of the other arms.

An intelligent understanding of "the other man's job" is the first essential of successful cooperation. To obtain the best results from the vast and complex machine composing a modern army, deep study of work other than one's own is necessary for all arms. For this study much time is needed, as well as much practical application of the principles evolved, and for reasons already explained, opportunity sufficient for adequate training could not be found. None the less, the best possible use was made of such opportunities as offered, and much was in fact accomplished.

As a natural corollary to the general increase of our forces, the signal service, required alike for the proper coordination of supply and for the direction and control of the battle, has grown almost out of recognition. From an original establishment of under 2,400 officers and men, trained and equipped chiefly for mobile warfare, at the end of 1918 the personnel of the signal service had risen to 42,000, fully equipped with all the latest devices of modern science to act efficiently under all conditions as the nervous system to the whole vast organism of our army.

The commencement of trench warfare and the greater use of artillery led to a rapid development of the signal system, which, as fresh units were introduced, became more and more elaborate. At the same time, the increase in the power and range of artillery made the maintenance of communications constantly more difficult. Many miles of deep trenches were dug in which cables containing 50 to 100 circuits were buried to gain protection from shell fire. The use of wireless communication gradually became more widely spread and finally constituted part of the signal establishment of all formations down to divisions. To provide an alternative method of communication with front-line troops, in 1915 carrier pigeons were introduced and a special branch of the signal service was formed controlling ultimately some 20,000 birds. In 1917 a messenger-dog service was started for similar purposes and did good work on a number of occasions.

The expansion of the work of the signal service in the more forward areas was accompanied by a similar development on the lines of communication, at general headquarters, armies, and corps. Construction and railway companies were formed and about 1,500 miles of main telegraph and telephone routes constructed in the lines of communication area alone, in addition to many miles in army areas. Provision had to be made for communication with London, Paris, and Marseille, as well as between the different allied headquarters. On the advance of our forces to the Rhine telephone communication was established between general headquarters at Montreuil and Cologne. Signal communication entailing the putting up of many thousands of miles of wire was provided also for the control of railway traffic, while to supplement electric communication generally a dispatch rider letter service was maintained by motorcyclists.

The amount of signal traffic dealt with became very great, and on the lines of communication alone more than 23,000 telegrams have been transmitted in 24 hours. Similarly, at general headquarters as many as 9,000 telegrams have been dealt with in 24 hours, besides 3,400 letters carried by dispatch riders; and army headquarters has handled 10,000 telegrams and 5,000 letters in the same space of time, and a corps, 4,500 telegrams and 3,000 letters. In addition to telegrams and letters, there has been at all times it great volume of telephone traffic.

Something of the extent of the constructional work required, in particular to meet the constant changes of the battle line and the movement of headquarters, can be gathered from the fact that as many as 6,500 miles of field cable have been issued in a single week. The average weekly issue of such cable for the whole of 1918 was approximately 3,300 miles.

The immense expansion of the army, from 6 to over 60 infantry divisions, combined with the constant multiplication of auxiliary arms, called inevitably for a large increase in the size and scope of the services concerned in the supply and maintenance of our fighting forces.

As the army grew and became more complicated the total

feeding strength of our forces in France rose until it approached a total of 2,700,000 men. The vastness of the figures involved in providing for their needs will be realized from the following examples. For the maintenance of a single division for one day, nearly 200 tons dead weight of supplies and stores are needed, representing a shipping tonnage of nearly 450 tons. In an army of 2,700,000 men, the addition of 1 ounce to each man's daily ration, involves the carrying of an extra 75 tons of goods.

To cope with so great a growth, the number of existing directorates had gradually to be added to or their duties extended, with a corresponding increase in demands for personnel. The supervision of ports was intrusted to the directorate of docks, which controlled special companies for the transshipping of stores. By the end of November 1918, the number of individual landings in France at the various ports managed by us exceeded ten and one-half million persons. During the 11 months, January to November 1918, the tonnage landed at these ports averaged some 175,000 per week.

To the directorate of transport, originally concerned with the administration of horse vehicles and pack animals, fell the further duty of exploiting mechanical road traction. Despite the employment of over 46,700 vehicles, including over 30,000 lorries, the number of horses and mules rose greatly, reaching a figure exceeding 400,000. The replacement, training, and distribution of these animals was the duty of the directorate of remounts. The directorate of veterinary services reduced losses and prevented the spread of disease, while the inspector of horse feeding and economies insured that the utmost value was obtained from the forage and grain consumed.

To meet the requirements of mechanical and horse traffic, the upkeep or construction of a maximum of some 4,500 miles of roadway was intrusted to the directorate of roads. Some idea of the work involved may be obtained from the fact that for ordinary upkeep alone, 100 tons of road material are required per fortnight for the maintenance of 1 mile of road. Under this directorate were organized a number of road construction companies, together with quarry companies to supply the necessary metal. In the month of October, 1918, over 85,000 tons of road material were conveyed weekly by motor transport alone, involving a petrol mileage of over 14,000,000 weekly. The total output of stone from the commencement of 1918 to the date of the armistice amounted to some 3,500,000 tons.

For the working of the existing railways and for the construction or repair of many miles of track both normal and narrow gauge, railway troops of every description, operating companies, construction companies, survey and reconnaissance companies, engine-crew companies, workshop companies, wagon-erecting companies, and light railway forward companies had to be provided. Under the directorate of railway traffic, the directorate of construction and the directorate of light railways, these and other technical troops during 1918 built or reconstructed 2,340 miles of broad-gauge and 1,348 miles of narrow-gauge railway. Throughout the whole period of their operation they guaranteed the smooth and efficient working of the railway system. In the six months of May to October 1918, a weekly average of 1,800 trains were run for British Army traffic, carrying a weekly average load of approximately 400,000 tons, while a further 130,000 tons were carried weekly by our light railways. The number of locomotives imported to deal with this traffic rose from 62 in 1916 to over 1,200 by the end of 1918, while the number of trucks rose from 3,840 to 52,600.

The inland water transport section were organized under a separate directorate for the working in France and Flanders of the canal and cross-channel barge traffic. On inland waterways alone an average of 56,000 tons of material were carried during 1918, the extent of waterways worked by us at the date of the armistice being some 465 miles.

The wonderful development of all methods of transportation had an important influence upon the course of events. No war been fought with such ample means of quick transportation as were available during the recent struggle. Despite the huge increase in the size of armies, it was possible to effect great concentrations of troops with a speed which, having regard to the numbers of men and bulk of material moved, has never before been equalled. Strategic and tactical mobility has been the guiding principle of our transportation arrangements; but this was itself at all times vitally affected by questions of supply and by the necessity of providing for the evacuation and replacement on a vast scale of the sick and wounded.

The successful coordination and economic use of all the various kinds of transportation requires most systematic management, based on deep thought and previous experience. So great was the work entailed in the handling of the vast quantities of which some few examples are given above, so complex did the machinery of transport become and so important was it, that the highest state of efficiency should be maintained, that in the autumn of 1916 I was forced to adopt an entirely new system for running our lines of communication. The appointment of inspector general of communications was abolished, and the services previously directed by that officer were brought under the immediate control of the adjutant general, the quartermaster general, and the director general of transportation. The last mentioned was a new office created with a separate staff composed for the greater part of civilian experts to deal specifically with transportation questions. At the same time, the command and administration of the troops on the lines of communication were vested in a "general officer commanding the lines of communication area."

The huge bulk of the supplies to be handled was due not merely to the size of our army. It arose also from the introduction of new weapons and methods of war, and from the establishment of a higher standard of comfort for the troops. The incessant demands of the fighting forces for munitions were supplied by the directorate of ordnance services, combined with a great expansion of ordnance workshops; while the directorate of engineering stores provided on a vast scale the materials required for the construction of trench defenses and kindred purposes. For the comfort and well-being of the troops, the directorate of supplies stored and distributed in sound condition fresh food, to take the place as far as possible of tinned rations. Through the agency of an inspectorate of messing and economies, regular schools of cookery gave instruction to nearly 25,000 cooks, and careful measures were taken for the recovery of kitchen byproducts. In August 1918, over 860,000 pounds of dripping were received from armies and consigned to England, while the cash value of the by-products disposed of from all sources has exceeded £60,000 in a single month. Provision was made for baths, and a new inspectorate supervised the running of army laundries on up-to-date lines.

The expeditionary force canteens made it possible to obtain additional comforts close up to the front. During 1918, the value of the weekly sales in the different canteens averaged eight and one-half million francs. These canteens were valuably supplemented by the various voluntary institutions ministering to the comfort and recreation of our troops, such as the Y. M. C. A., the Church Army, the Scottish Churches Huts, the Salvation Army, the Soldiers' Christian Association, the Catholic Women's League, and Club Huts, the United Army and the British and Navy Board, the Wesleyan Soldiers' Institute, and the British Soldiers' Institute. In many cases these organizations carried on their work almost in the actual fighting line, and did much to maintain the high morale of our armies. To permit the troops to avail themselves of the opportunities so offered, methods devised by the paymaster in chief enabled soldiers to obtain money anywhere in the field. Parcels and letters from home have been delivered by the army postal service with remarkable regularity.

As the effects of the enemy submarine warfare began to be felt and the shortage of shipping became more and more acute, so it became increasingly necessary for the army in France to be self-supporting. To meet this emergency vast hospitals and convalescent depots capable of accommodating over 22,000 men were erected west of the Seine at Trouville. Additional general hospitals with accommodation for over 7,000 patients were established in the neighborhood of Boulogne, Etaples, and elsewhere. Between January 1916 and November 1918, the total capacity of hospitals and convalescent depots in France grew from under 44,000 to over 157,000 persons.

Great installations were set up for the manufacture of gun parts and articles of like nature, for the repair of damaged material as well as for the utilization of the vast quantities of articles of all kinds collected from the battlefields by the organization working under the direction of the controller of salvage. The forestry directorate, controlling over 70 Canadian and other forestry companies, worked forests all over France, in the northwest, central and southwest departments, the Vosges, Jura, and Bordeaux country. As the result of its work our armies were made practically independent of oversea imported timber. The directorate of agricultural production organized farm and garden enterprises for the local supply of vegetables, harvested the crops abandoned by the enemy in his retreat, and commenced the reclamation of the devastated area.

At the same time a great saving of shipping was effected by the speeding up of work at the docks. The average tonnage discharged per hour in port rose from 12 1/2 tons in January 1917, to 34 1/2 tons in July 1918; while the average number of days lost by ships awaiting berth at the ports fell from some 90 ship days per week at the beginning of 1917 to about 9 ship days per week in 1918.

For the accommodation of so wide a range of services, installations of all kinds, hutments, factories, workshops, storage for ammunition, clothing, meat and petrol, power houses and pumping stations, camps and hospitals, had to be planned and constructed by the directorate of works. Our business relations with the French, the obtaining of sites and buildings, called for the establishment of a directorate of hirings and requisitions; while my financial adviser in France assisted in the adjustment of financial questions connected with the use of French railways and harbours, the exploitation of French forests and similar matters. The safeguarding from fire of the great number of buildings erected or taken over by us and of the masses of accumulated stores was intrusted to a definite staff under the supervision of a fire expert.

The creation and maintenance of the great organization briefly outlined above made big demands upon our available supply of personnel. Though these demands so far as possible were met, under the supervision of the controller of labour, by imported labour or prisoners of war. It was not practicable at any time to supply more than a proportion of our needs in this manner. Many fit men who might otherwise have reinforced the fighting line had also to be employed, especially during the earlier stages of the war.

As, however, our organization arrived at a greater state of completion and its working became smooth, so it began to be possible to withdraw considerable numbers of fit men from the rearward services. In many cases it was possible, where replacement was necessary, to fill the places of the fit men so withdrawn by women or unfit men. In this way, when the man-power situation became acute a considerable saving was effected. During the great British attacks of 1918, of a total male feeding strength of a little over two and one-quarter million, one and one-half million were in front of railhead. Even so, as has been found to be the case in the armies of all other belligerents, so in our army the number of fit men employed in the rearward services has at all times been large and necessarily so.

It is hardly too much to assert that, however seemingly extravagant in men and money, no system of supply except the most perfect should ever be contemplated. To give a single example, unless our supply services had been fully efficient the great advance carried out by our armies during the autumn of last year could not have been achieved.

Wars may be won or lost by the standard of health and morale of the opposing forces. Morale depends to a very large extent upon the feeding and general well-being of the troops. Badly supplied troops will invariably be low in morale, and an army ravaged by disease ceases to be a fighting force. The feeding and health of the fighting forces are dependent upon the rearward services, and so it may be argued that with the rearward services rests victory or defeat. In our case we can justly say that our supply system has been developed into one of the most perfect in the world.

The preceding paragraph illustrates the demands which the conduct of operations made on the staff and directorates controlled by the quartermaster general. The parallel development of the adjutant general's branch, while concerned with matters less patent to the casual observer, has been no less remarkable. The problem of insuring the supply of reinforcements at the times and places at which they will be required to replace casualties is present in all warfare, and is difficult in any circumstances. In operations conducted on the scale reached in this war it is exceedingly intricate. The successful solution of this problem alone entitles the adjutant general and his staff to the greatest credit. It has formed, however, but a small part of their work.

Owing to the impossibility of foretelling what claims would be made on man power by industry or by other theaters of war, it was necessary to prepare elaborate forecasts of the personnel likely to be required at various dates, and to work out in advance the best manner of utilizing reinforcements in the event of their being available in greater or less numbers. We were faced with an unexpected contraction in man power in the winter of 1917 and an unexpected expansion in the summer of 1918. Both these developments were encountered with a success which could only have been attained by the greatest forethought and application on the part of the staff concerned.

To reduce to cadre a depleted division, to fill it up when men became available, to break up a battalion and redistribute its personnel, to comb out a certain number of fit men from the rearward services, all sound simple operations. In reality each requires immense amount of sympathetic treatment and clerical labour, the extent of the work involved being instanced by the fact that in the month of April 1918, over 200,000 reinforcements were sent up to the fighting forces. The carrying out of measures of this nature was made more difficult by the continual formation of new types of unit to meet new requirements. It was necessary to find the personnel for those units with the least possible dislocation elsewhere, and with an eye to the most advantageous employment of the individual in regard to his medical category and special qualifications. The following figures will give some indication of the magnitude of the task. The adjutant general's office at the base has prepared over 8,000,000 records containing the military history of individual soldiers in France, and has received and dispatched over 22,000,000 letters.

Whatever the quality of the troops a just and efficient administration of military law is an indispensable adjunct to a high standard of discipline. I gratefully acknowledge the care with which officers of the adjutant general's branch in all formations have insured the observation of every safeguard which our law provides against injustice. They have seen to it that every plea which an accused or convicted soldier wishes to bring forward is heard, and that commanders are advised as to the suitability of sentences. I take this opportunity of recording my satisfaction at the success which has attended the operation of the suspension of sentences. The number of men under suspended sentence who by good conduct and gallant service in the field have earned remission of their sentence has been most encouraging.

Closely related to the administration of military law is the work of the military police under the provost marshal and of the military prisons in the field. In the battle zone, where frequently they had to do duty in exposed positions under heavy fire and suffered severe casualties, the military police solved an important part of the problem of traffic control, by preventing the unavoidable congestion of troops and transport on roads in the vicinity of active operations from degenerating into confusion. In back areas their vigilance and zeal have largely contributed to the good relations maintained between our troops and the civilian population.

Although the number of soldiers undergoing sentences of imprisonment in France has at no time amounted to one per thousand, the size of the army has necessitated a considerable expansion of the military prisons in the field. The director of military prisons, his governors and warders have sought, not retribution, but to build up the self-discipline of the prisoner. They have been rewarded by seeing a large percentage of the men committed to their charge subsequently recover their characters as good soldiers.

Under the general control of the adjutant general, the base stationery depot, which went to France in 1914 with a personnel of 10, has expanded into the directorate of army printing and stationery services, employing over 60 officers and 850 other ranks. In addition to the printing and distribution of orders and instructions, it undertook the reproduction on a vast scale, of aerial and other photographs, the number of which grew from 25,000 in 1916 to two and a quarter million in 1918. Other examples of administrative success are the prisoners of war section and the directorate of graves registration and inquiries.

Of the care taken for the physical and moral welfare of the troops I can not speak too highly.

In the former domain, the achievements of the director

general of medical services and his subordinates have been so fully recorded by me in previous dispatches that they need no further emphasis. It is sufficient to say that, in spite of the numbers dealt with, there has been no war in which the resources of science have been utilized so generously and successfully for the prevention of disease, or for the quick evacuation and careful tending of the sick and wounded.

In the latter sphere, the devoted efforts of the army chaplains of all denominations have contributed incalculably to the building up of the indomitable spirit of the army. As the result of their teaching, all ranks came to know and more fully understand the great and noble objects for which they were fighting.

Under the immediate direction of the adjutant general in matters concerning military administration, the principal chaplain for members of all churches except the Church of England, and the deputy chaplain general for members of the Church of England administer to the greatest harmony a very complete joint organization. Provided with a definite establishment for armies, corps, and divisions, as well as for the principal base ports, base camps, hospitals, and certain other units, they insure that the benefit of religion is brought within the reach of every soldier.

In all the senior offices of this joint organization down to divisions the principal chaplain and deputy chaplain general each have their representatives, the appointments to those offices in the principal chaplain's section being apportioned between the different churches, Protestant and Roman Catholic, in proportion to the numbers of their following in the army as a whole. This organization has worked for the common good in a manner wholly admirable and with a most noteworthy absence of friction. It has undoubtedly been much assisted, both in its internal economy and in its relations with commanders and troops, by being at all times in direct touch with the adjutant general's branch.

No survey of the features of the war would be complete without some reference to the part played by women serving with the British Armies in France. Grouped also under the adjutant general's branch of the general staff, Queen Alexandra's Imperial Military Nursing Service, the Nursing Sisters of the Canadian Army Medical Corps, and of the Australian, New Zealand, South African, and Territorial Force Nursing Services and the British Red Cross Society have maintained and embellished a fine tradition of loyalty and efficiency. Those services have been reinforced by members of Voluntary Aid Detachments from the British Isles, the Oversea Dominions, and the United States of America, who have vied with their professional sisters in cheerfully enduring fatigue in times of stress and gallantly facing danger and death.

Women in the British Red Cross Society and other organizations have driven ambulances throughout the war, undeterred by discomfort and hardship. Women have ministered to the comfort of the troops in huts and canteens. Finally, Queen Mary's Auxiliary Army Corps, recruited on a wider basis, responded with enthusiasm to the call for drafts and by the aid they gave to our declining man power contributed materially to the success of our arms.

The experience gained in this war alone, without the study and practice of lessons learned from other campaigns, could not have sufficed to meet the ever-changing tactics which have characterized the fighting. There was required also the sound basis of military knowledge supplied by our training manuals and staff colleges.

The principles of command, staff work and organization elaborated before the war have stood the test imposed upon them and are sound. The military educated officer has counted for much, and the good work done by our staff colleges during the past 30 years has had an important influence upon the successful issue of the war. In solving the various strategic and tactical problems with which we have been faced, in determining principles of training and handling of troops and in the control and elaboration of army organization generally, the knowledge acquired by previous study and application has been invaluable. Added to this have been the efficiency and smoothness of working resulting from standardization of principles, assisted in many cases by the previous personal acquaintance at the staff college of those called upon to work together in the field.

The course of the war has brought out very clearly the value of an efficient and well-trained high command, in which I include not merely commanders of higher formations, but their staffs also.

This has been the first time in our history that commanders have had to be provided for such large forces. Before the war, not one of our generals had commanded even an army corps such as has been used as a subsidiary formation in the battles of the last few years. In consequence, commanders have been faced with problems very different to those presented by the small units with which they had been accustomed to train in peace. That they exercised their commands with such success as most of them did shows, I venture to think, that their prior training was based on sound principles and conducted on practical lines.

Similarly as regards the staff, the magnitude of our operations introduced a situation for which no precedent existed. The staff colleges had only produced a reserve of staff officers adequate to the needs of our army on a peace footing, and for the mobilization of the expeditionary force of six divisions. Consequently, on the expansion of the army during the war many officers had to be recruited for staff appointments – from good regular officers chiefly, but also from officers of our new armies – and trained for the new duties required of them. Though numbers of excellent staff officers were provided in this way, it was found as a general rule that the relative efficiency in staff duties of men who had passed through the staff colleges, as compared with men who had not had that advantage, was unquestionably greater.

Good staff work is an essential to success in all wars, and particularly in a struggle of such magnitude as that through which we had just passed. No small part of the difficulty of achieving it lies in the possibility that officers on the staff of higher formations may get out of touch with the fighting forces, and so lose sense of proportion and become impractical. Every endeavour was made to avoid this by maintaining a constant interchange of such officers with others from the front, so that all might keep abreast with the latest ideas and experience both in the fighting line and elsewhere. In pursuance of this principle, in addition to 18 officers from army or corps staffs and other officers from the intelligence corps or general list, there were brought in during the period of my command some 50 officers direct from active duty with divisions or smaller units to hold for longer or shorter periods appointments in the general staff branch at general headquarters.

It may be accepted as a general rule that previous organizations should be upset as little as possible in war. As each war has certain special conditions, so some modification of existing ideas and practices will be necessary, but if our principles are sound these will be few and unimportant. In the present war new organizations and establishments for dealing with the demands of both the fighting and the rearward services have been brought into being continually and added to or absorbed by our existing organization and establishment.

The constant birth of new ideas has demanded the exercise of the greatest care, not only to insure that no device or suggestion of real value should be overlooked or discouraged, but also to regulate the enthusiasm of the specialist and prevent each new development assuming dimensions out of proportion to its real value. As the result of our own experience and that of the French during the fighting of 1915, all kinds of trench weapons were invented, bombs, bomb throwers, mortars and even such instruments as trench daggers. In those days the opinion was freely expressed that the war would be finished in the trenches and every effort was made to win victories in the trenches themselves. In consequence, rifle shooting was forgotten and was fast becoming a lost art. Similarly as regards artillery, the idea of dominating and defeating the hostile artillery before proceeding to the infantry attack was considered an impossibility.

Then followed the experience of the Battle of the Somme in 1916, which showed that the principles of our prewar training were as sound as ever. That autumn a revival of old methods was inaugurated. Musketry shooting was everywhere carried out, and bayonet-fighting was taught as the really certain way of gaining supremacy in hand-to-hand fighting. At the same time, as pointed out in paragraph 17 above, the greatest care was devoted to artillery shooting, as well as to the training of all arms for open fighting. The events of the next two years fully confirmed the lessons drawn from the Battle of the Somme. In short, the longer the war has lasted the more emphatically has it been realized that our original organization and training were based on correct principles. The danger of altering them too much, to deal with some temporary phase, has been greater than the risk of adjusting them too little. Some idea of the extent of the organization built up during the war for the training of our armies can be gathered from a survey of the different schools actually established.

In the armies important schools were maintained for the instruction of officers and noncommissioned officers of infantry and artillery in their several duties, for training in scouting, observation and sniping, in the use of trench mortars, in signaling, musketry, and bayonet fighting, antigas precautions, mining and defense against tanks. The different corps controlled a similar series of schools. Added to these were the special schools of the cavalry corps including a school of equitation; the tank corps mechanical school, and the different courses instituted and managed by divisions, which were largely attended whenever the battle situation permitted.

Other schools under the direct supervision of general headquarters provided instruction in the machine gun, Lewis gun and light mortar, in anticraft gunnery, in observation for artillery, in sound ranging and flash spotting, wireless, bridging and other engineering duties, in firing and bombing from aeroplanes, and in physical and recreational training. At the base depots big training and reinforcement camps were set up for infantry, artillery, cavalry, engineers, machine gunners, cyclists, tank corps, signal and gas personnel. Further, a regular succession of staff officers and others were sent home to take part in the various schools and courses established in England.

In the course of the past year it was found desirable to make provision for the more thorough coordination of effort among these various schools and also for assisting commanders, especially during battle periods, in the training and instruction of such troops as might from time to time be in reserve. For this purpose an inspectorate of training was established. Training and organization must always go hand in hand; for while tactical considerations dictate the organization of units and methods of training, upon sound tactical organization and training depend the development and effective employment of good tactics.

In the early spring of 1918 the foundations were laid of an educational scheme which might give officers and men throughout the army an opportunity to prepare themselves for their return to civil life. Delayed in its application by the German offensive and the crowded events of the summer and autumn of that year, since the conclusion of the armistice the scheme has been developed with most excellent results under the general direction of the training subsection of my general staff branch, and generously supported in every possible way by the educational department at home. Divided into a general and a technical side every effort has been made both to give opportunities for the improvement of general knowledge and to enable trained men to "get their hands in" before returning to civil life. In this way between 400,000 and 500,000 persons have been brought under instruction, while the number of attendances at lectures has approached a million in the course of a month.

The feature of the war which to the historian may well appear the most noteworthy is the creation of our new armies.

To have built up successfully in the very midst of war a great new army on a more than continental scale, capable of beating the best troops of the strongest military nation of prewar days, is an achievement of which the whole Empire may be proud. The total of over 327,000 German prisoners captured by us on the western front is in striking contrast to the force of six divisions, comprising some 80,000 fighting men all told, with which we entered the war. That we should have been able to accomplish this stupendous task is due partly to the loyalty and devotion of our Allies and to the splendid work of the Royal Navy, but mainly to the wonderful spirit of the British race in all parts of the world.

Discipline has never had such a vindication in any war as in the present one, and it is their discipline which most distinguishes our new armies from all similarly created armies of the past. At the outset the lack of deep-seated and instinctive discipline placed our new troops at a disadvantage compared with the methodically trained enemy. This disadvantage, however, was overcome, and during the last two years the discipline of all ranks of our new armies, from whatever part of the Empire they have come, was excellent. Born from a widespread and intelligent appreciation of the magnitude of the issues at stake and a firm belief in the justice of our cause, it drew strength and permanence from a commonsense recognition of what discipline really means from a general realization that true discipline demands as much from officers as from men, and that without mutual trust, understanding and confidence on the part of all ranks the highest form of discipline is impossible.

Drawn from every sphere of life, from every profession, department, and industry of the British Empire, and thrust suddenly into a totally new situation full of unknown difficulties, all ranks have devoted their lives and energies to the service of their country in the whole-hearted manner which the magnitude of the issues warranted. The policy of putting complete trust in subordinate commanders and of allowing them a free hand in the choice of means to attain their object has proved most successful. Young officers, whatever their previous education may have been, have learned their duties with enthusiasm and speed, and have accepted their responsibilities unflinchingly.

Our universities and public schools throughout the Empire have proved once more, as they have proved time and again in the past, that in the formation of character, which is the root of discipline, they have no rivals. Not that universities and public schools enjoy a monopoly of the qualities which make good officers. The life of the British Empire generally has proved sound under the severest tests, and while giving men whom it is an honour for any officer to command, has furnished officers of the highest standard from all ranks of society and all quarters of the world.

Promotion has been entirely by merit, and the highest appointments were open to the humblest provided he had the necessary qualifications of character, skill, and knowledge. Many instances could be quoted of men who from civil or relatively humble occupations have risen to important commands. A schoolmaster, a lawyer, a taxicab driver, and an ex-sergeant-major have commanded brigades; one editor has commanded a division, and another held successfully the position of senior staff officer to a regular division; the undercook of a Cambridge college, a clerk to the metropolitan water board, an insurance clerk, an architect's assistant, and a police inspector became efficient general staff officers; a mess sergeant, a railway signalman, a coal miner, a market gardener, an assistant secretary to a haberdasher's company, a quartermaster-sergeant and many private soldiers have risen to command battalions, clerks have commanded batteries; a schoolmaster, a collier, the son of a blacksmith, an iron molder, an instructor in tailoring, an assistant gas engineer, a grocer's assistant, as well as policemen, clerks and privates, have commanded companies or acted as adjutants.

As a body and with few exceptions, new officers have understood that the care of their men must be their first consideration, that their men's comfort and well-being should at all times come before their own, that without this they can not expect to win the affection, confidence, loyalty, and obedience of those they are privileged to command, or to draw the best from them. Moreover, they have known how to profit by the experience of others and in common with their men they have turned willingly to the members of the old regular army for instruction and guidance in all branches of their new way of life.

On their part, officers, noncommissioned officers, and men of the old regular army have risen to the demands made upon them in a manner equally marvelous. Their leaven has pervaded the whole of the mighty force which in four and one-half years of war has, gathered from all parts of the world round the small, highly trained army with which we entered the war. The general absence of jealousy and the readiness to learn, which in the field has markedly characterized all ranks of our new armies, is proof both of the quality of our old army and of the soundness of our prewar training. If further proof were needed, it is found in the wonderful conduct and achievements of our armies, new and old, and in the general pride with which they are universally regarded.

In the earlier stages of the war the regular army was called on to provide instructors and cadres round which the new armies could be formed. All that was best in the old regular army, its discipline, based on force of character, leadership, and mutual respect, its traditions and the spirit that never knows defeat have been the foundations on which the new armies have been built up. Heavy demands were necessarily made upon our establishment of trained regular officers, most regrettably depleted by the heavy sacrifices of the early days of the war. The way in which such demands have been met by those who survived those days has justified our belief in them.

Neither have the officers of the new armies, whether drawn from the British Isles or the Dominions, risen with less spirit and success to the needs of the occasion. The great expansion of the army, and the length of the war, necessitated an ever-increasing demand being made on them for filling responsible positions, in command, staff and administrative appointments. The call has been met most efficiently. The longer the war continued, the greater became the part played in it by the new armies of the Empire.

THE SIGNING OF THE TREATY OF VERSAILLES, 28 June 1919

Harold Nicolson, British diplomat

After the capitulation of Germany on 11 November 1918 she was required by the victorious Allies to sign a punitive peace treaty. The signing took place in the Hall of Mirrors at Versailles Palace – the Hall which had witnessed the humiliation of France and proclamation of the German Empire in 1871.

La journée de Versailles. Lunch early and leave the Majestic in a car with Headlam Morley. He is a historian, yet he dislikes historical occasions. Apart from that he is a sensitive person and does not rejoice in seeing great nations humbled. I, having none of such acquirements or decencies, am just excited.

There is no crowd at all until we reach Ville d'Avray. But there are poilus at every crossroad waving red flags and stopping all other traffic. When we reach Versailles the crowd thickens. The avenue up to the Château is lined with cavalry in steel-blue helmets. The pennants of their lances flutter red and white in the sun. In the Cour d'Honneur, from which the captured German cannon have tactfully been removed, are further troops. There are Generals, Pétain, Gouraud, Mangin. There are St Cyriens. Very military and orderly. Headlam Morley and I creep out of our car hurriedly. Feeling civilian and grubby. And wholly unimportant. We hurry through the door.

Magnificent upon the staircase stand the Gardes Républicains – two caryatides on every step – their sabres at the salute. This is a great ordeal, but there are other people climbing the stairs with us. Headlam and I have an eye-meet. His thin cigaretted fingers make a gesture of dismissal. He is not a militarist.

We enter the two anterooms, our feet softening on to the thickest of savonnerie carpets. They have ransacked the Garde Meubles for their finest pieces. Never, since the Grand Siècle, has Versailles been more ostentatious or more embossed . . .

We enter the Galerie des Glaces. It is divided into three sections. At the far end are the Press already thickly installed. In the middle there is a horseshoe table for the plenipotentiaries. In front of that, like a guillotine, is the table for the signatures. It is supposed to be raised on a dais but, if so, the dais can be but a few inches high. In the nearer distance are rows and rows of tabourets for the distinguished guests, the deputies, the senators and the members of the delegations. There must be seats for over 1,000 persons. This robs the ceremony of all privilege and therefore of all dignity. It is like the Aeolian Hall.

Clemenceau is already seated under the heavy ceiling as we arrive. "Le roi", runs the scroll above him, "gouverne par luimême." He looks small and yellow. A crunched homunculus.

Conversation clatters out among the mixed groups around us. It is, as always on such occasions, like water running into a tin bath. I have never been able to get other people to recognize that similarity. There was a tin bath in my house at Wellington: one turned it on when one had finished and ran upstairs shouting "Baath ready" to one's successor: "Right ho!" he would answer: and then would come the sound of water pouring into the tin bath below, while he hurried into his dressing-gown. It is exactly the sound of people talking in undertones in a closed room. But it is not an analogy which I can get others to accept.

People step over the Aubusson benches and escabeaux to talk to friends. Meanwhile the delegates arrive in little bunches and push up the central aisle slowly. [Woodrow] Wilson and Lloyd George are among the last. They take their seats at the central table. The table is at last full. Clemenceau glances to right and left. People sit down upon their escabeaux but continue chattering. Clemenceau makes a sign to the ushers. They say "Ssh! Ssh! Ssh!" People cease chattering and there is only the sound of occasional coughing and the dry rustle of programmes. The officials of the Protocol of the Foreign Office move up the aisle and say, "Ssh! Ssh!" again. There is then an absolute hush, followed by a sharp military order. The Gardes Républicains at the doorway flash their swords into their scabbards with a loud click. "Faites entrer les Allemands," says Clemenceau in the ensuing silence. His voice is distant but harshly penetrating. A hush follows.

Through the door at the end appear two huissiers with silver chains. They march in single file. After them come four officers of France, Great Britain, America and Italy. And then, isolated and pitiable, come the two German delegates Dr Müller, Dr Bell. The silence is terrifying. Their feet upon a strip of parquet between the savonnerie carpets echo hollow and duplicate. They keep their eyes fixed away from those 2,000 staring eyes, fixed upon the ceiling. They are deathly pale. They do not appear as representatives of a brutal militarism. The one is thin and pink-eyelidded: the second fiddle in a Brunswick orchestra. The other is moon-faced and suffering: a privat-dozent. It is all most painful.

They are conducted to their chairs. Clemenceau at once breaks the silence. "Messieurs," he rasps, "la sèance est ouverte." He adds a few ill-chosen words. "We are here to sign a Treaty of Peace." The Germans leap up anxiously when he has finished, since they know that they are the first to sign. William Martin, as if a theatre manager, motions them petulantly to sit down again. Mantoux translates Clemenceau's words into English. Then St Quentin advances towards the Germans and with the utmost dignity leads them to the little table on which the Treaty is expanded. There is general tension. They sign. There is a general relaxation. Conversation hums again in an undertone. The delegates stand up one by one and pass onwards to the queue which waits by the signature table. Meanwhile people buzz round the main table getting autographs. The single file of plenipotentiaries waiting to approach the table gets thicker. It goes quickly. The officials of the Quai d'Orsay stand round, indicating places to sign, indicating procedure, blotting with neat little pads.

Suddenly from outside comes the crash of guns thundering a salute. It announces to Paris that the second Treaty of Versailles has been signed by Dr Müller and Dr Bell. Through the few open windows comes the sound of distant crowds cheering hoarsely. And still the signature goes on.

We had been warned it might last three hours. Yet almost at once it seemed that the queue was getting thin. Only three, then two, and then one delegate remained to sign. His name had hardly been blotted before the huissiers began again their "Ssh! Ssh!" cutting suddenly short the wide murmur which had again begun. There was a final hush. "La séance est levée," rasped Clemenceau. Not a word more or less.

We kept our seats while the Germans were conducted like prisoners from the dock, their eyes still fixed upon some distant point of the horizon.

Musing on the signing of the treaty, Marshal Foch declared, "It is not a peace, it is an armistice for twenty years". The Marshal was right to the year.

SOURCES & ACKNOWLEDGMENTS

The editor has made every effort to locate all persons having rights in the selections which appear in this anthology, and to secure permission from the holders of such rights to reprint material. The editor apologises in advance for any errors or omissions inadvertently made. Queries regarding the use of material should be addressed to the editor c/o the publisher.

Part One: 1914

Jevtic, Borijove, *New York World*, 29 June 1924

Sulzbach, Herbert, *With the German Guns*, Leo Cooper, 1973

Kurnakov, Sergyei N., *Savage Squadrons*, Boston, Hale, Cushman & Flint, 1935

Asquith, H.H., *Memories and Reflections*, Vol II, Little, Brown and Co., 1928

George V, *King George V*, John Gore, Murray, 1941

Kokoschka, Oskar, *My Life*, Thames & Hudson, 1974

Graves, Robert, *Goodbye to All That*, Penguin Books, 1960, copyright © Robert Graves 1929, 1957. Reprinted by permission of A.P. Watt Ltd

"The Tommy", quoted *The Long March of Everyman*, ed. Theo Barker, Andre Deutsch, 1975

Bennett, Arnold, *The Journals of Arnold Bennett*, ed. Newman Flower, Cassell, 1932

Limmer, Walter, *German Students' War Letters*, ed. Dr Philipp Witkop, trans. A.F. Wedd, Methuen, 1929

Russell, Bertrand, quoted in *Voices from the Great War*, Peter Vansittart, Cape, 1981

Davis, Richard Harding, New York *Tribune*, 23 August 1914

Richthofen, Manfred Von, *The Red Baron*, trans. Peter Kilduff, Ace Books, 1969, copyright © Stanley M. Ulanoff, 1969

Denmore, Bernard, *True World War I Stories*, Robinson, 1997 (Originally published as *Everyman at War*, edited by C.B. Purdom, 1930)

O'Callaghan, D. quoted in *Voices from the Great War*, Peter Vansittart, Cape, 1981

Read, W.R., *People at War*, edited Michael Moynihan, David & Charles, n.d., copyright © Sunday Times Newspapers Ltd, 1973

Clark, Rev. Andrew, *Echoes of the Great War: The Diary of the Reverend Andrew Clark, 1914–19*, edited by James Munson, OUP, 1985

Morse, John, *An Englishman in the Russian Ranks*, Duckworth & Company, Duckworth, 1915

Hindenburg, Paul von, quoted in *Voices from the Great War*, Peter Vansittart, Cape, 1981

Richards, Frank, *Old Soldiers Never Die*, Anthony Mott Limited, 1983, copyright © the Estate of Frank Richards

Delius, Frederick, *A Life in Letters*, ed. Lionel Carley, Scolar Press, 1983

Spears, E.L., *Liasion 1914*, Heinemann, 1930

Sitwell, Osbert, *Great Morning*, Macmillan, 1948, copyright © Osbert Sitwell, 1948

Weddigen, Otto, quoted in *Source Records of the Great War*, Vol II, ed. Charles F. Horne, National Alumni, 1931

Wiegand, Karl von, UPI dispatch 1914

MacDonagh, Michael, *In London During the Great War*, Eyre & Spottiswoode, 1935

Bell, J.F. *True World War I Stories*, Robinson, 1997 (Originally published as *Everyman at War*, edited by C.B. Purdom, 1930)

Richards, Frank, *op. cit.*

Seegar, Alan, *Letters and Diary*, Charles Scribner's Sons, 1918

Richards, Frank, *op. cit.*

Meese, Fritz, *German Students' War Letters*, *op. cit.*

Grenfell, Julian, quoted in *Salute the Soldier*, Eric Bush, George Allen & Unwin, 1966

Hulse, Edward H.W., *The Albatross Book of English Letters*, The First Earl of Birkenhead, Albatross Verlag, 1936

Part Two: 1915

Goodbar, Montague, unpublished diary, Imperial War Museum

Hankey, Donald, *A Student in Arms*, Andrew Melrose, 1916

Britten, S.V., quoted in *Voices and Images of the Great War*, Lyn Macdonald, Penguin, 1988

Hossack, Anthony, *True World War I Stories*, Robinson, 1997 (Originally published as *Everyman at War*, edited by C.B. Purdom, 1930)

Bush, Eric, *Bless Our Ship*, George Allen & Unwin, 1958

Graves, Robert, *op. cit.*

Rhonda, Viscountess, *This Was My World*, Macmillan, 1933
Pankhurst, E. Sylvia, *The Home Front*, Hutchinson & Co., 1932
Bruckshaw, Horace, *The Diaries of Private Horace Bruckshaw*, edited and introduced by Martin Middlebrook, Scolar Press, 1979
H.S. Clapham, *Mud and Khaki: The Memories of an Incomplete Soldier*, Hutchinson, 1930
Horrocks, Brian, *A Full Life*, Collins, 1960
Walpole, Hugh, *Hugh Walpole: A Biography*, Rupert Hart-Davis, Macmillan, 1952, copyright © Rupert Hart-Davis, 1952
Thompson, Leonard, quoted in *Akenfield*, Ronald Blythe, Allen Lane, 1969
Graves, Robert, *op. cit.*
Von Buttlar Brandenfels, Treusch, *Zeppelins Over England*, George G. Harrap & Co. Ltd., 1931
Graves, Robert, *op. cit.*
Nevinson, H.W., *Last Changes, Last Chances*, Nisbet, 1928
Hogue, Oliver, *Love Letters of an ANZAC*, Andrew Melrose, 1916
Kokoschka, Oskar, *op. cit.*
Webb, Beatrice, *Beatrice Webb's Diaries*, ed. Margaret Cole, Longmans, 1952
Gahan, Stirling T., quoted in *Vain Glory*, Guy Chapman, Cassell, 1937
Tatham, M.I., Bell, J.F., *True World War I Stories*, Robinson, 1997 (Originally published at *Everyman at War*, edited by C.B. Purdom, 1930)
Greenwell, Graham, *An Infant in Arms*, L. Dickinson & Thompson, 1935
Keyes, Roger, *Naval Memoirs of Admiral of the Fleet: The Narrow Seas to the Dardanelles*, Thornton Butterworth, 1934
Griffith, Llewellyn Wyn, *Up to Mametz*, Faber & Faber, 1930
Falkenhayn, Erich von, *General Headquarters, 1914–1916, and Its Critical Decisions*, Hutchinson, 1919

Part Three: 1916

Tatham, J.S., quoted in *Hot Blood & Cold Steel*, Andy Simpson, Tom Donovan Publishing Ltd, 1993
Pétain, Artois, *Verdun*, Mathews & Marrot, 1930
Beumelburg, Werner, quoted in *The First World War*, Richard Thoumin, Martin Secker & Warburg Ltd, 1963, English translation copyright © Martin Secker & Warburg Ltd and G.P. Putnam's Sons
Noskoff, A.A., *The First World War*, Thoumin, *op.cit.*
Westmacott, T.H., unpublished diary, Imperial War Museum
Baucher, Pierre, *The First World War*, Thoumin, *op. cit.*
Spiegel, Adolf von, *U-Boat 202*, trans. Barry Domvile, Andrew Melrose, 1919
Sassoon, Siegfried, *Diaries, 1915–18*, ed. Rupert Hart-Davis, Faber & Faber, 1983, copyright © George Sassoon, 1983
Mounsley, E.O., *The Secrets of a Kuttite*, John Lane, 1921
Yeats-Brown, Francis, *Golden Horn*, Victor Gollancz, Gollancz, 1932
Cloete, Stuart, *A Victorian Son: An Autobiography*, Collins, 1972

Sassoon, Siegfried, *op. cit.*
Gregory, Henry, quoted *Hot Blood & Cold Steel*, Andy Simpson, *op. cit.*
Albert, Prince, *George VI, His Life and Reign*, J.W. Wheeler-Bennett, Macmillan, 1958
Francis, Ernest, *People at War*, edited Michael Moynihan, David & Charles, n.d., copyright © Sunday Times Newspapers Ltd, 1973
Hase, Georg Von, *Kiel & Jutland*, trans Arthur Champers and F.A. Holt, Skeffington & Son Ltd, 1921
Navigating Officer, HMS *Broke*, *The Fighting at Jutland*, ed. H.W. Fawcett and G.W.W. Hooper, Hutchinson & Co., 1921
Pétain, Artois, *Verdun*, *op. cit.*
Desagneaux, Henri, *A French Soldier's Diary*, Emfield Press, 1975
Brittain, Vera, *Testament of Youth*, Gollancz, 1933
Gerster, Matthaus, quoted in *Salute the Soldier*, Eric Bush, George Allen & Unwin, 1966
Walker, John Stanhope, *People at War*, edited Michael Moynihan, David & Charles, n.d., copyright © Sunday Times Newspapers Ltd, 1973
Rogerson, Sidney, *Twelve Days*, Arthur Barker Ltd, 1933
Part, Thomas, *The Diary of Thomas Reginald Part* web site, transcribed by Pauline Carter and David Jones, copyright © 1997 Pauline Carter
Gibbs, Philip, *Realities of War*, Victor Gollancz, Hutchinson, 1929
Graves, Robert, *op. cit.*
Anonymous, quoted in *First World War*, Martin Gilbert, Weidenfeld and Nicolson, 1994
Lawrence, D.H., *The Letters of D.H. Lawrence*, Heinemann, 1932
Graves, Robert, *op. cit.*
Richthofen, Manfred von, *The Red Baron*, trans. Peter Kilduff, Ace Books, 1969, copyright © Stanley M. Ulanoff, 1969
Steinbrecher, Friedrich, *German Students' War Letters*, ed. Dr Philipp Witkop, trans. A.F. Wedd, Methuen, 1929
Sturmer, Adolf, *German Students' War Letters*, *op. cit.*
Chaney, Bert, *People at War*, *op. cit.*
Steward, Bert, "The Taking of High Wood", The *Guardian*, September 1990
Richthofen, Manfred von, *The Red Battle Flyer*, trans. T. Ellis Barker, McBride & Co., 1918
George, David Lloyd, *War Memoirs*, Vol I, Nicholson and Watson, 1933
MacDonagh, Michael, *In London During the Great War*, Eyre & Spottiswoode, 1935
Carossa, Hans, *A Roumanian Diary*, Martin Secker, 1929
Gibbs, *op. cit.*
Charteris, J, *At GHQ*, Cassell, 1931
Paleologue, Maurice, *An Ambassador's Memoirs*, trans F.A. Holt, Hutchinson & Co., 1923
Samuel, Herbert, *Memoirs*, Cresset Press, 1945
Fielding, Rowland, *War Letters to a Wife*, Medici Society, 1929

Brittain, Vera, *op. cit.*
Pocock, Roger, *Chorus to Adventurer*, John Lane, The Bodley Head Ltd, 1931
Wilhelm II, Emperor, *The First World War*, Thoumin, *op. cit.*

Part Four: 1917

Owen, Wilfred, *Wilfred: Selected Letters*, ed. John Bell, OUP, 1985
Mack, Francis, *Trenches on the Web* internet site, n.d.
Marchant, Eric, unpublished letter, Imperial War Museum
Cooper, Ethel, quoted in *The Great World War 1914–45*, Vol II, John Bourne, Peter Liddle, Ian Whitehead, HarperCollins, 2001
Gibbons, Floyd, *Chicago Tribune*, 26 February 1917
Grandijs, L.-H., *The First World War*, Thoumin, *op. cit.*
MacDonagh, Michael, *In London During the Great War*, Eyre & Spottiswoode, 1935
Anonymous correspondent, *The First World War*, Thoumin, op. cit.
Coull, John, unpublished letter, Imperial War Museum
Denikin, Anton, *The Russian Turmoil: Memoirs, Military, Social, and Political*, E.P. Dutton and Company, 1922
Bishop, Billy (William A.), *Winged Warfare*, Pan Books Ltd., 1978, copyright © Stanley M. Ulanoff
Anonymous French Tank Officer, *The First World War*, Thoumin, *op. cit.*
Watson, W.H.L. *A Company of Tanks*, Blackwood, 1920
Spiess, Johannes, quoted in *The First World War*, Thoumin, *op. cit.*
Woodward, Oliver, unpublished memoir, Imperial War Museum
May, A.G., unpublished memoir, Imperial War Museum
Pressey, William, *People at War*, edited Michael Moynihan, David & Charles, n.d., copyright © Sunday Times Newspapers Ltd 1973
Gibbons, Floyd, *And They Thought We Wouldn't Fight!*, George H. Doran Company, 1918
Lawrence, T.E., *Seven Pillars of Wisdom*, Jonathan Cape Ltd, 1943, copyright © 1926, T.E. Lawrence
MacDonagh, Michael, *In London During the Great War*, Eyre & Spottiswoode, 1935
Downing, H.G., unpublished letters, Imperial War Museum
Floyd, Thomas H., *At Ypres with Best-Dunkley*, John Lane Company, 1920
Hare, A.S., quoted in *The Great World War 1914–45*, Vol II, John Bourne, Peter Liddle, Ian Whitehead, HarperCollins, 2001
Lapointe, Arthur, *Soldier of Quebec, 1916–17*, trans. R.C. Fetherstonhaugh, Edouard Garand, 1931
Hutton, I. Emslie, *With a Woman's Unit in Serbia, Salonika and Sebastopol*, Williams and Norgate Ltd, 1928
Bowen, Geoffrey, quoted in *Hot Blood & Cold Steel*, edited Andy Simpson, Tom Donovan Publishing Ltd, 1993, copyright © 1993 Tom Donovan Publishing Ltd and A. Simpson

Kobes, Albin, quoted in *Voices from the Great War*, Peter Vansittart, Cape, 1981
Lawrence, T.E., *op. cit.*
McCudden, James, *Five Years in the Royal Flying Corps*, Aeroplane & General Publishing Co., 1940
Wales, Henry G., International News Service, 19 October 1917
Lyne, C.E.L., unpublished diary, Imperial War Museum
Trotsky, Leon, *My Life*, Penguin, 1975
Reed, John, *Ten Days That Shook the World*, Lawrence & Wishart, 1926
Poincaré, Raymond, quoted in *The First World War*, Thoumin, *op. cit.*
Watson, W.H.L., *op. cit.*
Hindenburg, Paul von, *Out of My Life*, trans. F.A. Holt, Cassell & Co., 1920
Knight, Chris, *True World War I Stories*, Robinson, 1997 (Originally published as *Everyman at War*, edited by C.B. Purdom, 1930)
Allenby, Edmund, quoted in *How Jerusalem Was Won*, Constable & Co., 1919
Eccles, B.F., quoted in *Voices and Images of the Great War*, Lyn Macdonald, 1988
Lettow-Vorbeck, Paul von, *My Experiences of East Africa*, Hurst & Blackett, 1920

Part Five: 1918

Bultitude, R.G. *True World War I Stories*, Robinson, 1997 (Originally published as *Everyman at War*, edited by C.B. Purdom, 1930)
Grosch, Alfred, *True World War I Stories*, *op. cit.*
Osborn, Arthur, *Unwilling Passenger*, Faber & Faber, 1932
Sharp, William Graves, quoted in *The First World War*, Richard Thoumin, Martin Secker & Warburg Ltd, 1963, English translation copyright © Martin Secker & Warburg Ltd and G.P. Putnam's Sons
Censor, quoted in *The Long March of Everyman*, ed. Theo Barker, Andre Deutsch, 1974
Dartford, R.C.G., unpublished diary, Imperial War Museum
Charteris, J., *At GHQ*, Cassell, 1931
Keyes, Roger, *The Naval Memoirs of Admiral of the Fleet: Sir Roger Keyes*, Thornton Butterworth, Vol II, 1935
Carpenter, A.F.B., *The Blocking of Zeebrugge*, Houghton Mifflin Company, 1922
Monash, John, *War Letters of General Monash*, ed. F.M. Cutlack, Angus and Robertson, 1934
Sulzbach, Herbert, *With the German Guns*, Leo Cooper, 1973
Mitchell, F., *True World War I Stories op. cit.*
Russell, Bertrand, *Autobiography*, Allen & Unwin, 1967
Medvedev, Pavel, quoted in *Last Days of the Romanovs*, Thornton Butterworth, 1920

Hoffman, Robert C., *I Remember the Last War*, Strength and Health Publishing, 1940

Ludendorff, Erich von, *My War Memories*, Hutchinson, 1919

Haig, Douglas, *The Private Papers of Douglas Haig*, ed. Robert Blake, Eyre and Spottiswoode, 1952

Churchill, W.S., *The World Crisis*, Thornton Butterworth, 1927

Anonymous soldier, quoted *The First World War*, Thoumin, *op. cit.*

Hoffman, Robert C., *op. cit.*

Sherwood, Elmer, *Diary of a Rainbow Veteran*, Moore-Langen Company, 1929

Bowman, Rudolph, file 180920, World War I Document Archives web site

Pershing, John, *My Experiences in the World War*, Frederick A. Stokes Company, 1931

Lawrence, T.E., *Seven Pillars of Wisdom*, Jonathan Cape Ltd, 1943, copyright © 1926 T.E. Lawrence

Anonymous French cavalry officer, quoted in *The First World War*, Thoumin, *op. cit.*

Harvard Thomas, G., unpublished letters, Imperial War Museum

Lawrence, T.E., *op. cit.*

Rickenbacker, Eddie V., *Fighting the Flying Circus*, Stokes, 1919

Rilke, Rainer Maria, quoted in *Voices from the Great War*, Peter Vansittart, Jonathan Cape Ltd, 1981

Foch, Ferdinand, *The Memoirs of Marshal Foch*, trans. Colonel T. Bentley Mott, William Heinemann, 1931

Gibbs, Philip, *The Pageant of the Years*, Heinemann, 1946

Brittain, Vera, *Testament of Youth*, Gollancz, 1933

Cooper, Ernest Read, *People at War*, edited Michael Moynihan, David & Charles, n.d., copyright © Sunday Times Newspapers Ltd, 1973

Churchill, W.S., *The World Crisis*, Thornton Butterworth, 1927, copyright © the estate of Winston Churchill, 1927

Evans, Llewellyn, quoted in *The War the Infantry Knew 1914–1919*, Captain J.C. Dunn, Janes, 1938

Part Six: 1919

Nicolson, Harold, *Peacekeeping 1919*, Constable, 1933

Other titles available from Robinson Publishing

The Mammoth Book of How It Happened World War II Ed. Jon E. Lewis **£7.99 [ ]**
Six years that changed the world forever, here are 200 first-hand accounts from World War II, including Heinz Guderian rolling his Panzer tank into Poland in 1939 to the execution of Nazi war criminals at Nuremberg in 1946. This collection gives an insight into how the repercussions of war have shaped our modern world and how nothing from geo-politics to rock 'n' roll can really be understood without it.

The Mammoth Book of True War Stories Ed. Jon E. Lewis **£7.99 [ ]**
The 50 stories in this unique compilation are about men and war, ranging in time from the Ancient Greeks to Operation Desert Storm; from the Crusades to the killing fields of Vietnam; from the Battle of Trafalgar to the dropping of the atomic bomb. They reveal all the faces of war – heroism, savagery, excitement and terror, on land, sea and in the air and all are true in every detail.

The Mammoth Book of SAS & Elite Forces Ed. Jon E. Lewis **£7.99 [ ]**
Shrouded in mystery and feared throughout the world, very little is known about the elite fighting forces of the world including the Special Air Services – the soldier's soldier. Exploits in the Falklands and breaking the siege at Princes Gate are described in detail. Other first-hand accounts of the astonishing bravery of the elite forces of the world, including Delta Force, the Green Berets and the French Foreign Legion are also covered.

The Mammoth Book of Soldiers at War Ed. Jon E. Lewis **£7.99 [ ]**
Laying bare the truth behind the adventures of Flashman and Sharpe, *The Mammoth Book of Soldiers at War* includes eyewitness accounts of battles, the privations and the adventure of armed service during the French Revolutionary War, the Napoleonic Wars and the Wars of 1812 – a time of hussars, artillery, musket, sword, patriotic fervour, inspired commanders, heroes and always, bloody carnage on the field.

Robinson books are available from all good bookshops or direct from the publisher. Just tick the titles you want and fill in the form below.

TBS Direct
Colchester Road, Frating Green, Colchester, Essex CO7 7DW
Tel: +44 (0) 1206 255777
Fax: +44 (0) 1206 255914
Email: sales@tbs-ltd.co.uk

UK/BFPO customers please allow £1.00 for p&p for the first book, plus 50p for the second, plus 30p for each additional book up to a maximum charge of £3.00.
Overseas customers (inc. Ireland), please allow £2.00 for the first book, plus £1.00 for the second, plus 50p for each additional book.

Please send me the titles ticked above.

NAME (Block letters) . . . .

ADDRESS. . . . .

. . . .

POSTCODE. . . . .

I enclose a cheque/PO (payable to TBS Direct) for . . . .

I wish to pay by Switch/Credit card

Number . . . .

Card Expiry Date . . . .

Switch Issue Number . . . .

Other titles available from Robinson Publishing

The Mammoth Book of War Correspondents Ed. Jon E. Lewis **£7.99 [ ]**
Giving more than 100 eyewitness accounts of the reality of human conflict, this collection offers examples of fine writing by men and women who have overcome the danger and deprivation of life at the front, often boldly confronting obstructive military and perfidious politicians to show their dedication and their desire to reveal the true face of war to the world at large.

The Mammoth Book of Fighter Pilots Ed. Jon E. Lewis **£7.99 [ ]**
Relive the exploits of Manfred von Richthofen, Eddie Rickenbacker, Richard Hillary, Johnnie Johnson, Luftwaffe WWII aces Heinz Knoke and Johannes Steinhoff, and over 20 others. This is a comprehensive and fascinating book about a form of combat that has changed beyond recognition over the last hundred years. It gives vivid insights into both the daily round and the dangers, such as bailing out over enemy territory, surviving in an Iraqi POW camp, or getting shot down in a blazing Spitfire.

The Mammoth Book of Heroes Ed. Jon E. Lewis **£7.99 [ ]**
True courage is one of the most highly valued attributes of humanity. Gathered together in this volume are over 70 accounts, many of them in the words of those who were there, about men and women who showed real courage, often with their lives on the line. No fictional hero can match the true courage of Ernest Shackleton, the bravery of British soldiers at Rorke's Drift, or the spirit of Annie Sullivan teaching the deaf and blind Helen Keller to speak and read. This is an inspiring collection that celebrates the brave of heart through the ages.

The Mammoth Book of How It Happened Battles
Ed. Richard Russell Lawrence **£7.99 [ ]**
This book of collected accounts of famous battles is much more than the sum of its parts. Taken all together the whole changing nature of recorded warfare is explored, from Thermopylae in Ancient Greece, to Operation Desert Storm. Here are the words of those who fought in history's greatest battles in the words of the commanders and the non-commissioned officers and men. With over 50 maps showing the location of the battlefields and strategic development of the campaigns.

Robinson books are available from all good bookshops or direct from the publisher. Just tick the titles you want and fill in the form below.

TBS Direct
Colchester Road, Frating Green, Colchester, Essex CO7 7DW
Tel: +44 (0) 1206 255777
Fax: +44 (0) 1206 255914
Email: sales@tbs-ltd.co.uk

UK/BFPO customers please allow £1.00 for p&p for the first book, plus 50p for the second, plus 30p for each additional book up to a maximum charge of £3.00.
Overseas customers (inc. Ireland), please allow £2.00 for the first book, plus £1.00 for the second, plus 50p for each additional book.

Please send me the titles ticked above.

NAME (Block letters) . . . .

ADDRESS. . . . .

. . . .

POSTCODE. . . . .

I enclose a cheque/PO (payable to TBS Direct) for . . . .

I wish to pay by Switch/Credit card

Number . . . .

Card Expiry Date . . . .

Switch Issue Number . . . .